DATE			

BAKER & TAYLOR BOOKS

The Economics of Growth and
Technical Change

The Economics of Growth and Technical Change

Technologies, Nations, Agents

Edited by
Gerald Silverberg and Luc Soete

Edward Elgar

Published by
Edward Elgar Publishing Limited
Gower House
Croft Road
Aldershot
Hants GU11 3HR
England

Edward Elgar Publishing Company
Old Post Road
Brookfield
Vermont 05036
USA

British Library Cataloguing in Publication Data
Economics of Growth and Technical Change:
Technologies, Nations, Agents
I. Silverberg, Gerald II. Soete, Luc
338.9

Library of Congress Cataloguing in Publication Data
The economics of growth and technical change: technologies, nations, agents /
edited by Gerald Silverberg and Luc Soete.
368pp. 23cm.
Includes bibliographical references and index.
1. Technological innovations—Economic aspects. 2. Economic
Development. I. Silverberg, Gerald. II. Soete, Luc.
HC79.T4E254   1994
338'.064—dc20   93–32248
                                                                      CIP

ISBN 1 85278 958 1

Printed and bound in Great Britain by
Hartnolls Limited, Bodmin, Cornwall

Contents

List of Figures   ix

List of Tables   xiii

List of Contributors   xv

1   Introduction   1
    Gerald Silverberg and Luc Soete

PART I   THE TECHNOLOGY–GROWTH INTERACTION

2   The Production and Distribution of Knowledge   9
    Kenneth J. Arrow

3   Endogenous Growth Theory, Convergence and Divergence   20
    Bruno Amable

4   Do Economies Diverge?   45
    Richard H. Day

    Comment on Day   64
    Paul David

5   Growth Fluctuations in an Evolutionary Model of
    Creative Destruction   74
    Gerald Silverberg and Doris Lehnert

    Comment on Silverberg and Lehnert   109
    Paul Romer

PART II INTERNATIONAL DISPARITIES IN GROWTH AND
          TECHNOLOGICAL PERFORMANCE

6   Convergence and Divergence in the Long-term Growth of
     Open Economies   119
     Giovanni Dosi and Silvia Fabiani

     Comment on Dosi and Fabiani   147
     Franz Palm

7   Technology and Growth: the Complex Dynamics of Convergence
     and Divergence   154
     Bart Verspagen

     Comment on Verspagen   182
     Jan Fagerberg

8   Productivity Growth and Capital Intensity on the Sector
     and Industry Level: Specialisation among OECD Countries,
     1970–1988   185
     Edward N. Wolff

     Comment on Wolff   212
     Thijs ten Raa

PART III MICROECONOMIC FOUNDATIONS OF GROWTH AND
          TECHNOLOGY DIFFUSION

9   Dynamic Oligopolistic Pricing with Endogenous Change in
     Market Structure and Market Potential in an Epidemic
     Diffusion Model   217
     Thomas Ziesemer

     Comment on Ziesemer   240
     Gene Grossman

10   Games with Changing Payoffs   244
     Reinoud Joosten, Hans Peters and Frank Thuijsman

     Comment on Joosten, Peters and Thuijsman   258
     Kenneth J. Arrow and Fernando Vega-Redondo

11 The Method of Generalised Urn Schemes in the Analysis of
Technological and Economic Dynamics   261
Giovanni Dosi and Yuri Kaniovski

Comment on Dosi and Kaniovski   285
Sidney Winter

12 What has been the Matter with Neoclassical Growth Theory?   290
Richard R. Nelson

Author Index   325
Subject Index   331

Figures

C4.1a Classical demographic equilibria 67

C4.1b Population dynamics 67

C4.2 The 'Malthus space' 67

C4.3 The 'Solow-Boserup Space' 69

C4.4 Dynamics of the system with a unique stable attractor 70

C4.5 Dynamics of system with two regimes (non-intersecting) 70

5.1 Contours of equal selective potential in the a–c (Fig. 5.1a) and a–m (Fig. 5.1b) planes 79

5.2 Schematic representation of the capital stock dynamics 81

5.3a An empirical case of multiple replacement taken from the primary energy sector in the US (after Nakicenovic 1987) 83

5.3b Multiple replacement in our artificial economy 84

5.3c Multiple replacement in the same run as in 5.3b but with an ST investment parameter s of 0.5 84

5.4 Artificial time series for unemployment, average profitability and growth rate of productivity for a run with $\omega = 2$ years and $\tau = 2\%$ 85

5.5a Spectral density of aggregate productivity growth rate with $\omega = 2$ years, $\tau = 2\%$ / yr 86

5.5b Autocorrelation function of productivity and GNP growth rates 86

5.6 Spectral density of productivity growth rate of the same run as in Figure 5.4 but with an ST parameter value of 2 89

5.7 Time series of aggregate productivity growth rate and innovation dates (vertical dotted lines) for a run with $\omega = 8$ years 89

5.8 Cross correlation of the productivity growth rate and a 28-year moving average of the annual number of innovations 90

5.9 Time series of productivity growth rate and a 28-year moving average of innovations for the benchmark run 90

5.10 The spectral density of a 28-year moving average of the innovation rate 91

5.11 Correlation dimension for 28-year moving average of Poisson-distributed innovation rate ($\omega = 1$) 93

5.12 Correlation dimension for productivity growth rate ($\omega = 2$, $\tau = 2\%$) calculated with 6000 data points 93

5.13   Correlation dimension for benchmark run and Soete-Turner
       investment function with s = 1   94
5.14   Z-statistic of nonlinear predictability for the benchmark run
       (8192 data points) and different embedding dimensions and
       time delays for the phase-space reconstruction   95
5.15   Power spectrum of rate of productivity growth plotted against
       log of frequency   96
5.16   Spectrum of productivity growth rate when profits are allowed
       to feedback with a lag on the probability of innovation   97
5.17   Histogram of Haustein–Neuwirth innovation time series with
       two fitted Poisson distributions   99
5.18a Haustein–Neuwirth innovation time series, 1764–1975   101
5.18b Detrended Haustein–Neuwirth time series after eliminating
       exponential trend by nonlinear stretching of time axis   101
6.1   Dynamics of real income, two countries (log scale)   137
6.2   Per capita incomes in a sample of countries, simulation results 139
6.3   Standard deviation in growth rates   139
7.1   Convergence and divergence in per capita GDP in the twentieth
       century   157
7.2   Growth of output and total R&D stock, 1970–1985, the cross-
       country sample   163
7.3   Growth of output and business R&D stock, 1970–1985, the
       cross-country sample   164
7.4   The value of V, 1953–1989   174
7.5   Sources of convergence over the period 1970–1985   176
8.1   Japanese labour productivity relative to the US by major
       sector, 1970 and 1988   198
8.2   German and other OECD labour productivity relative to the
       US by major sector, 1970 and 1988   198
8.3   Japanese labour productivity relative to the US by
       manufacturing industry, 1970 and 1988   200
8.4   German and other OECD labour productivity relative to the US
       by manufacturing sector, 1970 and 1988   200
9.1   p' is the introductory price, p^* is the long-run price under
       dynamic optimisation   223
9.2   Under dynamic optimisation the logistic curve leading to D' is
       generated by p'   223
9.3   Jorgenson's (1989) case   224
9.4   (a) Metcalfe's (1981) case and (b) Glaister's (1974) case of
       intertemporal price differentiation   225
9.5   Dynamics of market quantity y with threshold value y^* 231

9.6   If initial value $y_1(0)$ and $y_2(0)$ are above the no-growth line and $c_1=0$, both firms arrive at the zero-profit line at t_1, the finite endogenous horizon value   231

9.7   If $c_1>0$ and $y_2>y_1(0)$ the price of firm 1 will be so low that it reaches the zero-profit line and exits or becomes a Stackelberg-follower with a zero-profit strategy   231

9.8   If $c_1<0$, small $|c_1|$ and $y_2>y_1(0)$ drive firm 2 towards its zero-profit line and either to exit or to a Stackelberg-follower position   231

9.9   After firm 1 reaches the zero-profit line 11 firm 2 extends its market share in the Stackelberg phase   235

9.10   The differential game produces diffusion between 0 and t_2 235

10.1   Proposition 2   254

11.1   Dependence of prices of A and B on the market share of A   271

11.2   Probability of choosing A depending on its market share   274

11.3   The price of the cheapest of the two technologies as a function of x_A 277

Tables

5.1	Proportion of spectral variance in the range 40 to 80 years for runs of length 1024 years and a range of relevant parameters	87
5.2	Proportion of spectral variance in the range 40 to 80 years for runs of length 1024 years and different values of ß and τ	88
5.3	Proportion of spectral variance in the range 40 to 80 years for the benchmark run with different values of ST parameter	88
5.4	Lag and moving average order for maximal cross correlation between innovation and productivity growth rate time series with and without ST investment term	91
5.5	Tests of Poisson distribution of original and detrended innovation time series	102
6.1	Estimates of pre-industrial per capita GNP (in 1960 US dollars)	122
6.2	Estimates of trends in per capita GNP 1750–1977 (in 1960 US dollars)	123
6.3	Real GDP growth rates (in % p.a.) in various regions, 1965–89	123
6.4	Real per capita GDP growth rates (in % p.a.)	124
6.5	Autocorrelation of residuals: 'evolutionary' simulation, 'real business cycle', US data	138
7.1	Correlation matrix of the variables in the regressions	163
7.2	Regressions explaining growth of output 1970–1985 by growth of various inputs (same period) and initial labour productivity gap	166
7.3	Embodied knowledge spillovers and growth	168
7.4	Panel dataset regressions	172
7.5	Decomposition of convergence trends, 1971–1985	176
8.1	Labour productivity levels relative to the US for the total economy among OECD countries, 1970–1988	188
8.2	Labour productivity levels relative to the US for total manufacturing among OECD countries, 1970–1990	190
8.3	Translog total factor productivity (TFP) levels relative to the US for the total economy and total manufacturing among OECD countries, 1970–1988	191
8.4	Capital–labour ratios (K/L) relative to the US and average annual growth rates for the total economy and manufacturing among OECD countries, 1970–1988	193

8.5   Labour productivity levels relative to the US, by major
      sector and manufacturing industry among OECD countries,
      1970–1988   196
8.6   TFP and capital–labour (K/L) levels relative to the US, by
      major sector and manufacturing industry among OECD
      countries, 1970–1988   202
8.7   Regression of relative TFP growth on relative TFP level and
      growth in relative capital intensity (manufacturing industry
      sample)   207
8.8   Regression of relative TFP growth on relative TFP level and
      growth in relative capital intensity (major sector sample)   208

List of Contributors

Bruno Amable
MERIT and INRA
Unité de recherche HEDM
63–65 Boulevard de Brandeburg
F-94205 Ivry Cedex
France

Kenneth J. Arrow
Department of Economics
Stanford University
Encina Hall
Stanford, CA 94304
USA

Paul David
Department of Economics
Stanford University
Encina Hall
Stanford, CA 94304
USA

Richard H. Day
Department of Economics
University of Southern California
University Park
Los Angeles, CA 90089-0035
USA

Giovanni Dosi
Universita Degli Studi di Roma
'La Sapienza'
Dipartimento di Scienze
Economiche
Via Nomentana, 41
I-00161 Rome
Italy

Silvia Fabiani
University of Cambridge
Darwin College
Cambridge CB3 9EU
UK

Jan Fagerberg
Norwegian Institute of Foreign
Affairs
PO Box 8159 DEP
N-0022 Oslo
Norway

Gene Grossman
Princeton University
Woodrow Wilson School of Public
and International Affairs
Robertson Hall
Princeton, NJ 08544
USA

Reinoud Joosten
MERIT
Rijksuniversiteit Limburg
PO Box 616
6200 MD Maastricht
The Netherlands

Yuri Kaniovski
V.M. Glushkov Institute of
Cybernetics, Kiev, and
International Institute for Applied
Systems Analysis
A-2361 Laxenberg
Austria

Doris Lehnert
Universität Stuttgart
Institut für Sozialforschung
Keplerstrasse 17
D-7000 Stuttgart 1
Germany

Richard R. Nelson
Columbia University in
the City of New York
School of International
and Public Affairs
Public Policy Research Center
420 West 118th Street
New York, NY 10027
USA

Franz Palm
MERIT/Faculty of Economics
Rijksuniversiteit Limburg
PO Box 616
6200 MD Maastricht
The Netherlands

Hans Peters
MERIT/Faculty of Economics
Rijksuniversiteit Limburg
PO Box 616
6200 MD Maastricht
The Netherlands

Thijs ten Raa
Faculty of Economics
Katholieke Universiteit Brabant
PO Box 90153
5000 LE Tilburg
The Netherlands

Paul Romer
Center for Advanced Study in
Behavioral Sciences
202 Junipero Serra Blvd
Stanford, CA 94305
USA

Gerald Silverberg
MERIT
Rijksuniversiteit Limburg
PO Box 616
6200 MD Maastricht
The Netherlands

Luc Soete
MERIT/Faculty of Economics
Rijksuniversiteit Limburg
PO Box 616
6200 MD Maastricht
The Netherlands

Frank Thuijsman
MERIT/Faculty of General
Sciences
Rijksuniversiteit Limburg
PO Box 616
6200 MD Maastricht
The Netherlands

Fernando Vega-Redondo
Facultad de Economicas
Universidad de Alicante
E-03071 Alicante
Spain

Bart Verspagen
MERIT
Rijksuniversiteit Limburg
PO Box 616
6200 MD Maastricht
The Netherlands

Sidney Winter
Wharton School
University of Pennsylvania
Philadelphia, PA 19104
USA

Edward N. Wolff
Department of Economics
New York University
269 Mercer Street, 7th Floor
New York, NY 10003
USA

Thomas Ziesemer
MERIT/Faculty of Economics
Rijksuniversiteit Limburg
PO Box 616
6200 MD Maastricht
The Netherlands

1. Introduction

Gerald Silverberg and Luc Soete

In 1987, when MERIT[1] was set up, the economics of growth and technical change still meant, for most practical purposes, growth accounting in the tradition of Solow, Denison and Kendrick. True, economists had also dealt with technological diffusion, the interrelation of technical change and market structure, and the economics of innovation, but these remained for the most part separate areas of study largely unconnected with the broader concerns of macroeconomics and growth theory. While growth accounting provided a convenient, if not undisputed, framework for comparing the experience of different nations or identifying changes of growth regime such as the productivity slowdown of the 1970s, it was widely felt to be running into decreasing returns with respect to the fundamental insights it could provide.

Other insights and traditions did float in the background of the mainstream discussion, but the cross fertilisation was at best only sporadic. These included the role of increasing returns and specialisation (insights indeed going back to Adam Smith, but long known to be difficult to reconcile formally with his invisible hand view of economic equilibrium, whose mathematical realisation in the theory of general equilibrium was dependent on diminishing returns) or the more evolutionary vision of Joseph Schumpeter predicated on creative destruction and disequilibrium. In 1988 we edited, together with Giovanni Dosi, Christopher Freeman and Richard Nelson, a voluminous 'state of the art' book bringing together some of these more evolutionarily inspired, but often disparate contributions.[2] Despite the size of the book, it did not pretend to be complete, nor to cover all new, emerging contributions in the field of economic theory and technical change. Yet it was precisely during these early planning years of the MERIT enterprise that growth theory began its remarkable renewal, drawing on innovations in the neoclassical analytical framework to incorporate at last the neglected notion of increasing returns and some elements central to the economics of technical change, such as spillovers, learning by doing, appropriability and creative destruction.

Thus it now seems appropriate and timely to confront those two streams of literature. It is not our intention to provide in this short introduction a systematic overview of the resurgence of interest in growth and technology and its possible convergence with evolutionarily inspired

1

visions of technology (the chapters in this volume by Bruno Amable and Richard Nelson do this admirably and critically, we believe). Let us merely list some of the salient points and refer to the other contributions in this volume for further elaboration and references.

Within the Solow growth modelling and general equilibrium tradition, under the name endogenous growth, a new class of models has been advanced since the mid-1980s which accomplishes a neoclassical *tour de force*. Instead of relegating technical change entirely to an unexplained residual (a total factor productivity shift factor), a new, produced factor of production is introduced, whether this be called knowledge, designs, differentiation, quality or human capital, not subject to diminishing returns and thus permitting open-ended growth. By appending an appropriately formulated, monopolistic economic sector to the pure competition model, it is then possible to derive the level of innovative activity from the nature of the economic incentives while retaining the prized rationality and intertemporal equilibrium assumptions. Whether this is not just a brilliant intellectual artifice to reconcile the peculiar and previously abhorrent characteristics of technology and innovation into the general equilibrium framework, or genuinely captures fundamental aspects of the growth process and will inspire a new level of empirical investigation, is something that still remains to be seen. The other side of the endogenous growth coin – the evolutionary one – deriving from the seminal work of Nelson and Winter in which agents invest in innovative activity, but not necessarily with perfect foresight and in market equilibrium, has also been pushed further by a number of authors, including Giovanni Dosi and Silvia Fabiani in this volume.

The question 'why do growth rates differ', which has dominated the international growth accounting literature, has also given way in this period to a new and even more voluminous literature on catching up, overtaking, falling behind and convergence. This rapidly growing empirical literature is not just the result of new theorising, but is also and in large part due to the availability of more systematic and internationally comparable data. These data are the product of international organisations, such as the World Bank and the OECD, and individual economists, both in the comparative growth field[3] and the more specific 'technology measurement' area. Thus whereas the former growth-accounting literature tended implicitly to regard each country in isolation, most of the more recent empirical contributions in this area take their point of departure from the concept of technology transfer and spillovers. What is remarkable about this literature (or at least a good part of it) is its implicit break with the notion that all countries in the world economy are on the same production function, differing only in their factor prices and in their rates of accumulation of these factors. Technology thus partakes of the nature of a semiprivate or semipublic good, exploitable for a while by its creators, but also conditioned on the expenditure of resources and learning exertions, and with a delay, prone to imitation. The initial results indicated that, at least for the OECD, convergence seemed to be the rule in the postwar period, but this has given way to a much more differentiated picture for larger country samples. This confusing picture in turn has led to a search for additional factors and more complex models of the catchup phenomenon. While Bruno Amable's survey also deals with this question, Part II is totally given over to these issues. The above-mentioned chapter by Dosi and Fabiani develops a disaggregated model of firm-based differential national development and compares it to some known aspects of national product time series. Bart Verspagen provides a multifaceted view of the empirical situation, disentangling the forces operating for convergence and divergence. Finally, Edward Wolff examines the productivity performance of industrialised countries at the industry level, and argues that the trend to across-the-board convergence predominant until the 1970s has been replaced by a more differentiated process of specialisation.

The convergence debate has revived the question of the nature of technological capability, its creation and transmission. This is the starting point of Kenneth Arrow's keynote address, which concluded the conference and placed some of the central issues into a remarkably coherent context. Arrow particularly emphasises technology as knowledge, tracking down the conditions under which knowledge arises and the means by which it spreads, as well as the implications for modelling and forecasting. An equally important aspect of technology, dual to knowledge, so to speak, as Arrow himself points out, is technology as artifacts, tools, distinct capital and consumer goods. This is the focus of the contribution by Gerald Silverberg and Doris Lehnert, which investigates stochastically generated, capital-embodied innovations in a nonlinear dynamic framework. Nonlinear dynamics also provides the basis for Richard Day's analysis of the growth process in the very long term, as a possibly chaotic succession of stages of civilisation resulting from the complex interdependence of infrastructure and population. Both of these contributions emphasise that growth is much more likely to be a structured but fluctuating affair rather than a stable steady state. Finally, and as the concluding Chapter 12, Richard Nelson rounds out the contributions on growth in the aggregate with a masterly overview of the insights and shortcomings of the growth literature since the 1950s. Much of what was at the centre of 'appreciative theorising' years ago is only being rediscovered today, he argues.

While learning, increasing returns and imperfect competition have been increasingly employed by macro theorists in highly stylised ways, these are concepts that must be rooted in microeconomic behaviour and interaction to be adequately understood. This is the focus of Part III, which consists of three contributions broadly representative of the different methodological approaches at the forefront of contemporary economic theory. First, Thomas Ziesemer's chapter analyses oligopolistic competition in a market with epidemic demand diffusion for a new product using dynamic optimisation. This is followed in the chapter by Reinoud Joosten, Hans Peters and Frank Thuijsman by a dynamic game model of technological choice when both learning and *unlearning* by doing are possible. Finally, Yuri Kaniovski and Giovanni Dosi present a review of the mathematical foundations of the Polya urn approach to technological competition and some simple economic illustrations.

A few words should be said about the genealogy of the individual contributions. As mentioned, they derive from a conference held in December of 1992. We were in the fortunate position of being able to assign a distinguished scholar as discussant for each paper, copies of which were available sufficiently far in advance to both discussants and conference participants to allow for a very high level of interaction. Although the chapters themselves were subsequently revised by the authors, we have endeavoured to preserve as much as possible of the spontaneity and wit of the original discussions, which were recorded and subsequently transcribed by Anthony Arundel.[4] We proceeded along similar lines with respect to Kenneth Arrow's keynote speech, which was transcribed and edited by Paul Diederen. The chapters by Bruno Amable and Richard Nelson are substantially different from the ones they delivered at the conference, so that the comments of Elhanan Helpman and Theo van de Klundert, respectively, were no longer germane. Finally, we are in the fortunate position to have two commentators focusing on different aspects of the work of Joosten, Peters and Thuijsman, since this was originally presented as two related papers.

A book and a conference, just like a technology, also have a dual nature. In this case the material and aesthetic aspects of this book could only have been realised thanks to the unstinting efforts of Mieke Donders in preparing the manuscript and the camera-ready copy. And the almost deceptive smoothness of the conference itself could only have been the success it was due to the logistic expertise behind the scenes of Wilma Coenegrachts and Corien Gijsbers.

NOTES

1. The Maastricht Economic Research Institute on Innovation and Technology of the University of Limburg, The Netherlands, whose fifth anniversary was the occasion 10–12 December 1992, for the conference from which this volume is derived, alongside two other volumes edited by Ben Dankbaar and John Hagedoorn, both forthcoming with Edward Elgar.
2. Dosi, G. *et al.* (eds), *Technical Change and Economic Theory*, London: Pinter.
3. Most influential have been Summers and Heston's readily available purchasing power parity estimates, Maddison's painstaking reestimates of official data, crucial to productivity measurement, and Griliches and his NBER-coworkers.
4. Of course, the discussants were permitted to revise their texts to reflect the changes made by the authors in their final drafts. A certain amount of editing of the contributions from the floor proved necessary to eliminate comments made superfluous by these revisions.

PART I

The Technology–Growth Interaction

2. The Production and Distribution of Knowledge

Kenneth Arrow

Since knowledge is connected with the idea of technical advance, it is an intrinsic part of any understanding of the growth process. Therefore, I should like to deal with some reflections on the classification, logical status and alternative theoretical formulations of the concept of knowledge, as it has recurred over and over again in discussions of growth theory. I shall consider four aspects of the role of knowledge in production. My first topic, and probably the primary one, is the idea of knowledge as an input and as an output in production. Next, I deal with the role of knowledge in the process of diffusion. Thirdly, I deal with tacit knowledge, and finally with the development of knowledge as a complex process.

1. KNOWLEDGE AS INPUT AND OUTPUT

Let me first note that knowledge is an extremely complex, multivariate concept. There is knowledge about all sorts of things and at all sorts of levels. However, in models, whether neoclassical or evolutionary, knowledge usually gets reduced from this extremely complex and multidimensional concept to one number: factor productivity.

The main idea is that knowledge is an input into production of other goods. In order to produce goods, you have to know how to produce, what to produce and many other dimensions. But as we are increasingly emphasising, knowledge is also an output, knowledge itself is produced. The essential feature is that the knowledge which is available, whether seen as factor productivity or otherwise, tends to increase with time. So, somehow, more of it is being created. The process by which it is created should also be captured by our models.

I should like, in particular, to point out the way knowledge concepts are used in growth theory in its earlier phases, the way the input and output aspects of knowledge are modelled there, and compare them with those in the evolutionary models.

9

1.1 Knowledge as Input

The first approach which, from a theoretical point of view, had quite a bit
of effect and has given rise to so many other researches is the idea
represented by the formula $Y = AF(K,L)$. Output is some constant times a
function F. The typical assumption here is that F is a well-behaved
neoclassical production function, concave homogeneous of degree one. It
can be thought of as the output you would get from a given K and given L
at some point in time. As time goes on, or if countries vary (it could be in
comparison to a base country), then we think of F as multiplied by a
factor A, a measure of total factor productivity. However, with less loading
of theory, F can also be thought of as simply a measure of resources, as
an index number of the inputs and need not necessarily be interpreted as a
production function.

This model was first used by Tinbergen in a paper in 1942, published
during the war in a German journal (*Weltwirtschaftliches Archiv*), so it
possibly did not attract the attention it might otherwise have done (Tinbergen 1942). Solow redeveloped this idea from an empirical point of view in
1957 (Solow 1957). There are variations that say that instead of multiplying the whole production function, we think of multiplying the factors,
and in effect we thus get more out of a given factor. This is called factor
augmenting rather than neutral technological progress. Therefore, instead
of Hicks-neutral technical progress we distinguish between various kinds
of factor augmentation and we may have Harrod-neutral and Solow-neutral
technical change, depending on whether it was assumed that progress took
place in one factor or the other. So one way to interpret this model is that
A is one more input into production, say the knowledge required to use the
other two. So you stay with three factors: capital, labour and knowledge,
into production.

In the new growth economics, we have a different kind of story. In
order to produce a new good you have to know how to produce the good.
A fixed amount of information is necessary to produce that good and you
have to pay a fixed cost to acquire this information, say from nature or
from R&D. After you have paid this fixed cost to obtain the production
knowledge, you produce at constant costs.

This approach is a bit more compatible with the economics of information. In fact, this aspect of new growth economics is based on the idea
that by higher scales one can get more than proportional increases of
output. There are a number of reasons why there can be increasing returns,
but even if you look in the work of Adam Smith (1776), a good part of
the reasons he gives why division of labour increases productivity are
information acquisitions. A worker develops skills: a worker who does the

same things over and over again learns better how to do it. This is repeated by Allyn Young in his 1928 presidential address to the Royal Economic Society (Young 1928). Whenever you have to have technical information about a product and how to produce it, you have a fixed cost. It need not be a rigid fixed cost: you can have more information and less information. Suppose you are doing work on process innovation, because you want to reduce the cost of production. You can imagine that the more you expend, the more likely you are to reduce the cost of production. As the budget goes up, you search among a wider set of alternatives and the probability that one of them will be good increases. So, even though the amount of information may be variable, you still can get increasing returns to scale. There are other aspects of increasing returns, other than information acquisition, but it certainly is a basic one, and the models that are used in the new growth economics represent a special case of this general principle.

1.2 Knowledge as Output

Now let me turn to the production of knowledge, to the question where does it come from. Solow and Tinbergen assumed that knowledge A increased exponentially over time, or equivalently, that the rate of change of A is proportional to A itself. Kennedy (1964) and von Weizsäcker (1966) considered the model $Y = F(AK, BL)$, where the change in A represents augmentation of capital and the change in B augmentation of labour, and assumed that there was a trade-off to augmenting capital versus labour. Silverberg and Lehnert's paper, presented at this conference [this volume], amounts to a stochastic version of Solow (1960). They have innovations coming along as a random process. Each innovation multiplies productivity of the previous innovation by a given factor, the same for all innovations. But the intervals by which they come along are random, say a Poisson variable, or a variation of that.

In all of these there is a particular interesting point: knowledge is produced. The new knowledge is a produced good, but the only input into that good is previous knowledge. So far this is a story in which knowledge produces knowledge, knowledge along with material resources produce material outputs, but there is no feedback from material outputs into the creation of knowledge. Shell (1967), proposed a variation of the Solow model in which the rate of increase in knowledge is a function of the resources devoted to R&D. New knowledge is produced jointly by existing knowledge and by resources: knowledge is only one input into knowledge. Thus, the rate of growth of the knowledge can be increased by devoting more resources to it. The more resources you give, the greater the probability of a breakthrough or discovery. Moreover, there is a trade-off between material inputs and knowledge in the equation of the production of new knowledge. In many respects, the paper presented here by Dosi and his collaborators at this conference [this volume] could be thought of as a particular realisation of the Shell method. It is a search model: the more resources you give, the greater the probability of a breakthrough or discovery. Given the kind of discovery, the expenditure of resources is stochastically related to the size of the improvement in productivity.

Now in the typical form of Romer's articles (Romer 1986, 1990), and some others, the essential expansion of output takes the form of new products. The launching of this new product tends in the formal representations of the models to be a cost of entry. This can be seen as a cost of information, which tends to be given once and for all. Therefore, in this significant stream, knowledge is a function of resources devoted to knowledge, not a function of the existing knowledge.

One kind of categorisation of theories is whether growth is endogenous or exogenous. In the Solow model, growth of course is partly endogenous through capital formation, but some other driving factor is the exogenous growth in labour. In this model, everything is produced out of something. Since knowledge is produced out of knowledge, it is not a reasonable thing to consider it an exogenous factor from the point of view of the rest of the system: it would be a peculiar definition of an exogenous variable.

I think the conclusion which seems to emerge from all this is that there is some exogenous stock of knowledge. To some extent knowledge creation in this view functions somewhat like the ideal university does: to make new knowledge out of old knowledge. If you put it that way, a great deal of science, basic science, is self-generated. Nevertheless, although the stock of knowledge is a very important factor in the growth of new knowledge, I think most of us would tend to feel that the resources devoted to it are also significant. Indeed, the question of whether there is room for policy seems to depend largely on this feature. But even if resources are not needed for new knowledge, if the basic determinant of new knowledge is old knowledge, even then there may be some question of how knowledge is being used in different directions.

1.3 Externalities and Policy

If we think that resources do affect production of knowledge then we have to model that more explicitly. One interesting point is that knowledge is not a commodity like other commodities: it is non-rivalrous in the terminology of Paul Romer. If I take my knowledge and give you some, I still have got the same knowledge as I had before. On the other hand, when I know something and you tell it to me, then I do not know more than I did before. So the algebra of information is not like the algebra of ordinary commodities. That not only means that the pricing of knowledge becomes a tricky business, but also that its spreading cannot be avoided. You cannot exclude others from acquiring information, even if you try to. An obvious example is the development and marketing of a new product. Consider somebody who is thinking of going into the business of a new product. He does not know whether this product can be produced at all and therefore he may be deterred from engaging in the R&D necessary to determine that. As soon as somebody else would put this product on the market, however, the first competitor understands that it can be produced, and the probabilities that he enters the business will have changed radically. There are certainly various ways of restricting access to information and knowledge: there are patent laws, there is secrecy. However, these only add something to the cost; they cannot offer insuperable barriers. Knowledge cannot be made private property in the sense other things are made private property.

Because knowledge has these public good features, it must be that in some sense the motives for producing information are, maybe not of a different nature, but of a different order of magnitude than those for producing other goods. It implies that the value of the goodwill does not end up fully in the hands of the producer. It is essential, though, that the producer may hold on to some of it. Even Schumpeter discusses this question: the prospect of acquiring this value in the form of temporary monopoly profits is the incentive to engage in a race to be the first to produce the new information. The period of monopoly might not be very long, may typically be pretty short when compared to the life of the product in society, and thus the share of the value of the knowledge accruing to its producer may be small.

Just to illustrate the public good character of knowledge, consider the following quick calculation. About 2.5% of total US resources are devoted to R&D. Suppose all growth of the national product is due to R&D. Then easy calculation shows that the (average) benefit–cost ratio equals 40 times g/r (where g is the rate of growth and r is the rate of return, such that g/r is somewhere in the order of one-half). This tremendous benefit–cost ratio would suggest, at least from a social point of view, an enormous underinvestment in the generation of new knowledge. Obviously growth will take place for other reasons than R&D, and acquisition of knowledge and learning are not confined to organised R&D, so that this figure is probably too high. Nevertheless, these rough figures suggest that the public goods character of knowledge is hurting us quite badly. Since we do seem to have had past growth success, motives of a noneconomic character must be playing a major role.

2. DIFFUSION AND THE AGGREGATE PRODUCTION FUNCTION

I want to discuss a further aspect which is very important in the question of the role of knowledge in production. That is the question of its diffusion. It is a fact that knowledge, once it enters the system, once it is acquired from nature, is in one place, and we are interested in the way it tends to spread to other places. So we have the question of acquisition of knowledge in particular places, of diffusion of knowledge. There are several mechanisms possible: information may spread through some mechanical means; its spread may be a result of deliberate policy; if people are aware that there is knowledge somewhere else, they may acquire it by special activities of one kind or another.

2.1 Mechanisms of Diffusion

Evolutionary theory stresses that the spread of new knowledge is often connected to capital expansion. The argument is that when knowledge is located somewhere, say in a firm, it is not so much that the knowledge spreads to other places, as that the firm with the knowledge gets bigger and the other firms get smaller. The expansion of the firm which has a command over the knowledge takes place because it earns a profit, allowing it to invest. The mechanism works in particular if there is the opportunity to transfer wealth, through capital markets or some other mechanism, from less to more profitable areas, the more profitable area being the one where the knowledge has been acquired. This capital expansion plays a big role in the Silverberg and Lehnert model referred to earlier.

There are many other mechanisms of diffusion at work, though, in particular ones in which the emphasis is on imitation (Chapter 6 by Dosi and Fabiani illustrates this). Here the firm goes out and looks at other firms and finds out what they are doing and what can be good for them. They look at why their competitors are doing better than they are, and try to find out why they do better and take over that technique. It is a different mechanism, in that the first mechanism is based on the resources expended by the leading firm, whereas the second is based on the use of resources by the firm that is behind.

These two mechanisms also figure in a somewhat speculative study by Albert Ammerman and Luigi Cavalli-Sforza (1984) on diffusion of agriculture in prehistoric Europe. They have evidence on certain genes connected to blood type and their distribution in parts of Europe. From this evidence they inferred a gradient of specific genes from Asia Minor through Europe. The gradient traces out a pattern of migration. Since we know that agriculture was invented in the Near East, this suggests that agriculture was brought to Europe by migrants from the Near East. To describe this process, they have a model which combines migration, which is like capital expansion, with imitation. Some of the previous European settlers saw their neighbours doing these strange things, like putting seeds in the ground, and imitated. Ammerman and Cavalli-Sforza thus, on the basis of fairly fragmentary data, infer something about the relevant importance of migration and imitation as mechanisms driving the diffusion of agriculture, and argue that both mechanisms in fact took place.

There is a third important mechanism of diffusion, somewhat similar to the second but not quite the same, and that is the one assumed in epidemic models, which have been so commonly used in diffusion studies. The difference from the imitation mechanism is related to the idea of search. In imitation models search tends to be active search, where agents engage in action to find the information they can use. In epidemic models, people having the new information run into those who do not, and somehow knowledge transfer takes place, such as by hiring away the engineers from the other firm.

2.2 Distribution of Knowledge

Having dwelt on the diffusion of information and knowledge, let me now return to the aggregate production function approaches to growth analysis mentioned before. What the diffusion story points out is that what is being disseminated is not factor productivity. What diffuses is very particular knowledge of how to do things. At any moment in time, this knowledge will be very unequally distributed. It is not as if we always have it everywhere, but there is a process in which knowledge is being created all the time in different places, and is then being diffused. This evolving distribution of knowledge should be reflected in a model of production, if it is to describe an entire economy in which different people know different things. As a consequence, the idea of an aggregate production function becomes very dubious, unless a new variable is introduced, representing the distribution and diffusion of new knowledge.

One of the consequences, by the way, and this is pointed out by Silverberg and Lehnert (Chapter 5), is that you would expect the gains in productivity to be greater, the bigger the variance of the distribution of knowledge. This is similar to a model in a paper by Stephen Marglin (1969) about the allocation of some given resource among a number of different users. He assumed a redistribution mechanism reallocating resources from the low marginal productivity areas to the high productivity areas. It turned out that the rate of growth of total output is proportional to the variance of the marginal productivities. Thus, the greater the spread in marginal productivities, the more gain you will be getting per unit time by these transfer processes. This is comparable to what was referred to as the capital expansion mechanism of diffusion. Also with an imitation mechanism you get qualitatively the same thing, the possibility of gain proportional to the variance. This might give a very interesting explanation of why it is not just the average level of knowledge that is relevant, but also its distribution.

3. TACIT KNOWLEDGE AND LEARNING BY DOING

There is another complicating aspect to the role of knowledge in production that needs to be touched upon in this context. Not all knowledge is of such a form that it can be transferred in that form easily, that it may diffuse in the ways as described above. There is so-called tacit or personal knowledge. You can know how to do things, without necessarily being able to describe how you do it.

It seems to me that there is in fact no knowledge that can be fully codified and transferred at the level of consciousness. Even a formal thing like doing mathematics depends to some extent on tact, feel and intuitive understanding, on things you cannot put down. Ways of doing these types of things are transferred by teachers to students by doing things together and by working through examples. There is a certain element of tacit knowledge in every knowledge. This tacit knowledge of course will not diffuse in the same way as non-tacit knowledge. For example, imitation may be much harder with tacit knowledge. The capital expansion mechanism will work perfectly well, although there the problem is to transfer the tacit knowledge within the organisation. This is a matter of practical concern. As there are organisations with more and more people, there have to be ways of assimilating new workers to the knowledge base of the organisation. If the rate of expansion is high enough, one expects to have a lot of trouble with the ratio of experienced people and inexperienced people regarding this transfer of tacit knowledge.

There are a number of fields, including quite high-tech fields, where the role of tacit knowledge is very high. An example would be a company making modern vacuum tubes. Making vacuum tubes of reliable quality is something that nobody can really explain how to do. Typically, a team of experienced people works together, making tubes with very few errors, but they cannot explain what they are doing. New people are brought into the team without much formal training and learn on the job. There is no other reasonable way that the skill can be transferred. Learning by doing is one way of reproducing tacit knowledge. It reproduces it not by spending resources in any explicit way, but as a by-product or joint product of production. Thus one expects the diffusion of tacit knowledge to have different properties.

4. DEVELOPMENT OF KNOWLEDGE AS A COMPLEX PROCESS

The main conclusion to be drawn from the foregoing reflections about knowledge as a determinant of production is the fact that knowledge is a multidimensional concept. This again stresses the inappropriateness of identifying it with one number, with factor productivity. An implication of this intricate nature of knowledge is that the creation of knowledge is a complex process. This can be defined here as a process that necessitates you to go sequentially through the whole chain of stages of its development to see where it ends up. It is like a difference equation. A non-complex difference equation can be solved, whereas a complex one requires you to compute the entire process to see where it goes. Attempting to predict the outcome of the complex process of developing new knowledge puts you in a similar situation. If you have a sufficiently nonlinear system, the only way to be able to predict the outcome is to go through all the intermediate stages, which in fact takes just as long as the knowledge itself takes to develop.

Let me give you an example from my own experience. I was a weather forecaster during the Second World War. Our group was summoned once and informed that Japanese balloons were crossing the ocean and dropping firebombs on the western part of the United States. It was a very ingenious mechanism, ingenious because it was extremely inexpensive. The problem was that they had alerted the anti-aircraft batteries on the West Coast of this phenomenon, and the batteries were shooting at everything in sight, such as the planet Venus rising in the morning. They thought that this was a little wasteful. The question was if we could tell them, given the winds, where along the coast the balloons would pass. They would then only alert that stretch of the coast and the wastage would be considerably reduced. We did not know then that an MIT meteorologist years later would say this is an intrinsically chaotic process. But we knew perfectly well we could not forecast six days in advance. In fact, we could not say any more than that they would land on the West Coast.

We did have weather observers behind the Japanese lines in China, they would send up balloons which we could track, and we would then know where the Japanese balloons would be. In other words, the only way to predict where the Japanese balloons would be was to observe them when they came. It was a complex problem. The prediction time was equal to the performance time.

Now, predicting an innovation is an intrinsically self-contradictory statement. If we could know what an innovation would be, we could make it today. Why wait? If we want to know what the state of electric cars will be in the year 2000, there is one certain way to find out: wait until the year 2000. After all, every prediction takes time. A somewhat extreme version is that it takes as much time to predict as the performance. There is nothing illogical about that. It is in this sense that the whole idea of modelling technological progress is something we have to be very modest about. It is an intrinsically complex process in a very well-defined sense of the word complexity. This insight is not original with me. It was already advanced by Karl Popper in his book *The Poverty of Historicism* (1957). He attacked the idea that it is possible to predict history, and he gave innovations as an example.

Let me conclude by mentioning that we even have historians *postdict*. They go back and tell us how a certain invention came to pass. What is very bothersome, I find, even if it may be correct, is that the stories tend to have a very accidental character about them. We know that Pascal, although he may not be a modern historian, claimed that if Cleopatra's nose had been a quarter of an inch longer, the history of the Roman Empire would have been different. My colleague Paul David examined why reapers were much slower to be introduced to England than to the United States, and argued that it was because the fields in England, after 600 years of cultivation, had much steeper furrows. You would not think about this unless you knew all the specific facts, and in that sense it has an accidental character. Most likely this is telling us something about how things really are; we are not going to know general principles. This does cast a shadow on the idea of forecasting in this area of research.

REFERENCES

Ammerman, A.J. and Cavalli-Sforza, L.L. (1984), *The Neolithic Revolution and the Genetics of Populations in Europe*, Princeton: Princeton University Press.

Kennedy, C. (1964), 'Induced Bias in Innovations and the Theory of Distribution', *Economic Journal*, 74, 541–547.

Marglin, S. (1969), 'Information in Price and Command Systems of Planning', in J. Margolis and H. Guitton (eds), *Public Finance*, New York: St. Martin's Press.

Romer, P. (1986), 'Increasing Returns and Long Run Growth', *Journal of Political Economy*, 94, 1002–1037.

Romer, P. (1990), 'Are Nonconvexities Important for Understanding Economic

Growth?', *American Economic Review*, Paper and Proceedings, 80, 97–103.

Shell, K. (1967), 'A Model of Inventive Activity and Capital Accumulation', in K. Shell (ed.), *Essays on the Optimal Theory of Growth*, Cambridge, MA: MIT Press.

Smith, A. (1776), *An Inquiry into the Nature and Causes of the Wealth of Nations*, Book I, Chapter I.

Solow, R. (1957), 'Technical Progress and the Aggregate Production Function', *Review of Economics and Statistics*, 39, 312–320.

Solow, R. (1960), 'Investment and Technical Progress', in K. Arrow, S. Karlin and P. Suppes (eds), *Mathematical Methods in the Social Sciences, 1959*, Stanford: Stanford University Press.

Tinbergen, J. (1942), 'Zur Theorie der langfristigen Wirtschaftsentwicklung', *Weltwirtschaftliches Archiv*, 55, 511–549. English translation: 'On the Theory of Trend Movements', in L.H. Klassen, L.M. Koyck and H.J. Witteveen (eds), *J. Tinbergen, Selected Essays*, Amsterdam: North-Holland, 1959.

von Weizsäcker, C.C. (1966), 'Tentative Notes on a Two Sector Model with Induced Technical Progress', *Review of Economic Studies*, 33, 245–251.

Young, A. (1928), 'Increasing Returns and Economic Progress', *Economic Journal*, 38, 527–542.

3. Endogenous Growth Theory, Convergence and Divergence

Bruno Amable[*]

1. INTRODUCTION

Just before the mid-1980s, interest in growth theory was somewhat limited, but it has revived with the appearance of 'new' or endogenous growth models. There have been quite a few surveys published on endogenous growth theory recently.[1] The renewed interest in the literature must, in this case at least, be taken as a sign that an important change of perspective has been adopted as far as the *sources* of growth are concerned. The new approaches stress the role played by technical progress as well as its determinants. In contrast to the traditional neoclassical growth model (Solow 1956, 1957), where technical progress is no more than a simple time trend, the new growth models take into account an endogenous determination of technical change, which actually means an endogenous determination of the sources of growth. Indeed, Solow's neoclassical growth model is characterised by a constant returns production function – an hypothesis compatible with perfect competition – with capital and labour as its arguments. The former is an accumulable factor, the latter may not be so. This means that without a labour-augmenting trend or a constant rate of technological progress, growth vanishes because of the unbounded decreasing marginal returns on the only accumulated factor, capital. Indeed the accumulation of capital brings a decreasing return that dries up any incentive to invest in the long run. Therefore, only exogenous influences can save growth. In such a framework the equilibrium growth rate is exogenous too, and independent of economic influences.

One may of course overcome this 'weakness' by endogenising technical progress. Kaldor (1957) and Arrow (1962) did precisely that by focusing on learning effects as a source of improvement in technology. Some endogenous growth models adopt more or less this approach, where technical progress is a by-product of production or investment.

* This paper owes much to collaboration with D. Guellec.

Growth is truly made endogenous this way, but another meaning is sometimes attached to the word endogenous, in reference to 'micro-foundations'. In a typically neoclassical tradition, technical change is made endogenous because economic agents choose to allocate a certain amount of resources to its development, for instance R&D expenditures or time for education. This approach may find support in many studies in the fields of industrial economics or microeconomics, but the endogenous character of growth is independent of whether one can find microeconomic motives behind technical change.

Perpetual growth is made possible by the presence of increasing returns to scale or externalities, which guarantees that marginal productivity in the accumulation of factors does not go to zero when these factors are accumulated. Most models then adopt a particular specification of accumulation: a certain quantity of resources produces a given percentage increase of a factor, not a given quantity. In fact, the specification of the production function of the consumption good is immaterial if this good is not used for accumulation purposes. What matters is the technology of production of the accumulated factor(s).

Following Amable and Guellec (1992), one can classify endogenous growth models according to several criteria. A first typology may be established based on the type of competitive mechanism on which the models are based. Increasing returns are also implicated in many endogenous growth models. Of course, in such a framework, the assumption of perfect competition present in the traditional neoclassical growth model cannot always be retained. Some models resort to Marshallian externalities, but many endogenous growth models display imperfect competition. A second typology could be devised based on the concept of growth adopted. Most models consider a traditional definition (growth of output or productivity), but some models rely on the growth of utility of a representative consumer. In fact, the difference is purely formal as argued in Grossman and Helpman (1991). A third typology is based on the sources of growth. The first source lies in investment in a certain factor. Romer (1986) considers a growth model not restrained by constant returns, but where the economies of scale are external to the firm. This model can support perfect competition.

Other models of endogenous growth have insisted on the particular role played by technological innovation and on the importance of the resources devoted to R&D. Romer (1990a) presents a model in which capital is not a homogeneous good, but rather a set of different intermediate goods. New inputs are discovered when one devotes R&D resources to a search process. Aghion and Howitt (1992) offer a different framework in which innovation consists of a series of 'creative destructions' rather than an increase in the range of available inputs of production. Each new in-novation takes the place of the preceding one, putting an end to the monopoly power attached to it.

A third source of endogenous growth may be found in the accumulation of human capital. In Lucas (1988), individuals accumulate human capital in a context of increasing returns. Moreover, the productivity of each worker in the production of the final good is all the higher the higher the average level of human capital. This constitutes a positive externality related to the individual accumulation of human capital.

A fourth source of growth may take the form of public goods and infrastructure: communication networks, information services, and so on. These goods are characterised by the fact that they increase the productiv-ity of private factors. The possibility of a simultaneous use of such goods by a large number of agents makes them public goods in the traditional sense. They will accordingly be produced by social institutions financed through taxes. The public goods policy of the state will of course have a tremendous importance. Several models of Barro (1990) and Barro and Sala-i-Martin (1992) tackle this problem. This last source of growth will not be addressed in the present paper. The first section stresses the difference between endogenous and 'exogenous' growth. Section 3 presents the main models of endogenous growth, making no attempt to be exhaustive.

Endogenous growth models have entered their diffusion phase. One can now see applications of endogenous growth theory rather than simply the development of new growth models. The major area of application is probably international economics. Grossman and Helpman have developed several models of international economics in a number of papers as well as in a book (Grossman and Helpman 1991). In these models of endogenous growth, international trade not only affects the level of international activity but its growth rate as well. Comparative advantage may thus become endogenous, and trade and research policy measures can have an effect on growth rates. Moreover, there is a possibility of persis-tent growth rate differentials.

This last point has been the focus of the empirical discussion of the impact of new growth theory. Broadly speaking, traditional neoclassical growth theory says that if all countries have access to the same tech-nology, they should all converge to the same level of per capita GDP provided tastes are identical across countries. Many endogenous growth models say that there is no tendency for countries to converge to the same level of development. A brief survey of the empirical literature is presented in section 4.

2. WHAT IS ENDOGENOUS GROWTH?

2.1 The Limits of the Neoclassical Model

The simplest neoclassical model of growth posits a constant returns production function with two factors, capital (K) and labour (L):

$$Y = F(K,L) \tag{3.1}$$

One may add to this specification an exogenous trend of technical progress as well as a constant growth rate of the population.

An equation representing the accumulation of capital is added to the model. Capital is homogeneous to the output, so that the same good may be used for investment or consumption purposes. Agents are confronted with an allocation decision between the two possible uses. The simplest assumption is to suppose that agents save a constant proportion s of their income, so that investment is equal to sY. Nevertheless, it is widely held that the 'proper consumption' Solow model (Hahn 1990) is its 'Ramseyification', whereby agents optimise their consumption flow over time and the saving propensity is made endogenous.

The growth process may be represented as follows. The variation in the level of capital K depends on the level of output Y, that is, on the level of K since Y and K are linked by a functional relationship. Since the marginal productivity of K in the production of Y decreases with the level of K, the higher this level is, the less capital contributes to increasing production. This means that capital accumulation is more and more difficult, so that growth stops in the long run. This result stems from the particular specification of the savings behaviour, and is in fact a typically neoclassical result. Incentives to invest shrink with the accumulation of capital.

The neoclassical growth model, thus specified, is unable to explain growth. A positive growth rate of per capita income can only exist if there is an exogenous trend due to technical progress. Otherwise, growth in Solow's basic model is limited to transitory dynamics. Other features of Solow's model are worth noting. The level of the savings rate influences the equilibrium capital/worker ratio, but not the equilibrium growth rate, which is exogenous by definition. In fact, at the equilibrium, all savings are used to build up capital for incoming workers, not to increase capital for the existing workers. A policy affecting the level of savings will thus only have a level effect, and a transitory effect, when the economy converges towards the equilibrium level of capital per worker, but it will not have any effect on the growth rate.

Second, in an international framework, all countries must converge towards the same level of capital and income per capita under the hypothesis that all agents have the same tastes, that is, they have the same savings rate. Poor countries will thus 'catch up' to rich countries. It seems rather difficult to reconcile this forecast with the observed facts of the last forty years, as many empirical studies demonstrate.

In fact, in order to obtain unceasing growth, one must take into account an external factor that increases the productivity of the inputs of production over time. The integration of exogenous technical progress T in a production function,

$$Y = F(K,L;T), \tag{3.2}$$

allows this under the assumption that T is not a production factor like K or L. The assumption of constant returns in the production function would mean that the marginal returns to capital and technology would have to be decreasing, preventing them from contributing to growth in the long run unless additional specific assumptions are introduced.[2]

The simplest way to introduce technical progress as an exogenous trend is in the form

$$Y = T_0 \, e^{\mu t} \, K^{\alpha} \, L^{1-\alpha}, \tag{3.3}$$

where μ represents the rate of growth of productive efficiency. The rate of growth of per capita income is thus non-zero:

$$g = \frac{\mu}{1 - \alpha}, \tag{3.4}$$

and capital accumulation occurs at the same rate. Technical progress has two effects. The first one is a direct increase in productivity (μ), the second one is an increase in the return to capital, leading to additional investment and thus extra income (the multiplier is $\alpha\mu(1 - \alpha)$). Accumulation of capital is a direct consequence of technical change, which is then the only source of growth. Since technical progress is not itself explained, one may say that growth in this model is exogenous.

2.2 The 'Technical Conditions' for Endogenous Growth

This section focuses on the formal conditions that allow growth to be endogenous. It was seen previously that the unbounded decrease of the marginal productivity of capital prevents long-run growth. In order to obtain unceasing growth, the accumulated factors of production must together have an elasticity of production at least equal to one. Endogenous growth comes from a factor that prevents the unbounded decrease of the marginal productivity of a factor of production that is indispensable to growth. If some indispensable factors are not accumulable, endogenous growth is only possible in the presence of increasing returns, this last characteristic leading possibly to the consideration of other market structures than perfect competition.

The role of returns to scale

Some recent models solve the problem of returns to scale by supposing that there is only one factor of production. The elasticity of production of this factor is one, and there are constant returns to scale. A simple case is the model of Rebelo (1990), where the production function is

$$Y = AK. \tag{3.5}$$

The marginal productivity of capital thus is constant. If there were non-accumulable factors of production alongside K in the above production function, unceasing growth would require the existence of increasing returns to scale. In the above formula, labour is assimilated to human capital and is therefore accumulable and subsumed under physical capital.

Investment is equal to the difference between production and consumption,

$$\dot{K} = Y - c. \tag{3.6}$$

Savings are supposed to be determined as a result of an intertemporal maximisation of the utility of consumption, utilising the following utility function for a representative agent:

$$U(c) = \int_t^\infty e^{-\rho\tau} \frac{c^{1-\sigma}}{1-\sigma} \, d\tau, \tag{3.7}$$

where ρ is the rate of time preference and σ the intertemporal elasticity of substitution, which is equal to the risk aversion.

With a population of fixed size, there is no exogenous source of growth. One can obtain from the above specifications an equilibrium of regular growth where income, capital and consumption grow at the same rate. This rate of growth is

$$g = \frac{A - \rho}{\sigma}. \tag{3.8}$$

This framework allows us to obtain endogenous growth while retaining the assumption of constant returns to scale, perfect competition and optimality of the market equilibrium.

If capital and final product are the same good, and if the production of the latter requires non-accumulable factors (for example, labour or any non-depletable natural resource), then increasing returns are a necessary condition for endogenous growth. But if capital is a specific good produced with a different technology than the final good, then the characteristics of the technology of production of the capital good do matter.

An elementary model of endogenous growth

The introduction of factors such as 'human capital' or knowledge can overcome the limitations present in the Solow model, because their accumulation does not depend on the final product, whose marginal returns to accumulated factors are decreasing. Technical progress may then be permitted by the accumulation of human capital, the per capita level of which is able to grow without limits. Taking such a variable into account allows us to keep a public good aspect to the factor responsible for growth, and to retain the assumption of perfect competition.

A very simple model of endogenous growth is presented below.[3] The basic equations are

$$Y = A^{\alpha} L^{1-\alpha}, \tag{3.9}$$

$$\dot{A} = \delta A^{\gamma} (\bar{L} - L)^{\beta}. \tag{3.10}$$

Y is the final product, L is labour and A is the level of knowledge. Population is fixed at $\bar{L}$. The technology of production of the final good exhibits constant returns to scale and includes a non-accumulable factor.

The production of 'knowledge' differs from that of the final good. What is saved is not a fraction of total output, as in models based on physical investment, but a fraction of the time of the labour force. The agent splits her time between producing the final good, which gives utility through consumption, and accumulating knowledge that will guarantee an increased production of the final good and hence future utility. Knowledge enters both the final good production function and its own. It cannot be assimilated to physical capital, the use of which is said to be 'exclusive', that is, cannot be used for two simultaneous purposes.

The non-exclusive character of knowledge is not enough to allow for endogenous growth. Indeed

$$\frac{\dot{A}}{A} = \delta \, A^{\gamma-1} \, (\bar{L} - L)^{\beta}, \tag{3.11}$$

so that

$$\frac{\dot{A}}{A} \leq \delta \, \bar{L}^{\beta} \, A^{\gamma-1}. \tag{3.12}$$

Therefore, if $\gamma < 1$, then $\dot{A}/A$ goes to zero when A grows.

The process of knowledge accumulation will eventually become exhausted. In order to obtain unceasing growth, it is necessary that $\gamma \geq 1$. Since $\beta > 0$, one has $\gamma + \beta > 1$. Thus knowledge is produced with increasing returns, for otherwise long-term growth cannot occur. In order to rule out explosive growth, which will happen if $\gamma > 1$, one must have $\gamma = 1$, which yields the following knowledge accumulation equation (with $\beta = 1$):

$$\frac{\dot{A}}{A} = \delta \, (\bar{L} - L). \tag{3.13}$$

This means that the production of a given extra proportion of A, not a given extra level of A, always requires the same effort, whatever the level of A is. L thus becomes increasingly more efficient in the production of the final good. The increasing returns in the knowledge accumulation equation may also be interpreted as an intertemporal externality. By accumulating more knowledge today, society elevates its future productivity.

Taking the same utility function as in the previous section, eq. (3.7), the optimal rate of knowledge accumulation is

$$\frac{\dot{A}}{A} = \frac{\alpha \, \delta \, \bar{L} - \rho \, (1 - \alpha)}{\alpha \, [1 - (1 - \sigma) \, (1 - \alpha)]}, \tag{3.14}$$

so that the economy's growth rate is

$$g = \frac{\alpha \, \delta \, \bar{L} - \rho \, (1 - \alpha)}{1 - (1 - \sigma) \, (1 - \alpha)}. \tag{3.15}$$

One thus obtains endogenous growth with constant returns in the final good production and in the presence of a non-accumulable factor, thanks to the possibility of an endogenous improvement of knowledge at a constant rate. Nevertheless, the model presented above, as well as the one presented in the previous section, is too simple to allow for a discussion of the sources of endogenous growth. This is why it is indispensable to look more closely at the main endogenous growth models.

3. THE SOURCES OF ENDOGENOUS GROWTH

3.1 Investment and Growth

Positive externalities linked to the accumulation of a particular factor are a first possible source of endogenous growth. Learning phenomena have been explored in the economic growth literature before endogenous growth models appeared. Kaldor (1957) proposed a technical progress function where productivity increased with the rate of investment I/K. Arrow (1962) took into account the effects of learning by doing, inspired by Kaldor. Sheshinski (1967) proposed a production function of the form

$$y = F(k, Al), \tag{3.16}$$

where y is the output of a firm, l the labour input and A is a function of the available knowledge in the economy, specified as

$$A = K^\gamma, \quad \gamma < 1, \tag{3.17}$$

with $K = Nk$, N being the number of firms in the economy. There is thus an externality, each firm benefiting from the knowledge accumulated by other firms. However, as in Arrow's (1962) model, the economy's growth rate goes to zero without population growth, so that growth remains exogenous because of the presence of decreasing returns in knowledge accumulation.

The models of Arrow and Sheshinsky took into account the positive externalities linked to knowledge accumulation. Externalities are a way of dealing with increasing returns to scale without having to relinquish the assumption of perfect competition. Following Marshall, one supposes that economies of scale are external to the firm, for which production occurs under non-increasing returns. Technical progress linked to an increase in the economy-wide division of labour permitted by an extension of the market (Young 1928) are represented through a positive technological externality.

Romer (1986) considers a model in which positive technological externalities are a by-product of the accumulation of a factor K, knowledge. One could also consider K to contain a non-physical component. Two distinct mechanisms can provide a foundation for the externalities. The first one is related to the 'learning spillover'. By accumulating capital, the firm accumulates knowledge through learning by doing, knowledge that can also benefit other firms. The second mechanism concerns capital itself. There exist complementarities between activities and firms when markets are incomplete (Rosenberg 1982; Durlauf 1991). Some activities require a simultaneous development of several industries, an idea featured in the model of Murphy, Shleifer and Vishny (1989).

Romer's (1986) model can be summarised briefly. k_j is the level of capital per head in firm j. The production function is

$$Y_j = f(k_j, K),$$ (3.18)

where

$$K = \sum_j k_j.$$ (3.19)

N, the number of firms in the economy, is fixed, and there is perfect competition. Specifying the production and utility functions by

$$u(c) = \ln(c)$$ (3.20)

and

$$F(k,K) = k^{\alpha} K^{\eta},$$ (3.21)

there are three solutions:

1. $\alpha + \eta < 1$. This case corresponds to decreasing returns to scale on accumulable factors, in this case firm knowledge and global knowledge, as in an exogenous growth model. The positive externality is not strong enough to offset the effects of marginal decreasing returns. In the long run, this model behaves like the models of Solow and Arrow.
2. $\alpha + \eta = 1$. This case corresponds to constant returns to scale on the accumulated factors. Therefore, growth is possible. One may notice that with this specification, there is no transitory dynamics. Every growth trajectory is characterised by a constant rate g, whatever the initial condition:

$$g = \alpha N^{\eta} - \rho,$$ (3.22)

and the production function may be written in the form

$$F(K,L) = T_0 \, e^{gt} \, K^{\alpha} \, L^{1-\alpha}.$$ (3.23)

The reduced form above shows that the model is observationally equivalent to a traditional neoclassical growth model with an exogenous technical progress trend g. The properties of the model are different, however. In particular, there is an effect of the savings rate on the rate of growth, in contrast to the traditional neoclassical growth model.

3. $\alpha + \eta > 1$. This case corresponds to a production function with increasing returns on the accumulated factors alone. The economy's growth rate keeps increasing all the time and growth is explosive. Therefore, regular growth is a razor's edge possibility in this model, since the elasticity of production on all the accumulated factors must equal exactly one. Actually, this characteristic is common to all growth models based on the accumulation of factors, and is not specific to this model.

An important feature of this model is that the market equilibrium is suboptimal on account of the externality in the accumulation of knowledge, which is not considered by the individual firm in making its production plan. In fact, market equilibrium is characterised by a lower growth rate and level of investment than the social optimum.

3.2 Innovation and Growth

The models presented so far, with the exception of Rebelo (1990), were based on an externality linked to the accumulation of a factor. This approach raises the problem of returns to scale. Another approach is possible, based on innovation. The latter is conceived mostly as the outcome of the activity of research and development (R&D), an activity to which specific resources are dedicated. R&D expenditures allow for the development of new goods, either intermediate or final, depending on whether one focuses on the growth of production or utility. One can distinguish two classes of models of endogenous growth based on innovation, the expanding product variety and the rising product quality classes, in the terminology of Grossman and Helpman (1991). In the former type, new products are aggregated with old ones in the production or the utility function, and dynamic increasing returns to scale or preference for variety is assumed. In the latter type, the new goods are of a superior quality and they take the place of the old goods. Their introduction raises utility or productivity.

Increasing product variety

The basic model is that of Romer (1990a). The source of growth lies in an increase in the economy-wide division of labour. This is made explicit in the formalisation of the production function. A larger number of intermediate goods used in final good production raises the level of productivity. Unlike the previous models, technical progress is not so much a by-product of accumulation as the result of a specific activity: research and development. Technological innovation is the basis of growth and results from an economic choice of the agents.

The model of Romer (1990a) has three sectors: research, intermediate goods and final good. There are four production inputs: physical capital, unqualified labour L, human capital H and technology. The technological level can grow without bounds, but the level of human capital H is fixed because human capital is embodied in a fixed-size population. Thus, there is an important difference between such a conception of human capital and the conception found for instance in the model of Lucas (1988). In Romer's model, human capital does not grow, and the problem is to find an optimal allocation of it between production and research.

The most original aspect of the model is the form taken by physical capital. It is not a homogeneous good but a collection of differentiated inputs on a continuum. Denoting by $x(i)$ the quantity of input i used in final good production, Romer posits the following production function:

$$Y(H_1,L,x_i) = H_1^{\alpha} L^{\beta} \int_0^A x(i)^{1-\alpha-\beta} \, di \, . \qquad (3.24)$$

An important point is that the growth of the stock of capital used in the production of the final good will take place under the guise of the growth of the number of intermediate inputs A, not the quantity of each input. The increase in the number of intermediate goods is identified with the increase in the economy-wide division of labour and the use of more and more roundabout methods of production that increase productivity. Such a production function had been used in Ethier (1982), but in a static framework.

New intermediate goods are produced with a design bought from the research sector and a certain amount of the final good. This sector has increasing returns because of the fixed cost of purchasing a new design. Each intermediate good is produced by a monopolist, so that innovation assures a monopoly rent to the intermediate good producer. In fact, all intermediate goods are produced under the same conditions. They only differ with respect to their design. They will be used in the final sector in the same quantity, so that $x(i) = \bar{x}$ for all i. The production function may thus be written in the form

$$Y = A \, H_1^{\alpha} \, L^{\beta} \, \bar{x}^{1-\alpha-\beta}. \qquad (3.25)$$

One may note that the $\bar{x}$ term is a constant, whereas the A term is not.

Research firms discover new intermediate goods. The number of these goods evolves according to

$$\dot{A} = \delta \, H_2 \, A \, . \tag{3.26}$$

There are increasing returns in the research sector. The more resources are dedicated to research, the higher the sector's productivity is. This hypothesis allows for the growth of technology: $\dot{A}/A$ does not go to zero with A increasing. There are increasing returns in the production of technology.

In order to justify this, Romer mentions the peculiar nature of knowledge as an economic good. It is non-rival: the use of a certain piece of knowledge by someone does not prevent the simultaneous use of it by someone else. Each researcher has access to the discoveries of all of his colleagues, contemporaneous or not, in making his own research. Spillovers from the total stock of knowledge enter the production function of new knowledge.

Firms must pay in order to have the right to produce the newly discovered inputs. A patent system prevents the undesired use of new knowledge and protects the inventor. Knowledge is thus an exclusive good. There is both a private return to knowledge obtainable by the sale of patents and a social return linked to the positive externality of knowledge in the creation of new designs.

The solution of the model is an equilibrium path where A, K (the intermediate goods) and Y grow at constant rate, for a fixed allocation of H between H_1 and H_2. With the same type of utility function as before, one obtains the following growth rate:

$$g = \frac{\delta \, H - \Lambda \, \rho}{\Lambda \, \sigma + 1} \, , \tag{3.27}$$

where

$$\Lambda = \frac{\alpha}{(1 - \alpha - \beta) \, (\alpha + \beta)} . \tag{3.28}$$

The growth rate of the economy does not depend on the size of the population but on the size of H. It does not depend on the technology of production of the intermediate goods. It is an increasing function of the amount of human capital dedicated to research, H_2. It is the pattern of allocation of human capital between research and production that determines the pace of growth. Other parameters (e.g., risk aversion) also enter into the determination of the growth rate.

H_2 grows more than proportionately with H:

$$H_2 = \frac{H - \rho \dfrac{\Lambda}{\delta}}{\Lambda \sigma + 1} . \tag{3.29}$$

An economy endowed with more human capital will grow more rapidly because a larger part of its human capital will be dedicated to research. If the level of human capital H is too low, only the solution $H_2 = 0$ is possible, so that human capital is completely dedicated to production. The economy's growth rate is then zero. This possibility represents a 'no-growth trap'.

It is no surprise that the optimal growth rate differs from the market outcome. The former is greater than the latter because a social planner would take into account the externalities linked to knowledge creation, and thus allocate a higher fraction of human capital to research activity.

Policy recommendations derived from this model vary. A policy favouring human capital (H) is efficient with respect to growth, as is a research subsidy policy (through δ), but a policy favouring investment will have no effect on growth.

One may advance two critical remarks regarding this model. First, the growth rate of an economy depends directly on the size of the country (measured with respect to human capital). Such a size effect appears too simple. Moreover, human capital is assumed to be of a fixed size, embodied in a constant population. This means that the model cannot admit both a positive growth rate in the level of human capital and a constant rate of growth of the economy. Second, technological change is cumulative to such an extent that all intermediate goods are used forever in the production of the final good. The number of intermediate products keeps growing and the relative weight of each one keeps decreasing with time. The Schumpeterian notion of 'creative destruction' is absent in this model.

Rising product quality
Aghion and Howitt (1992) have proposed an endogenous growth model in which creative destruction is present. There are three sectors in the economy: the intermediate good-producing sector, the final good-producing sector and the research sector. Technical progress does not manifest itself in an increase in the number of available intermediate goods but by a rise in the productivity that the intermediate good allows in final good production. Each innovation is thus an improvement of the intermediate good. The producer of the older intermediate product loses his monopoly profits and is replaced by the producer of the new good. There is thus a creative destruction aspect, manifested in the fact that each new product takes the place of the older one.

The final good production function is very simple:

$$y = A\, F(x), \quad F' > 0, \quad F'' < 0, \tag{3.30}$$

where x is the amount of intermediate product.

Each innovation is a new intermediate good that raises the productivity in the final good sector by a factor γ, so that after t innovations

$$A_t = A_0\, \gamma^t. \tag{3.31}$$

The production good is produced under a monopoly. Monopoly profits will cover the development costs of the new innovation. The arrival of an innovation is uncertain, its probability of arrival being characterised by a Poisson process with parameter $\lambda\phi(n)$, where n is the number of researchers. The time interval between two innovations is thus a random variable.

The value of making an innovation depends on its expected lifetime, itself a function of the number of researchers trying to discover the next innovation. The solution of the model is an allocation of the fixed population of qualified labour H between research (n) and production $(H - n)$. In equilibrium, qualified labour is paid the same wage in both activities, so that the model boils down to a difference equation between the number of researchers looking for the $t + 1$st innovation, n_t, and the number of researchers looking for the $t + 2$nd innovation, n_{t+1}:

$$n_t = \psi(n_{t+1}). \tag{3.32}$$

The producer of the intermediate good must take into account the possibility of its replacement by a more efficient good of another producer. Therefore, the expected benefit of an innovation depends negatively on the amount of research done for the next innovation.

The model admits three types of solutions. The first one is a stationary equilibrium, $\hat{n} = \psi(\hat{n})$, corresponding to a fixed allocation of research. In this framework, because of the stochastic nature of innovation, GDP follows a random walk around a trend. The average rate of growth is increasing with the amount of resources dedicated to innovation and the size of innovations. The second solution follows from the inverse relationship between any two successive allocations of qualified personnel, a higher n at one period being followed by a lower n the next period. This effect may discourage research altogether, in which case the economy enters a 'no growth trap'. The last type of solution is a cyclic allocation between high and low values of n.

The number of researchers n depends negatively on the interest rate, positively on the size of the innovation γ, the parameter λ and the size H of the qualified labour population.

As in many other endogenous growth models, the presence of externalities linked to the accumulation of knowledge implies that the market outcome is suboptimal. The externalities are not, however, of the same nature as in the expanding product variety model. There is no instantaneous positive externality of research, since innovation follows a memoryless process. But there is an intertemporal externality, since each innovator improves productivity forever.

An important difference from the expanding product variety model is that market mechanisms may lead to a lower as well as a higher growth rate than would be socially optimal. The second possibility is linked to the fact that each innovator does not take into consideration the loss of rents incurred by the previous innovator, a negative externality linked to innovation. When the size of each innovation γ is variable, market equilibrium always leads to a smaller than socially optimal innovation rate.

3.3 Human Capital and Growth

Taking human capital into account as a factor of growth is not specific to the endogenous growth literature. Growth accounting studies (Maddison 1987) also introduced a labour force quality indicator. Endogenous growth models go one step further, however, sometimes making human capital an accumulable factor and, in some models, the engine of growth.

Human capital may be defined as the sum of the abilities specific to individuals. These may be varied: health, strength, different types of knowledge or intellectual abilities, and so on. Human capital is appropriable by individuals since it is embodied in them. It is in large part produced by itself, and many positive externalities may be associated with it, so that the possibility of increasing returns to scale linked to its accumulation arises. Nevertheless, unlike knowledge, it is not a public good.

Lucas (1988) has proposed an endogenous growth model based on human capital. This model is very much like the simple model presented in the first section, with, in addition, the presence of physical capital and an externality running from human capital to production.

An individual accumulates human capital h exponentially,

$$\dot{h} = \delta \ (1 - u) \ h, \tag{3.33}$$

where u is the fraction of time spent by an individual on the production of the final good. Thus, $(1 - u)$ is the fraction of time spent on the acquisition of skills.

The linear specification, leading to a constant growth rate in equilibrium, is necessary for unbounded growth as was seen previously in section 2. The nature of this externality differs from the other models. It is intertemporal and not interindividual, as would be the case if the accumulated factor were knowledge or technology.

The production function of the final good is assumed to be of the following form:

$$Q = A \ K^\beta \ [u \ h]^{1-\beta} \ h_a^\gamma \tag{3.34}$$

where K is physical capital and h_a the average level of human capital. All agents being assumed identical, only cases where $h_a = h$ will be considered.

The interpretation of the h_a term is based on the idea of a collective capability linked to exchanges of information between agents. An individual will be all the more efficient when he is in touch with people with a higher level of human capital. This is an interindividual positive externality. It should be noted that the external effect of human capital on final good production is not essential for endogenous growth.

Physical capital accumulation is described by the following equation:

$$\dot{K} = Q - c, \tag{3.35}$$

where c is consumption. One assumes the same utility function as before, eq. (3.7).

The solution of the model differs according to whether one considers the market or the socially optimal solution. The rates of growth of human capital for these two cases are respectively v and v^*:

$$v = \frac{(1 - \beta) \ (\delta - \rho)}{\sigma \ (1 - \beta + \gamma) - \gamma}, \tag{3.36}$$

$$v^* = \frac{(1 - \beta) \ (\delta - \rho) + \delta \ \gamma}{\sigma \ (1 - \beta + \gamma)}, \tag{3.37}$$

and the corresponding rates of growth of the final product are:

$$g = (1 + \frac{\gamma}{1 - \beta}) \, v, \qquad (3.38)$$

$$g^* = (1 + \frac{\gamma}{1 - \beta}) \, v^*. \qquad (3.39)$$

Because of the external effects linked to human capital accumulation, the optimal rate of growth is higher than the market rate of growth.

An interesting aspect of the model concerns international disparities in per capita income. Two countries with identical initial levels of the 'physical capital/human capital' ratio, but with different absolute values for the levels of these variables, will grow at different rates. The country with the higher level of each variable will have a higher return to physical capital. In the absence of obstacles to capital mobility, there will be a tendency for foreign capital to flow into this country. Capital accumulation and growth will thus be more rapid in countries that are initially better endowed, which is the opposite of what happens in the traditional neoclassical model. Moreover, the human capital externality implies that a worker will be more productive and thus better paid in a country that is better endowed with human capital, so that there is a tendency for labour to migrate as well. Market mechanisms will thus tend to widen initial differences.

4. CONVERGENCE AND DIVERGENCE

According to the neoclassical growth model, GDP per capita only differs between countries due to differences in investment rates, on the assumption that technology is a free good. In contrast, many endogenous growth models imply that each country will develop along its own growth path, with no tendency for GDP levels to converge. The availability of a database on GDP for over a hundred countries between 1950 and 1985 constructed by Summers and Heston (1991) has inspired economists to make empirical tests of the different propositions put forward by new growth theory. The central question of this empirical work is whether poor countries tend to grow faster than rich countries, that is, whether there is a tendency to convergence.

Many studies have tested variants of the following equation on a cross-section of countries:

$$\Delta \ln(Y/L) \Big|_{0}^{t} = a + b \, \ln(Y/L)_0 + C \, X, \qquad (3.40)$$

where X is a vector of explanatory variables. A negative b means that less-advanced countries tend to grow faster than advanced countries, and that catch-up occurs. Baumol (1986) showed that there was a negative b when such an equation was tested for OECD countries over a long period, but this result is much harder to obtain with a wider sample. In fact, the choice of the X variables is crucial. Barro (1991) considered variables on education and investment as well as less traditional indicators supposedly reflecting political stability. The inclusion of such variables is indispensable for a catch-up effect to appear, although the exact choice of the extra explanatory variables may be controversial (Levine and Renelt 1992; Levine and Zervos 1992).

Of particular interest are the variables concerning investment and technical progress. De Long and Summers (1991) have used the proportion of equipment investment in GDP as an explanatory variable. The restriction to equipment is justified by the belief that investment in structures is not characterised by the same positive externalities as equipment investment. According to neoclassical theory, there should be no long-run effect of investment on growth, but only transitory effects. The estimations of De Long and Summers show that a 1% increase in the investment rate would bring about a rise of 0.34% in GDP growth, a much larger effect than the neoclassical growth model forecasts. Romer (1990b) also points to an influence of the investment rate on growth. Other variables might be considered, particularly those directly related to technological change, such as R&D expenditure or patents. The introduction of patent-based technological explanatory variables in productivity growth equations proves generally to be fruitful (Fagerberg 1987; Amable 1993).

Mankiw, Romer and Weil (1992) acknowledge that the simple Solow model cannot account for international differences in GDP levels on a broad sample of developed and less-developed countries. They contend that an extended version of the Solow model provides a satisfactory explanation. They consider the following model:

$$Y = K^\alpha H^\beta (A L)^{1-\alpha-\beta} , \qquad (3.41)$$

where H is human capital. L and A grow at the exogenous rates n and g. Accumulation of the factors is specified by:

$$\dot{K} = -\delta K + s_K Y, \qquad (3.42)$$

$$\dot{H} = -\delta H + s_H Y. \qquad (3.43)$$

Solving the model, one obtains the equilibrium growth path:

$$\ln(Y/L) = \ln(A) - \frac{\alpha+\beta}{1-\alpha-\beta} \ln(n+g+\delta) + \frac{\alpha}{1-\alpha-\beta} \ln(s_K)$$
$$+ \frac{\beta}{1-\alpha-\beta} \ln(s_H). \tag{3.44}$$

This equation is estimated on a cross-section of 98 countries, taking as given the rates of exogenous technical change and depreciation. s_H is proxied by a school enrolment variable. The estimation is satisfactory, which leads the authors to conclude that an extension of the traditional growth model is sufficient to explain growth differentials. The implication is that international differences in levels of GDP per capita are attributable to differences in tastes (the savings proportions s_H and s_K) rather than differences in access to technology. If one supposes that countries are off their equilibrium path, one needs to add a term in $\ln(Y/L)_0$ to the equation above. Mankiw, Romer and Weil (1992) obtain a negative coefficient on this term, as expected. The main result is that no matter how different national growth paths may look, the differences can be explained by a simple extended Solow model. There is thus no need for endogenous growth models to explain the apparent divergence in GDP levels.

Durlauf and Johnson (1992) examine the significance of the negative sign of the b coefficient (the catch-up effect) in the estimations of equations such as eq. (3.40). They make an interesting observation. Some endogenous growth models exhibit multiple equilibria (Azariadis and Drazen 1990) and may therefore have many stable paths for an economy. Therefore, one may observe local convergence around each of the stable equilibria, so that a negative estimate for b in the above equation does not imply global convergence. In fact, Bernard and Durlauf (1991) show that a negative b is compatible with many endogenous growth specifications. The control variables X may play a role in the negativity of the b coefficient. If there is local convergence around a certain number of equilibria, the X variables may split the countries of the sample into different subgroups among which countries converge to a similar level of development.

Durlauf and Johnson (1992) attempt to test the idea of local convergence. They start from the same model as Mankiw, Romer and Weil (1992) but suppose that countries may follow different growth regimes according to their level of human or physical capital. For instance, if there is a human capital threshold to be able to use the most advanced techniques, their model could be the following:

$$Y_i = \begin{cases} \phi \, K_i^{\alpha} \, H_i^{\gamma} \, (A_i \, L_i)^{1-\alpha-\gamma} & \text{if } H_i < \bar{H}, \\[2mm] \psi \, K_i^{\eta} \, H_i^{\zeta} \, (A_i \, L_i)^{1-\eta-\zeta} & \text{if } H_i \geq \bar{H}. \end{cases} \tag{3.45}$$

They run tests of an equation similar to that used by Mankiw, Romer and Weil (MRW) over different subsamples defined by levels of income and literacy, and come to the conclusion that the coefficients are different according to the subgroups. They then proceed to determine endogenously the criteria to separate countries according to the growth regime they follow. By a regression tree estimation, they find that a first split is made according to whether the countries had a level of per capita GDP higher or lower than $800 in 1960. Taking the sample of countries whose per capita GDP was higher than $800, a second split can be made at a literacy rate of 46%. Among the countries whose literacy rate is above this figure, a third split is made according to the threshold value of $4850 per capita GDP in 1960. They thus obtain four groups of countries and then proceed to test the MRW-type equation for each subsample, obtaining very different estimates.

There is a negative b coefficient (the catch-up effect) for each sub-sample, so that there is local convergence, but the growth regimes are very different according to the subsamples used for the estimation. Therefore, the results found support the multiple equilibria/local convergence hypothesis rather than the global convergence implied by the Solow model.

5. CONCLUSION

Is new growth theory so new? Perhaps not. Not only are some of the major ideas well known in the economic literature,[4] but some early models (Uzawa 1965) were endogenous growth models *avant la lettre*. Furthermore, growth was endogenous in Harrod's model, which could be interpreted as the '*AK*' model. However, what matters is not whether new growth theory is new or not, but rather the fact that it has highlighted the issue of the determinants of technical change in the growth debate, with all the related problems of external effects and the suboptimality of market outcomes. The diversity of the sources of growth and the presence of external effects may provide a theoretical justification for a wide variety of public policy interventions (for example, industrial, R&D or trade policy).

The range of dynamic behaviour encompassed by endogenous growth models is also richer than in Solow's models, with the possibility of multiple equilibria (King and Robson 1990; Weil 1989; Murphy, Shleifer and Vishny 1989; Matsuyama 1990) and the possibility of vicious circles of low growth or the existence of development thresholds (Becker, Murphy and Tamura 1990; Azariadis and Drazen 1990). Such models leave the impression that 'history matters' for the process of growth.

Cumulative mechanisms point to the major importance of small causes. Alternatively, the equilibrium of the economy may be affected by agents' expectations.

Nevertheless, new growth models suffer from a certain number of weaknesses. The first one is common to all growth models and concerns the razor's edge conditions necessary to obtain a steady-state growth. A slight modification of the parameters can be enough to make growth either collapse or explode. The second question revolves around the conception of technological change adopted in endogenous growth models. These models consider one source of technological change at a time, whereas historians of technology and many economists tend to stress that technical change is a mix of small improvements and radical change. Gille (1978) has proposed the concept of technical system defined as a set of complementary techniques around a limited number of major innovations. For Dosi (1982, 1984), technical progress follows 'paradigms', conceived as a focusing device for the advance of technology. Endogenous growth models incorporating some of these ideas could probably offer an interesting account of long-term growth.

More fundamentally, endogenous growth models, particularly those based on innovation, emphasise the 'linear' conception of technical change and neglect the feedback effects between its different stages. Technology still remains a 'black box'. For instance, the specification of external effects is vague. Of course, one must keep in mind that a growth model can only incorporate a simplified treatment of technological change. A third critique concerns the ahistoric character of the formalisations adopted. The regimes of technical change vary with time, influenced by institutional factors (North 1990), as expressed in the concept of socio-technical paradigms (Freeman and Perez 1988). A model of endogenous growth cannot hope to account for all of the complex factors affecting the relationship between technology and the economy. Thus the domain of validity of each model should be specified more precisely.

NOTES

1. One can cite Amable and Guellec (1992), Verspagen (1992), Van de Klundert and Smulders (1992), Sala-i-Martin (1990) and Laffargue (1992).
2. Such as a lower non-zero bound on the marginal returns.
3. Cf. Amable and Guellec (1992).
4. The importance of the division of labour is stressed in Adam Smith's *Wealth of Nations* as well as Xenophon's *Cyropedia*. The Kaldorian influence is present, if not always acknowledged, in many endogenous growth models. The importance of learning and human capital in explaining growth differentials is also found in Haavelmo (1954).

REFERENCES

Aghion, P. and Howitt, P. (1992), 'A Model of Growth Through Creative Destruction', *Econometrica*, 60(2), 323–351.

Amable, B. (1993), 'Catch-up and Convergence: a Model of Cumulative Growth', *International Review of Applied Economics*, 7(1), 1–25.

Amable, B. and Guellec, D. (1992), 'Les Théories de la Croissance Endogène', *Revue d'Economie Politique*, 102(3), 313–377.

Arrow, K. (1962), 'The Economic Implications of Learning by Doing', *Review of Economic Studies*, XXIX(2), 155–173.

Azariadis, C. and Drazen, A. (1990), 'Threshold Externalities in Economic Development', *Quarterly Journal of Economics*, 105, 501–526.

Barro, R.J. (1990), 'Government Spending in a Simple Model of Endogenous Growth', *Journal of Political Economy*, 98(5) pt 2, S103–S125.

Barro, R.J. (1991), 'Economic Growth in a Cross Section of Countries', *Quarterly Journal of Economics*, 106(2), 407–443.

Barro, R.J. and Sala-i-Martin, X. (1992), 'Public Finance in Models of Economic Growth', *Review of Economic Studies*, 59(4), 645–661.

Baumol, W. (1986), 'Productivity Growth, Convergence, and Welfare: What the Long-run Data Show', *American Economic Review*, 76(5), 1072–1085.

Becker, G.S., Murphy, K.M. and Tamura, R. (1990), 'Human Capital, Fertility and Economic Growth', *Journal of Political Economy*, 98(5) pt 2, S12–S37.

Bernard, A. and Durlauf, S. (1991), 'Convergence of International Output Movements', NBER Working Paper no. 3717.

De Long, J. and Summers, L. (1991), 'Equipment Investment and Economic Growth', *Quarterly Journal of Economics*, 106(2), 445–502.

Dosi, G. (1982), 'Technological Paradigms and Technological Trajectories', *Research Policy*, 11, 147–163.

Dosi, G. (1984), *Technical Change and Industrial Transformation*, London: Macmillan.

Durlauf, S. (1991), 'Nonergodic Economic Growth', mimeo, Stanford, NBER.

Durlauf, S. and Johnson, P. (1992), 'Local versus Global Convergence across National Economies', NBER Working Paper no. 3996.

Ethier, W. (1982), 'National and International Returns to Scale in the Modern Theory of International Trade', *American Economic Review*, 72, 389–405.

Fagerberg, J. (1987), 'A Technology Gap Approach to Why Growth Rates Differ', *Research Policy*, 16, 87–89.

Freeman, C. and Perez, C. (1988), 'Structural Crises of Adjustment: Business Cycles and Investment Behaviour', in Dosi *et al.* (eds), *Technical Change and Economic Theory*, London: Pinter.

Gille, B. (1978), *Histoire des techniques*, Paris: Gallimard.

Grossman, G.M. and Helpman, E. (1991), *Innovation and Growth in the Global Economy*, Cambridge, MA: MIT Press.

Haavelmo, T. (1954), *A Study in the Theory of Economic Evolution*, Amsterdam: North-Holland.

Hahn, F. (1990), 'Solovian Growth Models', in P. Diamond (ed.), *Growth, Productivity and Unemployment*, Cambridge, MA: MIT Press.

Kaldor, N. (1957), 'A Model of Economic Growth', *Economic Journal*, 67, 591–624.

King, M. and Robson, M. (1990), 'Endogenous Growth and the Role of History', Working Paper no. 63, London School of Economics.

Laffargue, J.P. (1992), 'Croissance Endogène et Développement: Points de Vue Récents', Working Paper no. 9209, CEPREMAP.

Levine, R. and Renelt, D. (1992), 'A Sensitivity Analysis of Cross-country Growth Regressions', *American Economic Review*, 82, 942–963.

Levine, R. and Zervos, S. (1992), 'Looking at the Facts: What We Know about Policy and Growth from Cross-country Analysis', Paper presented at the International Economic Association Conference on Economic Growth and the Structure of Long Term Development, Varenna.

Lucas, R. (1988), 'On the Mechanics of Economic Development', *Journal of Monetary Economics*, 22, 3–42.

Maddison, A. (1987), 'Growth and Slowdown in Advanced Capitalist Economies: Techniques of Quantitative Assessment', *Journal of Economic Literature*, 25(2), 649–698.

Mankiw, N.G., Romer, D. and Weil, D.N. (1992), 'A Contribution to the Empirics of Economic Growth', *Quarterly Journal of Economics*, 108, 407–437.

Matsuyama, K. (1990), 'Increasing Returns, Industrialization and Indeterminacy of Equilibrium', mimeo, Northwestern University.

Murphy, K., Shleifer, A. and Vishny, R. (1989), 'Industrialization and the Big Push', *Journal of Political Economy*, 97(5), 1003–1026.

North, D.C. (1990), *Institutions, Institutional Change and Economic Performance*, Cambridge: Cambridge University Press.

Rebelo, S. (1990), 'Long Run Policy Analysis and Long Run Growth', NBER Working Paper no. 3325.

Romer, P. (1986), 'Increasing Returns and Long–run Growth', *Journal of Political Economy*, 94, 1002–1037.

Romer, P. (1987), 'Crazy Explanations for the Productivity Slowdown', in *NBER Macroeconomics Annuals 1987*, Cambridge, MA: MIT Press.

Romer, P. (1990a), 'Endogenous Technological Change', *Journal of Political Economy*, 98(5) pt 2, S71–S102.

Romer, P. (1990b), 'Capital, Labor and Productivity', *Brookings Papers on Microeconomics*, 337–367.

Rosenberg, N. (1982), *Inside the Black Box: Technology and Economics*, Cambridge: Cambridge University Press.

Sala-i-Martin, X. (1990), 'Lecture Notes on Economic Growth (I): Introduction to the Literature and Neoclassical Models; (II) Five Prototype Models of Endogenous Growth', NBER Working Papers nos 3563 and 3564.

Sheshinski, E. (1967), 'Optimal Accumulation with Learning by Doing', in K. Schell (ed.), *Essays on the Theory of Optimal Growth*, Cambridge, MA: MIT Press.

Solow, R. (1956), 'A Contribution to the Theory of Economic Growth', *Quarterly Journal of Economics*, 70, 65–94.

Solow, R. (1957), 'Technical Change and the Aggregate Production Function', *Review of Economics and Statistics*, 39, 312–320.

Summers, R. and Heston, A. (1988), 'A New Set of International Comparisons of Real Product and Price Levels', *Review of Income and Wealth*, 34, 1–25.

Summers, R. and Heston, A. (1991), 'The Penn World Table (Mark 5): An Expanded Set of International Comparisons, 1950-1988', *Quarterly Journal of Economics*, CVI(2), 327–368.

Uzawa, H. (1965), 'Optimum Technical Change in an Aggregative Model of Economic Growth', *International Economic Review*, 6, 18–31.

Van de Klundert, T. and Smulders, S. (1992), 'Reconstructing Growth Theory: A Survey', *De Economist*, 140(2), 177–203.

Verspagen, B. (1992), 'Endogenous Innovation in Neoclassical Growth Models: A Survey', *Journal of Macroeconomics*, 14(4), 631–662.

Weil, P. (1989), 'Increasing Returns and Animal Spirits', *American Economic Review*, 79(4), 889–894.

Young, A. (1928), 'Increasing Returns and Economic Progress', *Economic Journal*, 38, 527–542.

4. Do Economies Diverge?

Richard H. Day[*]

My purpose here is to describe and illustrate in the simplest possible way a multiple-phase theory of economic growth and development that helps explain why human evolution has not been one of steady progress but one instead of fluctuating growth and changing forms, sometimes progressing to higher levels of complexity, sometimes reverting to earlier stages of organisation. In the form outlined here (in terms of macroeconomic growth theory) it is convenient to think of the analysis as involving the 'very long run'. But for reasons that will be suggested in the conclusion, the 'very long run' is of great interest for interpreting events in the 'very short run', in particular the processes of integration and disintegration currently at work in the world. Moreover, we can propose with some confidence an answer to the question posed in the title with which this discussion begins.

1. BACKGROUND

The Classical economists understood that a long-run stationary state at some culturally determined 'subsistence' income level could be avoided through inventiveness and improved productivity.

They emphasised that the latter in turn depended on a favourable institutional infrastructure which fostered education, private initiative and factor mobility, which maintained and enforced property rights, which adjudicated disputes, and which provided an acceptable legislative system for establishing the character of the system as a whole. In response to trends in the early industrial economies from mid-nineteenth to mid-twentieth centuries, economic theorists have often abstracted from infrastructural prerequisites in order to obtain the simplest models of resource allocation and capital accumulation consistent with the recent qualitative and quantitative macroeconomic picture of more or less steady exponential growth. Historians of the nineteenth century, however, noticed that prior to the industrial take-off economies had passed through distinct

[*] This chapter draws on work carried out over more than a decade, some of it in collaboration with graduate students at the University of Southern California, including Weihong Huang, Giovanni Lombardi, Larry Powell, Jean-Luc Walter, Zhigang Wang and Gang Zou.

stages of development characterised by differences in production technology, and in the organisation of exchange and governance. Archaeologists, aided by modern methods of dating materials, have extended
this picture backwards in time giving a proximate but coherent chronology
of major developments on a worldwide basis that stretches back to the
earliest evidence of a human presence.

To social scientists accustomed to the extensive data resources of 'advanced' economies, the archaeological record, no doubt, appears sketchy
and essentially qualitative. For purposes of understanding socioeconomic
evolution, however, there is a certain advantage in the very-long-run perspective it affords: salient features of the process stand out in bold relief.
Briefly, the great variety of human societies can be grouped into a relatively small number of forms or *stages* based on production technology
and social infrastructure. Any such grouping is to some extent arbitrary
and, by taking account of more and more details, a progressively finer
array of types can be identified. In order to describe the major developments throughout the entire span of *Homo sapiens sapiens* and to take
advantage of the known archaeological information a reasonable minimal
specification would be: hunting and gathering; extensive (slash and burn)
agriculture; intensive settled agriculture (complex societies); the city state
(civilisation); trading empires, industrial economies and information
economies.[1] Various geographical areas traversed these stages at very
different times and the advance through them did not increase uniformly
from lower to higher index. Rather, progress from one to another, especially in earlier times, was interrupted by reversions to lower-level
stages. Moreover, fluctuations in income, population and capital have been
typical. The overall picture is one of growth at fluctuating rates with
sometimes smooth, sometimes turbulent transitions when jumps and
reversions occurred until a 'higher' stage became firmly established.[2] It is
obvious that many complexly interacting forces are responsible for all this.
None the less, it is possible to capture the economic essence of the process
by augmenting the pure growth theory, which already incorporates savings,
capital accumulation, technological change and population growth, with an
explicit representation of diseconomies, socioeconomic infrastructure and
multiple regimes.

2. BEYOND CLASSICAL GROWTH

The basic ideas can be most simply presented by expanding upon the
classical framework of demoeconomic growth. The result is an even
'grander theory' than Baumol attributed to Smith, Malthus and Ricardo.

2.1 Household Behaviour, Technology and the Classical Story

Consider the classical time unit of a human generation, a quarter century, say. Each period is represented by a population of adults and of their children who inherit the adult world in the next generation. Assume that each generation must provide its own capital goods which only last the period. The output possible is then a function of the number of adults. The number of children who survive (that is, who become adults in the next period) depends on the per capita production of goods.

The first of these relationships is the production function which is assumed to possess eventually diminishing marginal returns to population and gives rise to the familiar curve of total output which rises monotonically as population grows but at a declining rate. The second is the demo-economic function which shows that (in our overlapping generation terms) the number of children of a given sex surviving to adulthood is nil below some very low-income threshold η, then rises rapidly, reaching a bound given by Ricardo's natural rate of growth. Putting these ingredients together, we obtain the standard classical results: if the threshold $\eta = 0$, then population, beginning at a small enough level, rises at an exponential rate during a phase of relative abundance; eventually, as diminishing returns lowers the marginal and average productivity of labour, a regime of scarcity is entered; population growth slows and converges to a stationary state at which the level of well-being is sufficient to motivate and sustain the formation of families just big enough to replace themselves generation after generation. Moreover, if a continuous, exponential advance in labour-augmenting productivity is incorporated, then the steady state gives way to 'geometric' growth. The iron law of wages is then postponed indefinitely, a fact appreciated already by the Classical writers.

Recently, a less-well-known conjecture of Malthus has been established, namely, that population growth could overshoot the stationary state and be followed by fluctuations in output, income and population numbers.[3] It is sufficient for the threshold η to be positive (and large enough). However, another cause of fluctuation will concern us here; one due to internal and external diseconomies.

2.2 Diseconomies of Population Size

The Classical economists emphasised that, given a fixed technology, marginal productivity declines as production expands due to the scarcity of land, water and other resources. But the scarcity of material resources is not the only cause of diseconomy in the production process. Another source is the increasing complexity of planning, communicating and co-ordinating as output expands. Diseconomies also accrue because the social goods and services on which market productivity rests become increasingly difficult to provide. We may call these *internal diseconomies* of population size. Recognising these diseconomies yields absolutely diminishing returns to population within an economy. Instead of a monotonic production function, a single-peaked function emerges in which production rises to a maximum as population increases, but then if population continues to rise, production diminishes. A negative-sloping segment in production cannot occur if resources are freely disposable, but *people* are not freely disposable so that the 'free disposal axiom' is not germane. It could be argued that people would never reproduce to such an extent as to depress absolute production, but this is a view supported more by faith than by facts. Over-population *within the context of a given technology or given stage of development* seems to have occurred, and very likely *is* occurring in a number of places so that its analysis would seem relevant indeed.

Setting aside technological advance for the time being (it will be reintroduced in due course), it is easy to see that diseconomies leading to absolutely diminishing productivity could cause – in addition to convergent growth – fluctuations (cyclic or irregular), and in the extreme, collapse; that is, growth and perhaps fluctuations followed by a fall in the standard of living below η and the demise of the economy, a prospect even more dismal than envisaged in the iron law of wages. This possibility poses a consideration for growth theory that goes beyond classical concerns, namely, that of *viability*. The conditions that enable an economy to persist cannot be taken for granted.

2.3 Infrastructure and Viability

Suppose that the technology can only be effective if a part of the population forms a social infrastructure upon which the use of the given technology depends. Such an infrastructure mediates the human energy devoted to co-ordinating production and exchange, to providing social cohesion for effective co-operation, for training and inculturating the workforce, and for producing the public goods, such as waste disposal and public safety required for the well-being of the workforce. Call the part of the population that makes up this infrastructure the *infrastructural force*. Ester Boserup (1981) called the knowledge upon which the infrastructure is based, the *administrative technology*. It must augment the production technology and, given that the social infrastructure requires a significant block of human resources, it follows that for an economy to be feasible, the population must exceed a given bound. The effect on the production function is to shift it to the right so that output can become positive only when the human resources have accumulated beyond a certain level. Combined with the possibility of absolute diseconomies introduced above, the problem of viability is clearly exacerbated, for population must not fall below the numbers required to keep the infrastructure intact. If it does, the economy is no longer viable. But this formulation raises the question, 'How could a society reach the required threshold in the first place?'. The answer, however, is obvious: only by having already passed through a growth process within a system or through a sequence of systems that required a less elaborate infrastructure and hence lower thresholds for positive production. Actually, there is somewhat more to the story than this, but let us consider it a step at a time.

2.4 Replication and Reorganisation

Very early human societies were built around very small groups so that families themselves could provide infrastructural requirements without the need for elaborate hierarchical organisations. The hunting and gathering band thus takes its place early in the process of economic development. Archaeologists have now traced its diffusion throughout the world. The mechanism that mediated this diffusion is that of *fission*. If and as a band gradually grew, it would eventually deplete the sources of game in its neighbourhood and the productivity of search became greatly reduced. By splitting, two much smaller, more or less independent bands could be formed that, moving apart, could greatly increase the total area supplying food while greatly increasing productivity with no significant change in technology or organisation. This growth and replication process can proceed until there is no vacant terrain left.

It is at this point that the Malthusian process of overshoot and undershoot might be expected to occur. Continuing growth is not possible without major technological change. One need not go back into prehistory to find this process at work. Indeed, the splitting up of societies into parts that become more or less independent is described already in Herodotus. It has now been established as a common process by which city states spread throughout the Mediterranean world. Such a process is easily explained by the presence of internal diseconomies and the requirements of infrastructure which, of course, played a much enlarged role in urban society. At some point in the expansion of human numbers within an economy when productivity has fallen enough, the population may reach a level at which a new society with a newly constituted infrastructure can be split off in such a way as to increase welfare, just as Herodotus describes, in this way overcoming the internal diseconomies of population size. Such a process can continue until again the known world is full of such units.

To see what is meant by the term 'full', to the *internal* diseconomies that operate within a given socioeconomic unit, take account of the *external* ones that derive from the total population of all the economies together. These are, for example, caused by the exhaustion of the environment's waste-absorbing capacity. This capacity can – for a given technology – be stated in terms of the space available which in turn depends on the population density. In addition, as resources become scarce and the cost of extracting and refining them grows, diminishing absolute returns to the work-force can eventually come to pass as the total world population gets large. The internal diseconomies can be overcome by fission, the external ones cannot. Once the world is full in the sense that external diseconomies become important, the replication of economies with the same basic structures must come to an end.

This is as true of the city state as it is of the hunting and gathering band. If, when this state is attained, a collapse occurs due to a very powerful drop in productivity, the population may reorganise itself by eliminating some of the previous groups and fusing into a smaller number. Then the stage is set for a new growth process, both through the internal growth of the individual economies and through the fission process just described. Fluctuations in total population as well as in the numbers of economies (or societies) could ensue, perhaps in a highly irregular way for a very long time.

2.5 Development Blocks, Fusion and Stages of Growth

Because of external diseconomies and in the absence of technological change, growth must ultimately be limited. But now consider the role of 'ways of life' or 'development blocks', such as those that underlie the great stages of development listed above. Each of these is structurally distinct, depending on distinct production and administrative technologies and correspondingly with very different infrastructural requirements.

It seems evident that the infrastructural requirements have grown as one proceeds through the order. That is, each successive stage requires a greater overhead of human capital as a prerequisite for production. This implies that for a switch to a more advanced stage to occur, existing economies must fuse to form larger, reorganised and elaborated infrastructures. Further growth in the total population is possible only if the external diseconomies are greatly diminished by such a change and for each successive regime a much larger worldwide population becomes possible before external diseconomies become acute. Such a change in regime is unlikely to occur unless average productivity is enhanced by doing so. This does not mean that each successive technology is uniformly more productive than the predecessor, but only that at a given total population the switch to a new regime will enhance the standard of living at that population level. In other words, 'local efficiency' is sufficient to drive the selection process of technological regime switching in much the same way that it drives the process of replication through fission.

2.6 The 'Grander' Multiple Phase Dynamics

The Classical theory has now been augmented by the following ingredients:

- absolute internal diseconomies
- infrastructural human capital
- the possibility of growth through fission
- absolute external diseconomies
- reorganisation through fusion
- multiple technological regimes
- a selection criterion of local efficiency.

The number of possible development patterns that can now be explained as an intrinsic process has grown literally without bound. Beginning with a very small population in an initial regime with highly restricted limits on the populations of individual economies, growth can proceed within existing units and by replicating economies through fission until a switch to an entirely new regime occurs. The process can be repeated on successively greater scales, but possibly as well, interrupted by periods of turbulent transitions when, instead of advancing, a collapse might occur that causes a reversion to a less-advanced regime. Then the relatively advanced economy splits into less-advanced ones with smaller infrastructural requirements. Thus, the development path need not be smooth or even monotonic but could be irregular. It can be characterised by changes in output, population and standards of living as in the classical model and also by the numbers and qualitative character of the economies making up the process as a whole. It is in this sense that a grander (multiple phase) dynamics is involved; a grander dynamics that can be given a precise mathematical expression but which seems to mimic the growth and vicissitudes of human economic activity through its many forms, as we understand them to have occurred in reality.

2.7 Continuous Productivity Advance and the Ultimate Population Bound

Suppose now that an exponentially growing productivity factor ('learning by doing') is added to the basic production function so that as experience within a given regime accumulates, the workforce is effectively augmented when measured in efficiency units. Suppose such a factor does *not* expand the ultimate limits on population merely allowed by the internal and external economies described above. Then, as output growth is enhanced, the process of output growth, fission and regime switching is accelerated. Over the long run the system becomes more unstable. Development is less likely to get 'stuck' within a given regime, but it will bump up against an ultimate population limit – if there is one – sooner than before. Such an ultimate bound was suggested by a National Academy of Sciences panel convened as long ago as 1968 as lying somewhere between 6 and 25 billion people. What happens is that the advancing regimes become progressively 'squashed' against this ultimate bound, with ever greater speed, with an ever greater likelihood of collapse.

3. BEYOND NEOCLASSICAL GROWTH

Human capital is not the only requirement for the social infrastructure. Material capital is also needed and, with each advancing regime, in growing amounts. Of course, capital should also be included in the basic production function.

Consider the growth theory, then, when material capital is incorporated explicitly. To do this in the simplest terms, population growth will first be considered to occur at a constant rate. We shall not include the fission and fusion process either. A variable demoeconomic function and technical bounds on population due to externalities can be introduced later.

3.1 Technology and the 'Neoclassical' Story

We return to the original classical production function with undifferentiated labour and augment it so the flow of output depends on the stock of capital as well as labour. Assuming a homogeneous production function of the first degree, and if there is a single regime and a constant savings rate (as in the simplest version of the Solow model), the picture of growth obtained is similar to the Classical one, but now, instead of converging to a stationary state, a steady state in the capital/labour ratio is approached with which is associated an exponentially balanced growth path for output and capital stock. The growing capital stock (workforce) makes up for the diminishing marginal returns to labour (capital) so that steady growth can occur forever. If continuous, labour-augmenting productivity is added, then the picture does not change very much, except that the rate of growth is, of course, accelerated.

3.2 Infrastructure, Restricted Factor Substitution and Viability

To take account of the infrastructural requirements, divide the total population into infrastructure forces and workforces as before. And, correspondingly, divide the capital stock into that devoted to the infrastructure and that devoted to the production of market goods. In the interest of simplicity, assume that the size of the capital stock required for the infrastructure is directly related to the population by a fixed proportion. Likewise, assume the size of the infrastructural force is directly related to the size of the capital stock by a fixed proportion. Then it can be shown that the effect on the production function is to compress the possibilities for capital/labour substitutions into a cone within the positive orthant. The range of feasible capital/labour ratios is compressed within an interval determined by the boundary rays of the cone. Gang Zou and I (Day and Zou 1992) call this the Restricted Factor Substitution (RFS) production function.

3.3 The Efficiency Cone and Fluctuations

A significant property of the RFS production function is that for any given output level, the efficient capital/labour combinations lie in a cone, say C^*, within the feasibility cone C, but the isoquant on which these combinations lie approaches the boundaries of C asymptotically and extends outside C^*. In other words, $C \setminus C^*$ contains capital/labour ratio combinations that are *inefficient*. Interpreted literally, this means that if the political and economic decision-makers, administrators and managers could perceive and understand society's production structure as a whole, more production and a higher standard of living could be achieved for any given combination outside of C^* by rearranging capital and labour so as to obtain a combination within C^*. *It seems to us unrealistic to suppose that they always manage to do this.* Viable trajectories of capital and labour must unfold within the viability cone, but now the growth paths need not be monotonic or convergent to balanced growth. At a given savings rate, over-investment can take place with a corresponding inefficiency in the use of capital and labour. Capital/labour ratios can fluctuate, and the paths of capital accumulation can follow a zig-zag path in the capital/labour space. The reason for this is that for any given population level, a sufficient capital stock must be allocated to infrastructure before production can occur and, for the same reason, for any given capital stock, a sufficient part of the population must be allocated to infrastructure. Capital/labour ratios are therefore constrained to lie in an interval. If the capital/labour ratio becomes too small – or too large – there must be a rapid decline in productivity. Consequently, it is possible to overshoot the balanced growth path and oscillation around it may follow. The multiplication of discrete economies through fission and fusion in the earlier model is replaced by a continuous reorganisation of labour and capital into production and infrastructural components in this one. None the less, similar possibilities for instability exist.

3.4 Multiple Phase Dynamics

Suppose now there exist completely different potential development blocks, each with its own basic production function and its own implied cone of substitution possibilities. These cones may or may not overlap. All the various parameters determine the possible growth trajectories. If the efficiency cones themselves overlap and if each succeeding regime is productive enough, growth will be monotonic and the transition between regimes will be smooth. If the efficiency cones do not overlap, but if each regime is productive enough, then each will possess an escape interval. Smooth transitions can occur in such a case, but turbulence is also a possibility with continued growth occurring only after a series of jumps and reversions. The latter will involve occasional periods of capital accumulation that are inefficient with respect to the current technology but which will eventually be substantial enough to permit a transition to the next regime. Still another possibility occurs if the 'gap' between adjacent regimes is great enough. A collapse can bring about a reversion to a less-complex regime with lower infrastructural requirements – or in a still more extreme situation – to the demise of the society altogether. Finally, if an asymptotically stable steady state exists within the dominance cone of a given regime, trajectories can become 'stuck' within that regime, structural change ceases, and growth – in the absence of exogenous shocks – converges to a balanced growth path. Evidently, evolution beyond a single neoclassical story can only occur if regimes are unstable.

3.5 Are There Limits to Growth?

As in the previous case, continuously augmented labour productivity accelerates growth but does not really change the picture a lot. All of the various possibilities for stability, instability and evolution still occur. Introducing a dependence of birth rates on the standard of living or per capita income level adds the realistic possibility of abatement of exponential population growth. Possibilities of the kind examined by Nelson (1956) can occur, including a Malthusian trap and cessation of development. If a diseconomy to total population places an ultimate bound on human numbers as considered in section 2, the analysis is somewhat complicated and the effects have not yet been studied. It seems reasonable to surmise, however, that the lower boundary of the cone of feasible capital/labour ratios and the production isoquants within the various regimes would be bent upward, eventually placing a limit on growth and increasing the possibility of fluctuations, collapses and reversions.

4. REFLECTIONS

4.1 Do Economies Diverge?

A look at the facts of economic growth in the very long run indicates that, 'Yes, economies do diverge.' They may approach steady states but eventually depart and head off in a new direction after perhaps a turbulent period of switching and reswitching. Jumps and reversions are not rare, according to the historical record. We think of the breakup and subsequent reconstituting of the Roman Empire as a prime example, but many other examples are described in the literature involving several of the stages of growth briefly alluded to at the beginning of this paper. Such divergences from any fixed patterns are explained in the present theory as the result of underlying instabilities in the way the demoeconomic forces interact in the presence of diseconomies, infrastructures and multiple regimes. Within this theory convergence could in principle take place. The facts, however, suggest that the qualitative properties of technology and behaviour that would lead to such an outcome are not the relevant ones. The instabilities responsible in theory for complex evolution provide an explanation for how patterns of growth in isolated regions could follow very different developments, even when beginning from similar but not identical initial conditions. Instability also explains how a relatively small 'perturbation' due to unexplained 'shocks' could induce a drastically different history from the one that would have followed without it. This phenomenon is sometimes referred to as 'path dependence'.

4.2 The Problem of Transition

The theory, as developed so far, rests on a principle of 'local economic efficiency'; it is assumed that at a given population level, a given economy will grow within itself, split, fuse or switch regimes so as to maximise total output. This is, of course, a radical simplification and many other socioeconomic forces, no doubt, play a role. At another extreme we can consider the existence and character of optimal growth paths that maximise some infinite horizon objective function in a consistent way that satisfies Bellman's principle of intertemporal optimality. This would be an interesting elaboration, but it is probably even more far-fetched than the local efficiency criteria used above and unlikely on the face of it to have much to do with the real world. It is the transition between regimes and the process of fission within a regime that is so completely glossed over in the theory developed so far. One may understandably not be sanguine about the possibility of adding much to our understanding of this transition using mathematical models – but that could just be sour grapes. After all, one may have doubted the possibility that pure growth theory could say *anything* about the stages of economic growth and the complex gyrations of historical evolution. But we have shown that it can. In any case, I shall not attempt to further the analysis here, except to say that once we have got this far, it is the mechanism of transition that is the essence of the problem.

4.3 A Florescent Regime: Are There Limits For Growth?

I hesitate to suggest that there are limits to growth. Economists like growth, politicians like growth and, indeed, almost everyone would like to envisage a long and healthy life for human kind. What then *are* the prospects for continual growth? It seems to me that there *is* some kind of bound perhaps one much bigger than the present world population – but perhaps also smaller. If so, continued growth could eventually lead to drastically strengthened externalities with all the attending instabilities and possibilities for collapse noted in our discussion. To prevent this squashing against the limits of growth, the theory above identifies three key parameters for attention:

1. the externality generating effects of aggregate population;
2. the propensity for a positive rate of reproduction;
3. the vast infrastructural complexities of advanced stages of development.

New technologies, behavioural rules and modes of organisation that can arrest the debilitating aspects of growth should have the highest priority for basic research. Without an abatement of the current florescent surge the likelihood of a collapse would seem to be very high, and because the current velocity of the process is so great, the timing may not be that far off – perhaps within a few generations – or, perhaps, even within our own time.

4.4 The Great Transition

Consider the current situation in the former Soviet bloc. Here we see something like the kind of reversion our theory predicts: a large complexly organised economy disintegrating into a number of smaller ones. The process surely looks turbulent, the prospects highly uncertain. In the terms spelled out here the causes are clear. The system outgrew the infrastructure required to continue growing in an effective manner. A population of such great size cannot persist within that kind of a regime. A new one is required and that is what the attempted transition is about. But this is no reason for those within the democratic capitalist countries to gloat. For reasons given in our theory, we, too, can expect a collapse and disintegration unless new, more effective infrastructural components and behavioural rules can be evolved. Various previews of possible disintegration due to excessive population combined with inadequate infrastructure are at hand. Although our theory explains economic evolution in the long run, the mechanisms of disintegration and of regime switching take place within a generational time-scale. When regime jumps or reversions occur, they often do so within a fraction of a biblical life. It is for this reason that the multiple phase theory of economic growth in the very long run holds lessons for us now.

TECHNICAL APPENDIX

A.1 The Multiple-phase Classical Model

The following is an abstract of the model described in Day (1991). Measure the size of an economic unit (band, tribe, nation, civilisation) by the number of families, x. Each household supplies one adult equivalent of effort to society, either as a part of the workforce or as part of the infrastructural force; one adult equivalent of effort is utilised in household production, childrearing and leisure. If the size of a 'production unit' is G, then $G = M + L$ where M is the number of adult equivalents in the infrastructural force and L the number in the workforce.

Let the maximum number compatible with an effective socioeconomic order be denoted by N. The term $N - G = S$ represents the social 'space' or 'slack'. If S is large the unit may increase in size without depressing productivity very much. When S is small, increases in size begin to lower productivity – at first marginally, then absolutely. When $S \leq 0$ the group cannot function. This is the internal diseconomy of group size.

Suppose now that the productive activity within a group can be represented by a group production function continuous in the arguments L and S. Thus, $Y = h(L,S)$. Substituting $S = N - G$ and $L = G - M$ we get

$$Y = h(G-M, N-G) \equiv g(G). \qquad \text{(A4.1)}$$

Allowing for the splitting of units, the current total population is organised into 2^k groups of average size $G = x/2^k$ in such a way as to achieve a maximum output,

$$Y = f(x) := 2^k g(x/2^k) = \max_{n \in \mathbb{N}^+} \{2^n g(x/2^n)\}. \qquad \text{(A4.2)}$$

This gives the output Y of a population x divided into 2^k economies that each possesses a given techno-infrastructure.

The external diseconomy, that becomes more and more important when the absorbing capacity of the environment is increasingly stressed, is expressed by a monotonically decreasing function

$$p(x,\bar{x})\begin{cases} = 1 & , \ x=0 \\ \in (0,1) & , \ 0<x<\bar{x} \\ = 0 & , \ x \geq \bar{x}. \end{cases} \qquad \text{(A4.3)}$$

The *social production function* is then defined to be

$$F(x) \equiv f(x)p(x,\bar{x}). \qquad \text{(A4.4)}$$

The family function $b(y)$ that determines the average number of surviving children per family is assumed to depend on the average level of well-being

$$y = Y/x \qquad \text{(A4.5)}$$

and satisfies

$$b(y) = \begin{cases} 0 & , \ 0 \leq y \leq \eta \\ \alpha(y-\eta) & , \ \eta \leq y \leq \eta + \dfrac{1+n}{\alpha} \\ 1+n & , \ \eta + \dfrac{1+n}{\alpha} \leq y. \end{cases} \qquad \text{(A4.6)}$$

The parameter η is called the birth threshold. The family function can be derived from the expansion path of an appropriate household preference function.

Now begin with an initial population x_0. Putting this into eq. (A4.1) we get the number of groups, and into eq. (A4.4) the total output. This takes account of both the internal and external diseconomies of population size. This gives average welfare y from eq. (A4.5) which using eq. (A4.6) yields the next generation of families x_1 and so on. This process, when carried out generation after generation, yields the difference equation

$$x_{t+1} = \theta(x_t) := \frac{1}{2}x_t b(F(x_t)/x_t). \qquad (A4.7)$$

Suppose there are several quite different techno-infrastructures available which we may denote by a set of indexes $T := \{1,2,3,...,j,...\}$. The various components and parameters are then indexed accordingly so that a given system can be indicated by

$$S^j := \{g_j(\cdot), M^j, N^j, x_j(\cdot), \bar{x}^j, b_j(\cdot), \eta^j, \lambda^j\}, j \in T.$$

Suppose as before that society is organised so as to maximise output for any given population. Then

$$f_{i,k}(x) := \max_{j \in T} \max_{n} \{2^n g_j(x/2^n)\} \qquad (A4.8)$$

and

$$F_{i,k}(x) := f_{i,k}(x) \cdot p_i(x, \bar{x}^i). \qquad (A4.9)$$

The index pairs $I(x) = (i,k)$ give the efficient techno-infrastructure i and the efficient number of economic units 2^k for each population x.

Using the birth function eq. (A4.6) indexed to indicate the system to which it applies, we get a difference equation for each regime:

$$x_{t+1} = \theta_{i,k}(x_t) := \frac{1}{2}x_t b_i(F_{i,k}(x_t)/x_t). \qquad (A4.10)$$

Let $X_{i,k}$ be the set of populations for which the efficient infrastructure and number of units is the pair (i,k). Then

$$I(x) = (i,k) \quad \text{for all} \quad x \in X_{i,k}. \qquad (A4.11)$$

In this way we arrive at a difference equation:

$$x_{t+1} = \theta(x_t) := \theta_{I(x_t)}(x_t). \qquad (A4.12)$$

Each phase structure $\theta_{I(x)}(\cdot)$ characterises growth in a given regime, which consists of a given number of economic units and a given techno-infrastructure, and determines the population in the succeeding generation when the current population x belongs to a phase zone $X_{i,k}$.

If $I(x_{t+1}) = I(x_t)$ then there is no structural change, just growth, fluctuation or decline as the case may be. If $I(x_{t+1}) \neq I(x_t)$ then there is a phase change, that is a switch in regime.

If $\theta^t(x)$ is the population of generation t when x is the initial condition, then the sequence

$$I(\theta^t(x)), \quad t = 0,1,2,\ldots \tag{A4.13}$$

gives the history in terms of the sequence of regimes and constituent numbers of economies. For a detailed analysis of how various qualitatively distinct development scenarios can occur, see Day and Walter (1989).

A.2 A Multiple-phase Model of Capital Accumulation

Following Day and Zou (1992), consider the standard 'neoclassical' homogeneous production function. Introduce explicitly the infrastructural capital requirement, $\bar{K}$. Total capital, Z, now consists of that part, K, employed in market production and that part employed in the social infrastructure, $\bar{K}$. That is, $Z=\bar{K}+K$. Setting $x=M+L$ as before, where M is the part of the population allocated to the infrastructure, the production function can be written

$$Y = \begin{cases} 0 \ , \ x \leq M \ or \ Z \leq \bar{K} \\[2ex] BF(x-M, Z-\bar{K}) \ , \ x > M, \ Z > \bar{K}. \end{cases} \tag{A4.14}$$

Suppose that the workforce required by the infrastructure is proportional to the total capital stock, $M = \frac{1}{v}Z$, and that the capital requirement for the infrastructure depends on the total population, $\bar{K} = \mu x$. The production function in the (Z,x) space is

$$Y = \begin{cases} 0 \ , \ (z,x) \notin C \\[2ex] BF(x - \frac{1}{v}Z, z - \mu x) \ , \ (z,x) \in C \end{cases} \tag{A4.15}$$

where

$$C := \{(z,x) \,|\, \mu x \leq Z \leq vx\} \equiv \{(z,x) \,|\, \frac{1}{v}Z \leq x \leq \frac{1}{\mu} \leq Z\}. \tag{A4.16}$$

Taking advantage of homogeneity, we get the production function in per family terms:

$$y = Bf(z) := \begin{cases} 0, & Z^0 := \{z | z \le \mu, \ z \ge v\} \\ BF\left[\frac{1}{v}(v-z), \ (z-\mu)\right], & Z := \{x | \mu \le z \le v\}. \end{cases} \quad \text{(A4.17)}$$

Assume (again, for simplicity) that savings is a constant fraction of income, then

$$s(z) := \begin{cases} 0, & z \in Z^0 \\ \sigma Bf(z), & z \in Z. \end{cases} \quad \text{(A4.18)}$$

Now consider the dynamic process of capital accumulation:

$$z_{t+1} = \theta(z_t) := \frac{1}{1+n}\{(1-\delta)z_t + s(z_t)\}. \quad \text{(A4.19)}$$

In terms of the explicit phase structures, it is

$$z_{t+1} = \theta(z_t) := \begin{cases} \theta_0(z_t) = \frac{1}{1+n}(1-\delta)z_t, & k \in Z^0 \\ \theta(x_t) = \frac{1}{1+n}\left[(1-\delta)z_t + \sigma Bf(z_t)\right], & k \in Z. \end{cases} \quad \text{(A4.20)}$$

Suppose now that there are several regimes denoted by the set of indexes, $T := \{1,...,j,...\}$. Each regime is characterised by a savings rate, σ_j, the natural rate of growth, n_j, a production function, $B_j F^j(K,L)$, and infrastructure parameters, (μ_j,v_j). Denote the regime by $\mathbb{R}^j := (n_j, F^j, B_j, \mu_j, v_j, \sigma_j)$.

Each regime is individually viable on the set of feasible capital/labour ratios, (μ^j, v^j), where positive output occurs. Suppose that the society chooses the locally efficient one. This *dominant regime* is given by the index, $i = I(z)$, defined in

$$f_i(z) := \min_k \{f_k(z) \ge f_j(z), j \in T\}.$$

Let

$$Z^i := \{z | f_i(z) \ge f_j(z), \ j \in T\}. \quad \text{(A4.21)}$$

It is possible without further restrictions that regimes might *not* overlap. If $z \notin (\mu^j, v^j)$ for some j, then define $I(z)=0$ and define $f_0(z) \equiv 0$. Then

$$Z^0 := \{z | \text{ there exists no } j \text{ such that } z \in (\mu^j, v^j)\}.$$

Given these definitions, we get the multiple phase dynamical system

$$z_{t+1} = \theta(z_t) := \theta_{I(z)}(z) := \frac{1}{1+n_{I(z)}} \Big[(1-\delta_{I(z)})z_t + s_{I(z)}(z)\Big], \quad (A4.22)$$

where

$$s_i(z_i) := \begin{cases} 0 \; , \; z_t \in Z^0 \\[2mm] \sigma_i B_i f^0(z_t) \; , \; z_t \in Z^{\,i} \end{cases} \quad (A4.23)$$

or, what is the same thing,

$$z_{t+1} = \theta(z_t) := \begin{cases} \theta_0(z_t) := \frac{1}{1+n_i}(1-\delta_i)z_t \; , \; z_t \in Z^0 \\[3mm] \theta_i(z_t) := \frac{1}{1+n_i}(1-\delta_i)z_t + \sigma_i B_i f_i(z_t) \; , \; z_t \in Z^{\,i}. \end{cases} \quad (A4.24)$$

Details of this model and empirical examples are given in Day and Zou (1992). Extensive elaborations of the theory are developed in Zou (1991).

NOTES

1. To emphasise: these seven names are, of course, only suggestive. It is not implied, for instance, that hunter-gatherers only hunt and forage or that agrarians never hunt or gather wild foods. Nor do we wish to imply by the term 'city state' that citizens never engaged in hunting or that hunter-gatherers were entirely absent in later stages. The division merely reflects the dominant forms of social organisation and economic activity.
2. All of this is summarised at somewhat greater length with references to the background literature in Day and Walter (1989).
3. See Day, Kim and Macunovich (1989).

REFERENCES

Boserup, E. (1981), *Population and Technological Change*, Chicago: University of Chicago Press.
Day, R.H. (1991), 'Infrastructure, External Diseconomies and Turbulent Economic Growth', *Journal of Economic Development*, 16, December, 7-24.
Day, R.H., Kim, K.H. and Macunovich, D. (1989), 'Complex Demoeconomic Dynamics', *Journal of Population Economics*, 2, 139–159.
Day, R.H. and Walter, J.L. (1989), 'Economic Growth in the Very Long Run: On the Multiple Phase Interaction of Population, Technology and Social Infrastructure', in W. Barnett, J. Geweke and K. Shell (eds), *Economic Complexity, Chaos, Sunspots, Bubbles and Nonlinearity*, Cambridge: Cambridge University Press.
Day, R.H. and Zou, G. (1992), 'Infrastructure, Restricted Factor Substitution and Economic Growth', Paper presented at the Annual Meeting of the American Economic

Association, January 1993.

Georgescu-Roegen, N. (1966), *Analytical Economics*, Cambridge, MA: Harvard University Press.

Nelson, R. (1956), 'A Theory of the Low Level Equilibrium Trap in Underdeveloped Countries', *American Economic Review*, 46, 894–508.

Solow, R. (1956), 'A Contribution to the Theory of Economic Growth', *Quarterly Journal of Economics*, 70, 65–94.

Zou, G. (1991), *Growth With Development*, PhD. Dissertation, University of Southern California.

COMMENT ON DAY

Paul David

Richard Day's paper sets out to provide a simple explanation for why human societies have not steadily evolved but, instead, have fluctuated between progressions to higher complexity and reversions to earlier stages of simpler organisational forms. Day's explanation also leads him to offer a positive answer to the question 'Do economies converge?'. I would suggest that the positive answer is clearer and more definite than the meaning of the question itself. Do economies 'converge': in their structural features? in their per capita real income levels? in their rates of growth? Do all economies 'converge', inevitably? It would be a lot to expect answers to all those very different questions, and I believe it is fair to say that this paper really is not undertaking to supply them.

Instead, Day's paper both provides an economic model that can generate quite complex dynamics, and seeks to address some of the central questions of economic history. This has created a special problem for me as I am both an economist and an economic historian. As an economist, I admire Day's attempt to simplify complex historical forces into a few equations. At the same time, however, as an economic historian, I want to protest and exclaim that the workings of human society cannot be depicted so simply.

One hundred years ago, another economic historian, William Cunningham, had these same concerns while reading Alfred Marshall's *Principles of Economics*. Cunningham made the awful mistake of giving full vent to his misgivings in his review article of Marshall's *Principles* in the *Economic Journal* for September 1892. Cunningham wrote:

> The course of economic history consists of a gradual, and by no means continuous progress... It is not easy to understand the steps in the process... There is no royal road by which we may get to comprehend the evolution of social structure and economic conceptions, which combine to bring about industrial progress... But there are some who do not feel these difficulties, who, with no practice in the weighing of historical evidence, and with the equipment of some two or three badly chosen books, will decide the most difficult problems off-hand, or sketch you the history of the world with easy confidence. (pp. 490–491)

This assault on Marshall, in addition to being an ungenerous reading of the chapters of *The Principles* on economic history, was a dreadful tactical mistake. Marshall and his allies were able to organise the Economics curriculum at the University of Cambridge and expel both Cunningham and the teaching of economic history from it. Those long-past skirmishes in the *Methodenstreit* contributed significantly to the separation of Economics from Economic History as academic disciplines – to their mutual detriment. I do not wish to make the same mistake. Instead, the best response I can make to Day's paper is to abandon both the strategy of the economic historian and that of the economist and to use a mixed strategy which combines recourse to some history and some economic theory.

To begin, what makes the story of mankind's economic progress interesting according to Day? The answer, in a word, is 'nonlinearities'. It is well known that a quite simple dynamical system, characterised by simple lags and nonlinearities, can produce unusual, complex behaviours.

It is often the case with attempts to develop a simple model that some of the most intriguing and subtle features of the world become blurred or obscured from view. I fear this has happened in the presentation of the simulation models on which Day's paper is grounded. This is unfortunate, first because a clear understanding of the details is needed to evaluate the results of these models and, second, because the assumptions and specifications of the full model need to be exposed and understood before one can understand the nature of the mechanism that generates the most interesting results. Without that exposure a reader who does not slog through the technical appendices may simply be left with a reaffirmation of Siever's law: 'With every simulation there is an equal and opposite amount of dissimulation'.

Day builds upon the simple classical model which predicts a Malthusian increase in the population whenever there is any economic surplus above a culturally determined subsistence wage. This simple dynamic process converges to a stationary state where the population level is the highest possible given the available resources. Day makes this classical model more interesting by introducing absolute decreasing returns. This generates overshooting and limits cycles.

If we wish to develop the model further, we have to specify the relationship between population size and per capita output. Alternatively, we could make population responsive to the real wage, as the classical economists did, in which case we can describe it as some fraction of per capita output (see Figure C4.1a where $(1-\theta_k)$ is the wage share of per capita output, y). Day models the relationship between population growth and production through a family function. This function assumes that there is a threshold level of capital accumulation below which the population will not grow.

My view (see Figure C4.1b) is that there are three regions of population dynamics that vary with income. There is a Malthusian region where the population increases with income and reaches an equilibrium population level at some wage. Beyond this the desire to better one's condition prevails and there is a demographic transition zone where fertility declines with increasing income. Further increases in per capita income lead to a region of below-replacement fertility, which is where most of the advanced countries of the world are found.

Day's model does not incorporate the full range of these possible demographic responses, but instead is based on a simplified Malthusian relationship between population and income. In addition to a population response function, we can describe a production relationship where the real wage is a function of the capital stock, which embodies some level of improvable technology. The rate of population growth is dependent upon the stock of capital and population at any moment. When graphed, this gives an area or 'Malthus space' – as it is described by Ronald Lee, of UC Berkeley – where the population will grow, and spaces where the population will decline (see Figure C4.2).

It is possible to add to this basic model Solow's neoclassical model of capital accumulation and Boserup's conjecture that population growth drives improvements in technology. It is simple enough to do this if we accept Maurice Scott's argument that investment activity provides occasions for learning something new, and the resulting technological/organisational innovations are all embodied in the stock of capital. The conditions under which population can increase will vary depending on the factors governing accumulation and consequent improvements in the technology, thus defining a 'Solow–Boserup space' that is analogous to the Malthus-space (see Figure C4.3a). For example, the population level could be either too sparse or too dense for capital accumulation to occur, there could be negative externalities that interfere with accumulation (see Figures C4.3b and C4.3c), or a minimum level of infrastructural capital could be needed before growth is possible (see Figure C4.3d).

As Ronald Lee has shown, using diagrams of this kind, it is possible to create a model with a stable attractor by combining the Solow–Boserupian and Malthusian dynamics. In this case different economies will converge in the long run towards the same per capita income level, though growth rates can diverge (see Figure C4.4).

Day's model goes one step further than this and imagines that there is not just one kind of Solow–Boserup space based on a particular relationship between population growth and capital accumulation, but several regimes, for example 1 and 2, where 2 requires a more developed infrastructure. We can also assume that these two regimes do not overlap. In this case there are two stable attractors at different per capita income levels and, of course, an unstable attractor somewhere in the middle (see Figure C4.5).

This type of model gives a different answer to the question: 'Do economies converge?'. In this model both convergence and divergence can

Figure C4.1a: Classical demographic equilibria

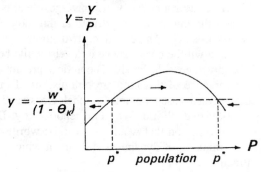

Figure C4.1b: Population dynamics: three 'regions' $\dot{p}/p = N(w)$

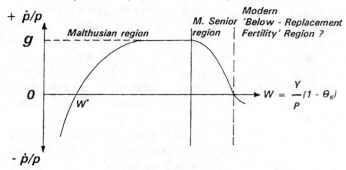

Figure C4.2 The 'Malthus space': the right-hand boundary must be crossed vertically, since it is a $\dot{p} = 0$*-locus.*

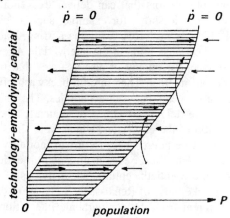

occur. Economies with very different technologies, but which fall within the region of the stable attractor 'A', will converge towards 'A', while economies which pass the minimum infrastructural threshold for attractor 'B' will converge towards 'B'. There will be two groups of economies. Within each group there will be convergence in levels, while between each group there will be divergence in levels. Theoretical predictions of both convergence and divergence of this kind are reminiscent of the results of recent econometric studies based on international cross-section data for growth in the post-Second World War era reported by Durlauf and Johnson. The point in common that would seem to be worth emphasising is that we should be thinking of dynamical systems in which there exist a multiplicity of attractors.

Of further interest is what happens to economies that are quite similar, in terms of technologies, labour productivity and per capita output, and therefore start in the unstable zone between the two attractors A and B, (that is, in the neighbourhood of C in Figure C4.5). These economies could either move towards the stable attractor at the lower per capita level or move towards the higher attractor. In this case there is extreme sensitivity to initial conditions where very small differences can give rise to quite different development histories, particularly because the present model does not assume the existence of stochastic influences on economic development.

   The question here is, can this kind of dynamic modelling account for the historical odyssey of mankind? Like Day's simulation structure, it is neat, but does its neatness really help us to understand the progression from hunting and gathering societies to modern economies with complex patterns of global competition? Surely not. We need to remind ourselves what has been left out of the model. For example, the model does not consider environmental factors that can deliver exogenous shocks. There are no plagues or climatic shifts, for example, such as changed the temperature of the Baltic sea and drove away the herring, leading to the commercial decline of the Hansa ports in the late Middle Ages. Moreover, the model includes only one economy or else assumes that there are a lot of economies that do not interact. There are no backwash effects from trade, or adverse factor movements between economies. The only type of development possible is efficient growth. Consequently the model cannot explain the expansion of the city states, which were sinks into which endless immigrants could be poured because urban mortality rates were very high; no major city in the world ever maintained an endogenous positive growth rate before the twentieth century. The activities of the city states of the Ancient World, like those of Renaissance Italy, were driven by a set of dynamics very different from the demographic interactions represented in

Figure C4.3: The 'Solow-Boserup space' under alternative savings and technology specifications: (a) Population may be too sparse or too dense for accumulation; (b) Upper limit to sustainable stock; (c) Cases (a) and (b) combined; (d) Case (c) plus necessary minimum level of stock

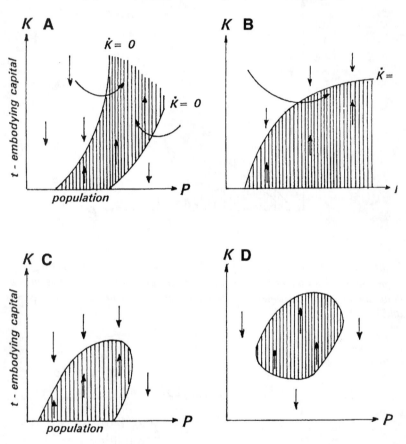

Day's models. Among other historically important factors that are not included in the model are conquest and politics, as well as the willingness to undertake economically inefficient measures, such as Peter the Great's efforts to modernise Russia on the backs of the peasantry.

Yet more than these problems, what plagues this model, and what is the essential problem for all stage theories such as the German stage theories of Hildenbrand, is the problem of transitions. Only Marx provided something like an internal dynamic to explain transitions. Endogenous technical

Figure C4.4: Dynamics of the System with a unique stable attractor: economies converge, in levels of y, Y.

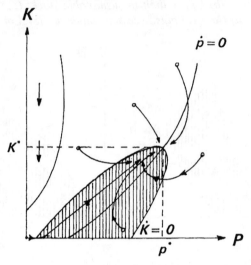

Figure C4.5: Dynamics of system with two regimes (non-intersecting) Some economies converge, others diverge in levels of y, Y; 'convergence-club' membership becomes manifest only among economies where $\dot{p} > 0$ and $\dot{k} > 0$.

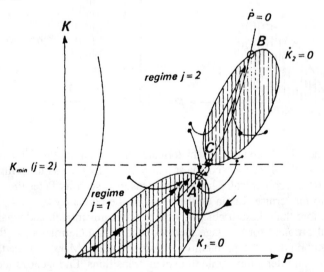

change, institutional change, or the psychosocial creation of tastes have all been left out of the story by the very device of defining pre-existing and distinct regimes of per capita incomes. In this model, the existence of two or more different regimes does not tell us how economies make the transition in which one regime grows out of another. The different regimes are already 'out there', beckoning the economies onward. However, major transitions, for example between hunting and gathering to sedentary agriculture over a period of 3000 years, did not occur because the population of hunters and gathers became too dense for their habitat. It involved the co-evolution between an increase in sedentary habits and a change in the demographic regime. One possibility is that sedentary life permitted higher fertility rates because women did not need to breast-feed their children, which they carried, for three years, as the ¡Kung people of the Kalahari do today. There was also a co-evolutionary process between gatherers and plants.

Economic history develops through a complicated and truly evolutionary kind of dynamic that can be set back or interrupted by ecological and cultural developments lying outside the economists' normal purview; and which requires much more complexity and subtlety in the modelling, of course. We need to go further with modelling experiments to explore how distinctive economic regimes are created and develop. For inspiring this, we are grateful to the pioneering efforts of Dick Day. But I am happy to tell you that there is still plenty left for economic historians to do.

Richard Day:
Historians often criticise models for ignoring important factors. We desire this kind of response because there is a need for a detailed critique based on historical evidence. However, a theoretical model at this level of sophistication is a cartoon that sketches out the essential aspect of an argument without going into the details. I don't think that it is possible in mathematical models to incorporate the richness that is actually there.

It is clear that economic development cannot be understood without studying economic history. It is a great pity that economics has gradually eliminated the study of economic history from the curriculum. History is very important because it provides a means of discussing all of the issues that are brushed aside in a simply theory.

There is one comment that I would like to make about Paul David's model with two attractors. This model requires a random external shock to push the economy from one regime to another and allow the process of growth to start over again. In effect, the model switches from discrete to continuous time. Conversely, my model includes a fundamental instability that explains the possibility for transition to a different regime. This instability is necessary because there are no random external shocks. Of course there are many complicating external factors that can provide a shock, and environmental factors do play a role. Yet, economists have tended to overlook the possibility of endogenous instability playing a role in the evolutionary process. I would argue that it is worthwhile to try to identify the sources of endogenous instabilities.

This theory does not explain the process of transition, but I doubt if it will ever be possible to explain this transition in mathematical terms. It may be possible, however, to describe how an economy mechanically manages to reorganise itself to make the jump. If we knew how economies did that, then we would be a lot more successful in advising our colleagues in economies that are attempting to change to a different infrastructural form in giant strides, which contrasts with gradual changes made by Western economies. So far we have not been very successful at this and we are more likely to learn about transitions through a process of trial and error. Hopefully this learning process can be compressed in time.

Richard Nelson:

I would have thought that the most remarkable economic transformation of all, which laid the foundation for modern economies, occurred during the nineteenth century and involved the development of the human, social and economic capacity to generate continuous technical change and improvement across a wide range of human needs. Neither Paul David nor Richard Day included in their models the development of science and engineering capabilities, which is an essential factor in the growth of modern economies.

Paul David:

One of the things that I would like to hear discussed is speed of transition, which appears to be increasing. Some of this increase in the rate of change is illusory. For example, there have been periods of rapid population growth in the past, but they were often followed by extinctions and a loss of knowledge, so the long-term rate of growth was very low. The question is how modern society can cumulatively learn and generate new technologies. This contrasts with earlier societies which had to struggle to maintain existing knowledge.

Perhaps the transition from societies which struggle to maintain existing knowledge to societies which generate new knowledge can be modelled. I think there have been some attempts to do this which have shown that the probability of extinction is a function of size for small populations. The diffusion of knowledge is easier in open societies and protects against extinction, though it does increase the probabilities of the diffusion of pathogens and of war.

5. Growth Fluctuations in an Evolutionary Model of Creative Destruction

Gerald Silverberg and Doris Lehnert

Evolution is the result of a sequence of replacements.
Elliott W. Montroll (1978)

1. INTRODUCTION

Schumpeter's concept of creative destruction has attracted increased theoretical attention in recent years. The interest in 'endogenising' economic growth (see Chapter 3 by Bruno Amable in this volume) has led researchers to try to characterise technical change in a more precise manner (for example, by focusing on increasing specialisation, product quality and variety, and imperfect competition). The specific features of creative destruction as a form of technical change are the emphasis on the qualitatively distinct nature of major innovations, the fact that technologies compete for 'niches' and thus replace one another, and that diffusion, imitation and differential profit rates are intricately bound up with the process of economic change. These observations accord well with the voluminous literature on technology diffusion, but they have only begun to form the cornerstone of models of economic growth and business cycles. While Schumpeter (1939) is an attempt to do precisely this, his intuitions have not been cast into a theoretically convincing form until now.

Let us begin by formulating a few basic points characterising innovation and productivity growth to which researchers of all persuasions would probably subscribe. First, the innovation process is inherently uncertain and irregular, and neither the exact nature nor the timing of innovations is under the control of the actors. For these reasons, a stochastic approach seems natural. Second, although the Schumpeterian description of entrepreneurship hinges on imperfect competition and appropriability, technical progress has very rarely been monopolisable for any length of time by a single party. Instead, it has generally been the joint product of the actions of many agents and therefore only imperfectly appropriable at best (thus the frequent necessity of patent pools, reverse engineering, strategic alliances and informal knowledge sharing).[1] Third, the productivity-enhancing effects of innovations only become manifest during diffusion. Investment and capital formation, learning and organizational change thus play a central role in translating innovation into ongoing technical change. And this diffusion often requires considerable time; its rate is usually proportional to profitability.[2] Fourth, it follows from the simultaneity of diffusion processes that the economy at any given time will consist of a superposition of different technologies inherited from the past, as well as a multitude of 'cutting edge' technologies competing for dominance on the frontier. The nature of competition determines replacement dynamics and choice of technique (see also Chapter 11 by Dosi and Kaniovski in this volume). Such an economy will look quite different from anything representable by a shifting, smooth, substitutable production function.

A number of authors of a neoclassical bent have begun incorporating elements of a creative destruction picture in models of economic growth and international trade (Aghion and Howitt 1992; Cheng and Dinopoulos 1992; Grossman and Helpman 1991; Segerstrom, Anant and Dinopoulos 1990). Thus, as in the model we shall present below, Aghion and Howitt assume that innovations arrive discretely and represent a fixed multiplicative jump in productivity. In the steady state they derive, the innovations will arrive according to a homogeneous Poisson process. However, they interpret creative destruction to mean that the advent of an innovation makes all previous technologies instantaneously obsolete. Moreover, because technologies are viewed as intermediate goods and not as capital embodied (a feature their model shares with most other endogenous growth models), diffusion is instantaneous and costless. This abstraction might be acceptable if one were solely interested in the steady-state properties of growth modelled as a patent race. However, as we have pointed out above, a patent race, with its winner-take-all connotations and its implicit assumption that participants know exactly what they are shooting at, may be a serious misrepresentation of the reality of technological competition. We shall adopt a more agnostic position here, focusing less on the microeconomic incentives to innovate and simply assume a certain stochastic pattern for the innovation process. Instead, the dynamics of diffusion will be shifted to centre stage in order to investigate the temporal properties of Schumpeterian economic growth and not just steady states. To this end we shall draw upon the more evolutionary approach to Schumpeterian dynamics represented by Henkin and Polterovich (1991), Iwai (1984a,b), Nelson (1968), Silverberg (1984), and Soete and Turner (1984).[3] The essence of this modelling perspective is to focus on 'mutation'/selection dynamics and the statistical distributions of heterogeneous populations, in contrast to the representative agent analysis typical of much economic thinking.

Schumpeter himself visualised the dynamics of a capitalist economy as intimately related to the long waves of economic development Kondratieff (1926) claimed to have identified in historical time series. While the well-known Schumpeterian 'hypothesis' relating the destabilising effect of basic innovations, the bandwagon dynamics of imitation and the gradual disappearance of older structures summarised by the expression 'creative destruction' has seemed intuitively appealing to many researchers, Kuznets (1940) already cast doubt on the logical coherence of this picture as an explanation of long waves. First, it would have to be shown that the rate of innovative activity was sufficiently irregular, making some provision for the varying macroeconomic significance of individual innovations. In particular, a bunching or clustering of innovations would seem to be called for. Second, assuming that clustering does characterise the innovation process, some reason would have to be given why the expansive effects would endure as long as 50 years, only to end in depression (see Freeman 1987 for a review of this debate).

The postwar period saw a slackening of interest in Kondratieff cycles and Schumpeterian dynamics, which ceded the stage to steady-state growth models and productivity accounting exercises. This gradually changed with the publication of Mensch (1975) and in the aftermath of the oil, inflation and productivity crises of the 1970s. Mensch presented empirical evidence purporting to demonstrate significant clustering of innovations in particular in the depression phases of 50-year cycles. He also advanced the hypothesis that there was indeed a causal connection, with the introduction of radical innovations being accelerated by desperate entrepreneurs in crisis periods to overcome the fall in the rate of profit (the 'depression trigger hypothesis'). Further evidence was presented by Kleinknecht (1981, 1987, 1990a,b) in support of the clustering hypothesis. These results were challenged by Freeman and his associates (Clark, Freeman and Soete, 1981; Freeman, Clark and Soete 1982) on both empirical and methodological grounds. First, they found much weaker evidence for clustering of innovations, and furthermore rejected the depression trigger hypothesis. Second, they called into question the significance of the timing of innovations *per se* as explanation of long waves, arguing that diffusion was the key mechanism mediating between innovations and their macroeconomic and structural impact, and that diffusion times were both variable and long, thus obscuring any fixed relationship between discovery and economic development.

The long-wave debate, at least in so far as technology is implicated,[4] has more or less stagnated conceptually since that time. Empirically, work has continued to find direct evidence of long waves in macroeconomic time series on the one hand (see, for example, Metz 1992), and better evidence of clustering of innovations and their correlation with profit rates on the other. Theoretically, various reformulations have been put forward to salvage the basic Schumpeterian inspiration while emancipating it from the Achilles heel identified by Kuznets. One insight that has emerged from this debate, however, is the necessity of embedding the diffusion process into the centre of any discussion of the technological determinants of long waves. In this respect the IIASA work on diffusion in the context of multistage technological substitution (following on the approach of Fisher and Pry 1971) is highly suggestive (see, for example, Nakicenovic 1987). It would appear not unreasonable at this stage of the international discussion to require that the disparate empirical studies of innovation rates, diffusion curves and time series first be incorporated into a complete dynamic model before their relative significance can be properly assessed.[5]

2. THE MODEL

Our approach is based on Silverberg (1984), which in turn is an extension of Goodwin (1967). First, a linear Phillips curve is postulated to govern the growth rate of real wages:

$$\dot{w} = -mw + nwv, \tag{5.1}$$

where m and n are constants and v is the rate of employment aggregated over all technologies. Second, the economy is assumed to be composed of a number of fixed-coefficient linear technologies. The rate of growth of the capital stock embodied in each technology is posited to be equal to that technology's own rate of (net) profit. Letting a_i, c_i, k_i, r_i be the labour productivity, the capital–output ratio, the capital stock and the rate of profit of any given technology i and γ the rate of exponential *physical* deterioration of capital (economically motivated scrapping is an endogenous component of the model) we have

$$\frac{\dot{k_i}}{k_i} = r_i - \gamma = \frac{1}{c_i}\left(1 - \frac{w}{a_i}\right) - \gamma. \tag{5.2}$$

Soete and Turner (1984) propose an extension of this mechanism to allow the profits made with one technology to be invested in another technology with superior profitability. If the probability of making this jump on the technology ladder is proportional to the difference in profitability on the one hand and the relative size of the capital stock of the target technology on the other, then they show that eq. (5.2) can be extended to

$$\frac{\dot{k}_i}{k_i} = r_i + s(r_i - \bar{r}) - \gamma = \frac{1}{c_i}\left(1 - \frac{w}{a_i}\right) + s(r_i - \bar{r}) - \gamma, \tag{5.3}$$

where s is a constant representing the strength of the cross technology investment flows and

$$\bar{r} = \sum_{i=1}^{n} k_i r_i / \sum_{i=1}^{n} k_i$$

is the capital stock weighted average profit rate. Employment using this technology will grow at the same rate as the capital stock, so that the share of the labour force employing this technology v_i is given by

$$\frac{\dot{v}_i}{v_i} = \frac{\dot{k}_i}{k_i} - \alpha = \frac{1}{c_i}\left(1 - \frac{w}{a_i}\right) + s(r_i - \bar{r}) - \beta, \tag{5.4}$$

where α is the growth rate of the labour force and $\beta = \alpha + \gamma$.

In Silverberg (1984) a criterion is derived that determines whether a new technology initially introduced in a small quantity will displace an existing technology. This is based on evaluating the sign of the eigenvalue associated with the employment share of the new technology in the neighbourhood of the old steady state. If it is positive, the old technology will be replaced by the new one; if it is negative, the new technology will not diffuse. This criterion reduces to comparing an expression specific to each technology based solely on technological and exogenous factors, independent of current relative prices and initial conditions:

$$T_i = a_i(1 - c_i(\alpha + \gamma)) = a_i(1 - c_i\beta). \tag{5.5}$$

If T_i, which we term the technology's evolutionary potential, is higher than those of previous technologies, it will survive and gradually dominate the economy (see Figures 5.1a, b). The difference in evolutionary potential $\Delta T = T_2 - T_1$ also determines the rate of replacement in the two-technology case:

$$v_2^{m_2}/v_1^{m_1} = \text{const} \cdot e^{\Delta T \cdot t}, \tag{5.6}$$

where $m_i = a_i c_i$ is the capital/worker ratio for each technology, as can be seen by simple algebraic manipulation of the two employment share equations to eliminate w, and subsequent integration.

Figure 5.1: Contours of equal selective potential in the a–c (Fig. 5.1a) and a–m (Fig. 5.1b) planes. Technologies above (below) the contour are superior (inferior) to ones on it.

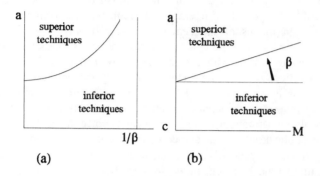

(a)   (b)

We now generalise the model to reflect the behaviour of the capital stock and employment shares in the case of a continuing stream of capital-embodied innovations entering the economy over time. We envision each technology as being 'seeded' with a fixed and very small employment share (say 0.01% of the labour force) at a specific moment in history. Formally this is tantamount to 'turning on' the corresponding employment share equation *à la* eq. (5.4) with the corresponding initial value for v_i at the time of innovation, thereby enlarging the dimension of the active state space of the system by one. Since the dimension of the state space is unbounded for such a process, we are forced in the numerical realisation to restrict attention to only a finite number n of technologies most recently introduced. If the size of this subset is made sufficiently large with respect to the rate at which new technologies are being introduced, there is in fact no danger in this procedure, since old technologies automatically decline asymptotically to zero with time as they become relatively obsolete. Thus in our implementation, when a new technology is introduced, the stack of technologies is pushed down by one, the oldest technology is eliminated, and the difference between the initial employment share of the new technology and the remaining employment share of the scrapped technology is proportionately removed from the rest of the economy to maintain a constant overall rate of employment. Then the economy is allowed to evolve as an $n+1$ dimensional dynamic system starting with the n new (or shifted) technological parameters and initial employment shares and the previous real wage rate until the next innovation comes along.

In contrast to the macrodynamics of sectoral employment and wage formation, which are modelled deterministically, we wish to focus on the *stochastic* character of the innovation process. To this end, the model can be completed by filling the innovation 'black box' with a fully specified stochastic process that can be either autonomous or subject to feedback from the economy. We have examined a number of stochastic models that are plausibly congruent with empirical studies of innovation and some hypotheses on modes of inducement in the economy. The first, which serves as a devil's advocate benchmark case, simply regards an innovation as a point event in time whose probability of occurrence is independent of other innovations and of time. This is precisely the definition of a time-homogeneous Poisson process. For simplicity we define an innovation to be a fixed proportional increase in labour productivity over the last inno-vation, with the capital/output ratio unchanged, since this is consistent with the main implications of our choice of technique criterion eq. (5.5).[6] The resulting stochastic process can be characterised by two parameters: ω, the mean waiting time between innovations (= $1/\rho$, the mean number of in-novations per unit time), and Δ, the proportional jump in labour produc-tivity between innovations. The approximate average growth rate of labour productivity τ will then be Δ/ω (more precisely, $\ln(1+\Delta)/\omega$), which we can use to calibrate the model to historically reasonable values. As is well known, a time-homogeneous Poisson process is associated with the fol-lowing distribution and probability density function:

$$\text{Prob } (n \text{ events during time interval } t) = \frac{(\rho t)^n}{n!}\, e^{-\rho t}, \qquad (5.7)$$

$$\text{Prob } (t < \text{ interval between events } < t+dt) = \rho e^{-\rho t} \cdot dt. \qquad (5.8)$$

For the time-homogeneous case the innovation process can be imple-mented exactly. The computer generates negative exponentially distributed variates for a given mean waiting time by appropriately transforming a standard uniformly distributed random number generator. The system of differential equations is solved starting with some set of initial values for the length of the randomly generated time interval. Then a stack updating is performed as outlined above and a new time interval is generated from our negative exponentially distributed variates, and the process iterates.

For the models described below involving a time-varying Poisson para-meter the process is discretely approximated as a Bernoulli process. The time axis is divided into small intervals, the Poisson parameter is scaled down proportionately, and a correspondingly weighted computer-generated 'coin' is flipped to determine if an innovation is introduced during this interval. If no, the system is solved until the end of the interval and the coin tossing is repeated. If yes, a stack updating is also performed at the end of the interval. In all versions of the model a fixed-step, fourth-order Runge–Kutta algorithm, which has proved more than adequate in accuracy for this well-behaved class of systems, is employed to solve the system of differential equations.

Figure 5.2: Schematic representation of the capital stock dynamics. Vertical bars represent the share of each technology in the total capital stock. As an innovation arrives at the left the entire distribution shifts one step to the right.

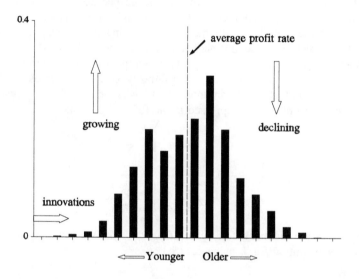

The operation of the model can be visualised by plotting the share of each technology in the total capital stock as a bar graph (Figure 5.2). Denoting the share of technology i by f_i ($= k_i/k$, where k is the total capital stock) and rates of growth of a variable by a hat over it, we have

$$\hat{f}_i = \hat{k}_i - \hat{k}$$
$$= r_i + s(r_i - \bar{r}) - \gamma - (\bar{r} - \gamma) \qquad (5.9)$$
$$= (1 + s)(r_i - \bar{r}).$$

In the absence of innovation, technologies with above-average profit rates will be growing in relative share; those with below-average profit rates will be declining. Eq. (5.9) is an example of so-called replicator dynamics (cf. Hofbauer and Sigmund 1988). $\bar{r}$ will increase monotonically in time (for constant wages) and is a Lyapunov function for the dynamics as the system converges to the most profitable technology. As innovations are introduced, however, the entire capital stock distribution shifts to the right. Thus an 'innovation wind' prevents the 'diffusion wave' from washing up on the shore.

Artificial time series were generated under quasi-stationary circumstances by first allowing transients induced by the initial conditions (in particular, the shape of the initial capital stock 'vintage' structure) to die out by removing the first 200 years of each run. The variables of interest are: the unemployment rate, the aggregate rate of gross profits, and the rate of growth of aggregate labour productivity. With respect to the last variable, only the 'deterministic' component, that is, the increase in labour productivity due to the shift in employment from existing low to existing high productivity sectors – the diffusion effect – was examined. The small, instantaneous jumps in productivity at the moment of introduction of a new technology, which can be made arbitrarily small by decreasing the initial employment share of an innovation, were neglected. This deterministic component can be expressed in the following form:

$$\hat{a} = \frac{d}{dt} \ln \left(\frac{\text{output}}{\text{labour}} \right) = \frac{d}{dt} \ln \left(\frac{\sum\limits_{i=1}^{n} \dfrac{k_i}{c_i}}{\sum\limits_{i=1}^{n} \dfrac{k_i}{a_i c_i}} \right) = \frac{\sum\limits_{i=1}^{n} \dfrac{\dot{k}_i}{c_i}}{\sum\limits_{i=1}^{n} \dfrac{k_i}{c_i}} - \frac{\sum\limits_{i=1}^{n} \dfrac{\dot{k}_i}{a_i c_i}}{\sum\limits_{i=1}^{n} \dfrac{k_i}{a_i c_i}}. \quad (5.10)$$

Since the c_i's are identical, and by defining $\alpha_i = 1/a_i$, we can simplify eq. (5.10) by substituting for $\dot{k}$ using eq. (5.3):

$$\hat{a} = \frac{w(1+s)}{c\bar{\alpha}} \sigma_\alpha^2, \quad (5.11)$$

where $\bar{\alpha}$ and σ_α^2 are the mean and variance of $\{\alpha_i\}$ over the distribution of technologies $\{f_i\}$. The proportionality between the rate of growth of average productivity and the variance of the technology distribution is fully parallel to the result derived in Soete and Turner (1984) for profit rates.

3. STRUCTURAL DYNAMICS AND LINEAR TIME SERIES ANALYSIS

As new technologies come online, they diffuse into the economy due to their superior profitability. In the course of time, as their profitability declines to the average value prevailing in the economy, their share saturates, until they begin to diffuse out of the capital stock due to relative unprofitability. If this diffusion (either in or out) proceeds according to the well-known logistic equation, the share f of a technology will obey the following equation:

$$\ln(f/(1-f)) = \alpha \cdot (t - t_0). \tag{5.12}$$

Marchetti and Nakicenovic (1979) have extended this framework to the multiple replacement case, where new technologies saturate in terms of market share due to the advent of even newer technologies. An example from the primary energy sector is shown in Figure 5.3a.

To analyse the structural dynamics we have plotted the transformed share of successive innovations (as measured by their share in the total capital stock) over time for a typical run with pure ploughback investment in Figure 5.3b. Indeed, we do recover the characteristic features of the multiple replacement case uncovered in the empirical literature. Notice that both the rate of diffusion (the slope of the quasi-linear segments) and the ultimate penetration levels vary between innovations, and are determined endogenously by the exact historical timing of preceding and subsequent innovations. Figure 5.3c shows the replacement pattern for a positive value of the ST investment term s. As expected, diffusion proceeds more rapidly in this case, and technology lifecycles become correspondingly shorter.

Figure 5.3a: An empirical case of multiple replacement taken from the primary energy sector in the US (after Nakicenovic 1987)

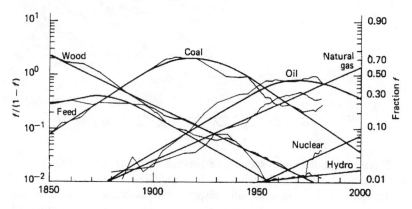

Figure 5.3b: Multiple replacement in our artificial economy (ω = 15, τ = 2%)

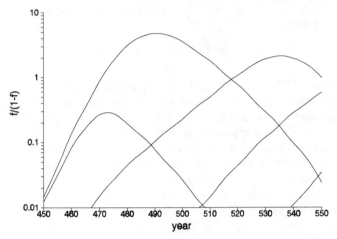

Figure 5.3c: Multiple replacement in the same run as in 5.3b but with an ST investment parameter s of 0.5

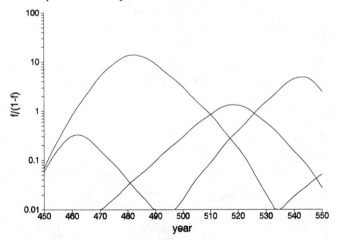

Figure 5.4 shows times series for a benchmark run of some of the macro-economic variables of primary interest. The unemployment and profit rate variables may initially display short (Goodwin) cycles, which die out unless a period of constant productivity growth is encountered. Otherwise they reflect the underlying long period fluctuations in productivity growth. These are irregular but far from a random walk.

Figure 5.4: Artificial time series for unemployment, average profitability and growth rate of productivity for a run with $\omega = 2$ *years and* $\tau = 2\%$

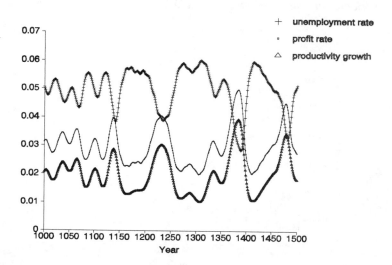

As opposed to the search for long waves in the historical statistics, where nonstationarity and the limited length and reliability of the data impose severe restrictions on the applicability of spectral methods, the model allows the unlimited generation of artificial data from a known stationary mechanism (assuming a constant innovation probability). In Figure 5.5a the spectral density of the productivity growth rate is presented generated by running the model for 200 periods to allow transients to die off and performing a spectral analysis on the following 1024 periods. What is remarkable is the sharp rise in spectral density in the 40–80 year region. Thus, in contrast to a naive expectation of sharply defined 50–60 year Kondratieff cycles, our model also seems to provide strong evidence for long-period behaviour, but in a spectrally distributed sense. In Figure 5.5b we have plotted the related autocorrelation function for two key macrovariables, which both display the characteristic *persistence* of empirical macroeconomic time series, that is, the slow tapering off of autocorrelation with increasing lags.

To see whether this result was not an artefact of the specific parameter values of this run, we ran the model through a range of relevant points in parameter space. Table 5.1 summarises these experiments and shows the proportion of total spectral power concentrated between 40 and 80 years for a range of values of the three most significant parameters, for runs of length of 1024 periods. The capital–output ratio c has a direct effect on

Figure 5.5a: Spectral density of aggregate productivity growth rate with ω = 2 years, τ = 2%/yr. The spectral plots for the other macroeconomic variables are quite similar

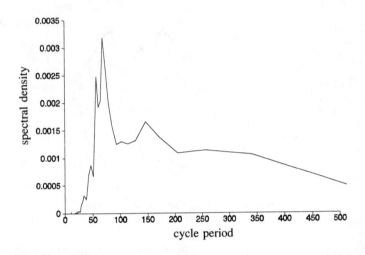

Figure 5.5b: Autocorrelation function of productivity and GNP growth rates. The horizontal lines give the 5% significance bounds

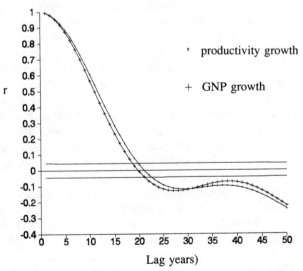

diffusion time (cf. Silverberg 1984) and thereby on the spectral pattern. The interaction of τ and ω also affects diffusion times, whereby the mean waiting time between innovations in the Poisson process ω does not itself directly determine the periodicity of the cycle. This is not the case if innovations are introduced nonstochastically with the precise period of ω; in this truly driven case the macro variables will also show a sharp spike in the spectrum at period ω, rather than in the long-range region.

The parameters m and n, which control labour market dynamics, only have an effect on the period of the Goodwin cycle, but none at all on the long-wave dynamics. The effect of varying ß is shown in Table 5.2. Very large values of ß tend to diminish the relative importance of the Kondratieff region in total variability.

By turning on the ST investment parameter diffusion is progressively accelerated, which leads to a shortening of the cyclical pattern due to the emergence of an increasing number of time series peaks. Table 5.3 shows the proportion of spectral variance between 40 and 80 years for different values of the ST investment parameter for our benchmark run. A plot of spectral density for a Soete/Turner run is presented in Figure 5.6. It is

Table 5.1: Proportion of spectral variance in the range 40 to 80 years for runs of length 1024 years and a range of relevant parameters

τ	ω	c	2	3	4	5
0.01	1		0.309	0.309	0.215	0.142
	2		0.385	0.219	0.143	0.116
	5		0.478	0.320	0.177	0.121
	10		0.378	0.259	0.139	0.098
0.02	1		0.422	0.426	0.369	0.307
	2		0.398	0.403	0.310	0.216
	5		0.423	0.467	0.406	0.291
	10		0.346	0.368	0.307	0.211
0.03	1		0.358	0.430	0.414	0.365
	2		0.309	0.397	0.375	0.302
	5		0.338	0.437	0.445	0.381
	10		0.295	0.357	0.343	0.276

Table 5.2: Proportion of spectral variance in the range 40 to 80 years for runs of length 1024 years and different values of β and τ

β \ τ	0.01	0.02	0.03
0.01	0.320	0.467	0.437
0.05	0.249	0.455	0.448
0.10	0.168	0.395	0.441
0.20	0.054	0.139	0.203

Table 5.3: Proportion of spectral variance in the range 40 to 80 years for the benchmark run with different values of ST parameter

s	0.0	0.2	0.5	2.0	5.0
	0.568	0.562	0.534	0.343	0.183

apparent that the effect of turning on this investment mode is to shift the spectrum towards the shorter periods.

In our model causality runs from innovations to the macro dynamics. Our null hypothesis until now has been that the innovations are generated by a Poisson process, that is, by white noise. The model transforms this white noise into a particular long-wave spectral pattern, as we have seen above. To examine more closely the relationship between innovations and macro dynamics, Figure 5.7 plots innovation times against average productivity growth rate. It is readily apparent that 'clusters' of innovations translate with a delay into a surge of productivity growth. By computing the cross correlation between moving averages of different orders of the time series of number of innovations per period, and the productivity growth rate, an optimal order and lag between the two time series can be determined. In the case of a run with $\omega = 2$ years and $\tau = 2\%$/year (which will serve as our benchmark in the following) the cross correlation reaches a value as high as 83% for a 28-year moving average and a lag of 24 years (that is, innovations leading productivity, as is to be expected, see Figure 5.8). The plot of the productivity growth and innovation moving average time series in Figure 5.9 confirms this relationship. The introduction of the ST investment term, not unexpectedly, shortens both the order of the moving average and the lag (Table 5.4).

This observation sheds some light on the so-called productivity paradox. If we attempt to predict the productivity growth rate of the present

Figure 5.6: Spectral density of productivity growth rate of the same run as in Figure 5.4 but with an ST parameter value of 2

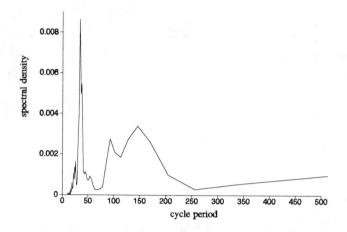

Figure 5.7: Time series of aggregate productivity growth rate and innovation dates (vertical dotted lines) for a run with ω = 8 years

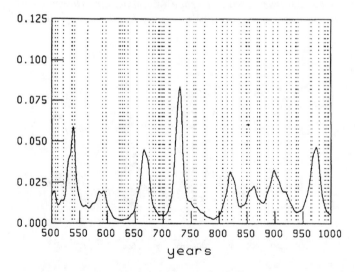

with a moving average of the innovation activity of the recent past, Figure 5.8 indicates that the two are essentially uncorrelated (lagged value at −14 years). The moving average of past innovation activity is only a good predictor of productivity growth for a point in time ten years into the

Figure 5.8: Cross correlation of the productivity growth rate and a 28-year moving average of the annual number of innovations

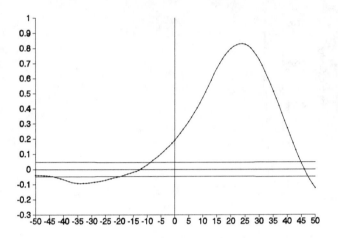

Figure 5.9: Time series of productivity growth rate (upper curve, left scale) and a 28-year moving average of innovations (lower curve, right scale) for the benchmark run. The lagged correlation is apparent.

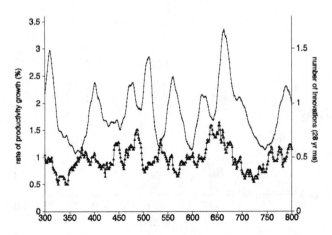

future in this case. This is not entirely unexpected, since our model makes clear that diffusion introduces significant time delays.

Our high-dimensional, nonlinear dynamic system thus appears to a certain extent to be imitating a moving average process in converting the white noise innovation input into the macrovariable cyclical output. It is

Figure 5.10: The spectral density of a 28-year moving average of the innovation rate. Notice that it differs significantly from the productivity spectrum despite the high cross correlation.

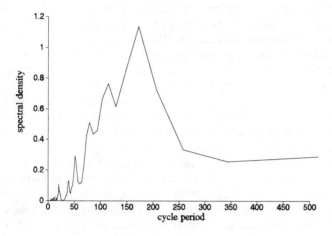

Table 5.4: Lag and moving average order for maximal cross correlation between innovation and productivity growth rate time series with and without ST investment term

ω	s	0			2		
		MA	lag	r	MA	lag	r
2		28	24	0.83	16	14	0.79
5		26	27	0.66	18	13	0.65

well known that a moving average process will extract a cyclical structure from white noise (the Slutsky–Yule effect). However, an examination of the spectrum of such a moving average process reveals that it is still far from the characteristic long-wave pattern we have discovered for the macrovariables (Figure 5.10). For this reason we extended the analysis by drawing upon some of the relatively recent methods of the theory of non-linear dynamical systems.

4. NONLINEAR TIME SERIES ANALYSIS

It is by now well known that even very simple nonlinear dynamic systems can show an incredible richness of behaviour, in particular, the resulting time series may mimic the properties of a stochastic process even though they are generated deterministically. The standard methods of linear time series analysis are not in general sufficient to distinguish the two types of mechanisms (see, for example, Baumol and Benhabib 1989; Lorenz 1989; Brock and Malliaris 1989; Brock and Dechert 1991). In recent years, however, a number of new, specifically nonlinear methods have been developed that permit deterministic systems (so-called 'low dimensional chaos') to be distinguished from truly stochastic ones based solely on an analysis of univariate time series.

A stumbling block in the application of these methods to real-world economics has been the paucity of data: in general they require rather long time series to yield significant results. Once again we are in the fortunate position to be able to generate unlimited artificial data for analysis. One of the main tools employed in nonlinear time series analysis has been the calculation of the Grassberger–Procaccia correlation dimension (see Grassberger 1986 for an overview). By embedding a time series in successively higher dimensional spaces using the method of time-delay reconstruction and calculating the correlation integral for a range of correlation lengths, it is possible to determine if convergence occurs and thus if a finite correlation dimension exists. In general, a stochastic process will be infinite dimensional (that is, no convergence will be observed), while a deterministic process will be characterised by a finite dimension (bounded from above by the dimension of the state space). Nonintegral values of the correlation dimension (as well as positive values of the largest Lyapunov exponent; see Wolf 1986) are indicative of chaotic behaviour on a strange attractor. Finite data sets introduce a severe restriction, however, since the upper limit on the calculated dimension increases approximately with the log of the number of data points.

In Figures 5.11 and 5.12 we have reproduced the calculation of the correlation dimensions for the 28-year innovation moving average and the productivity growth rate of our benchmark run using 6000 data points.[7] As we have pointed out above, these two series are highly correlated. Nevertheless, the correlation dimension plots permit them to be clearly differentiated. The moving-average series shows only weak convergence over a narrow scaling range at a value above 4. The productivity-growth rate data, in contrast, show convergence over a fairly wide range of scaling lengths to an estimate of the correlation dimension of approximately 2.9. In Figure 5.13 we also present the correlation dimension calculation

Figure 5.11: Correlation dimension for 28-year moving average of Poisson-distributed innovation rate (ω = 1)

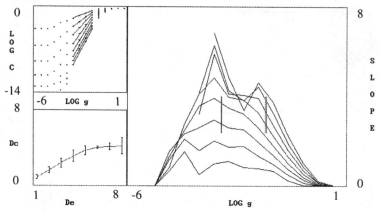

Figure 5.12: Correlation dimension for productivity growth rate (ω = 2, τ = 2%) calculated with 6000 data points. $D_c \approx 2.9$

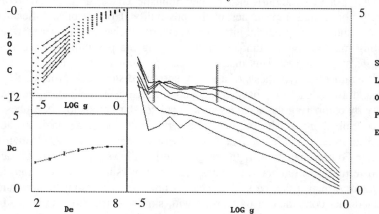

for the same case, but with an ST investment parameter of 1. A number of other measures of nonlinearity and chaos can be applied to these data, such as the spectrum of Lyapunov exponents and the BDS-statistic. Both of these again provide evidence of low-dimensional chaos; for more details see Silverberg and Lehnert (1993).

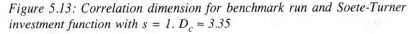

Figure 5.13: Correlation dimension for benchmark run and Soete-Turner investment function with s = 1. $D_c \approx 3.35$

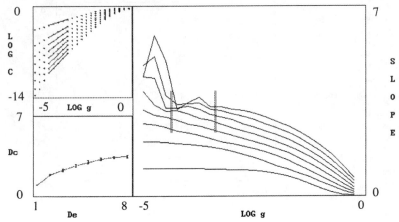

The 'practical' significance of deterministic chaos, as opposed to its purely conceptual appeal, lies in the possibility it offers of significantly greater short-term predictability over standard stochastic time-series forecasting methods, while fundamentally denying the possibility of accurate long-term prediction. This distinction can be turned into a test of chaos itself against the hypothesis of a highly correlated stochastic process. Kennel and Isabelle (1992) have developed a statistic of nonlinear predictability by comparing the accuracy of a 'local constant predictor' of a phasespace embedding of the original time series with the same predictor applied to an ensemble of derivative time series generated to have a roughly similar Fourier spectrum. If the original series allows significantly greater short-term prediction based on extrapolations from similar constellations in its history, then it can be said to possess nonlinear deterministic structure beyond that contained in its cousins with similar correlation structure. In Figure 5.14 we present the values of this *z*-statistic for a range of embedding dimensions and time lags of the phase-space reconstruction, for oneperiod forecasting on a benchmark series of 8192 data points, where data points within the characteristic autocorrelation time of the current point (in the present case 22 years) are excluded in making the forecasting to eliminate pure correlation effects. The results are highly significant for an embedding dimension of two onwards.

What are we to make of these indications of chaotic, low-dimensional nonlinear behaviour? Our model can be characterised as a high-dimensional system of nonlinear ordinary differential equations whose coef-

Figure 5.14: Z-statistic of nonlinear predictability for the benchmark run (8192 data points) and different embedding dimensions and time delays for the phase-space reconstruction

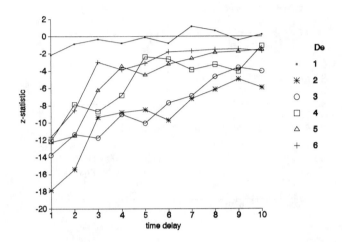

ficients are perturbed in a systematic way at random times. Thus strictly speaking it is neither a deterministic dynamical system nor a stochastic system with additive noise. Nevertheless, its behaviour seems to be reducible to a small number of degrees of freedom, but it is neither strictly periodic nor representable by linear time-series procedures. For this reason we have chosen to denote it as 'evolutionary chaos'.

A clue to unravelling the behaviour of this system can be gleaned by examining a log-log plot of the spectral density against frequency for a very long data set (Figure 5.15). At very low frequencies the spectrum is simply white noise. Starting at around 0.02 (corresponding to cycles of 50-year length) the spectrum becomes a declining straight line before gradually reverting to white noise at a low level (corresponding to the innovation driving term?). This power law region of the spectrum is reminiscent of the so-called $1/f$-noise characteristic of many physical systems (see, for example, Takayasu 1990). This power law behaviour of the spectrum over only a limited range before reverting to white noise is especially characteristic of a phenomenon recently termed self-organised criticality (Bak, Tang and Wiesenfeld 1988; Bak and Chen 1991). A sandpile with sand constantly falling on to the centre and falling off the edges of a finite table provides the best intuitive illustration of this phenomenon. The pile will eventually organise itself into a heap with a characteristic slope, and ad-

Figure 5.15: Power spectrum of rate of productivity growth plotted against log of frequency. The upper curve is the log of the spectrum (left scale), the lower curve the spectrum itself (right scale)

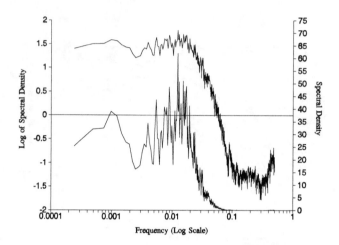

ditions of sand will trigger avalanches of all sizes (in fact, distributed according to a power law). In some respects, the capital stock of our model economy bears a certain resemblance to a sandpile (cf. Figure 5.2). The finite lifetimes of technologies tracked in the model correspond to the finite size of the table. The nonlinear Lotka–Volterra dynamics of the technologies corresponds to the rearrangement of sand down the pile, and the innovation process corresponds to the addition of new sand to the pile at random times. The fluctuations in the rate of productivity growth correspond to fluctuations in the variance of the capital stock distribution and thus the shape of the pile. The analogy is less precise than suggestive, but the log-log spectrum does seem to imply that we are dealing with a qualitatively similar kind of phenomenon.

5. EXTENSIONS OF THE MODEL

Until now we have assumed that the probability of making an innovation per unit time was constant and independent of economic variables. While this is an intriguing null hypothesis for discussing explanations of the long wave, it is an empirical question whether it can be maintained. It is intuitively plausible that the innovation Poisson parameter will in fact be influenced by economic variables, for example investments in R&D in previous periods. To see what effect such assumptions may have on the robustness of the long-wave result, we have modified the model to allow for such feedbacks from economic activity to innovation.[8]

The simplest assumption is to make the innovation Poisson parameter a linear function of lagged profitability:

$$p = \max[p_{min}, a<r> +p_o],$$ (5.13)

where p is the innovation Poisson parameter, $<r>$ is lagged profitability, and p_o and p_{min} are constants. For simplicity we have used an exponential lag on profitability:

$$\frac{d}{dt}<r> = \frac{1}{T}(r-<r>),$$ (5.14)

where T is the exponential lag and r is the current average profit rate.

Spectral analysis of this feedback case for certain parameter values indicates that the long-wave structure may emerge even more distinctly (Figure 5.16).

The other half of our original null assumption – constancy of the under-lying innovation probability – is not borne out by the empirical record, as we shall show in the next section. The frequency of innovation has in fact grown over the last two centuries more or less exponentially. To inves-

Figure 5.16: Spectrum of productivity growth rate when profits are al-lowed to feedback with a lag on the probability of innovation (T = 10, $p_{min} = 0, p_o = 0.1, a = 1$)

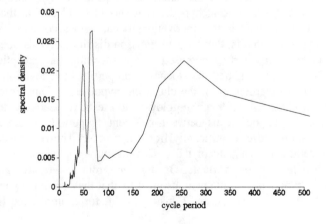

tigate this case, we have also allowed the innovation parameter to grow logistically:

$$p = p_0 + \frac{p_1}{1 + e^{-a(t-t_0)}},\qquad(5.15)$$

where p_0 and p_1 are the lower and upper bounds of the innovation Poisson parameter, a is the growth rate, and t_0 is the date of the inflection point of the logistic growth process. Thus the Poisson parameter will initially grow exponentially but eventually saturate at an upper bound. The resulting growth process will no longer be stationary, however, but will accelerate with time. The long-wave pattern still persists, but with strong preponderance of very long-period spectral power due to the nonstationarity.

6. ANALYSIS OF EMPIRICAL INNOVATION TIME SERIES

Beginning with Mensch (1975), a considerable literature has arisen investigating whether innovations have occurred in more or less regular clusters (Kleinknecht 1981, 1987, 1990a,b; Haustein and Neuwirth 1982; Freeman, Clark and Soete 1982; van Duijn 1983; Solomou 1986). In contrast to the 'shocks' of traditional stochastic macroeconomic modelling, the innovations in our model are in principle identifiable as historical events of measurable magnitude. Although all of the innovation time series proposed in the literature are marred by considerable subjectivity with respect to selection and dating, we shall simply re-examine the main series investigated to date and concentrate on the statistical methodology employed.

In discussing the clustering hypothesis it should be clear that the null hypothesis to be refuted is that innovations occur with a constant probability per unit time, that is, that they are Poisson distributed. This does not seem to have been clearly recognised in the literature (an exception is Sahal 1974, who investigated the stochastic properties of innovation time series, but not in the context of the clustering hypothesis). Thus Solomou (1986) and Kleinknecht (1990a,b) employ z and t tests, respectively, to test the hypothesis that the means between different subperiods of the innovation time series differ significantly from each other. The first objection to this procedure is that both of these tests are only applicable to a normally distributed random variable. On *a priori* grounds we have argued that the null hypothesis on innovations must be that they are homogeneous Poisson distributed, however, and a histogram of, for example, the Haustein–Neuwirth data (as well as any of the other series we have examined) confirms that they are anything but normally distributed (Figure 5.17).

Figure 5.17: Histogram of Haustein–Neuwirth innovation time series with two fitted Poisson distributions. ($\rho = 0.84$ is maximum likelihood estimate, $\rho = 0.683$ obtained by equating value for zero innovations)

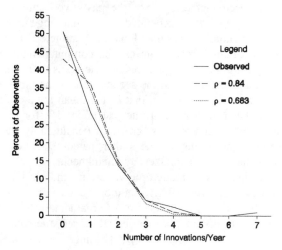

Second, both authors apply their tests to subsamples they claim have been selected on the basis of *a priori* criteria (it is well known that means tests are inapplicable if the subsamples have been chosen with regard to the means themselves). In general, the periodisations employed derive from previous authors such as Mensch, whose use of a runs test did not depend on it, or on the examination of growth rates and the addition of a time lag. In the latter case, however, as our Figure 5.8 demonstrates, growth rates and a moving average of the innovation data may be highly (cross) correlated, so that the selection of a proper lag against variations in the growth rate series may simply be a method to select subperiods of above- and below-average innovation activity even from a completely random series. This fact would further invalidate any means test (even one appropriate to a Poisson process, such as a binomial statistic). For this reason we have elected to analyse the innovation time series without attempting to impose any periodisation into subsamples of high and low activity.

The raw data of the Haustein–Neuwirth series are presented in Figure 5.18a. The existence of a trend cannot be rejected out of hand, so that we

have tested the null hypothesis that the various series are Poisson processes with zero exponential trend against the alternative hypothesis of a non-
zero trend (see the notes to Table 5.5 for details of the test). For all but
the very short Clark *et al.* (1981) series a homogeneous Poisson (trendless)
process is rejected at very high levels of significance, and in all cases a
growing trend is indicated. Indeed, it does not seem surprising that the rate
of innovation has been increasing over the past two centuries. On the
assumption that the series were generated by an inhomogeneous Poisson
process with exponentially growing Poisson parameter, a maximum
likelihood estimate of this growth rate can be computed numerically by
solving the implicit transcendental eq. (5.4) of the notes to Table 5.5.

These growth rates are shown in the second part of the table and seem
to lie between 0.5 and 1% per annum, that is, the mean number of innovations per year has been growing at a rate just under 1% for the last two
centuries, with product innovations growing considerably faster than
process innovations (according to the Baker patent statistics, where a
separation by type has been undertaken by Kleinknecht).

Before the question of systematic time variations and clustering (in the
sense of a significant departure from a homogeneous Poisson process as
the benchmark for a – in the sense of mathematical statistics –
nonclustering stationary distribution) can be addressed, the data must first
be detrended. This can be accomplished by defining a new time scale that
'stretches' the time axis as the Poisson parameter grows to maintain a
constant (in the mean) number of innovations. If an inhomogeneous Poisson process is characterised by a time-dependent Poisson parameter $p(t)$,
then with respect to the new time index

$$v(t) = \int_{t_0}^{t} p(u) \, du, \qquad (5.16)$$

the series becomes an homogeneous Poisson process with constant unit
rate (Cox and Lewis 1966, p. 29). Since our data are given as numbers of
innovations in each year instead of exact dates for each event (something
that would be meaningless anyway, given what they represent), we have
detrended the series by redefining the time axis as in eq. (5.14) and reas-
signing the innovations randomly within the new 'bins' of nonuniform
size. The results of this detrending for the Haustein–Neuwirth series are
shown in Figure 5.18b. Only after this detrending has been performed does
it make sense to apply tests of the null hypothesis of random generation.

The two tests employed in Table 5.5 – the dispersion and the H-test –
were used in a formulation with nonuniform intervals, so that the random
reassignment of events within the new 'bins' has no effect. The hypothesis
of a Poisson process is not surprisingly rejected for the undetrended data.

Figure 5.18a: Haustein–Neuwirth innovation time series, 1764–1975

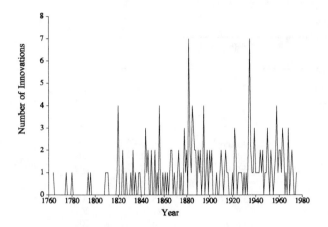

Figure 5.18b: Detrended Haustein–Neuwirth time series after eliminating exponential trend by nonlinear stretching of time axis

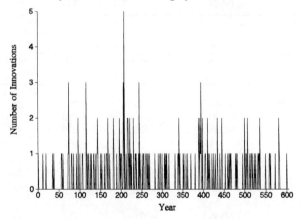

Significant is the fact that it is still rejected for the detrended data at the 1% or 5% levels. Examination of the data (as in Figure 5.17) reveals that the deviations from Poisson are due to a slight but significant excess of periods with large or with zero events, and a deficiency of periods with intermediate values (near the expectation). This is in fact indicative of clustering in the statistical sense but not necessarily in the sense of a systematic time variation in the process (one interpretation of the proposed Schumpeterian swarming of innovations). The alternative hypothesis would

Table 5.5: Tests of Poisson distribution of original and detrended innovation time series

Original innovation time series					
	Dispersion d	H-Test	df	Growth rate (%)	z-Trend
Baker					
Product	741.08**	731.59**	273	0	8.11**
Process	465.67**	442.84**	273	0	7.93**
all	775.17**	815.21**	273	0	9.19**
Baker 1769–					
Product	438.66**	465.69**	202	0	1.88**
Process	304.17**	308.17**	202	0	2.66**
all	422.05**	443.79**	202	0	1.09**
Baker Kleink.					
Product	336.27**	287.75**	201	0	7.11**
Process	236.94*	214.91	201	0	1.11
all	295.98**	305.15**	201	0	6.15**
Clark	76.39	86.99*	64	0	0.77
Haustein	336.20**	310.24**	211	0	6.68**
van Duijn	195.58**	171.79**	115	0	2.29*

Detrended innovation time series					
	Dispersion d	H-Test	df	Growth rate (%)	z-Trend
Baker					
Product	381.01**	380.79**	273	1.24	2.43*
Process	374.41**	378.44**	273	0.63	0.80
all	402.24**	426.68**	273	0.99	2.06*
Baker 1769–					
Product	288.78**	320.09**	202	1.00	1.20
Process	288.14**	301.09**	202	0.28	0.05
all	298.49**	318.64**	202	0.72	0.66
Baker Kleink.					
Product	245.79*	235.12*	201	1.15	1.16
Process	234.56*	213.68	201	0.20	0.07
all	246.90*	266.72**	201	0.73	0.58
Clark	76.43	86.41*	64	0.52	0.13
Haustein	300.00**	264.48**	211	0.86	0.83
van Duijn	179.26**	166.48**	115	0.78	0.28

* significant at 5% level   ** significant at 1% level

Notes

Statistical tests employed in Table 5.5:

Dispersion test of Poisson distribution (Cox and Lewis 1966, p. 232):

$$d = \sum_{i=1}^{k} \frac{n_i^2}{t_i \lambda} - n, \tag{N5.1}$$

where λ is the sample mean, n the number of events, n_i is the number of events in the ith interval of length t_i. This is chi-square distributed with $k-1$ degrees of freedom under the null hypothesis of a Poisson distribution.

H-test of Poisson distribution (Cox and Lewis 1966, p. 236):

$$H = 2\left[\sum_{i=1}^{k} n_i \ln\left(\frac{n_i}{t_i}\right) - n \ln \lambda \right]. \tag{N5.2}$$

This is also chi-square distributed with $k-1$ degrees of freedom under the null hypothesis.

Test for a trend (Basawa and Rao 1980, p. 104; Cox and Lewis 1966, p. 47):

$$z = \frac{\sum_{i=1}^{n} t_i - \frac{n\tau}{2}}{\tau\sqrt{n/12}}, \tag{N5.3}$$

where the t_i are now the epochs (dates of the ith event), τ is the length of the series, and n is the number of events. z is approximately standard normal for large n on the hypothesis of a Poisson distribution with 0 exponential trend.

Maximum likelihood estimate of exponential trend θ (Basawa and Rao 1980, p. 104):

$$\frac{1}{\theta} + \frac{\tau e^{\theta\tau}}{1 - e^{\theta\tau}} = -\frac{1}{n}\sum_{i=1}^{n} t_i. \tag{N5.4}$$

Sources: All Baker series: Kleinknecht (1987)
Clark: Clark, Freeman and Soete (1981)
Haustein: Haustein and Neuwirth (1982)
van Duijn: van Duijn (1983)

be one of several generalised Poisson processes that admit a higher degree of clustering, a subject we intend to investigate further in the future.

As can be seen by examining the z-trend column of the second part of Table 5.5, our exponential detrending procedure does seem to capture fully the trend component of the innovation series except for the full Baker dataset. This would imply either that an acceleration in the growth rate of innovation activity had taken place between the first and second halves of the eighteenth century, or that the Baker patent data are deficient for the preindustrial period.

Runs tests on the original data series quite clearly demonstrate significant departures from randomness, something that is already dictated by the existence of trends in the series. After detrending, the results are somewhat ambiguous, since a certain element of arbitrariness is introduced by the necessity of rebinning the events into the nonlinearly deformed time scale. In most instances runs tests cannot reject the hypothesis of randomness, and those departures that remain are very much below the levels detected in the undetrended data. The first autocorrelation also fails to detect significant departures from independence. Thus the question whether the innovation time series after detrending are characterised by significant time variation in mean levels, by a renewal or other process displaying a higher degree of clustering than the Poisson process, or some combination of the two, remains a subject for further research. Whatever the precise answer to this question, it is clear that the innovation time series investigated until now in the literature do seem to correspond to a discrete stochastic process of approximately Poisson nature with exponentially increasing trend.

7. CONCLUSIONS

The combination of a stochastic innovation process with a dynamic model of Schumpeterian competition and 'endogenous' diffusion patterns yields a model of creative destruction which is neither a steady state nor a random walk with drift (the two extremes which have dominated the endogenous growth literature). Instead, the model robustly generates temporal patterns with an aperiodic long-wave character beginning in the Kondratieff region of 40–60 years.

The debate Schumpeter first set in motion on the relationship between purported long waves of economic activity and the innovation process has focused on clustering of innovations in the trough phases of the wave. Because Schumpeter and subsequent authors in this controversy did not argue within the context of a fully specified model connecting innovation, diffusion, investment and macrodynamics, critics have rightly aimed at weak links at various points in this chain of reasoning. Much empirical research has focused on demonstrating or refuting intrinsic clustering in the innovation process.

Our model demonstrates, however, that no intrinsic clustering of innovations is necessary to produce long-period fluctuations of economic activity. It suffices that the innovation process is stochastic. This seems to be a remarkably robust result. Whether innovations are produced autonomously according to a Poisson process of different 'frequencies', or are subject to feedbacks from economic activity or time-varying trends in means, it seems to be the manner in which the economy incorporates innovations rather than the time pattern of any forcing term that is responsible for this result. Moreover, the time pattern of the macrodynamics appears intrinsically nonlinear with characteristics of low-dimensional chaos with dimension, depending on parameter constellation, between 2.5 and 3.5. Finally, the global spectral pattern contains a region governed by a power law relationship and suggests a connection to the class of phenomena known as self-organised criticality.

Our review of the empirical literature confirms that innovations have indeed followed a stochastic process that to the first order can be approximated by a Poisson process with exponentially growing trend. However, the deviations from Poisson are significant and indicate that a somewhat more clustering stochastic process is at work. Whether a systematically varying mean of this process on a time scale of the order of a long wave can be demonstrated remains an open question. However, for theoretical reasons this no longer seems to be such a central question in the long-wave debate.

NOTES

1. Very suggestive on this latter point are Allen (1983) and von Hippel (1988).
2. The classic study of factors influencing innovation diffusion is Mansfield (1961). The voluminous literature since then does not seem to have changed this picture in any essential way.
3. Nelson and Winter (1982) and Winter (1984) are the most complete expositions of the evolutionary approach in economics. However, their elaborate model of search, selection and imitation is not based on *capital-embodied* innovation, and thus investment enters primarily into the search and learning process. We hope to combine the elements of accumulation dynamics presented here with a model of search and learning in future research.
4. We shall not discuss other approaches here which do not focus explicitly on technology, such as Sterman (1985), which emphasises the 'capital self-ordering' principle as a nonlinear extension of the multiplier/accelerator mechanism, even though there are many points of methodological tangency. (Recently Sterman and Mosekilde 1992 have extended this framework to demonstrate how nonlinear entrainment between capital self-ordering and the short-period business cycle, regarded as a forcing term, can lead to complex dynamics.) The ability of a model to generate cycles of a certain length under certain circumstances does not seem to us sufficient evidence in itself to establish the primacy of its assumptions over other, possibly competing, possibly complementary assumptions of other models as the ultimate explanation of long waves. This is a deep problem of model identification which we can only touch on in the body of the paper. In any event we consider the study of technological evolution worthwhile in its own right, regardless of its status with respect to the long-wave controversy.

5. Thus we share the critique of Rosenberg and Frischtak (1984, pp. 10–11), who write:
   > In spite of this long listing of possible influences, we are left without a precise knowledge of what are the necessary and sufficient changes in the environment which, even conceptually, can bring out a bandwagon-like diffusion of some number of basic innovations. In other words, there is no well-specified set of elements that effectively link and elucidate the direction of causality between the basic innovations, the 'general level of profitability and business expectations', and their diffusion in the form of a swarm of new products and processes. More generally, nowhere in the literature is there to be found an unambiguous treatment of causality within a neo-Schumpeterian framework, which establishes the precedence of innovation clusters over investment outlays and aggregate movements in the economy.

6. One could obviously regard the size and direction of an innovation jump in a–c space as themselves random variables, something we have opted not to do for the time being in order to leave the analysis as transparent as possible.

7. The box in the upper left corner shows the log of the correlation integral as a function of the log of the scaling length for different embedding dimensions. The slope of the regression line within the scaling range is an estimate of the correlation dimension. The accuracy of this estimate can be judged by examining the right-hand box, where the slope between consecutive points is plotted. The scaling range is selected by determining where these slopes converge with increasing embedding dimension. The estimated correlation dimension, with error bars, is displayed as a function of the embedding dimension in the lower left corner.

8. Ideally, one would like to extend the model to a full-fledged treatment of evolutionary 'endogenous' growth, that is, to provide an economic accounting for the realised rate of innovation in terms of competitive self-organisation or expected rates of return on R&D investment. We have refrained from this step here and restrict ourselves to an analysis of the robustness of the spectral results to different specifications of the variations in the innovation arrival rate.

REFERENCES

Aghion, P. and Howitt, P. (1992), 'A Model of Growth through Creative Destruction', *Econometrica*, 60, 323–351.

Allen, R. (1983), 'Collective Invention', *Journal of Economic Behavior and Organization*, 4, 1–24.

Bak, P. and Chen, K. (1991), 'Self-organized Criticality', *Scientific American*, January, 26–33.

Bak, P., Tang, C. and Wiesenfeld, K. (1988), 'Self-organized Criticality', *Physical Review A*, 38, 364–374.

Basawa, I.V. and Rao, B.P. (1980), *Statistical Inference for Stochastic Processes*, London: Academic Press.

Baumol, W. and Benhabib, J. (1989), 'Chaos: Significance, Mechanism, and Economic Applications', *Journal of Economic Perspectives*, 3, 77–105.

Brock, W.A. and Dechert, W.D. (1991), 'Non-linear Dynamical Systems: Instability and Chaos in Economics', in W. Hildenbrand and H. Sonnenschein (eds), *Handbook of Mathematical Economics, Volume IV*, Amsterdam: North-Holland.

Brock, W. and Malliaris, A. (1989), *Differential Equations, Stability, and Chaos in Dynamic Economics*, Amsterdam: North-Holland.

Cheng, L. and Dinopoulos, E. (1992), 'Schumpeterian Growth and International Business Cycles', *American Economic Review. Papers and Proceedings*, 82, 409–414.

Clark, J., Freeman, C. and Soete, L. (1981), 'Long Waves, Inventions, and Innovations', *Futures*, 13, 308–322.

Cox, D.R. and Lewis, P. (1966), *The Statistical Analysis of Series of Events*, London and New York: Methuen/John Wiley.

Fisher, J. and Pry, R. (1971), 'A Simple Substitution Model of Technological Change', *Technological Forecasting and Social Change*, 3, 75–88.

Freeman, C. (1987), 'Technical Innovation, Diffusion and Long Cycles of Economic Development', in T. Vasko (ed.), *The Long-Wave Debate*, Berlin: Springer-Verlag.

Freeman, C., Clark, J. and Soete, L.L. (1982), *Unemployment and Technical Innovation: A Study of Long Waves in Economic Development*, London: Pinter.

Goodwin, R. (1967), 'A Growth Cycle', in C.H. Feinstein (ed.), *Socialism, Capitalism and Economic Growth*, London: Macmillan.

Grassberger, P. (1986), 'Estimating the Fractal Dimensions and Entropies of Strange Attractors', in A.V. Holden (ed.), *Chaos*, Manchester: Manchester University Press.

Grossman, G.M. and Helpman, E. (1991), *Innovation and Growth in the Global Economy*, Cambridge, MA: MIT Press.

Haustein, H.-D. and Neuwirth, E. (1982), 'Long Waves in World Industrial Production, Energy Consumption, Innovations, Inventions, and Patents and their Identification by Spectral Analysis', *Technological Forecasting and Social Change*, 22, 53–89.

Henkin, G.M. and Polterovich, V.M. (1991), 'Schumpeterian Dynamics as a Nonlinear Wave Theory', *Journal of Mathematical Economics*, 20, 551–590.

Hofbauer, J. and Sigmund, K. (1988), *The Theory of Evolution and Dynamical Systems*, Cambridge: Cambridge University Press.

Iwai, K. (1984a), 'Schumpeterian Dynamics. I: An Evolutionary Model of Innovation and Imitation', *Journal of Economic Behavior and Organization*, 5, 159–190.

Iwai, K. (1984b), 'Schumpeterian Dynamics. II: Technological Progress, Firm Growth and "Economic Selection" ', *Journal of Economic Behavior and Organization*, 5, 321–351.

Kennel, M.B. and Isabelle, S. (1992), 'A Method to Distinguish Possible Chaos From Colored Noise and Determine Embedding Parameters', *Physical Review A*, 46(6), 3111–3118.

Kleinknecht, A. (1981), 'Observations on the Schumpeterian Swarming of Innovations', *Futures*, 13, 293–307.

Kleinknecht, A. (1987), *Innovation Patterns in Crisis and Prosperity: Schumpeter's Long Cycle Reconsidered*, London: Macmillan.

Kleinknecht, A. (1990a), 'Are There Schumpeterian Waves of Innovations?', *Cambridge Journal of Economics*, 14, 81–92.

Kleinknecht, A. (1990b), 'Schumpeterian Waves of Innovation? Summarizing the Evidence', in T. Vasko, R. Ayres and L. Fontvieille (eds), *Life Cycles and Long Waves*, Berlin: Springer-Verlag.

Kondratieff, N. (1926), 'Die langen Wellen der Konjunktur', *Archiv für Sozialwissenschaft und Sozialpolitik*, 56. English translation: *Review*, 2 (1979), 519–562.

Kuznets, S. (1940), 'Schumpeter's Business Cycles', *American Economic Review*, 30, 257–271.

Lorenz, H.-W. (1989), *Nonlinear Dynamical Economics and Chaotic Motion*, Berlin: Springer-Verlag.

Mansfield, E. (1961), 'Technical Change and the Rate of Imitation', *Econometrica*, 29, 741–766.

Marchetti, C. and Nakicenovic, N. (1979), *The Dynamics of Energy Systems and the Logistic Substitution Model*, Research Report RR-79-13, Laxenburg, Austria: IIASA.

Mensch, G.O. (1975), *Das technologische Patt*, Frankfurt: Umschau.

Metz, R. (1992), 'A Re-examination of Long Waves in Aggregate Production Series', in A. Kleinknecht, E. Mandel and I. Wallerstein (eds), *New Findings in Long-Wave Research*, London: Macmillan.

Montroll, E. (1978), 'Social Dynamics and the Quantifying of Social Forces', *Proceedings of the National Academy of Sciences, USA*, 75, 4633–4637.

Nakicenovic, N. (1987), 'Technological Substitution and Long Waves in the USA', in T. Vasko (ed.), *The Long-Wave Debate*, Berlin: Springer-Verlag.

Nelson, R. (1968), 'A "Diffusion" Model of International Productivity Differences in Manufacturing Industry', *American Economic Review*, 58, 1218–1248.

Nelson, R. and Winter, S. (1982), *An Evolutionary Theory of Economic Change*, Cambridge MA: The Belknap Press of Harvard University Press.

Rosenberg, N. and Frischtak, C.R. (1984), 'Technological Innovation and Long Waves', *Cambridge Journal of Economics*, 8, 7–24.

Sahal, D. (1974), 'Generalized Poisson and Related Models of Technological Innovation', *Technological Forecasting and Social Change*, 6, 403–436.

Schumpeter, J. (1939), *Business Cycles: A Theoretical, Historical and Statistical Analysis of the Capitalist Process*, New York: McGraw-Hill.

Segerstrom, P. S., Anant, T. and Dinopoulos, E. (1990), 'A Schumpeterian Model of the Product Life Cycle', *American Economic Review*, 80, 1077–1091.

Silverberg, G. (1984), 'Embodied Technical Progress in a Dynamic Economic Model: the Self-organization Paradigm', in R. Goodwin, M. Krüger and A. Vercelli (eds), *Nonlinear Models of Fluctuating Growth*, Berlin: Springer-Verlag.

Silverberg, G. and Lehnert, D. (1993), ' "Evolutionary Chaos": Growth Fluctuations in a Schumpeterian Model of Creative Destruction', in W. Barnett and M. Salmon (eds), *Nonlinear Dynamics in Economics*, Cambridge: Cambridge University Press (in press).

Soete, L. and Turner, R. (1984), 'Technology Diffusion and the Rate of Technical Change', *Economic Journal*, 94, 612–623.

Solomou, S. (1986), 'Innovation Clusters and Kondratieff Long Waves in Economic Growth', *Cambridge Journal of Economics*, 10, 101–112.

Sterman, J. (1985), 'A Behavioral Model of the Economic Long Wave', *Journal of Economic Behavior and Organization*, 6, 17–53.

Sterman, J. and Mosekilde, E. (1992), 'Business Cycles and Long Waves: A Behavioral Disequilibrium Perspective', in W. Semmler (ed.), *Business Cycles: Theory and Empirical Methods*, Dordrecht: Kluwer.

Takayasu, H. (1990), *Fractals in the Physical Sciences*, Manchester and New York: Manchester University Press.

van Duijn, J. (1983), *The Long Wave in Economic Life*, Boston: Allen & Unwin.

von Hippel, E. (1988), *The Sources of Innovation*, Oxford: Oxford University Press.

Winter, S. (1984), 'Schumpeterian Competition in Alternative Technological Regimes', *Journal of Economic Behavior and Organization*, 5, 137–158.

Wolf, A. (1986), 'Quantifying Chaos with Lyapunov Exponents', in A.V. Holden (ed.), *Chaos*, Manchester: Manchester University Press.

COMMENT ON SILVERBERG AND LEHNERT

Paul Romer

Richard Nelson's last paper in this session discusses the mechanisms by which we learn things in economics and he emphasises the importance of interacting between the different levels of economics. Richard identifies a pure theoretical level, which is mathematical, and appreciative theory which is less mathematical. Appreciative theory is hard to describe, even though most of us probably know what he means. An interesting question about this paper by Jerry Silverberg and Doris Lehnert and about some other papers in this conference is if we are going to generate an entirely different level of theory – theory on the computer. It is interesting to speculate what the implications of this will be, especially for the process of interacting.

One of Dick's points, which I think is correct, is that formal mathematical theorists tend to stop communicating with anyone else.

(Interjection by **Richard Nelson**): My complaint was that formal theorists weren't listening, not that they weren't communicating.

Paul Romer:

OK, we weren't listening to others, other than picking up a stylised fact here and there and then running with it.

Silverberg and Lehnert's paper identified the Kondratieff wave, a 50-year cycle driven by innovation and ending in a depression. The discussion in the paper takes this as a kind of stylised fact to motivate the theoretical work. This reminded me of when I was an undergraduate exposed to a really long wave in physics class. I had a professor who described the long wave associated with the big bang. He said that the universe will either stop expanding and then contract, or it will expand forever. His attitude was that it was impossible to tell which option was right. He then said that if this was really true – that it is impossible to tell – then why should we care? What difference would it make?

The Kondratieff wave operates on a shorter time-scale than the big bang, but for economic purposes, in terms of the data we have, it is not that much shorter. I would suggest that as a profession we should set this question aside. I do not see how we can possibly determine if there is or is not a 50-year wave, given the data available.

Fortunately, the paper covers many other issues which I think are more interesting than the existence of Kondratieff waves. The paper tries to say that the model gives some support for them, but this support is dependent on redefining the Kondratieff waves as not sharply defined at a 50-year frequency. Setting aside the historical context, I should like to discuss several interesting aspects of the paper.

One is the theoretical mechanism that converts innovations, even Poisson-derived innovations, into very long waves of productivity. The paper gives you some ability to predict the future based on placing yourself in what looks like a similar historical context. The key feature of this theoretical mechanism is diffusion, which is tied to capital accumulation, which in turn is driven by the rate of profit. This feature is not original to this paper. The mechanism has been explored in earlier papers and also by Soete and Turner.

This mechanism has a large number of implications. For example, I found the discussion of the productivity slowdown very interesting. There is a widespread tendency among macroeconomists to explain the productivity slowdown using contemporary variables, for example through analysing R&D and its returns in the 1970s. This analysis has not been successful. In contrast, Silverberg and Lehnert's paper looks back much further. This makes the exercise much more difficult, but opens interesting lines of investigation.

To give a provocative example, perhaps the productivity slowdown in the 1970s is due to the introduction of peer-reviewed basic research after World War II and the redirection of substantial amounts of research funds from the business-oriented R&D that dominated before World War II towards peer-reviewed basic research. Before I read this paper, I would not have taken this idea very seriously, but the paper makes me take it a tiny bit seriously.

Another interesting aspect of the paper is the description of the time series of innovation. There is some evidence of bunching, though not very strong. But the strongest fact in the innovation series is an upward trend in the number of innovations. This is perhaps an important stylised fact that all theorists should be thinking about. An interesting question is why growth is speeding up over human history. This is a trend which does not fit easily with simple-minded economic theory about diminishing returns, limits to growth and scarcity. I was encouraged to see that this innovation data fits with other historical data, for example on per capita income growth.

I have a brief comment on Paul David's discussion of Day's paper. As Paul mentioned, Ron Lee, the demographer, has a good paper where he explains the link between the long-run exponential trend in population growth and the innovation rate. The rate of innovation increases because there are more people to innovate. Another explanation is that the more you do of it, the faster you go. Once paper is invented, it is possible to record things, once there are computers you can search much faster than before. These two lines of investigation need to be pursued further.

One final issue here is the use of computers to develop theory. This opens up exciting possibilities where computer models can teach us new things. When macroeconomists first found out that they could use computers to generate things such as business cycles, that led to a programme of building larger and larger macroeconomic models. But no one is doing this any more; we have returned to very simple analytical models.

Why? We felt that the large computer models prevented us from learning about the fundamental questions. It may have been a recognition that we didn't know enough about the basics involved here to move to the computer. The answer may be first to figure out the underlying frictions in the economy and then run computer simulations. Or it may be a tougher lesson about the difficulty of learning something from these very complicated models. By definition there is an enormous number of possible complicated models that one can investigate. I am a little bit afraid that an enormous amount of work on complex systems will lead to the conclusion that complex systems are very complex and that there aren't very many robust generalisations that can be drawn from them. Moreover, this raises the possibility that in the future not only could mathematical theorists not listen to other people, but there could be a whole new branch of computer theorists who don't listen to others, though this paper does not suffer from any of these problems. The computer theorists will work with lots of simulated data and form a coalition with the econometricians who will generate more and more complicated statistical techniques. The two will be freed from any further constraints about sample size and will go off dancing together.

Kenneth Arrow:

I have an observation and a question. First, I once dealt with a complex system, the weather, when I worked for a few years doing research on weather forecasting. They thought then that it was possible to predict the future by finding a similar condition in the past. They spent a lot of time coding weather data over 40 years. The effort was a total failure. There were a number of rival methods of long-term forecasting, but none was any good and did not improve on simply using averages. One could do slightly better, but that was all.

The problem with a nonlinear system of unknown structure is that you only have local observations. Linear systems permit you to take observations in one region and extrapolate them to another, but with nonlinear systems with an unknown structure, the best you can do is to predict that the same situations will give the same results, but even that isn't very good. Incorrect variables, long lags or stochastic noise can obliterate whatever values you have.

My question concerns the wage equation. It seems that this is very elementary, compared to the other parts of the system, but it plays an essential role because profitability is affected by it. The wage equation is independent of productivity because the dynamics depend on the employment rate. Since in advanced economies the employment ratio varies from 0.0 to 0.97, you don't get much action out of this, so you get an exponential wage rate. But it seems to me that what evidence we have indicates that productivity has a great deal of influence on the wage rate over moderate periods of time, for example over ten years.

Frank Englmann:

With respect to labour productivity and the wage bargaining equation, if you include it as I did in a paper published this year in the *Journal of Evolutionary Economics*, then you see that the employment effects vanish during the diffusion process and this has an impact on the output growth, but I don't think that it changes the cyclical pattern of the story. I have three more points to make.

First, you pointed out that there is a multitude of cutting-edge technologies, but are these at a macro level or a sectoral level? In your study they are always at a macro level and I wonder if this is a good representation of a real economy.

Second, you point out that there is a lag between R&D expenditure and productivity growth because the latter depends on diffusion, which depends on profitability. One further explanation for a productivity slowdown is that, as Stiglitz among others has pointed out, right at the beginning at market entrance, a new technology is not usually mature and its profitability may be lower than already existing technologies. This can occur because people think that there is a learning curve during the diffusion process. You have not included this in your model. This is a problem because you have a strong correlation between the diffusion rate and the rate of profit, even though there are no technological expectations in the model.

Third, you allow for some sort of imitation using the ST parameter, but how do you make sure that this ST parameter is not too high, because there is a maximum rate of accumulation connected with every technology, which is equal to its output/capital ratio.

Richard Nelson:
If we could, avoid technical questions if possible.

Gerald Silverberg:
There are a few technical questions that do need a response. In particular, I did not understand Kenneth Arrow's question because wages, in fact, track productivity in this model, because the equation is a dynamic one. Productivity does not have to be put into the equation since employment is generated by the rest of the system, which represents investment, and therefore wages more or less have to track productivity over the long term. You could make the additional step of introducing productivity explicitly in the wage-bargaining equation, but . . .

Kenneth Arrow:
There is no labour scarcity there?

Gerald Silverberg:
You have the employment rate. The first equation says that if labour is scarce wages start going up. Therefore, there is a natural level of employment at a given level of productivity change, and this leads to wages rising in step with productivity.

Richard Nelson:
Otherwise profits will soar and . . .

Gerald Silverberg:
That's right, otherwise profits will soar and investment will soar. It's a simple Lotka–Volterra system – when profits are very high employment goes up because businessmen are hiring workers, which drives up the wage rate. This cuts into profits and causes employment to fall. On average the two things are tracking each other. You don't have to explicitly put that into the model. As Frank Englmann mentioned, you could explicitly model this, but it is a question of how explicit you want to be. What is important in this model is that wages only track productivity, they are not identical to productivity growth.

In terms of complex systems analysis, as raised by Paul Romer and Kenneth Arrow, there are some important and relevant points here. Ken's analogy to the weather is quite accurate. Many people have argued that the weather is a chaotic system. Chaos is only a valuable concept for low-dimensional chaotic systems. A high-dimensional system is essentially stochastic – every random-number generator on a computer is a high-dimensional chaotic system. The important point that most people working on complex systems are making is that a complex system can often be generated by using only a few variables. The correlation dimension tells us how many active variables are driving the system. You don't know *a priori* what those variables are – they could be complex transformations of the observables, but in essence they are the principal dimensions in some subspace in which the real action is happening. The entire arsenal of methods to deal with complex dynamics is designed to reduce the large *a priori* complexity to something compact. It may be highly nonlinear and lead to surprising behaviour, but in principle one may be able to model a complex system using a very small number of variables.

We do know that the economy consists of lots of dimensions; there are lots of agents and lots of possible behaviours. Intrinsically it is a high-dimensional system. If you want to use small models but you don't want to be *ad hoc*, it may pay to look at it in terms of complex systems and see what the crucial variables may be. Our intuition is not a good guide to the crucial variables. It would be useful to find a class of low-dimensional models that corresponded to some intrinsic features of the data. The data used in this particular paper is artificial, except for the innovation time series. It is a big problem in economics that we shall probably never have the data needed to do this type of analysis in a fully satisfactory way, as Paul Romer noted, although I see nothing cosmological about fluctuations of the order of 50 years, well within the lifetime of a single individual. There is a tendency in the statistical literature to apply asymptotic methods to small sample sizes. In principle, this will never produce accurate results about the system, but we may get revealing clues.

In terms of Ken's analogy to the weather, this could be taken further. You cannot look at history naively, but must look at several years before an historical event and try to recreate event histories with enough data in the past to be able to make historical analogies. What chaos tells you is that the accuracy of your prediction declines exponentially. Historical analogy will never give you a long-term forecast even if the system is truly a nonlinear deterministic system. If you use the simplest stochastic rule that the weather tomorrow will be the same as the weather today, you will be right about 65% of the time. Even with the best computers, one-day forecasting only improves the accuracy by about 5%. This is an intrinsic barrier that we shall probably never be able to overcome.

Paul Romer:

On the issue of sample size, the interaction could be quite important. We might learn more about these effects through looking at detailed historic cases, such as Paul David's study of the dynamo. This may be a more effective way of understanding what is going on than trying to use statistics to get at a small set of data.

My sense of what is going on in modern macroeconomics is that we have retreated into trying to come up with concepts such as a cold front or a low-pressure zone. There was an attempt to define a few key concepts and then figure out how they interact. This is what I think the authors are trying to do. Maybe there is room for this.

Paul David:

I welcome two particular results of Jerry Silverberg and Doris Lehnert's paper. One is the pure theory of historical analogies, which suggests going back to 1900, for example, and trying to show the coincidence of structural features and the time-scales of events. An example is the parallel between the productivity paradox related to the introduction of microcomputers and the history of the electrical dynamo. This latter story matches the current situation with the one where the United States and Great Britain were *circa* 1900, about 20 years after the introduction of a central dynamo station. By following this story you get some notion of the diffusion process and the time-scale for an upswing in productivity.

The second thing in this model is that the authors emphasise the same thing that I was stressing, that the translation of an innovation into productivity growth is bound up with the diffusion process. But then I would agree with Frank Englmann in emphasising the positive interaction between diffusion and learning and the positive feedback features. Perhaps it is the characteristics of the learning process which is more important in delaying the realisation of rapid productivity growth, rather than the Phillips curve macroeconomic cycle which is central in this paper. This curve possibly tends to delay the onset of enough investment to realise the new innovations in a rapid buildup of a wave of cutting-edge technology.

I think that exploring these kinds of mechanisms is an interesting way in which historical analysis can work hand in hand with the insights that you get from nonlinear simulations, and help develop our intuitions about some of these processes. This is one of the benefits from really cheap computing – being able to acquire stronger and more accurate intuitions about the behaviour of nonlinear systems. We understand linear systems but we don't have such good intuitions about nonlinear systems, and we can acquire them from computing.

PART II

International Disparities in Growth and Technological Performance

6. Convergence and Divergence in the Long-term Growth of Open Economies

Giovanni Dosi and Silvia Fabiani[*]

1. INTRODUCTION

This work attempts to explore the evolutionary foundations of the differentiated patterns of growth one observes in the international economy. Economic historians such as Abramovitz (1989, 1992), David (1975), Landes (1969), Rosenberg (1976) and Maddison (1982, 1991, 1992) have devoted considerable attention to 'catching up' as well as divergence ('forging ahead' and 'falling behind') in economic development. Relatedly, a good deal of effort by economists has been devoted to the explanation of 'why growth rates differ' – as the famous contribution by Denison and Poullier (1967) was entitled. One of the central topics of this work is the analysis of the determinants of both convergence and divergence in the levels and rates of growth of per capita income amongst countries.

This also implies a search for the underlying determinants and processes which might have generated the diverse patterns of development we observe. Economic historians have stressed the role of technical and institutional change (or lack of it), together with broad country-specific factors such as education, geography and political events. Moreover, some of them have pointed to the importance of capital accumulation (although this remains a somewhat controversial issue) and to the dynamic interaction between trade performance and growth performance.

The theoretical account which the economic discipline provides captures only some of the elements which historians have identified as the major determinants of development, and little of the 'action' which they

[*] Part of this work draws upon an ongoing research project also involving D. Marinucci at the University of Rome 'La Sapienza'. We also want to thank D. Mandeng for his help in accessing the CAN Data Bank (CEPAL, Santiago) on trade flows. We gratefully acknowledge research support to G.D. by the National Research Council of Italy (CNR) and by the Consortium on Cooperation and Competitiveness (CCC) at the Center for Research in Management, UC Berkeley; and to S.F. by Fondazione Rosselli, Turin, Italy.

have described. Consider, for example, technological change. Neoclassical models since the pioneering work of Solow (1957) have pointed – at least by default – to the crucial importance of technical and institutional change as expressed in a relatively large 'residual factor'. But until recently little progress was being made in the formal modelling of technical change itself. New growth theory does attempt to incorporate some measures of technological innovation (despite the significant limitations in the ways technology itself is represented, which we discuss below). However, possibly the most striking difference between historians' and economists' interpretations is that the former heavily rely on the joint identification of variables and processes affecting development, while the latter usually assume an invariant (and indeed quite peculiar) economic 'process', implicitly summarised by the properties of the postulated production function. The standard Solow production function, $Y(t) = A(t)F(\cdot)$, relates output to an invariant allocation process and to a time-drift $(A(t))$, which supposedly captures all the action that economic historians are talking about. In many respects, 'new growth' theories push this analytical strategy even further.

The thrust of most recent developments in growth theory is indeed to squeeze the drift into the production function itself either as an externality or as the outcome of an allocative decision *vis-à-vis* the production of a particular input – 'knowledge'. While in Solow-type models one has implicitly two major explanatory headings, namely optimal allocations of inputs (the PF) and 'learning' (what is left out), many contemporary growth models attempt to model learning, too, as the equilibrium outcome of an optimal allocation mechanism (Lucas 1988 is a lucid and extremist statement of this research programme).

In this work we shall pursue a quite different line of inquiry and explore some dynamic properties of economic systems driven by processes of learning, while neglecting – in a first approximation – optimal resource allocation issues. That is, we focus on the process driving the $A(t)$ dynamics, assuming that whatever pattern of resource allocation emerges it is, too, a highly imperfect outcome of innovation, imitation and diffusion. The exercise finds a major source of inspiration in the evolutionary models of Nelson and Winter (1982). The approach is 'evolutionary' in the sense that (a) the microfoundations rest upon boundedly rational agents; (b) the general presumption is that interactions occur away from equilibrium; (c) markets and other institutions perform as selection mechanisms amongst heterogeneous agents and technologies.

To do so, we develop a model showing how evolutionary microfoundations easily allow for the emergence of divergent patterns of growth and their persistence. In particular, we show how agent-specific technological 'shocks' entail country-wide effects, yielding a rich variety of growth patterns (catching up, falling behind, overtaking). We also discuss the overlapping and complementarities between these evolutionary microfoundations and other, often non-microfounded, models which attempt to explain the differentiated patterns of growth on the grounds of broad country-specific characteristics and some non-linearity in the development process (models of Kaldorian inspiration, some of the catching-up literature as well as various strands of dynamic-increasing-returns models fall into this category).

2. DIVERGENCE, CONVERGENCE AND PERSISTENT DIFFERENCES: SOME 'STYLISED FACTS'

It might be helpful to start with the broad historical picture. Consider the last three centuries as the unit of observation. What must be striking for any external observer is the explosion of diverging development patterns, starting from quite similar pre-industrial levels of per capita incomes. Table 6.1, from Bairoch (1981, p. 5), presents estimates showing that before the industrial revolution 'the income gap between the poorest and the richest country was certainly smaller than the ratio 1.0 to 2.0 and probably of the order of only 1.0 to 1.5'. The dominant pattern after the industrial revolution is one with rapidly increasing differentiation among countries and overall divergence (see Table 6.2). Even in the post-Second World War period, commonly regarded as an era of growing uniformity, the hypothesis of 'global' convergence (that is, convergence of the whole universe of countries toward increasingly similar income levels) does not find support from the evidence (De Long 1988; Easterly *et al.* 1991; Verspagen 1992).

Rather, one finds some – although not overwhelming – evidence of local convergence, that is within subsets of countries grouped according to some initial characteristics such as income levels (Durlauf and Johnson 1992) or geographical location (Soete and Verspagen 1992). Still, across-group differences in growth performances appear to be strikingly high. Clearly, convergence in the end-period levels of income ought to show up in an inverse correlation between rates of growth and initial levels, but the evidence does not support this proposition (for recent regional data see Tables 6.3 and 6.4).

Acknowledging a 'post-selection bias' (De Long 1988), the performance of OECD countries displays much stronger convergence characteristics. It is well known that after the Second World War, one observes a strong catching-up process by other OECD countries in per capita income and labour productivity *vis-à-vis* the United States

Table 6.1: Estimates of pre-industrial per capita GNP (in 1960 US dollars)

	Period	GNP per capita
Countries now developed		
Great Britain	1700	160–200
United States	1710	200–260
France	1781–1790	170–200
Russia	1860	160–200
Sweden	1860	190–230
Japan	1885	160–200
Countries now less developed		
Egypt	1887	170–210
Ghana	1891	90–150
India	1900	130–160
Iran	1900	140–220
Jamaica	1832	240–280
Mexico	1900	150–190
Philippines	1902	170–210

Note: It is probably safe to assume nearly constant per capita incomes in the years which precede the estimates, so that for example the figure of Ghana 1700 should not have been significantly different from that of Ghana 1891 (if anything it could have been higher before the slave trade). Clearly, the figures should be taken as rough orders of magnitude.
Source: Bairoch (1981).

(Maddison 1982; Abramovitz 1989). At least since 1870, the OECD followers have become increasingly homogeneous in the sense that the standard deviations of their relative distance from the USA have steadily fallen. However, the mean gap itself increased until the Second World War and fell thereafter.

An interesting phenomenon concerns the persistence of relative growth performances over time. Historical evidence regarding specific countries seems to suggest the persistence of above/below-average growth rates at least within particular phases of development. Compare, for example, the below-average performance of the UK after the Second World War (and indeed throughout this century) with the above-average performance of Japan, Germany and Italy. However, long-term persistence of growth rates systematically different from the mean world growth rate, somewhat surprisingly, does not appear to be a general characteristic of the whole set

Table 6.2: Estimates of trends in per capita GNP 1750–1977 (in 1960 US dollars)

Year	Developed Countries		Third World			Gaps
	(1)	(2)	(3)	(4)	(5)	(6)
	Total ($bn)	per capita	Total ($bn)	per capita	= (2)/(4)	Ratio of most-developed to least-developed
1750	35	182	112	188	1.0	1.8
1800	47	198	137	188	1.1	1.8
1830	67	237	150	183	1.3	2.8
1860	118	324	159	174	1.9	4.5
1913	430	662	217	192	3.4	10.4
1950	889	1054	335	203	5.2	17.9
1960	1394	1453	514	250	5.8	20.0
1970	2386	2229	800	380	7.2	25.7
1977	2108	2737	1082	355	7.7	29.1

Source: Bairoch (1981), pp. 7–8.

Table 6.3: Real GDP growth rates (in % p.a.) in various regions, 1965–89

	1965–80	1980–89
East Asia[*]	7.3	7.9
South Asia	3.9	5.1
Africa (Sub-Sahara)	4.0	2.1
Latin America	5.8	1.6

[*] including China
Source: World Bank, *World Development Report 1991*.

of countries. Easterly *et al*. (1991) find a rather low cross-period correlation in relative growth rates (around 0.3), with a greater instability amongst developing countries.

This also implies that countries which appear to catch up in one period

Table 6.4: Real per capita GDP growth rates (in % p.a.)

East Asia[*]	5.0	6.3
South Asia	1.5	2.9
Africa (Sub-Sahara)	1.1	−1.2
Latin America	3.5	−0.5

[*] including China
Source: World Bank, *World Development Report 1991.*

fall behind in another one. This is broadly confirmed by a new study of the long-term evidence concerning both developed and developing countries by Angus Maddison (1992). We do not wish to pursue the empirical debate any further here, and refer to Verspagen's contribution to this volume for more empirical evidence.[1]

One could summarise the empirical evidence on international patterns of growth along the lines of the following seven 'stylised facts' (SFs):

SF1:   Economies have grown over the past two centuries probably faster than during any previous period in recorded history.

SF2:   However, they have grown at different and variable rates (sometimes negative for particular periods and particular countries – Argentina, a few less-developed countries, the USSR, etc., or for many countries for particular periods, e.g., deep recessions).

SF3:   The long-term pattern for the whole set of countries shows an increasing differentiation, highlighted by a secular increase in the variance in per capita income.

SF4:   Catching up with forging ahead has been relatively rare (Britain overtaking Holland in the eighteenth century; the USA, Germany and others overtaking Britain in the late nineteenth and twentieth centuries; Japan overtaking almost everyone in the late twentieth century).

SF5:   Progress in catching up has been more widespread (Western-Central Europe in the nineteenth century; Scandinavia and Italy in the twentieth; East Asian countries in the late twentieth century; the EEC catching up with the USA during the 1960s and 1970s).

SF6:   Falling behind has also been a rather frequent phenomenon (many less-developed countries in the 1970s and 1980s; a few countries falling behind after a considerable 'spurt' of catching up – compare the 1950s with the 1980s in Latin America and Eastern Europe; Britain's long-term relative decline).

SF7:   One is, in general, not able to identify persistent features of national growth patterns on the basis of initial levels alone (e.g. 'all laggard countries will tend to grow faster', or 'those that have grown faster will also grow faster in the future'). Closer inspection of particular economies or groups of economies does appear to show long-term persistence (e.g., Japan or Britain), but the causes of the phenomenon are plausibly country-specific rather than a common feature of the world economy.

3. 'INGREDIENTS' VS. PROCESSES OF DEVELOPMENT: TOWARDS EVOLUTIONARY MICROFOUNDATIONS

In general terms, moving from stylised evidence to theory involves the identification of both some basic 'ingredients' of growth – what Abramovitz would call the 'proximate causes' of development – and some underlying processes which shape the dynamics of these 'ingredients' and link them together, hence generating the observable patterns of development – Abramovitz's 'deeper causes' (cf. Abramovitz 1989).

Significant progress has been made in recent years towards a more satisfactory theoretical understanding of both 'ingredients' and 'processes' (although some of the novel directions of inquiry are inconsistent with each other). For the purposes of our analysis let us just mention the following streams of analysis:

1. The 'Schumpeterian' acknowledgement that a good deal of innovative exploration is endogenous to the activities of business firms has led to a variety of models in which growth is driven by technological innovation undertaken by profit-motivated agents (see, among others, Romer 1990; Grossman and Helpman 1991; and nearer to a Schumpeterian spirit, Aghion and Howitt 1992; Segerstrom *et al.* 1990; Cheng and Dinopoulos 1992). As mentioned above, the methodological thrust of 'new growth' theories has been to endogenise Solow's time-dependent drift within an 'enlarged' production function – a special 'production function of knowledge' yields increasing returns to knowledge itself, while at the same time preserving general equilibrium microfoundations.

2. The 'impactedness' of knowledge may lead to nonlinearities in the relationship between inputs and outputs, and this may be captured by 'technological externalities with threshold properties' in an otherwise standard production function (Azariadis and Drazen 1990), or by big indivisibilities and structural changes associated with development

(Justman and Teubal 1991).

3. In a somewhat parallel fashion to new growth theories, 'new trade' theories have incorporated some forms of increasing returns and imperfect competition into open economy models. They demonstrate that the welfare-enhancing properties of free trade cease to hold in general (see Grossman and Helpman 1991 and Young 1991, among others).

4. Both 'old' and 'new' growth theories do not allow for any country specificity, except those already captured by the inputs in the production function (whether 'standard' or 'enlarged'), and also assume instantaneous intra-country diffusion of innovations. An alternative route to the explanation of why levels and growth rates of income differ (which has a few points of tangency with the model we shall present below) focuses, on the contrary, on national determinants of the dynamics of the 'shifts' in the production function itself. Building upon an early model of Nelson and Phelps (1966), Benhabib and Spiegel (1992) interpret economically the $A(t)$ dynamics as dependent on country-specific variables such as proxies for human capital. Note that the latter enters the production function of knowledge, as in Romer, while also determining the country-specific rates of diffusion of knowledge. That is, 'education' influences both the rate at which knowledge is generated and the catching up of laggard countries to frontier technologies. In a model with strong evolutionary features, Verspagen (1992) shows how a nonlinear interaction between the potential of imitation, determined by technological lags *vis-à-vis* the frontier countries, and domestic capabilities can produce either catching up dynamics or falling behind.

Benhabib and Jovanovic (1991) and Jovanovic and Lach (1991) interpret persistent international differences in growth rates (as well as the time-series variations) as the outcome of imperfectly correlated country shocks and non-instantaneous diffusion. Rates of diffusion are assumed to be identical across countries, and in Jovanovic and Lach (1991) are calibrated on the micro US data from Klepper and Graddy (1990). The production function itself is a Solow constant-returns function. As Benhabib and Jovanovic emphasise, in these models the relation goes from knowledge to capital accumulation and not the other way round (as for example in new growth theories).

5. It was mentioned earlier that an important finding from the economics of innovation is the distinction between relatively incremental (or 'normal') technical progress vs. paradigmatic changes. That distinction is also captured to a certain extent in various equilibrium models of invention and growth: Jovanovic and Rob (1990) distinguish between 'intensive' and 'extensive' search; Cheng and Dinopoulos (1992) between 'breakthroughs' and improvements; Brezis, Krugman and Isiodon (1991), despite extremely parsimonious references to the innovation

literature, is in fact an equilibrium model of change in international leadership associated with changes in 'technological paradigm'. In general, the presence of both incremental and radical changes generates persistent fluctuations in aggregate time-series and/or persistent international differentiation (see also Amable 1992 and Chapter 5 by Silverberg and Lehnert in this volume).

6. Two features which most of the models reviewed so far have in common (with the exception of evolutionary models) are microfoundations based on perfectly rational agents and equilibrium interactions. An immediate objection to such microfoundations is that one is bound to lose a lot of the 'action' (that is, the microeconomic process of change) on which the historical interpretation of development is grounded. We shall return to this point later but let us just point out here that even without abandoning equilibrium and rationality *tout court*, some important insights can already be gained by relaxing the most restrictive assumptions on general equilibria (of the Arrow–Debreu type) and on perfect foresight.[2] In this regard, two directions of inquiry are worth mentioning for our purposes.

The first one points to the importance of coordination failures and demand externalities resulting simply from the absence of Arrow–Debreu contingency markets. In this vein, Murphy, Shleifer and Vishny (1989) formulate an argument, familiar in development literature, about the importance of 'big pushes' (Rosenstein–Rodan) and intersectoral demand linkages (Hirschman) in order to switch from one growth path to another one. Durlauf (1992) models an economy with endogenous cyclicity due to changing intersectoral demand flows (but the argument can in principle be extended to multi-economy worlds).

The second direction studies the aggregate implications of microeconomic behaviours based on various informational imperfections (e.g. in the market for finance) and local learning. Stiglitz (1992) shows that these conditions are sufficient to generate multiple-growth trajectories (and he also argues that the transitional dynamics between them squares with some of the stylised facts on growth and catching up).

To summarise, we can say that in recent years diverse endeavours have enriched growth theory by bringing into the picture some forms of increasing returns, threshold effects, demand complementarities, country- and technology-specific shocks, and in some cases a more satisfactory microeconomics based on informational asymmetries.

Still, it seems to us that progress towards a better understanding of the 'deeper sources' of growth is hindered by an obstinate adherence to equilibrium microfoundations and to the attempt by many to incorporate learning within the familiar framework of optimal allocation by an unboundedly rational representative agent.

Indeed, the tension between dynamic phenomena – such as technical change – and the static allocative properties summarised by a Solow-type production function shows up in the empirical estimations which often yield quite weird coefficients for marginal productivities and factors shares.[3] One may obtain, for example, in unconstrained estimates negative marginal social products of capital or negative labour shares! In some respects these exercises are reminiscent of the story of Procrustes' bed in Greek mythology: if you pull the blanket to protect your head from being cut off, you uncover your feet, and *vice versa*.

Moreover, the quest to maintain traditional microfoundations restricts the analysis of increasing returns and non-convexities to those forms which can be reconciled – at least in principle – with some underlying general equilibrium. It might be noted that for similar reasons, firm-specific technological 'shocks' have been largely neglected, even if they are a crucial part of the historical interpretation of development. Not surprisingly, company-specific learning has been mainly considered within the evolutionary tradition.[4]

In line with the latter approach, the following section will explore the properties of evolutionary microfoundations of growth in open economies which continuously undergo innovation and imitation by heterogeneous agents.

4. AN ATTEMPT AT MODELLING THE EVOLUTIONARY MICROFOUNDATIONS OF DEVELOPMENT

We start from the Schumpeterian intuition that technical change is in its nature a disequilibrium phenomenon and focus on the aggregate properties of economies in which innovative learning never reaches a state wherein resources are optimally allocated and prices reveal relative efficiencies. In fact, we shall make our argument even more extreme and suppose that each economic system is never constrained by scarcities either in terms of notional technological opportunities or in terms of labour supply. Under these extreme circumstances we shall ask, will each system self-organise through fluctuations far from equilibrium and generate some of those regularities which we empirically observe?[5]

Benhabib and Jovanovic conclude in their work by saying that 'no doubt, a quantum leap in our understanding of growth will occur only when the engine of growth namely the stochastic process driving country-specific technological shocks is successfully endogenized' (Benhabib and Jovanovic 1991, p. 102). This model tries to move some steps in this direction by providing a microfoundation of country dynamics using some stylised company-specific processes of innovation and imitation.

More specifically, we shall show that:

1. initially identical countries may well differentiate in ways that are persistent over time;
2. 'local' (company-specific) fluctuations may determine long-term aggregate (country-wide) effects;
3. 'evolutionary' microfoundations and heterogeneous learning are sufficient to sustain Kaldorian 'virtuous' and 'vicious' feedbacks;
4. on different time-scales and during different 'phases' one may observe 'catching up', forging ahead or divergence.

The modelling strategy is inspired by the seminal work of Nelson and Winter (1982) and draws on a previous (closed-economy) model by one of us (Chiaromonte and Dosi 1992). The current version has been elaborated together with R. Aversi (for more details on an earlier model, cf. Fabiani 1990). In view of the highly nonlinear structure of the model, its properties are explored via simulations.

4.1 The Model

The 'world' economy is composed of two sectors, m countries and n firms per country per sector. Each firm i of country j undertakes two activities, namely 'search' (via innovation and imitation of other firms) and 'production' of either of the two final (homogeneous) goods (1,2). Labour is the only input in both search and production. (Fixed) coefficients of production are company-specific, $1/\pi_{ij}(t)$, where $\pi(\cdot)$ is labour productivity. In the version of the model presented here, for simplicity labour is homogeneous and can be indifferently applied to search and production. However, similar results are obtained through more reasonable formulations with two types of labour, 'skilled' for research and 'unskilled' for production.

Search and imitation

'Search' is a two-stage stochastic process and applies to both innovation and imitation. A first stage determines whether search is successful:

$$Pr\{I_{ij}(t) = 1\} = 1 - \exp\{-a_1 IN_{ij}(t)\}, \tag{6.1}$$

where I_{ij} is a binary variable which takes the value one if the event 'success' occurs, IN_{ij} is the investment in search by firm i of country j measured in terms of a current and lagged number of searching workers (Inn),[6]

$$Inn = \sum_{\tau=0}^{2} Inn_{ij} \ (t - \tau).$$

The parameter a_1 captures the level of technological opportunities.

If 'success' is drawn, the firm adds a per cent productivity increment by accessing a Poisson distribution with mean λ:

$$E \ [\ \pi_{ij}^{I} \ (t + 1)] \ = \ \pi_{ij} \ (t) \ (\ 1 + \frac{\lambda}{100} \ ). \tag{6.2}$$

The value of λ, too, is a proxy for the richness of unexplored opportunities.

Technological knowledge, in our model, is neither a purely public good nor perfectly appropriable. New techniques can be imitated, but with a search cost. Just as innovation, imitation is modelled as a two-stage stochastic process, and dependent on the 'technological gap' *vis-à-vis* the imitated technique.

Define the set of techniques that can be imitated as $\Pi \ (t) = \bigcup_{j=1}^{m} \pi_j \ (t)$.

Next, define the differences (that is the 'distance') between the technique already used by firm i and any one technique belonging to $\Pi(\cdot)$:

$$d(\pi_{ij}(t), \pi(t)) = \begin{cases} \max\{0, \pi - \pi_{ij}\} \text{ if } \pi \in \Pi_j, \\ \\ \xi\max\{0, \pi - \pi_{ij}\} \text{ otherwise,} \end{cases}$$

where ξ (>1), increases the 'distance' (i.e., decreases the use of imitation) of the techniques belonging to firms of other countries.

Hence the imitation search set for the i-firm is defined by

$$\Pi \ M_{ij} \ (t) = \{ \ \forall \pi \varepsilon \Pi \ | \ d(\pi_{ij}(t), \pi) > 0 \ \}. \tag{6.3}$$

Like the innovation process, success in imitation is a stochastic variable

$$Pr \{ M_{ij} \ (t) = 1 \} = 1 - \exp\{ -a_{2j} \ IM_{ij} \ (t) \}, \tag{6.4}$$

where, denoting the number of workers involved in imitative search by $Imi(\cdot)$,

$$IM_{ij}(t) = \sum_{\tau=0}^{2} Imi_{ij}(t-\tau) + \alpha_{3j} \sum_{i} \sum_{\tau=0}^{2} Imi_{ij}(t-\tau) + \alpha_{4j} \sum_{j} \sum_{\tau=0}^{2} Imi_{ij}(t-\tau).$$

(6.5)

The parameter a_{2j} is an inverse measure of appropriability, while α_{3j} and α_{4j} capture country-wide and world-wide externalities, respectively. (In the simulations we shall present below we shall put α_{3j} and α_{4j} equal to zero). In the case of 'imitative success', the imitated technique is drawn from the imitation search set with a probability proportional to the distance from the technique currently used by firm i, $\forall \pi \in \Pi\, M_{ij}(t)$:

$$Pr\{\,\pi_{ij}^{M}(t) = \pi\,\} = \frac{[d\,(\pi,\pi_{ij})]^{-1}}{\displaystyle\sum_{\pi\in\Pi M_{ij}(t)} [d\,(\pi,\pi_{ij})]^{-1}}.$$

(6.6)

The intuition behind this formulation is that learning is 'local' and knowledge is partly tacit, so that the probability of instantaneous catching up to best practice techniques is inversely proportional to the laggard's distance (although, of course, the scope for catching up is higher).

The rule determining the technique actually applied to production is straightforward:

$$\pi_{ij}(t+1) = \max\{\,\pi_{ij}(t),\, \pi_{ij}^{I}(t),\, \pi_{ij}^{M}(t)\}.$$

Behavioural rules

We make the rather extreme and unorthodox assumption that behaviour is totally 'routinised', that is, based on fixed and event-independent rules. There are indeed good empirical and theoretical reasons to expect behaviours to be rather inertial in highly uncertain and nonstationary environments (see Nelson and Winter 1982; Heiner 1988; Dosi and Egidi 1991, in addition of course to the 'behaviourist tradition' of Herbert Simon and James March). In any case, the reader who is more inclined to 'rational' characterisations of microbehaviours may well consider this assumption as an extreme version of bounded rationality cum myopic expectations.

Investment in 'search' is determined by a rule linking it to the previous period's turnover:

$$R\&D_{ij}(t) = a_{3ij} Y_{ij}(t-1). \tag{6.7}$$

The number of workers undertaking search is defined by

$$I_{ij}(t) = \frac{R\&D_{ij}(t)}{w_j(t)},$$

where w_j is the wage in country j at time t.

Another rule subdivides search between innovation, Inn_{ij} and imitation, Imi_{ij}:

$$Inn_{ij} = (1 - \mu_{ij}) I_{ij}, \tag{6.8}$$

$$Imi_{ij} = \mu_{ij} I_{ij}. \tag{6.9}$$

Pricing is based on a mark-up procedure:

$$P_{ij}(t) = \frac{w_j(t)}{\pi_{ij}(t)} (1 + a_{4ij}). \tag{6.10}$$

Finally, production by firm i at time t responds to the 'orders' received at the beginning of each 'period' (through a mechanism which we shall define below).

The process of change of individual productivities, together with the fixed mark-up rule for pricing, determines the level of firm-specific competitiveness, E_{ij}:

$$E_{ij}(t) = \frac{1}{P_{ij}(t)} \rho_j(t), \tag{6.11}$$

where ρ_j is the exchange rate of country j.

Workers consume in period $(t+1)$ all the wages they have earned in t. Firms invest their surpluses in search via the mechanism of eq. (6.7), and deposit their net cash flow in an interest-free account with a 'financial sector' which is not modelled here, or they can draw interest-free advances up to a limit proportional to their current turnover and past cash flows.[7]

Market dynamics
Domestic demand in each market (at current prices and exchange rates), D^j, aggregates *ex post* over the whole wage bill paid to workers employed

in both production and search:

$$D^j(t) = \sum_i w_j N_{ij}(t),\qquad(6.12)$$

where N_{ij} is total employment in firm i.

In this version of the model we also assume a constant-share demand function

$$D^{1k} = (1 - a_{6j})\, D^k,$$
$$D^{2k} = a_{6j}\, D^k,\qquad(6.13)$$

where the superscripts 1 and 2 stand for the sectors and k for the national markets.

Demand is distributed among individual producers according to their relative competitiveness, $E^{1k}{}_{ij}$, where $\bar{E}^{1k}$ is the average competitiveness of product 1 on market K (of course, if $j \neq k$ it means that a firm is exporting):

$$\bar{E}^{1k}(t) = \sum_i \sum_j f_{ij}^{1k}(t)\, E_{ij}(t).$$

$f^{1k}{}_{ij}$ is the market share of firm i belonging to country j on the market K in product 1 (below, subscripts and superscripts will be dropped when that does not engender confusion).[8]

Market share dynamics in each sector is governed by

$$\dot{f}_{ij}^{1k}(t,t+1) = a_{7j}\left[\frac{E_{ij}^{1k}(t)}{\bar{E}^{1k}(t)} - 1\right] f_{ij}^{1k}(t),\qquad(6.14)$$

subject to the constraint in note 7 (the dot stands for the rate of change).[9]

This replicator dynamics associated with market selection entails, in general, the co-existence of firms characterised by different levels of efficiency and different behaviourial rules.[10] The parameter a_7 represents market 'selectiveness', that is, loosely speaking it determines the speed at which successful innovators are rewarded and laggards are punished. Firms die when their market share falls below a certain critical level:

$$\sum_k f_{ij}^k < f_{min}.$$

The model also allows for the entry of new firms. Dead firms are replaced by new entrants with an initial productivity equal to the average productivity in that sector in the country where birth occurs, $\pi^1_j(t)$ or $\pi^2_j(t)$, plus white noise.

Production decisions follow the 'orders' received in each national market, determined via eq. (6.14). Thus the output (= income) of each firm operating in sector 1 is

$$Y^1_{ij}(t) = \sum_k f^{1k}_{ij}(t) \, D^{1k}(t-1) \, \rho_j(t). \qquad (6.15)$$

The same applies to firms in sector 2.

The demand for labour employed in production by firm i is just its real output divided by its labour productivity:

$$N^P_{ij}(t) = \frac{Y_{ij}(t)}{P_{ij}(t) \cdot \pi_{ij}(t)}. \qquad (6.16)$$

Aggregate dynamics and national accounts

National aggregate variables sum up (very much like national accounts) over their corresponding microeconomic values. Total employment is

$$N_j(t) = \sum_i (N^{P1}_{ij}(t) + N^{P2}_{ij}(t) + I^1_{ij}(t) + I^2_{ij}(t)), \qquad (6.17)$$

that is, the sum of all labour demanded in the country, in the two sectors, for production and for research.

National income, at constant prices is

$$Y^*_j = \sum_i (Y_{ij} / P_{ij}). \qquad (6.18)$$

Exports are

$$(EXP)_j = \sum_{k \neq j} \sum_i [(f^{k_1}_{ij} D^{k_1} + f^{k_2}_{ij} D^{k_2})] \, \rho_j, \qquad (6.19)$$

and imports are

$$(IMP)_j = \sum_i [(f^{j_1}_{ij} D^{j_1} + f^{j_2}_{ij} D^{j_2})] \, \rho_j, \qquad (6.20)$$

that is, sales of domestic firms in every country different from their own. The balance of trade (which in this model is taken to be identical to foreign payment balances) is

$$B_j \equiv (EXP)_j - (IMP)_j.$$

We have already mentioned that we assume an unlimited supply of labour. This hypothesis (*à la* Lewis 1954) can be rationalised by imagining that developing countries can always draw on labour from a large backward (subsistence) sector not explicitly represented here, and that developed countries can always open up their frontiers to immigration.

The (monetary) wage dynamics is driven by labour productivity growth ($\dot{\pi}$), consumer price changes ($\dot{\bar{P}}_j$), and changes in the levels of employment ($\dot{N}_j$):

$$\dot{w}_j\ (t,t+1) = a_{8j}\dot{\bar{\pi}}_j\ (t-1,t) + a_{9j}\dot{\bar{P}}_j\ (t-1,t) + a_{10j}\dot{N}_j\ (t-1,t). \quad (6.21)$$

The variable P stands for a sort of consumer price index and thus includes prices charged in j by firms which export from other countries; $\bar{\pi}_j$ is the average productivity across the two sectors weighted by the real product of each firm; a_{8j}, a_{9j} and a_{10j} are bounded in the interval [0,1]. Exchange rates vary as a function of current and past cumulated foreign balances.[11]

Before discussing the simulation results, let us consider some general properties of this model. First, note that the dynamic behaviour is driven by endogenously generated, company-specific technological shocks, but the latter exert their influence on incomes via a 'Keynesian' mechanism of demand formation. Second, the propagation of these shocks occurs via (a) imperfect adjustments on the product markets, through changes in market shares, and (b) inter-firm imitation. This also implies, of course, that diffusion of innovation is never instantaneous, and that rates depend jointly on market selection amongst heterogeneous firms and on the appropriability of innovations. Further, financial market rationing may put a ceiling on the expansion of the most successful firms. Third, the model embodies different sources of persistence. At the company level, (a) probabilities of innovation and imitation also depend on lagged expenditures in search; (b) innovation success feeds upon itself by increasing the amount of resources devoted to search in the future; and of course, (c) the dynamics of firm-specific levels of productivity implies a non-dissipating memory (indeed, productivity *for the single firm* displays a behaviour like a random walk with drift). Fourth, imitation plus market selection introduces nonlinear interactions between firms. Moreover, adjustments in wages and exchange rates can be considered as negative feedbacks which curb, at least to some extent, the ability of firms to expand indefinitely on the world market.

Finally, a few things are missing in this model that are very important in reality and crucial in determining the observed cross-sectional and time-series regularities in incomes. There is no fixed investment, and thus the model rules out all those sources of irreversibility associated with capital-embodied technical change and vintages effects (cf. Silverberg and Lehnert, Chapter 5 in this volume). There is also no room for expectations formation and thus for the amplifying or dampening effects that might result *vis-à-vis* past dynamics. There is no room for those general factors such as education, levels and composition of investment, and so on, which, as we argued at greater length in Dosi, Freeman and Fabiani (1992), are of paramount importance in development. Under these circumstances, one of the crucial questions is precisely whether firm-specific sources of persistence are sufficient to explain country-level differentiation, that is, persistent diversity in the levels and growth rates of incomes. A positive result, of course, would *a fortiori* hold were such fundamental country-specificities taken into account.

5. PRELIMINARY SIMULATION RESULTS

Let us start by emphasising that what we report in the following are preliminary results, which none the less suggest in our view the heuristic promises of an evolutionary microfoundation of growth. In all simulations presented here, the initial conditions are set to correspond to a homogeneous world economy in stationary equilibrium: all firms and all countries are identical and foreign account balances and all exchange rates are equal to one. In order to minimise any built-in bias toward differentiation, we do not allow any country-wide externalities and assume that the adjustment parameters (on the labour and product markets) and the behavioural parameters (for example, mark-ups, propensity to invest in innovation, and so on) are identical across firms and across countries.

We have experimented with a few different parameterisations. The results that we shall present appear to be robust to rather wide parameter variations. The analytical strategy guiding the simulation exercises was to explore the major regularities which the model generates as emergent properties, that is, as aggregate outcomes of the positive and negative feedback mechanisms embedded in the behaviours and interactions of the micro units.

A first general feature of the model is that it produces persistent inter-firm *asymmetries* in productivities, profits and market shares, a fact which certainly fits the microeconomic 'stylised facts' of industrial economics and the economics of innovation. Detailed analyses of the econometric properties of the time series generated by the model are beyond the scope of this paper. However, let us just mention that persistence in shock

Figure 6.1: Dynamics of real income, two countries (log scale)

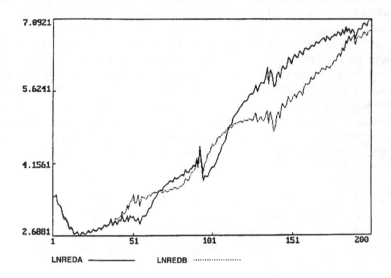

LNREDA ———————   LNREDB ·····················

propagation appears to be a general outcome. Consider a highly simplified version of the model, with one sector and two countries, A and B. Figure 6.1 presents one 200-period simulation, parameterised with $\lambda = 8$ (that is, the average 'jump' in productivity drawn from the Poisson distribution is 8%), selection parameter a_7 equal to unity, $\xi = 0$ (no greater difficulty in imitating in the other country) and $\psi = 0$ (no greater difficulty or cost in exporting to the other country).

OLS estimates of a deterministic trend yield the following results (standard errors are in brackets):

$$\ln Y_A = \underset{(0.053)}{2.115} + \underset{(0.0004)}{0.025\, t} \quad R^2 = 0.94 \quad F = 3117.4 \; DW = 0.065$$

$$\ln Y_B = \underset{(0.037)}{2.319} + \underset{(0.0003)}{0.021\, t} \quad R^2 = 0.95 \quad F = 4421.3 \; DW = .119$$

Table 6.5 presents the autocorrelation function of the residuals and compares them with those generated by the 'real business cycle' model of King, Plosser and Rebelo (1988) and the actual data from the US economy reported there.[12]

Clearly, the observer of the time series unaware of the process which generated them could easily interpret the strong trend component as the outcome of exogenous technical progress (as in Solow-type production functions). However, it follows from the structure of the model outlined above that if anything this is an important aggregate property emerging from endogenous technical changes cum heterogeneous agents and far from equilibrium diffusion. This very structure also yields a very high persistence, without exogenously imposing autocorrelation in the shocks. (Also note that our 'shocks' are firm-specific.) Indeed, in all the simulations that we have run, the detrended residuals are autocorrelated above 0.1 up to at least lag 20. Finally, it is worth stressing that these basic properties hold for rather different 'technological opportunities' (we have experimented with values of λ, the mean of the Poisson distribution, between 4 and 16).

Table 6.5: Autocorrelation of residuals: 'evolutionary' simulation, 'real business cycle', US data

| | Autocorrelation coefficients [a] | | |
Lags	1	2	3
KPR[b]($\beta = 0$)	0.03	0.03	0.03
KPR[b]($\beta = 0.9$)	0.93	0.86	0.80
USA(1948-1986)	0.96	0.91	0.85
'Evolutionary model':			
Country A (LNRED A)	0.95	0.90	0.85
Country B (LNRED B)	0.93	0.90	0.83

Notes
[a] Autocorrelation of residuals after detrending.
[b] King, Plosser and Rebelo (1988): $\beta = 0$, uncorrelated shocks; $\beta = 0.9$, correlated shocks ($u_t = 0.9u_{t-1} + \varepsilon_t$).

More central to the argument of this paper is the long-term convergence/divergence in per capita incomes. The experiment we shall now discuss concerns a 'world' economy with two sectors and 55 countries. Again we start with identical firms and a stationary state. The parameterisation of 'opportunities' and selection is the same as above. (However, we allow for positive ξ and ψ.) The evolutionary model generates increasing differentiation in both levels and rates of growth of per capita incomes: Figure 6.2 presents the dynamics of per capita incomes in a sample of simulated countries and Figure 6.3 the standard deviations in the rates of growth.

Simple tests of convergence from some intermediate date to the end period on the whole sample generally show divergence as the dominant

Figure 6.2: Per capita incomes in a sample of countries, simulation results

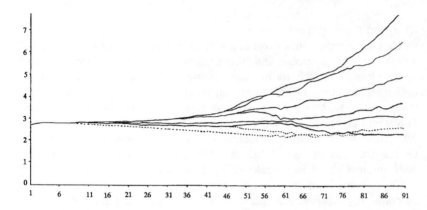

Figure 6.3: Standard deviation in growth rates

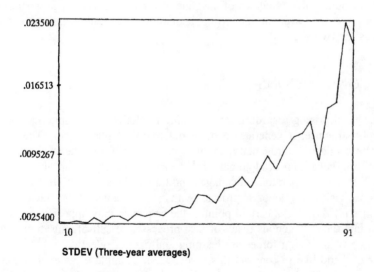

STDEV (Three-year averages)

pattern. Estimates of the form:

$$\ln \frac{Y_i(t)}{Y_i(0)} = \alpha + \beta \ln Y_i(0)$$

over the period 31–90 yield

$$\ln(Y_i(t)/Y_i(0)) = \quad -8.25 + \quad 3.67 \ln Y(0) \qquad R^2 = 0.06 \qquad F = 4.33$$

$$(5.07) \qquad (1.76)$$

(β is significant at the 5% level).

Of course, one can always explicitly introduce a 'post-selection bias' and test for the subgroups which turn out at the end to be 'developed' and 'undeveloped'. In the former case (same period, top 25 countries) we obtain a negative (-0.59) but statistically insignificant β coefficient (t-ratio: -0.23, $R^2 = -0.04$). For the bottom 20 countries β is positive (1.80) and highly significant (t: 3.06; $R^2 = 0.31$). One implication of these estimates is the relative weakness of systematic forces in leading to convergence on the one hand, and the tendency of some countries to 'self-organise' in vicious circles of backwardness on the other.

The dynamics of imports and exports are, in this model, the *ex post* outcome of sector-specific international competition together with country-wide adjustments, which in turn affect the competitiveness of single firms. Thus, 'comparative advantages' are the *ex post* outcome of innovation, imitation and selection. In some countries this process leads to specialisation. In others, the dynamics of absolute advantage/disadvantage is similar across sectors (with an increasing technology gap rather homogeneous across the two sectors).

6. CONCLUSIONS

What is surprising regarding the foregoing model is that, despite its rather simple structure, it generates a quite rich array of phenomena. They encompass micro heterogeneity, innovation and diffusion, the cyclical and long-term behaviour of aggregate time series, convergence and divergence, absolute and comparative advantages and trade. The story which the model tells is basically one of a process with no 'ingredients' or 'factors' to begin with. What at a certain point in the sequence may appear to be such is in fact the endogenous result of past processes of self-organisation. And the two twin driving forces are learning and market selection.

We would like to consider this model as an example of an evolutionary microfoundation consistent, at least in principle, with other more structured, more aggregate and not necessarily microfounded analyses. This evolutionary microstructure is certainly consistent with and complementary to the intuitions which have inspired a number of developments in growth theory regarding country-specific characteristics and institutions, threshold effects and externalities. We suggest that these properties are, if anything, magnified whenever one does not attempt to force them into the standard microeconomic framework.

Moreover, the emphasis on learning de-coupled from optimal allocation processes is a common element shared by evolutionary models and models of Kaldorian inspiration. For example, it is easy to imagine co-evolutionary processes of innovation and capital accumulation (or lack of them) leading to self-reinforcing divergent patterns of development which might rest on microfoundations of the kind outlined above. In a similar vein, one could envision fruitful links with models of cumulative divergence and catching-up and with growth models which derive the long-term properties of the economy from some general assumptions about the nature of learning and of innovation-embodying capital accumulation.

These suggestions, of course, entail a rich research agenda. It overlaps with a few equilibrium-cum-rationality agendas in the thrust to place knowledge, innovation and increasing returns at the centre of growth theory, but it departs from them above all in the assumptions about how agents behave, how learning takes place and how markets work. Putting it somewhat loosely, evolutionary approaches focus on the analysis of what in standard production functions is the $A(t)$ dynamics and, further, claim that this is sufficient to incorporate all the microeconomic action without invoking any underlying notion of general equilibrium. In this preliminary study we have tried to demonstrate that this approach holds the promise of interpreting a few stylised facts and 'stylised processes' of international economic development.

NOTES

1. See also Dosi *et al.* (1992).
2. Most new growth endeavours have, if anything, increased the demands on the rational abilities of their 'representative agents'. For example, the predictions of many of these models stand or fall with rational technological expectations. Moreover, in the 'new-growth' literature it is very difficult to get any intuition on the nature of out-of-equilibrium adjustments, while stability results have yet to be obtained.
3. On this issue see, for example, Durlauf and Johnson (1992) and Benhabib and Jovanovic (1991).
4. See Nelson and Winter (1982), Iwai (1984a,b), Metcalfe (1988), Silverberg, Dosi and Orsenigo (1988), Conlisk (1989), Chiaromonte and Dosi (1992).
5. This interpretative conjecture – according to which some form of 'order' is a disequilibrium property – although quite revolutionary in economics, is increasingly corroborated in quite a few other disciplines.
6. In another version of the model, not presented here, we impose a learning externality, so that the probability of innovation also depends on the amount of search undertaken by all other firms within the country and in the world:

$$IN_{ij} (t) = \sum_{\tau=0}^{2} Inn_{ij} (t-\tau) + \alpha_{1j} \sum_{\tau=0}^{2} Inn_{totj} (t-\tau) + \alpha_{2j} \sum_{\tau=0}^{2} Inn_{tot} (t-\tau).$$

7. This is like saying that credit is rationed for individual firms and may constrain individual growth. Note that there is no aggregate ceiling to credit (say, via exogenous money supply). Our assumption is near the Kaldorian idea of 'endogenous money'. Call $C_{ij}(t)$ the net cash flows. The (credit-constrained) maximum growth of a firm is:

$$Y_{ij} (t+1)_{max} \leq (1 + a_{5j})(Y_{ij} (t) + \sum_{\tau=0}^{t} C_{ij} (\tau))$$

where a_{5j} is a leverage parameter.
8. In one of the implementations of the model, we assume that $E_{ij}^{lk} = E_{ij}(1-y)$ if $i \neq k$. The parameter y ($0<y<1$) stands for various 'imperfections' on export markets, e.g. transport costs, set-up obstacles in foreign markets, etc.
9. A way of visualising the mechanism is by imagining that, at the beginning of each period, firms announce their prices on every market and correspondingly receive their orders which they prepare to fulfil (up to some maximum growth constraint; if the latter is binding, then unfulfillable demand is distributed to the other suppliers, in proportion to their market shares). In turn, customers do not instantaneously move to the lowest price producers, due to, for example, imperfect information, brand loyalties, adjustment costs, and so on (of course, this would apply, *a fortiori*, in the more general case of differentiated products).
10. This selection dynamics draws on Silverberg, Dosi and Orsenigo (1988). In the particular case in which the best techniques are stationary, it entails sigmoid diffusion patterns.
11. Define an 'income-normalised' balance as $S_j = B_j / Y_j$. Then define

$$\dot{r} (t,t+1) = a_{11} S_j (t) \exp \{a_{12} \mid \sum_{\tau=0}^{t} S_j (t) \mid \},$$

and

$$r_j (t+1) = [1 + \dot{r} (t,t+1)] r_j (t).$$

12. Unit roots tests not shown here reject, at the 5% level, the hypothesis that neither the original series nor the detrended ones are a random walk.

REFERENCES

Abramovitz, M. (1989), *Thinking about Growth*, Cambridge: Cambridge University Press.

Abramovitz, M. (1992), 'American Economic Growth in the Twentieth Century. Historical and International Perspectives', Stanford University, mimeo.

Aghion, P. and Howitt, P. (1992), 'A Model of Growth through Creative Destruction', *Econometrica*, 60, 323–351.

Amable, B. (1992), 'National Effects of Learning, International Specialization and Growth Paths', in C. Freeman and D. Foray (eds), *Technology and the Wealth of Nations*, London: Pinter.

Aoki, M. and Dosi, G. (1992), 'Corporate Organization, Finance and Innovation', in V. Zamagni, *Finance and the Enterprise*, New York: Academic Press.

Azariadis, C. and Drazen, A. (1990), 'Threshold Externalities in Economic Development', *Quarterly Journal of Economics*, 105, 501–526.

Bairoch, P. (1981), 'The Main Trends in National Economic Disparities since the Industrial Revolution', in P. Bairoch and M. Levy-Loboyer (eds), *Disparities in Economic Development since the Industrial Revolution*, London: Macmillan.

Benhabib, J. and Jovanovic, B. (1991), 'Externalities and Growth Accounting', *American Economic Review*, 81, 82–113.

Benhabib, J. and Spiegel, M.M. (1992), 'The Role of Human Capital and Political Instability in Economic Development', New York University, mimeo.

Boyer, R. (1988a), 'Technical Change and the Theory of Regulation' in G. Dosi, C. Freeman, R. Nelson, G. Silverberg and L. Soete (eds), *Technical Change and Economic Theory*, London: Pinter.

Boyer, R. (1988b), 'Formalizing Growth Regimes', in G. Dosi, C. Freeman, R. Nelson, G. Silverberg and L. Soete (eds), *Technical Change and Economic Theory*, London: Pinter.

Brezis, E., Krugman, P. and Isiodon, D. (1991), 'Leapfrogging: a Theory of Cycles in National Technological Leadership', *NBER Working Paper*, No. 3886.

Cheng, L.K. and Dinopoulos, E. (1992), 'Schumpeterian Growth and International Business Cycles', *American Economic Review, Papers and Proceedings* 82, 409–414.

Chiaromonte, F. and Dosi, G. (1992), 'The Microfoundation of Competitiveness and their Macroeconomic Implications', in C. Freeman and D. Foray (eds), *Technology and the Wealth of Nations*, London: Pinter.

Conlisk, J. (1989), 'An Aggregate Model of Technical Change', *Quarterly Journal of Economics*, 104, 787–821.

David, P. (1975), *Technical Choice, Innovation and Economic Growth*, Cambridge: Cambridge University Press.

De Long, B.J. (1988), 'Productivity Growth, Convergence and Welfare', *American Economic Review*, 78, 1138–1154.

De Long, B.J. and Summers, L.H. (1991), 'Equipment Investment and Economic Growth', *Quarterly Journal of Economics*, 106, 445–502.

De Long, B.J. and Summers, L.H. (1992), 'How Robust is the Growth–Machinery Nexus', Harvard University, mimeo.

Denison, E.F. and Poullier, J.P. (1967), *Why Growth Rates Differ*, Washington, DC: Brookings Institution.

Dosi, G. (1982), 'Technological Paradigms and Technological Trajectories', *Research*

Policy, 11, 147–162.

Dosi, G. (1988), 'Sources, Procedures and Microeconomic Effects of Innovation', *Journal of Economic Literature*, 26, 1120–1171.

Dosi, G. and Egidi, M. (1991), 'Substantive and Procedural Uncertainty', *Journal of Evolutionary Economics*, 1, 145–168.

Dosi, G., Freeman, C., Fabiani, S. and Aversi, R. (1992), 'On the Processes of Development', CCC Working Paper, Berkeley, CA: Center for Research in Management.

Dosi, G., Freeman, C., Nelson, R., Silverberg, G. and Soete, L. (eds) (1988), *Technical Change and Economic Theory*, London: Pinter.

Dosi, G., Pavitt, K. and Soete, L. (1990), *The Economics of Technological Change and International Trade*, London: Wheatsheaf/Harvester Press.

Durlauf, S.N. (1992), 'Path Dependence in Aggregate Output', Stanford University, mimeo.

Durlauf, S.N. and Johnson, P.A. (1992), 'Local versus Global Convergence across National Economies', Stanford University, mimeo.

Easterly, W., King, R., Levine, R. and Rebelo, S. (1991), 'How do National Policies affect Long Run Growth?', *World Bank Working Paper*, WPS 794.

Fabiani, S. (1990), *Dinamica Tecnologica e Commercio Internazionale: Il Processo di Differenziazione tra Paesi*, Graduation Thesis, University of Rome, Department of Economics.

Fagerberg, J. (1988), 'Why Growth Rates Differ', in G. Dosi, C. Freeman, R. Nelson, G. Silverberg and L. Soete (eds), *Technical Change and Economic Theory*, London: Pinter.

Fagerberg, J. (1991), 'The Impact of Technology on Why Growth Rates Differ', Paper prepared for the Workshop on International Macro-Dynamics, November 1991, MERIT, Maastricht.

Freeman, C. (1982), *The Economics of Industrial Innovation*, London: Pinter.

Freeman, C. (1987), *Technology Policy and Economic Performance*, London: Pinter.

Freeman, C. and Perez, C. (1988), 'Structural Crises of Adjustment', in G. Dosi, C. Freeman, R. Nelson, G. Silverberg and L. Soete (eds), *Technical Change and Economic Theory*, London: Pinter.

Grossman, G.M. and Helpman, E. (1991), *Innovation and Growth. Technological Competition in the Global Economy*, Cambridge, Mass.: MIT Press.

Heiner, R.A. (1988), 'Imperfect Decisions and Routinized Production: Implications for Evolutionary Modelling and Inertial Technical Change', in G. Dosi, C. Freeman, R. Nelson, G. Silverberg and L. Soete (eds), *Technical Change and Economic Theory*, London: Pinter.

Iwai, K. (1984a), 'Schumpeterian Dynamics: an Evolutionary Model of Innovation and Imitation', *Journal of Economic Behaviour and Organization*, 5, 159–190.

Iwai, K. (1984b), 'Schumpeterian Dynamics, Part II: Technological Progress, Firm Growth and "Economic Selection" ', *Journal of Economic Behaviour and Organization*, 5, 321–351.

Jovanovic, B. and Lach, S. (1991), 'The Diffusion of Technology and Inequality among Nations', *NBER Working Paper*, No. 3732.

Jovanovic, B. and Rob, R. (1989), 'The Growth and Diffusion of Knowledge', *Review of Economic Studies*, 56, 569–582.

Jovanovic, B. and Rob, R. (1990), 'Long Waves and Short Waves: Growth Through Intensive and Extensive Search', *Econometrica*, 58, 1391–1409.

Justman, M. and Teubal, M. (1991), 'A Structuralist Perspective on the Role of Technology in Economic Growth and Development', *World-Development*, 19.

Kaldor, N. (1985), *Economics without Equilibrium*, Cardiff: University College Cardiff Press.

King, R.G., Plosser, C.I. and Rebelo, S.T. (1988), 'Production, Growth and Business Cycles', *Journal of Monetary Economics*, 21, 195–232 and 309–341.

Klepper, S. and Graddy, E. (1990), 'The Evolution of New Industries and the Determinants of Market Structure', *Rand Journal of Economics*, 21, 27–44.

Landes, D. (1969), *The Unbounded Prometheus*, Cambridge: Cambridge University Press.

Lewis, W.A. (1954), 'Economic Development with Unlimited Supply of Labour', *The Manchester School*.

Lucas, R.E.B. (1988), 'On the Mechanisms of Economic Development', *Journal of Monetary Economics*, 22, 3–42.

Lundvall, B.-Å. (1988), 'Innovation as an Interactive Process: from User–Producer Interactions to the National System of Innovation', in G. Dosi, C. Freeman, R. Nelson, G. Silverberg and L. Soete (eds), *Technical Change and Economic Theory*, London: Pinter.

Lundvall, B.-Å. (ed.) (1992), *National Systems of Innovation – Toward a Theory of Innovation and Interactive Learning*, London: Pinter.

Maddison, A. (1982), *Phases of Capitalist Development*, Oxford: Oxford University Press.

Maddison, A. (1991), *Dynamic Forces in Capitalist Development*, Oxford: Oxford University Press.

Maddison, A. (1992), 'Explaining the Economic Performance of Nations: 1820–1989', in W.J. Baumol, R.R. Nelson and E.N. Wolff (eds), *International Convergence of Productivity*, New York: Oxford University Press (forthcoming).

Metcalfe, S. (1988),'The Diffusion of Innovation: an Interpretative Survey', in G. Dosi, C. Freeman, R. Nelson, G. Silverberg and L. Soete (eds), *Technical Change and Economic Theory*, London: Pinter.

Murphy, K.M., Shleifer, A. and Vishny, R.W. (1989), 'Industrialization and the Big Push', *Journal of Political Economy*, 97, 1003–1026.

Nelson, R.R. (ed.) (1992), *National Systems of Innovation*, Cambridge: Cambridge University Press.

Nelson, R. and Phelps, E.S. (1966), 'Investment in Humans, Technological Diffusion and Economic Growth', *American Economic Review*, 56, 69–75.

Nelson, R. and Winter, S. (1982), *An Evolutionary Theory of Economic Change*, Cambridge, MA: The Belknap Press of Harvard University Press.

Pasinetti, L. (1982), *Structural Change and Economic Growth*, Cambridge: Cambridge University Press.

Pavitt, K. and Soete, L. (1981), 'International Differences in Economic Growth and the International Location of Innovation', in Herbert Giersch (ed.), *Emerging Technologies: Consequences for Economic Growth, Structural Change and Employment*, Tübingen: Mohr.

Perez, C. and Soete, L. (1988), 'Catching up in Technology: Entry Barriers and Windows of Opportunity', in G. Dosi, C. Freeman, R. Nelson, G. Silverberg and L. Soete (eds), *Technical Change and Economic Theory*, London: Pinter.

Romer, P.M. (1986), 'Increasing Returns and Long-run Growth', *Journal of Political Economy*, 91, 1001–1037.

Romer, P.M. (1990), 'Endogenous Technological Change', *Journal of Political*

Economy, 98, 71–102.

Rosenberg, N. (1976), *Perspectives on Technology*, Cambridge: Cambridge University Press.

Rosenberg, N. (1982), *Inside the Black Box*, Cambridge: Cambridge University Press.

Scott, M.F.G. (1991), 'A New View of Economic Growth', *World Bank Discussion Paper*, No. 131.

Segerstrom, P.S., Anant, T.C.A. and Dinopoulos, E. (1990), 'A Schumpeterian Model of the Product Life Cycle', *American Economic Review*, 80, 1077–1091.

Silverberg, G., Dosi, G. and Orsenigo, L. (1988), 'Innovation, Diversity and Diffusion. A Self-Organization Model', *Economic Journal*, 98, 1032–1054.

Soete, L. and Verspagen, B. (1992), 'Technology and Growth. The Complex Dynamics of Catching Up, Falling Behind and Taking Over', in A. Szirmai, B. van Ark and D. Pilat (eds), *Explaining Economic Growth*, Amsterdam: Elsevier.

Solow, R. (1956), 'A Contribution to the Theory of Economic Growth', *Quarterly Journal of Economics*, 70, 65–94.

Solow, R. (1957), 'Technical Change and the Aggregate Production Function', *Review of Economics and Statistics*, 39, 312–320.

Stiglitz, J.E. (1992), 'Explaining Growth: Competition and Finance', Paper prepared for the Villa Mondragone International Economic Seminar on 'Differences in the Rates of Growth', July 1992, Rome.

Verspagen, B. (1991a), 'A New Empirical Approach to Catching Up or Falling Behind', *Structural Change and Economic Dynamics*, 2, 359–380.

Verspagen, B. (1991b), 'Specialization, Competitiveness and Growth Rate Differentials: a Multi-Sector Evolutionary Model with Neo-Keynesian Characteristics (MARK II)', *MERIT Research Memorandum 91-020*.

Verspagen, B. (1992), 'Technology and Growth: The Complex Dynamics of Convergence and Divergence', Paper prepared for the Conference on 'Convergence and Divergence in Economic Growth and Technical Change', Maastricht, MERIT, December 1992.

Young, A. (1991), 'Learning by Doing and Dynamic Effects of International Trade', *Quarterly Journal of Economics*, 106.

Zamagni, V. (ed.) (1992), *Finance and the Enterprise*, New York: Academic Press.

COMMENT ON DOSI AND FABIANI

Franz Palm

Let me start by congratulating the authors for having written a very stimulating and interesting paper which, because of its preliminary nature, is but a first step along a potentially fruitful line of research. I welcome alternative microfounded approaches to explain the dynamics of growth.

In the paper, the authors develop a large-scale, dynamic, stochastic model based on the evolutionary approach and they show by simulation that the model is capable of producing trend-stationary income series, high positive first-, second- and third-order autocorrelations of the detrended income series, strong evidence of diverging growth for the countries as a whole, for the developing countries and some evidence, although not significant, of convergent growth for developed countries.

My comments can be subdivided into three parts. First, I briefly comment on the structure of the theoretical model. Second, a few remarks will be made on the fit of the model to the stylised facts. Third, I discuss the approach in relationship with alternative approaches and possible extensions of the current work.

C1 The Theoretical Model

The world economy is represented using a large-scale multicountry two-sector model. The simulation experiments are obtained for 55 countries. From the beginning, the reader gets the impression that the insight becomes blurred by an abundance of details and that the main features of the behaviour of the model could be generated without including the details for 55 countries.

The model is dynamic and stochastic. Several features of the model immediately appear. The decision rules or routines are quite simple and mechanic. Feedback mechanisms and learning do not play an important role. Forward-looking behaviour is almost absent despite the fact that uncertainty is an intrinsic part of the model. Much emphasis, possibly too much, is put on the importance of inertia in the system. The rationale for this is adjustment costs, uncertainty, routine. Also, it is not clear which objective economic agents pursue according to the model. Are they striving for survival? Obviously, they are not profit maximisers.

While I am a proponent too of using simple rules and assumptions whenever appropriate, I have some difficulty in accepting some of the assumptions made. Let me give a few examples:

1. A fixed proportion of the labour force employed in R&D is involved in innovation (re)search. Should this proportion not depend on expected opportunities for progress? If, for instance, innovations have been made recently outside the firm it may become profitable to shift additional resources into search for imitation instead of looking for decreasing returns to scale from innovative (re)search.
2. For the exchange rates and for wages, sophisticated adjustment processes are postulated. For prices, a simple mark-up rule is applied. Would it have been difficult to assume that the mark-up factor varies with the market share or some other indicator of market power?
3. The economic system is not constrained in terms of labour supply. This assumption may be reasonable as far as unskilled labour is concerned. Once different types of labour with different skills are introduced in the model, this assumption may no longer be appropriate. Physical capital is absent from the model. With labour being abundantly available and no physical capital being required for production, the economies in the model can enjoy the use of unlimited resources.
4. Assuming that dead firms are replaced by new entrants with average productivity and not allowing for additional entry is not what I understand by Schumpeter's concept of creative destruction.

These examples illustrate how the model could be enriched and made more realistic in a straightforward way without leaving the world of evolutionary economics.

C2 Fitting Stylised Facts

Next I should like to comment on the extent to which the model fits the stylised facts. In the simulations, the model generates the kinds of patterns which have been found in the data for several countries. In particular, the model generates divergent growth patterns, deterministic trends in income, and high positive serial correlation in detrended income.

When the latter two measures are taken, the model behaves as well as real business cycle models augmented with an exogenous autoregressive process for technology shocks. It would be interesting to investigate whether this model or variants of it and alternative models such as the new growth models behave in a similar fashion when the other overidentifying restrictions are checked against the information in macroeconomic and sectoral time series using an extended econometric analysis. The interesting question then would be which model explains facts that until now were left unexplained.

With respect to the time-series properties of income generated by the model, I am not convinced that the finding that income is trend-stationary (as opposed to difference-stationarity) is really in line with the current state of our knowledge about dynamic properties of GNP for many countries. The properties of the model could be compared with the empirical evidence for several countries, not just the US. For instance, for eight out of sixteen OECD countries, Schotman and van Dijk (1990) report evidence in favour of a unit root in the log of real GNP for the sample period 1948–1987, whereas for the remaining eight countries the odds ratio of trend stationarity versus difference stationarity is approximately equal to one.

The test of the catching-up hypothesis in section 5 may not yield robust results. The test is applied in a situation where some countries converge, others do not. The test does not account for the effect of the different states to which the countries grow. In this case, as shown by e.g. Bernard and Durlauf (1992), the outcome of the test may be very sensitive to the type of data used.

As the graph in Figure 6.2 is dominated by series for which initial income is an indicator of future success, it is not surprising that the catching-up hypothesis is rejected. It would also be rejected – I guess – in most cases when the tests were applied to subsets of countries. The rich variety of growth pattern (catching up, falling behind, overtaking) promised in the introduction does not emerge in Figure 6.2. In the sample shown in Figure 6.2, while starting from the same per capita income level, some countries grow fast. Others follow for a while and then fall back. With one exception, no country really overtakes the others in terms of income per employed person. The graph does not exhibit convergence within groups of countries. The simulation experiment does not seem to generate the growth patterns found in real-life multicountry data on per capita income which exhibit within-group convergence and inter-group divergence. The findings shown in Figure 6.2 raise questions about the properties of the mechanisms which generate them. At the starting point, all firms are identical and unconstrained in their resources. Why then are some countries successful while other countries are faced with a worsening economic outlook? Could success be mainly determined by the stochastic process which generates the innovations and imitations, combined with an overdose of inertia? If a country experiences technological success at the beginning, its growth may take off, whereas if it gets confronted with technological failures at the start because of factors of inertia such as the absence of forward-looking behaviour and learning, the country gets locked into a path of slow growth, stagnation or decline.

C3 The Approach

Again, I think that analyses such as the present one are extremely useful to get insights into the dynamics of macroeconomic and sectoral data. But one should go beyond what the authors have done in trying to see whether the data allow us to discriminate among rival models, for instance growth models in the new classical tradition and models formulated in the spirit of evolutionary theory. Extensive simulation of these models may help us to understand their behaviour and to see what kind of patterns the outcomes of the simulations have.

Questions such as do the graphs in Figure 6.2 correspond to the mean of the distribution of the response of the model, what does this distribution look like, how robust are the simulation results, what type of equilibria and how many does the model generate, should be addressed. Will per capita income evolve monotonically over time or will it reach turning points? Is it really appropriate to take as a starting point a stationary situation with identical firms when the purpose of the analyses is to study typically nonstationary processes? What generates the nonstationarities? Would the introduction of additional feedback mechanisms modify the outcomes in an important way? Does the model generate obvious opportunities of unexploited profits which could lead to the entry of new firms or expansion of existing firms? Are the stochastic features really endogenous? These are a few of the exciting questions that could be addressed with the model using the technology developed by the authors. I would warmly welcome studies which take up some of these issues.

Michael Wolfson:

I have a few questions which concern the robustness of the model. The simulation begins with all countries being identical, though your stylised facts show that they are a bit different. How similar would the results be if you started with some differences? Second, can you think of one or two mechanisms in the model that would produce convergence rather than divergence? Third, would the results and the conclusions differ if you did fifty or a hundred replicates of exactly the same initial conditions?

Giovanni Dosi:

Both Michael Wolfson and Franz Palm ask one similar question: what is the feedback nature inside the model that produces either divergence or convergence? The model leads to convergence if imitation is made very easy or if the selection parameter is low, so that firms do not pay as dearly for their mistakes. My intuition is that countries would tend to be identical if imitation is made very easy and the rate of transition from technological success to growth is slow. In respect to the robustness of the model, we tried different simulations by varying the mean of the Poisson process between 4 and 16%. In general, the model still tended to produce divergence more than convergence.

Richard Nelson:

Does anyone want to respond to Giovanni's proposal in his presentation that this might be an ugly-looking model compared to the elegant new breed of neoclassical models by discussing if beauty and elegance are in the eyes of the beholder? It is a more complex model with more variables and more structure, but on the other hand it generates more output.

Michael Wolfson:

I was struck by the fact that even though this model is best thought of in computer science terms, you choose to illustrate it through a series of obscure mathematical equations. I wonder if the reason that you call the model ugly is because you look at it in terms of neoclassical mathematical formulae. I think that the model would appear much more elegant if it was presented, as in computer science, as a flow chart.

Paul Romer:

Giovanni has been hoping for a shoot-out between the new-growth guys and the evolutionary guys for some time and I am going to let him down again. I'm not a fan of shoot-outs, I'm very much a Maoist on this issue – let a thousand flowers bloom. I would like to state what motivates me and why there is room for a diversity of approaches.

One of the overriding problems of economics is that it is a non-experimental science. This creates problems for the big questions that we care about, such as what determines long-term growth or what we can do to enhance growth in a particular country, because we can't run large experiments. Our only hope for making progress is to have strong communication links between the large 'big picture' questions and the micro approach where it is possible to find a few naturally occurring small experiments or where we can even have a few controlled experiments. These experiments can help us to understand endogeneity and causality and perhaps allow us to make some robust inferences. I think that both Giovanni and I would agree that we need models that can span the whole distance from the micro to the macro.

I also have a strong belief in the cumulative nature of scientific inquiry. My job is to build as much as possible on all the evidence that we have built up in the last 100 years in economics and to try to expand our understanding. This makes my approach somewhat conservative. I tend to drop one or two restrictive assumptions at a time, rather than make a big leap by changing a large number of assumptions. For example, my current work is involved in a debate in the US on whether or not it is still acceptable to assume perfect price-taking. I argue that we must move away from this assumption. However, I'm not simultaneously debating how myopic or forward-looking agents are. Conversely, the evolutionary approach tries to make much bigger leaps.

Kenneth Arrow:
I have some comments in respect to diffusion processes in the model. I was struck by the figure which shows the enormous variation among countries which start out being identical and with no structural differences. It would be easy to understand these differences if the figure was for firms rather than countries, since the differences are due to an accumulation of stochastic events, but what is the justification for these differences among different countries? The only assumption that can support this difference is that cross-country diffusion is slower than diffusion within a country. This can occur if the probability of finding someone to imitate declines as the distance, in some sense, increases.

Distance is made of the difference across countries versus within the same country. As an aside, this difference may or may not be relevant in a modern world with multinational corporations and similar elites. Yet, imagine a world in which, by historical accident, countries are divided among a high and a low level of economic productivity. If a low-level country imitates at all, it is going to imitate the higher productivity level. In contrast, suppose that there are many different countries with different productivity levels. In this world the countries with the lowest productivity levels are going to gain much more slowly than in the first case because they are more likely to imitate countries with productivity levels close to their own.

Is there any empirical evidence to support the hypothesis that countries are more likely to imitate countries with a productivity level close to their own? Ten or so years ago the US was always taken as the country to imitate. No one said that Italy was imitating The Netherlands, or that Spain was imitating Italy. This also introduces a problem between similarity in knowledge and similarity in productivity because the two differ. A country may be better able to imitate another country with a similar level of knowledge, but productivity may not be the proper measure of knowledge.

Giovanni Dosi:

Ken has raised two questions. The first is what makes countries different as opposed to differences between firms in the same country? The answer is that the distance mechanism implies that it is easier to imitate within a country than outside of it and therefore this produces homogenisation within countries. How realistic this distance assumption is in a world of multinational companies is another matter. Another mechanism for differentiation between countries is as follows. A successful company can expand on international markets, leading to a type of Keynesian mercantilist feedback mechanism where the income of the country where the firm is based increases. This results in an increase in investment in R&D in that country and an increase in the probability, in the next round, of finding a new innovation.

The second question is whether countries imitate their neighbours or the country with the best practice? Latin Americans often discuss imitating Spain or Italy and comment that they will never be able to imitate the US or Japan because the corporate and institutional context there is too different. If one views learning as path-dependent and incremental, then countries should try to imitate their technological neighbours, even though they may aim for the best.

Richard Nelson:

Discussions of this type of model invariably lead to a call for more realistic assumptions. Yet of perhaps greater importance is what larger questions are raised by these models. This model raises important questions about the imitation target for firms in poor countries and strongly calls out for a theoretical–empirical dialogue on this issue.

References

Bernard, A.B. and Durlauf, S.N. (1992), 'Interpreting Tests of the Convergence Hypotheses', Stanford University technical report.

Schotman, P. and van Dijk, H.K. (1990), 'Posterior Analysis of Possibly Integrated Time Series with an Application to Real GNP', forthcoming in Parzen, E. *et al.* (eds), *New Directions in Time Series Analysis*, Berlin: Springer Verlag.

7. Technology and Growth: the Complex Dynamics of Convergence and Divergence

Bart Verspagen[*]

1. INTRODUCTION

The notion that investment in endogenous technological change is at the core of the wealth of nations was already present in the work of many classical economists (such as Smith, Ricardo and Marx), and has recently entered the mainstream neoclassical theory in the form of so-called new growth models (for an overview, see Verspagen 1992a). The basic question that these models, as their more heterodox counterparts in the so-called evolutionary or neo-Schumpeterian traditions,[1] try to answer is in what way technological change influences the growth of welfare in an economy.

The empirical literature on the interaction between technology and growth, which started long before endogenous innovation entered mainstream theoretical models, has also looked at this question. There are two large empirical streams of literature on the relation between growth and technology. The first one starts from the notion that R&D, that is, investment in science and technology, can be viewed as an additional production factor, entering the production function in much the same way as various types of fixed capital or labour. One specific characteristic of R&D in this approach, however, is that it brings some important externalities with it (as in the theoretical new growth models). The main contribution of this approach, which is reviewed in Mohnen (1992), is to estimate the marginal productivities of various types of R&D investment, either at the firm, sectoral or aggregate level, as well as to establish the influence of R&D spillovers.

The second stream of literature that tries to establish an empirical

[*] I thank Bronwyn H. Hall for helpful suggestions, Luc Soete for helpful suggestions and comments, Erik Beelen for research assistance, and Jan Fagerberg as well as participants at the conference for comments on the first draft. The usual disclaimer applies.

relation between knowledge accumulation and growth of output or productivity focuses on cross-country samples. Intercountry knowledge spillovers are the most important factor with regard to knowledge accumulation found here. One important hypothesis in this field is that relatively backward countries should grow faster than advanced countries, because they are able to imitate technological knowledge and thereby converge to the frontier value of per capita income rapidly. The issue of spillovers in this approach is not, as in the above-mentioned one, so closely connected to R&D, but instead relates in a general way to cross-country differences in (initial) (labour) productivity. Early examples of this approach are Gerschenkron (1962) and Cornwall (1977). More recently, the work of Abramovitz (1979, 1986, 1992) in this area is noteworthy.

With the advent of new growth theory, an additional factor that has been taken into account in these cross-country estimates of growth rates is human capital (for example, Mankiw, Romer and Weil 1992; Baumol, Batey Blackman and Wolff 1989). Patel and Soete (1985), Fagerberg (1988) and Lichtenberg (1992) take into account R&D as an explaining factor.

The aim of this paper is in a sense broader than the above-mentioned approaches. One way of interpreting the latter is to say that each of them focuses on a specific subset of knowledge accumulation modes, that is, either general intercountry spillovers leading to convergence, more specific R&D spillovers, or accumulation of (self-developed) R&D capital. The motivation for this paper lies in the fact that one can indeed relate these different aspects of the technological process to different technology indicators. I shall present and estimate an analytical model in which each of these aspects has its own influence on growth.

The inroad into this problem will be the question whether different aspects of technology have had a converging or diverging influence on the growth paths of OECD countries over the postwar period. In other words, which technological factors have led to a more even distribution of welfare in the world, and which ones have had the opposite effect?

Section 2 of the paper will therefore start with a sketch of the general empirical facts about convergence and divergence in per capita income over the twentieth century. The third section will then develop a model in which the different aspects of technological change and their influence on growth will be outlined. The model will be used in estimations for a cross-country sample of 1970–1985 growth paths, as well as in a panel dataset for yearly growth rates over the 1969–1987 period.

The fourth section will come back to the issue of convergence and divergence and try to develop an analytical framework identifying different empirical sources for any specific convergence or divergence trends in the data. This technique will be applied using some of the parameter estimates and data from section 3, thereby arriving at a suggested answer to the key problem of the paper. Section 5 will summarise the main arguments and conclusions

2. CONVERGENCE AND DIVERGENCE: THE HISTORICAL PERSPECTIVE

The history of postwar growth in the OECD area has been dominated by convergence. Numerous contributions[2] have shown that the poorest countries in the OECD have increased per capita GDP at the highest rate. At the same time, however, it is clear that in a sample larger than just the OECD, this simple negative linear relation between per capita income and subsequent growth rates is not valid (see, among others, Verspagen 1991). This paper will concentrate on the OECD,[3] thereby limiting the analysis to the industrialised, developed world. Recognising that the developing countries' problems are quite different from the ones that highly developed countries face, it is not suggested at any point that the conclusions have a more general, worldwide validity.

This section presents some empirical evidence on the growth trends in a sub-OECD sample of countries over the entire twentieth century. The specific aim is to find out to what extent the convergence trend is specific to the postwar period (as suggested, for example, by Abramovitz 1992), and whether convergence is likely to continue into the future.

In order to test for convergence or divergence trends over the twentieth century, the following simple statistical test is applied. First, define a variable W as follows:

$$W_{it} = \ln \frac{Q_{it}}{P_{it}} - \ln \left(\frac{Q_t}{P_t} \right)^*. \tag{7.1}$$

In this definition, Q denotes GDP, P is population, subscripts i and t denote a country and time, respectively, and superscript * denotes a sample average. W is the log of the ratio of per capita GDP in country i and the sample average. Following Ben-David (1991), it is assumed that for each period $t-t+1$, W changes according to the following process:

$$W_{it+1} = \Psi W_{it}. \tag{7.2}$$

If $\Psi > 1$, per capita income differences diverge; if $\Psi < 1$, convergence takes place.[4]

Using these definitions, Ψ is estimated for different periods for a sample of 16 countries.[5] The source for the data is Maddison (1991). For each of the years 1903–1987 (t), a 'moving' panel-dataset is constructed with $W_{t-2}..W_{t+2}$ as the dependent variables, and $W_{t-3}..W_{t+1}$ as the independent variables, leading to 80 datapairs for each year.[6]

Figure 7.1 presents the estimated values of Ψ using the above procedure. These values are indicated by the solid line. The dashed lines indicate the calculated values $\Psi \pm 2\sigma$, with σ denoting the standard error of the estimated Ψ. Thus, since Ψ has to differ from unity for convergence of divergence to take place, one can (roughly) say that a non-significant result is obtained whenever the dashed lines 'embrace' the horizontal line.

Figure 7.1: Convergence and divergence in per capita GDP in the twentieth century

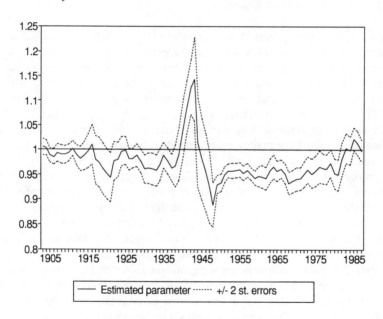

The figure shows that although in the prewar period there was some weak tendency towards convergence, the period 1950–1980 is the only one in which a *significant* convergence trend occurs. Moreover, convergence seems to have come to an end during the 1980s, with a trend break occurring in the late 1970s.

Two questions which arise from this analysis are: 'What factors can explain the convergence tendency over the postwar period?' and 'What factors can explain the slowdown in convergence since the late 1970s?'. In order to answer these questions, it is useful to start from two explanations for the convergence phenomenon found in the literature: capital accumulation and technological imitation (Helliwell 1992). A simple approach to long-run growth incorporating these two factors will be set out in the next section.

3. CONVERGENCE AND TECHNOLOGY: THE ROLE OF R&D, PATENTS AND TECHNOLOGY SPILLOVERS

3.1 Different Types of Knowledge

The recent renewed interest in (endogenous) growth theory has led to a large number of papers investigating the empirical role of various factors in explaining cross-country growth patterns.[7] Although many factors have turned up as significant in various regressions, there are only a few which seem to be able to stand out in more robust tests (see Levine and Renelt 1992). In spite of the attention in the new growth models to R&D as the key process in generating new technologies, empirical analyses of cross-country samples have mainly concentrated on human capital (education) as an indicator of the technological level of a country. As has already been mentioned in the introduction, Lichtenberg (1992), as well as some older studies (for example, Fagerberg 1988; Patel and Soete 1985), however, concentrate on R&D as a possible explanation of the growth process.

Empirical and theoretical models on the relation between R&D and growth at the firm or single-country level suggest that there is a relation between R&D and productivity growth.[8] In these studies, it has also been shown that R&D spillovers are a significant factor in explaining growth. Bearing these results in mind, a model is developed below in which different aspects of technological change will be measured by different technology indicators. The empirical analysis in this section therefore has two primary aims. The first is to see whether an empirical relation between differences in the rate of accumulation of knowledge and output growth can be observed in the data. The second is to see whether a distinction between various types of knowledge accumulation is significant in explaining growth rates.

While Lichtenberg (1992) estimates a model in the Solow (and more recently, Mankiw, Romer and Weil 1992) tradition, a much more technology-determined approach is presented here, incorporated in a simple Cobb–Douglas-based model. In a Solow-type model, the investment–output ratio (investment in fixed capital, human capital or research capital) determines the speed of the adjustment process which leads the growth path of an economy towards its long-run steady-state value. The model used here, in contrast to Lichtenberg (1992) and Fagerberg (1988), but similar to Patel and Soete (1985) and many firm-level studies, concentrates on differences in the *stock* of various types of knowledge and capital, rather than just the investment ratios. This approach is not in conflict with a Solow-type interpretation of the world, nor is it with a range of other interpretations, ranging from Romer-type new growth models to the more evolutionary inspired approaches to growth (Nelson and Winter 1982; Verspagen 1992b).

One useful distinction between different aspects of technological change is the one between innovation and imitation. The term innovation will be associated with an original contribution to the stock of knowledge in the (international) economy, while the term imitation will be used to represent the diffusion of knowledge to other agents than the original innovator. In this chapter, it will be assumed that it is possible to distinguish between technology indicators which measure these different aspects of technological change at the country level.

In light of this distinction, different technology indicators can be assigned different roles. R&D, perhaps the most widely used indicator, is clearly associated with both aspects, as it can be directed towards innovation as well as imitation (see, for example, Cohen and Levinthal 1989). Knowledge spillovers, however, are related exclusively to imitation, almost by definition. Patenting, on the other hand, can be considered to be connected more directly to innovation, as only truly new ideas can be patented.

With regard to knowledge spillovers, which are the prime way of measuring the effects of imitation, it will be assumed in this paper that they can take two forms: embodied and disembodied. Disembodied knowledge spillovers apply to general knowledge and principles, which can be used in some form or another in the production of (new) goods. An example is the knowledge found in engineering or science textbooks, which can be used by anyone who acquires them. Embodied knowledge spillovers, on the other hand, take place by using capital or intermediate goods developed by other, innovative producers. Viewed in this way, a computer embodies the knowledge developed (or applied) by its producer.

In the model below, a distinction between four different types of knowledge will be made: (general) R&D, new technologies appropriated by means of a patent, and embodied and disembodied knowledge spillovers. It will be assumed that the first three of these accumulate like a normal capital stock, with (gross) additions to the stock being formed by (gross) investment, and depreciation taking place with a fixed proportion each period. Disembodied knowledge spillovers are modelled as a flow, each period flowing from the advanced to the less-advanced countries.

3.2 A Model

The model used is similar with regard to structure to the one presented in Dowrick and Nguyen (1989). Uppercase symbols are used to express levels of variables, and lowercase symbols to express growth rates, defined for variable X as $\ln(X_t) - \ln(X_{t-1})$. The average annual growth rate of variable X over a period of length T is defined as x_T / T, and will be denoted by a lowercase symbol without a time index. Superscript *s are used to denote a variable which is scaled by its counterpart in some reference country, say country 1. Thus, $X^* = X_i / X_1$. The symbols Q, L, K and R_k are used to denote output, labour input, the capital stock and the knowledge stock of type k (representing the three types of 'accumulating' knowledge introduced above).

Assume that the production function is of Cobb–Douglas form, so that

$$\ln Q_{it} = A_i + \alpha \ln K_{it} + \beta \ln L_{it} + \sum_k \rho_k \ln R_{ikt} + \gamma t + \lambda \ln F_{it}. \quad (7.3)$$

A is a scale factor which is constant over time, γ is a constant component of the rate of growth of TFP, and F is a factor due to disembodied knowledge spillovers. Equation (7.3) differs from the one used in Dowrick and Nguyen in the sense that it regards the knowledge stock explicitly as a factor of production, thereby potentially making the TFP term smaller.

Assume next, as in Dowrick and Nguyen, that F is proportional to relative labour productivity (denoted by Y), so that

$$\frac{F_{it}}{F_{it-1}} = \frac{1}{Y^*_{it-1}}, \; Y_{it} = \frac{Q_{it}}{L_{it}}. \quad (7.4)$$

Substituting eq. (7.4) into (7.3), taking first differences of the resulting equation, expressing all variables relative to the reference country, and assuming that L, K and Q grow at a fixed rate, this expression can be rewritten to obtain

$$\ln Y^*_{it} = \alpha k^*_i + \sum_k \rho_k r^*_{ik} + (\beta-1) l^*_i + (1-\lambda) \ln Y^*_{it-1}. \quad (7.5)$$

In order to find an expression for long-run growth rates, this first-order difference equation can be solved to obtain

$$\ln Y_{iT}^* = (1-\lambda)^T \ln Y_{i0}^* + (\alpha k_i^* + \sum_k \rho_k r_{ik}^* + (\beta-1) l_i^*) \frac{1-(1-\lambda)^T}{\lambda}. \quad (7.6)$$

Solving this equation for the average annual growth rate of output over period $0-T$, one arrives at the following expressions:

$$q_i = c + \frac{\delta}{\lambda}(\alpha k_i + \sum_k \rho_k r_{ik}) + (1-\frac{\delta}{\lambda}(\beta-1))l_i - \delta \ln Y_{i0}^*,$$

$$c = (1-\frac{\delta}{\lambda})(\alpha k_1 + (\beta-1)l_1 + \sum_k \rho_k r_{1k}) + \gamma, \quad (7.7)$$

$$\delta = \frac{1-(1-\lambda)^T}{T} > 0.$$

This equation can be estimated. Note that the estimations obtained are not equal to the underlying Cobb–Douglas elasticities. Given the estimate of δ obtained on the last term on the rhs, however, one will be able to deduce estimates for α, β, ρ and λ.

3.3 Basic Estimations

First, some variants of eq. (7.7) including R&D stocks, the patent stock, disembodied knowledge spillovers, as well as the more conventional factors capital and labour will be estimated. Data on the growth rate of output, the growth rate of labour input, and initial labour productivity relative to the USA will be used.[9] Since a reliable dataset for capital stocks is not available for the cross-country sample used, the procedure used by Dowrick and Nguyen (1989), that is, taking the investment output ratio as a proxy for the growth rate of the capital stock, will be used. However, it is argued that while this procedure may be adequate in the case of fixed capital,[10] it is not for R&D. In fact, the data show that in general, the countries with low R&D-output ratios have realised the highest rates of growth of the R&D stock. To the extent that this argument is also valid for the case of fixed capital, the approach used probably misspecifies this part of the estimates. All variables, except initial labour productivity, are average growth rates over this period, defined in the manner described above.

  Studies at the firm level (see Mohnen 1992) have shown that the type of R&D and the source of funds matters (see also Lichtenberg 1992). Therefore, a distinction is made between total R&D (including government-financed and higher education R&D) and business enterprise

R&D (carried out by private firms, but possibly also financed partly by government). In the regressions, the growth rate of the business R&D stock ($R(bus)$), the non-business R&D stock ($R(nbus)$) and the total R&D stock (the sum of the two, denoted by $R(tot)$) are used separately. Other distinctions (for example, basic vs. applied R&D) are possible, but generally lead to fewer observations.

The equation is estimated for a cross-country[11] sample of 1970–1985 growth rates, which makes the results here quite different from the ones obtained in Dowrick and Nguyen (1989) or other similar regressions in earlier papers (for example, Abramovitz 1979; Baumol 1986), which look at growth over a longer period. The fact that the erratic growth path in the period under investigation here seems harder to explain than the 'stylised facts' of the 1950s and 1960s is therefore one source of the peculiar outcomes.

Table 7.1 gives the correlation coefficients between the variables in the analysis. The table shows that *a priori*, most variables have a fairly high degree of correlation to the dependent variable in the regressions, that is, the growth rate of output. Moreover, there are many cases in which the dependent variables themselves are highly correlated, for example initial labour productivity, which has strong (negative) correlations to almost any other variable in the table. The regressions are therefore likely to suffer from some degree of multicollinearity.

The results of the basic estimations are presented in Table 7.2. Following Levine and Renelt (1992), the effect of including or excluding various countries which have observations on the extremes of the (partial) scatterplot of R&D vs. growth has also been investigated (see Figures 7.2 and 7.3).[12] This is why the results in Table 7.2 are displayed for various samples of countries.

There are several features that emerge from Table 7.2. First, it is notable that the source of R&D funds matters: non-business R&D funds do not turn up as significant if put in a regression together with business R&D funds. If one uses the total R&D stock, however, this variable usually does turn up significantly. Second, the role of labour input is very significant.

The significance of the other variables differs with regard to the exact sample used, probably connected partly to multicollinearity in the data. The investment variable, the results of which are also influenced by the fact that the investment share of output is only a proxy for the actual growth rate, turns up significant in most cases, except in five equations where non-business R&D is included in some way, or whenever patents are indicated.

Table 7.1: Correlation matrix of the variables in the regressions

	q	i	l	$r(tot)$	$r(bus)$	$r(nbus)$	p	$\ln Y^*$
q	1.0							
i	0.35	1.0						
l	0.69	−0.12	1.0					
$r(tot)$	0.80	0.42	0.39	1.0				
$r(bus)$	0.83	0.29	0.58	0.90	1.0			
$r(nbus)$	0.51	0.36	0.17	0.83	0.72	1.0		
p	0.55	0.63	0.01	0.64	0.39	0.39	1.0	
$\ln Y^*$	−0.72	−0.36	−0.31	−0.78	−0.68	−0.54	−0.62	1.0

Figure 7.2: Growth of output and total R&D stock, 1970–1985, the cross-country sample

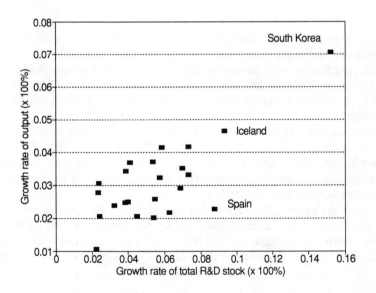

Figure 7.3: Growth of output and business R&D stock, 1970–1985, the cross-country sample

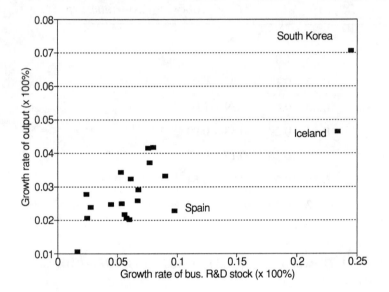

With regard to the innovation-related variables, the disembodied knowledge spillovers term has the correct sign, and is significant in most cases. Exceptions are cases where business R&D or business R&D and non-business R&D are the only other innovation variable(s). The role of the R&D variables, except for non-business R&D stock, is significant in all cases, except the equations excluding South Korea and Iceland (1c–4c). Patents are only significant in some cases, especially when investment is not included (this is not surprising, given the high correlation between patenting and investment in Table 7.1). This means that there is some, although limited, support for measuring different aspects of innovation by including both patents and R&D.

Using the estimated values of δ, one can deduct the 'true' underlying structural parameters in the Cobb–Douglas production function assumed. Given the results in Table 7.2, it appears that these values are quite close to (in fact, slightly higher than) the actual estimates obtained in the table.

3.4 Embodied Knowledge Spillovers

Following Mohnen (1992), the hypothesis that R&D spillovers can also be embodied in imported capital and intermediate goods will now be tested. Two different ways of measuring these knowledge spillovers will be applied. First, multiplying OECD-average sectoral R&D intensities[13] with national imports yields an assumed imported amount of embodied R&D (see the Appendix for data details). The yearly amounts that come out of this calculation are then used to construct the stock of imported R&D, using the above procedure. This stock is denoted by S_1. Second, technology payments to foreign countries (i.e., licences, technology transfer, etc.) are used to construct a stock of imported knowledge, again using the above procedure (see Appendix for data details). This stock is denoted by S_2.

The results of estimates including these two measures for embodied knowledge spillovers (separately) are documented in Table 7.3. Equations 1a–2a in the table show that neither of the estimates is significant. Therefore, a variant of the equation where the growth rates of embodied knowledge stocks are measured as the period–average ratio of yearly gross investment as a fraction of GDP (as has been done throughout with fixed investment) is presented. These estimates are documented as equations 1b–2b in the table. The results are basically the same, that is, no significant coefficient estimates are obtained.[14]

Although these results can be due to the limited way of measuring embodied spillovers, it is notable that contrary to Mohnen (1992), who uses more or less the same method as the one represented by S_1 here for the case of Canada, a positive influence of embodied knowledge spillovers does not turn up here. One speculation about the reason for this is that in a country sample as broad as the one used here, the role of these factors is too diffuse to turn up significantly in a regression.

3.5 Parameter Differences Between Countries

The regressions in Table 7.2, and the model underlying them, assume that the values of the estimated parameters are fixed over time and between countries. However, in light of the distinction between various types of knowledge, one may wish to challenge the latter assumption. One reason for this is closely related to the cumulativeness of the knowledge creation process (see Dosi 1988). If there are increasing returns to scale in knowledge production, one should expect that R&D aimed at pure innovation is more effective in the advanced countries than in the catching-up countries. Moreover, country-specific capabilities to assimilate knowledge spillovers may vary (see Verspagen 1991).

Table 7.2: Regressions explaining growth of output 1970–1985 by growth of various inputs (same period) and initial labour productivity gap

#	i	l	$\ln Y^*$	$r(bus)$	$r(nbus)$	$r(tot)$	p	c	R^2	n	F
Total sample											
1a	0.060 (0.027**)	0.770 (0.181***)	-0.009 (0.004**)	0.080 (0.034**)	-0.042 (0.054)			-0.004 (0.007)	0.79	20	15.60
2a	0.059 (0.029**)	0.815 (0.188***)	-0.009 (0.004**)	0.066 (0.031**)				-0.005 (0.007)	0.80	20	20.59
3a	0.048 (0.024*)	0.881 (0.134***)	-0.007 (0.003**)			0.157 (0.040***)		-0.006 (0.007)	0.82	23	26.30
4a	0.024 (0.035)	0.847 (0.181***)	-0.005 (0.002**)	0.070 (0.018***)			0.079 (0.023***)	-0.003 (0.009)	0.83	20	19.88
5a		0.808 (0.151***)	-0.004 (0.002**)	0.076 (0.015***)			0.076 (0.021***)	0.008 (0.002***)	0.84	20	25.74
Sample excluding South Korea											
1b	0.066 (0.028**)	0.753 (0.163***)	-0.006 (0.004)	0.060 (0.021***)	-0.019 (0.049)			-0.004 (0.008)	0.60	19	6.46
2b	0.066 (0.029**)	0.773 (0.167***)	-0.006 (0.004)	0.053 (0.017***)				-0.004 (0.007)	0.63	19	8.66
3b	0.053 (0.025**)	0.832 (0.131***)	-0.006 (0.003***)			0.129 (0.056**)		-0.005 (0.006)	0.65	22	10.68
4b	0.031 (0.050)	0.831 (0.188***)	-0.004 (0.002*)	0.066 (0.022***)			0.067 (0.064)	0.002 (0.010)	0.63	19	7.23
5b		0.821 (0.183***)	-0.004 (0.002*)	0.077 (0.013***)			0.097 (0.035***)	0.008 (0.003**)	0.65	19	9.31

Sample excluding South Korea and Spain

								R^2		
1c	0.058 (0.039)	0.738 (0.170***)	-0.004 (0.004)	0.106 (0.110)	-0.033 (0.057)			-0.003 (0.009)	0.47	18	4.07
2c	0.059 (0.040)	0.772 (0.169***)	-0.004 (0.004)	0.086 (0.103)				-0.004 (0.008)	0.51	18	5.44
3c	0.054 (0.025**)	0.787 (0.166***)	-0.007 (0.002***)			0.111 (0.077)		-0.004 (0.007)	0.56	21	7.37
4c	0.031 (0.050)	0.832 (0.192***)	-0.004 (0.004)	0.065 (0.098)			0.068 (0.074)	0.002 (0.010)	0.51	18	4.51
5c		0.820 (0.188***)	-0.004 (0.004)	0.082 (0.101)			0.095 (0.055*)	0.008 (0.004**)	0.53	18	5.81

Sample excluding South Korea, Iceland and Spain

								R^2		
1d	0.025 (0.035)	0.657 (0.192***)	-0.001 (0.004)	0.213 (0.099**)	0.001 (0.066)			0.001 (0.009)	0.57	17	5.18
2d	0.025 (0.035)	0.657 (0.174***)	-0.001 (0.003)	0.213 (0.090**)				0.001 (0.008)	0.60	17	7.07
3d	0.041 (0.023)	0.803 (0.154***)	-0.006 (0.002**)			0.195 (0.063***)		-0.004 (0.007)	0.65	20	9.80
4d	0.012 (0.041)	0.700 (0.197***)	-0.002 (0.004)	0.190 (0.105*)			0.037 (0.075)	0.004 (0.009)	0.58	17	5.38
5d		0.690 (0.190***)	-0.001 (0.005)	0.202 (0.108*)			0.046 (0.064***)	0.006 (0.003**)	0.61	17	7.27

Numbers between brackets are standard errors (robust to the presence of heteroscedasticity). Three, two and one asterisk(s) point to significance at the 1, 5 and 10% level in a 2-tailed t-test. R^2 is adjusted for degrees of freedom.

Table 7.3: Embodied knowledge spillovers and growth

#	i	l	$\ln Y^*$	$r(bus)$	S_1	S_2	p	c	R^2	n	F
Total sample – embodied spillovers as a stock											
1a	0.034 (0.052)	0.824 (0.182***)	-0.004 (0.003)	0.051 (0.072)	0.016 (0.063)		0.073 (0.071)	0.001 (0.011)	0.61	19	5.62
2a	0.067 (0.018***)	0.786 (0.122***)	-0.007 (0.001***)	-0.079 (0.061)		-0.116 (0.019)	0.060 (0.018***)	0.005 (0.003)	0.81	16	11.77
Total sample – embodied spillovers as a flow relative to GDP											
1b	0.043 (0.048)	0.913 (0.159***)	-0.003 (0.002)	0.063 (0.021***)	-10.119 (3.09)		0.061 (0.048)	0.004 (0.010)	0.71	19	8.44
2b	0.086 (0.033**)	0.741 (0.128***)	-0.007 (0.002***)	-0.078 (0.047)		-0.611 (0.314*)	0.057 (0.056*)	-0.001 (0.006)	0.71	16	7.02

Numbers between brackets are standard errors (robust to the presence of heteroscedasticity). Three, two and one asterisk(s) point to significance at the 1, 5 and 10% level in a 2-tailed t-test. R^2 is adjusted for degrees of freedom.

As a very crude way of testing for these possibilities, a panel dataset is constructed, in which there are yearly observations (1969–1987) for each of the variables in Table 7.2. Note that in the case of initial labour productivity, R&D and patent stocks, variables are used with time lag one. With this dataset, the equations in Table 7.2 are re-estimated, including also two (additive) time dummies, one for the years 1974–1975, and one for the years 1980–1982, in order to incorporate business-cycle effects. The variables representing embodied knowledge spillovers are no longer included.

The assumption of equal parameters between countries is challenged by introducing multiplicative country-group dummies. The following equation is estimated:

$$q_{it} = \sum_u (1+D_{xi})X_{it} + \sum_w (1+D_{xi})X_{it-1} + DT_1 + DT_2 + c, \qquad (7.8)$$

with X_t being the set of variables which is not lagged, X_{t-1} the set of lagged variables, D_{xi} a set of country-group dummies to be estimated, and DT_1 (1974–1975) and DT_2 (1980–1982) two time dummies.

In estimating country-wise dummies, the approach chosen was not to estimate one dummy for each country, but rather to group countries, and include dummies for each of the groups (there are, however, some groups which include only one country). Although several groupings were used in the estimations, the outcomes of only one particular grouping are presented (due to space considerations). The country-groups that were used in these estimations are as follows:[15]

Group 1: United States
Group 2: Japan
Group 3: Switzerland
Group 4: Germany, France, United Kingdom (the dominant European countries)
Group 5: Australia, New Zealand
Group 6: Austria, Belgium, Denmark, Italy, Netherlands, Norway, Sweden (the smaller developed European countries)
Group 7: Canada
Group 8: Spain, Finland, Greece, Ireland, Iceland, Portugal, Turkey, Yugoslavia (the less-developed European countries)
Group 9: South Korea.

First, two basic equations not including any country dummies were estimated. These are documented as eqs 1 and 2 in Table 7.4. Basically, the results from the pure cross-country regressions are repeated, yielding significant results and correct signs. The proportion of variance explained is lower, but still adequate. Note that the time dummies are also highly significant, indicating that, on average, growth was 2–3% lower during the recession years, and that the patent variable and the investment variable are *both* significant.

Next, estimations with country dummies for each of the variables investment, labour, business R&D, patents, and initial labour productivity were carried out. For all these variables, except patenting, regressions were run including all variables except patents, plus one country dummy. For patenting, regressions including all variables except R&D, plus one country dummy were done. Of these 45 equations, there were 13 in which the country dummy turned up significantly (at the 10% level or higher). These equations are documented as eqs 3–15) in Table 7.4. For each of the regressions, a dummy name is listed, which consists of a letter describing the variable it was multiplied by (R for R&D, I for investment, L for labour, Y for relative labour productivity, P for patents), the abbreviation DUM, and a number, corresponding to the country group.[16]

In general, the degree of variance explained is not very much higher in the case of country dummies, but in spite of this, some of the dummies are quite significant. In the case of business R&D, it appears that R&D in the USA is much more effective (a high positive value of RDUM1), while R&D in the less-developed (European) countries is less effective, but still has a positive influence (a negative value of RDUM8, of which the absolute value is smaller than the coefficient on R&D itself, however). With regard to investment, these conclusions are very much the same, while in addition investment seems to be more effective in Japan (RDUM2 is positive). Labour input seems to be much more effective in the USA and Japan, but the values of the dummy variable are so high as to yield quite implausible conclusions in this regard.

The conclusion with regard to the dummies of the relative labour productivity variable are particularly interesting. They show that for Japan and the larger European countries (Germany, France, United Kingdom), the catch-up coefficient has a much larger absolute value, while for the less-developed (European) countries, the absolute value is smaller, but still larger than zero. First, this points to the conclusion that even the more-developed economies have benefited from disembodied knowledge spillovers. Second, it shows that the less-developed countries are less effective in assimilating these spillovers. These conclusions are broadly in accordance with the approach in Verspagen (1991). Lastly, the results for the patent dummies show that patents are less effective in the less-developed countries, and more effective in South Korea. The first of these conclusions seems to indicate that the quality of an average patent in the less-developed countries is low (in fact, the 'net' coefficient for these countries is very close to zero). The second result is a bit harder to interpret, especially since the patent variable itself is not significant in eq. 15 in the table.

Overall, these results show that in some cases it is important to distinguish between countries when estimating the relations between various inputs and the growth rate of output. The parameters in the production function assumed in the above model seem to be subject to international differences.

4. HOW MUCH OF THE CONVERGENCE SLOWDOWN CAN BE EXPLAINED BY TECHNOLOGY?

The issue of convergence is now put back to the centre of the analysis. As shown in section 2, the strong postwar convergence tendency seems to have slowed down recently. On the basis of the previous results, this section tries to obtain an answer to the question which factors can be found to explain this event. First define the indicator V:

$$V \equiv \sum_{i=1}^{n} (\ln Y_i - \ln \bar{Y})^2,$$

$$\bar{Y} = \frac{1}{n} \sum_{i=1}^{n} Y_i. \tag{7.9}$$

This indicator, which is basically a variance indicator, falls in periods of convergence, and rises in periods of divergence.

Figure 7.4 presents the value of V over the 1953–1989 period for a sample of 20 countries.[17] As could be expected from the results in section 1, a trend reversal occurs at the end of the 1970s, when convergence becomes much slower, and V follows an almost horizontal time path. The question the rest of this section will try to answer is 'What factors can explain this tendency?'. The approach followed is to decompose the time derivative of V into the separate factors which have been used in the above regression explaining cross-country growth.

In order to decompose the change of V over time, start by differentiating with respect to Y_i:

$$\frac{\partial V}{\partial Y_i} = \frac{2}{Y_i} (\ln Y_i - \ln \bar{Y}) - \frac{2}{\bar{Y} n} \sum_{j=1}^{n} \ln Y_j + \frac{2 \ln \bar{Y}}{\bar{Y}}. \tag{7.10}$$

From the model in section 3, the following equation for the change in

Table 7.4: Panel dataset regressions

#	i	l	$\ln Y^*$	r(bus)	DT1	DT2	p	Dummy name	Dummy value	c	R^2	n	F
Equations without country dummies													
1	0.119 (0.026***)	0.562 (0.200***)	-0.012 (0.005***)	0.092 (0.025***)	-0.029 (0.005***)	-0.023 (0.003***)				-0.011 (0.007)	0.33	411	35.19
2	0.103 (0.027***)	0.584 (0.199***)	-0.009 (0.005*)	0.091 (0.025***)	-0.029 (0.005***)	-0.021 (0.003***)	0.043 (0.019**)			-0.008 (0.007)	0.34	411	31.43
Equations with country dummies													
3	0.129 (0.027***)	0.538 (0.201***)	-0.013 (0.005***)	0.090 (0.025***)	-0.028 (0.005***)	-0.022 (0.003***)		RDUM1	0.345 (0.155**)	-0.014 (0.007**)	0.34	411	30.79
4	0.115 (0.026***)	0.548 (0200***)	-0.012 (0.005**)	0.126 (0.030***)	-0.028 (0.005***)	-0.022 (0.003***)		RDUM8	-0.066 (0.028**)	-0.011 (0.007)	0.34	411	31.53
5	0.135 (0.028***)	0.457 (0.210**)	-0.014 (0.005***)	0.095 (0.025***)	-0.029 (0.005***)	-0.022 (0.003***)		IDUM1	0.094 (0.033***)	-0.016 (0.007**)	0.34	411	31.39
6	0.110 (0.027***)	0.582 (0.201***)	-0.012 (0.005**)	0.091 (0.025***)	-0.028 (0.005***)	-0.023 (0.003***)		IDUM2	0.027 (0.015*)	-0.009 (0.007)	0.34	411	30.51
7	0.134 (0.025***)	0.546 (0.199***)	-0.017 (0.005***)	0.090 (0.024***)	-0.029 (0.005***)	-0.022 (0.003***)		IDUM8	-0.040 (0.013***)	-0.015 (0.007***)	0.35	411	32.69
8	0.132 (0.028***)	0.458 (0.216**)	-0.013 (0.005***)	0.096 (0.026***)	-0.029 (0.005***)	-0.022 (0.003***)		LDUM1	0.701 (0.325**)	-0.015 (0.007***)	0.34	411	30.91
9	0.108 (0.027***)	0.577 (0.200***)	-0.012 (0.005**)	0.091 (0.025***)	-0.028 (0.005***)	-0.023 (0.003***)		LDUM2	1.240 (0.514**)	-0.009 (0.007)	0.34	411	30.83
10	0.116 (0.026***)	0.676 (0.219***)	-0.147 (0.005***)	0.096 (0.025***)	-0.028 (0.005***)	-0.022 (0.003***)		LDUM8	-0.504 (0.254**)	-0.012 (0.007*)	0.34	411	31.36

											R^2	N	
11	0.108 (0.027***)	0.583 (0.201***)	−0.012 (0.005**)	0.091 (0.025***)	−0.028 (0.005***)	−0.023 (0.003***)		YDUM2	−0.016 (0.008**)	−0.009 (0.007)	0.34	411	30.71
12	0.129 (0.027***)	0.656 (0.212***)	−0.012 (0.005**)	0.092 (0.025***)	−0.029 (0.005***)	−0.022 (0.003***)		YDUM4	−0.015 (0.008**)	−0.016 (0.008**)	0.34	411	30.61
13	0.118 (0.025***)	0.576 (0.201***)	−0.022 (0.007***)	0.071 (0.025***)	−0.029 (0.005***)	−0.022 (0.003***)		YDUM8	0.014 (0.005**)	−0.012 (0.007*)	0.35	411	32.37
14	0.118 (0.027***)	0.654 (0.175***)	−0.019 (0.04***)		−0.025 (0.006***)	−0.021 (0.003***)	0.080 (0.027***)	PDUM8	−0.076 (0.029***)	−0.012 (0.007*)	0.31	475	31.11
15	0.136 (0.027***)	0.594 (0.180***)	−0.016 (0.04***)		−0.024 (0.006***)	−0.023 (0.003***)	0.006 (0.018)	PDUM9	0.134 (0.039***)	−0.012 (0.007*)	0.32	475	32.26

Numbers between brackets are standard errors (robust to the presence of heteroscedasticity). Three, two and one asterisk(s) point to significance at the 1, 5 and 10% level in a 2-tailed t-test. R^2 is adjusted for degrees of freedom.

Figure 7.4: The value of V, 1953–1989

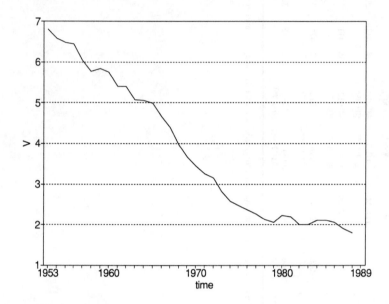

labour productivity can be obtained:

$$y_i = \gamma + \alpha k_i + (\beta - 1)l_i + \sum_k \rho_k r_{ik} - \lambda \ln Y_i^*. \tag{7.11}$$

This is the equation estimated in section 3 using the panel dataset in section 3. Multiplying both sides of this equation by Y_{it-1} gives an approximation of the change in the level of Y_i. Multiplying this with the derivative in eq. (7.10) gives the following:

$$\frac{\partial V}{\partial Y_i} = Y_{it-1}[2(\alpha k_i + (\beta - 1)l_i + \sum_k \rho_k r_{ik})(\ln Y_i - \ln \overline{Y}) +$$

$$(\alpha k_i + (\beta - 1)l_i + \sum_k \rho_k r_{ik})C_{t-1}], \tag{7.12}$$

$$C = \frac{2\ln \overline{Y}}{\overline{\overline{Y}}} - \frac{2}{\overline{\overline{Y}}n} \sum_{j=1}^n \ln Y_j.$$

This expression can be summed over the n countries to obtain the total (predicted) change in V. In such an expression, terms with k, L, r_k and $\ln Y$ can be grouped together. The result gives an approximation of the influence of each of these factors on the change in V.

The variables in the panel dataset from section 3, as well as parameter

estimates obtained in that section (eq. 2 in Table 7.4),[18] have been used
to calculate the influence of the growth of labour inputs, investment
shares, growth of business R&D stocks, the growth of the patent stock,
and initial labour productivity on the change in the indicator V. The outcome of this exercise is compared to both the actual data on changes in V,
and predicted changes in V conditional on the value of the indicator in the
previous period. For the latter predictions, a simple AR(1) estimate for V
is applied, the outcome of which is the following (numbers between brackets are standard errors, estimated period is 1954–1988):

$$V_t = 0.97042 \ (0.014) \ V_{t-1} - 0.02906 \ (0.058) \ R^2 = 0.99, \text{ Durbin (1970)}$$
t-stat = 0.67.

The results of the calculations are in Table 7.5 and Figure 7.5. The
figure has the exact values of each of the factors for the years 1971–1985.
Because short-run growth rates of the underlying variables were used, the
lines in the figures show a high degree of variability from period to
period. Although this feature is clearly artificial, the general trend of the
lines, as well as their relative (vertical) positions display some useful
information. The table summarises this information, by giving averages
over two different periods.

The first feature that emerges from the table is the fact that there is a
considerable discrepancy between the actual, predicted (on the basis of an
AR(1) process), and calculated changes in V. This is caused by the fact
that short-term data are being used, which reflects all sorts of short-run
disturbances. Nevertheless, the general trend and the level of the predicted
change seems to match the actual data to some extent, such that comparing the outcomes of the calculations to either the actual or predicted
changes in V yields some interesting conclusions.

First, the results show that, in both periods used in the table, R&D and
disembodied knowledge spillovers are the most important sources for
convergence (that is, the fall of V). Labour inputs, patents and capital
investment play a much less important role in this respect. Labour has
even displayed a net diverging tendency over both periods. This supports
the argument of technological change as the driving force for convergence
(see also Helliwell 1992). Moreover, it supports the distinction between
different forms of technological change, with imitation being a much more
important source for convergence than innovation (as measured by
patents).

Moreover, the results clearly show that the two main factors behind the
slowdown of convergence are (again) business R&D stocks and disembodied knowledge spillovers, as measured by the initial labour productivity

Figure 7.5: Sources of convergence over the period 1970–1985

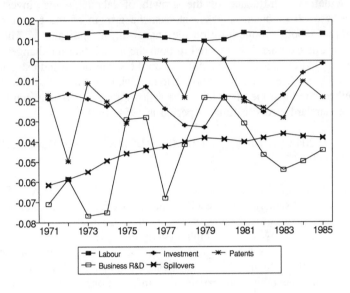

Table 7.5: Decomposition of convergence trends, 1971–1985

	1971–1979	1980–1985	Change
Investment share	−0.0203	−0.0170	−0.0034
Labour	0.0127	0.0126	−0.0000
Patents stock	−0.0183	−0.0128	−0.0054
Business R&D stock	−0.0559	−0.0376	−0.0183
Disembodied spillovers	−0.0496	−0.0382	−0.0114
Total above	−0.1315	−0.0929	−0.0385
True	−0.1647	−0.0046	−0.1601
Predicted	−0.1116	−0.0911	−0.0205

relative to the USA. In the case of the latter factor, this means that the
'catching-up potential', as measured by disparities in labour productivity,
has reached a low level at the end of the 1970s. With regard to R&D, one
can conclude that the catching-up process during the 1960s and 1970s also
seems to have come to an end.

5. CONCLUSIONS

This paper has looked at the postwar growth record of the industrialised world. Section 2 has shown that this period, contrary to the prewar period, has been characterised by convergence of per capita income levels. Since the beginning of the 1980s, however, this convergence seems to have stopped.

Section 3 has shown that different types of knowledge accumulation can be associated with different explanations for cross-country growth patterns. Estimating regressions for the 1970–1985 period, it was found that both traditional factors (labour and investment in fixed capital), and technology-related factors (R&D and patent stocks, disembodied knowledge spillovers) are positively related to growth. With regard to R&D, it was found that the part of R&D carried out by private firms is most relevant to economic growth. Knowledge spillovers embodied in technology payments or imports of capital and intermediate goods did not turn up significantly in the regressions.

Regressions using a panel dataset have shown that it cannot be assumed that the parameters in the basic model are equal for all countries. Especially in the countries very close to the technological frontier (Japan, USA, the larger European countries), many of the variables are more effective than average. In the countries lagging furthest behind (a number of less-developed European countries), these factors are generally less effective.

It was argued that the three different technology indicators used are related to different parts of the technology process. Patents can be associated with innovation itself, while knowledge spillovers are related to imitation. R&D can be related to both aspects of knowledge accumulation.

Section 4 has used the results of the regressions to calculate the sources of the convergence trend and slowdown found in section 2. It appears that R&D and disembodied knowledge spillovers are the two most important sources of this slowdown, as well as for convergence itself. This leads to the conclusion that technological imitation is indeed the primary factor explaining convergence in the industrialised world, while the recent slowdown in convergence can be attributed largely to the decreased influence of these factors.

APPENDIX: DATASOURCES

The data on the growth rate of output, labour input, population and investment output ratios are taken from Summers and Heston (1991). Labour input and population are measured in persons, and monetary variables are measured in 1985 prices and purchasing power parties vs. the USA.

The R&D data is taken from a database maintained at MERIT. The main source for the database is OECD, but additional data for total R&D expenditures for early years is taken from UNESCO (Statistical Year-books) and NSF (Science and Engineering Indicators). Additional data on business R&D is taken from NSF and Patel and Soete (1985). Korean R&D data is taken from the Korean National Bureau of Statistics. For years for which R&D data is lacking, R&D intensity (defined as R&D expenditures as a percentage of GDP) was interpolated, and the expenditures were estimated on the basis of this interpolation (no extra- or retrapolations were used).

Data on patents are taken from the US Patent Office (USA patents) and OECD (total external patents). USA patents are patents granted, and are dated by date of grant. Total external patents are patent applications, and are also dated by date of application. Because of space considerations, the regressions documented only include patent stocks on the basis of USA patents. The reason for this is that total external patents are not available for the period before 1973, and, moreover, patent requirements differ between countries, which makes the data harder to interpret. The regressions carried out with the total external patenting stock indicate that the results are slightly less significant but otherwise comparable. These latter regressions are available from the author.

The data for technology payments to foreign countries are taken from the OECD. Data on imported R&D is calculated by using sectoral (business) R&D intensities for a subset of OECD countries (Germany, France, United Kingdom, Italy, Japan, United States). The sectors for which imports were considered to add to the national knowledge stock are: Fabricated metal products; Office machinery and computers; Electrical machinery; Machinery not elsewhere classified; Electronic equipment and components; Ships and boats; Aerospace; Motor vehicles; Instruments.

NOTES

1. For example, Nelson and Winter (1982), Dosi *et al.* (1988), Dosi, Pavitt and Soete (1990).
2. Among which are Abramovitz (1979, 1986), Baumol (1986) and Dowrick and Nguyen (1989).
3. And in some cases, South Korea.
4. Moreover, one can calculate the relative strength of the convergence/divergence process by calculating the time it takes to halve the value of W as $\ln(0.5)/\ln(\Psi)$. If $\Psi > 1$, this value is negative, indicating that its absolute value should be interpreted as the time it takes to double the income difference.
5. These are Australia, Austria, Belgium, Canada, Denmark, Finland, France, Germany, Italy, Japan, Netherlands, Norway, Sweden, Switzerland, United Kingdom, USA.

6. For example, for the year 1905, datapairs $W_{1903}-W_{1902}$, $W_{1904}-W_{1903}$, $W_{1905}-W_{1904}$, $W_{1906}-W_{1905}$, $W_{1907}-W_{1906}$ are used for each of the 16 countries.
7. Baumol, Batey Blackwell and Wolff (1989), Barro (1991), Barro and Sala-i-Martin (1991) and Romer (1989) are but a few.
8. Some of the key references in this field are Griliches (1980a,b, 1986), Griliches and Mairesse (1983, 1984, 1990), Hall and Mairesse (1992), Wolff and Nadiri (1987), Bernstein and Nadiri (1990). For a survey and more references, see Mohnen (1992).
9. See the Appendix for data sources. As in Griliches (1990) and many other papers, a perpetual inventory method is used to construct the R&D and capital stocks, with a rate of depreciation of 0.15, and the initial stock estimated as the investment in the next year multiplied by 5. The results are not very sensitive to changing the rate of depreciation.
10. See Dowrick and Nguyen (1989) for some tests of this assumption.
11. The regressions include up to 23 countries. These countries are Australia, Austria, Belgium, Canada, Switzerland, Germany, Denmark, Spain, Finland, France, United Kingdom, Greece, Ireland, Iceland, Italy, Japan, Netherlands, Norway, Portugal, Sweden, United States, Yugoslavia, South Korea.
12. Other independent variables in the regressions generally do not have these extreme values.
13. R&D as a fraction of production.
14. Regressions (in turn) leaving out each of the other terms in the equations were also carried out, yielding roughly the same results for the coefficients on the embodied spillovers terms.
15. New Zealand and Turkey, for which data is available for a limited subset of the period 1970–1985, have been left out of the previous regressions, but are included now, yielding a sample of 25 countries.
16. For example, RDUM9 means a multiplicative R&D dummy for South Korea.
17. Austria, Belgium, Canada, Switzerland, Germany, Denmark, Spain, Finland, France, United Kingdom, Ireland, Iceland, Italy, Japan, Netherlands, Norway, Portugal, Sweden, United States, South Korea.
18. Although the other results in Table 7.4 show that there are significant differences between countries with regard to parameter values, non-documented calculations show that inclusion of the estimated country dummies in the calculations below do not change the outcomes to any significant degree.

REFERENCES

Abramovitz, M.A. (1979), 'Rapid Growth Potential and its Realisation: The Experience of Capitalist Economies in the Postwar Period', in E. Malinvaud (ed.), *Economic Growth and Resources*, vol. 1: *The major Issues*, proceedings of the fifth World Congress of the IEA, London: Macmillan.

Abramovitz, M.A. (1986), 'Catching Up, Forging Ahead and Falling Behind', *Journal of Economic History*, 46, 385–406.

Abramovitz, M.A. (1992), 'Catch Up and Convergence in the Postwar Growth Boom and After', Paper presented at the workshop on Historical Perspectives on the International Convergence of Productivity, New York, 23–24 April 1992.

Barro, R.J. (1991), 'Economic Growth in a Cross-section of Countries', *Quarterly Journal of Economics*, 106, 407–444.

Barro, R.J. and Sala-i-Martin, X. (1991), 'Convergence across States and Regions', *Brookings Papers on Economic Activity*, 1, 109–158.

Baumol, W.J. (1986), 'Productivity Growth, Convergence and Welfare: What the Long-run Data Show', *American Economic Review*, 76, 1072–1085.

Baumol, W.J., Batey Blackman, S.A. and Wolff, E.N. (1989), *Productivity and American Leadership: The Long View*, Cambridge, MA: MIT Press.

Ben-David, D. (1991), 'Equalizing Exchange: A Study of the Effects of Trade Liberalization', *NBER Working Paper*, no. 3706.

Bernstein, J.I. and Nadiri, I.M. (1990), 'Rates of Return on Physical and R&D Capital and Structure of the Production Process: Cross Section and Time Series Evidence', in Raj (1990).

Cohen, W.M. and Levinthal, D.A. (1989), 'Innovation and Learning: The Two Faces of R&D', *Economic Journal*, 99, 569–596.

Cornwall, J. (1977), *Modern Capitalism: Its Growth and Transformation*, London: Martin Robertson.

Dosi, G. (1988), 'Sources, Procedures and Microeconomic Effects of Innovation', *Journal of Economic Literature*, 26, 1120–1171.

Dosi, G., Freeman, C., Nelson, R., Silverberg, G. and Soete, L. (eds) (1988), *Technical Change and Economic Theory*, London: Pinter.

Dosi, G., Pavitt, K. and Soete, L. (1990), *The Economics of Technological Change and International Trade*, Brighton: Wheatsheaf.

Dowrick, S. and Nguyen, D.T. (1989), 'OECD Comparative Economic Growth 1950–85: Catch-up and Convergence', *American Economic Review*, 79, 1010–1030.

Fagerberg, J. (1988), 'Why Growth Rates Differ', in Dosi *et al.* (1988).

Gerschenkron, A. (1962), *Economic Backwardness in Historical Perspective*, Cambridge, MA: Harvard University Press.

Griliches, Z. (1980a), 'Returns to Research and Development Expenditures in the Private Sector', in Kendrick and Vaccara (1980).

Griliches, Z. (1980b), 'R&D and the Productivity Slowdown', *American Economic Review*, 70(2), 343–348.

Griliches, Z. (ed.) (1984), *R&D, Patents and Productivity*, Chicago: University of Chicago Press.

Griliches, Z. (1986), 'Productivity, R&D and Basic Research at the Firm Level in the 1970s', *American Economic Review*, 76, 141–154.

Griliches, Z. (1990), 'Patent Statistics as Economic Indicators: A Survey', *Journal of Economic Literature*, XXVIII, 1661–1707.

Griliches, Z. and Mairesse, J. (1983), 'Comparing Productivity Growth: An Exploration of French and US Industrial Firm Data', *European Economic Review*, 21, 89–119.

Griliches, Z. and Mairesse, J. (1984), 'Productivity and R&D at the Firm Level', in Griliches (1984).

Griliches, Z. and Mairesse, J. (1990), 'R&D and Productivity Growth: Comparing Japanese and US Manufacturing Firms', in Hulten (1990).

Hall, B.H. and Mairesse, J. (1992), 'Exploring the Relationship Between R&D and Productivity Growth in French Manufacturing Firms', *NBER Working Paper*, no. 3956.

Helliwell, J. (1992), 'Trade and Technical Progress', Paper presented at the Conference on Economic Growth and the Structure of Long-term Development, Varenna, Italy, 1–3 October 1992.

Hulten, C. (ed.) (1990), *NBER Studies in Income and Wealth*, 53, Chicago: University of Chicago Press.

Kendrick, J. and Vaccara, B. (eds) (1980), *New Developments in Productivity Measurement and Analysis*, Chicago: University of Chicago Press.

Levine, R. and Renelt, D. (1992), 'A Sensitivity Analysis of Cross-country Growth Regressions', *American Economic Review*, 82(4), 942–963.

Lichtenberg, F. (1992), 'R&D Investment and International Productivity Differences', Paper presented at the World Economics Conference on Economic Growth in the World Economy, Kiel, Germany, 23–25 June 1992 (also published as an NBER Working Paper).

Maddison, A. (1991), *Dynamic Forces in Capitalist Development. A Long-run Comparative View*, Oxford: Oxford University Press.

Mankiw, N.G., Romer, D. and Weil, D. (1992), 'A Contribution to the Empirics of Economic Growth', *Quarterly Journal of Economics*, 152, 407–437.

Mohnen, P. (1992), *The Relationship Between R&D and Productivity Growth in Canada and Other Major Industrialized Countries*, Economic Council of Canada.

Nelson, R.R. and Winter, S.G. (1982), *An Evolutionary Theory of Economic Change*, Cambridge, MA: Harvard University Press.

Patel, P. and Soete, L. (1985), 'Recherche-Développement, Importations de Technologie et Croissance Économique. Une Tentative de Comparaison Internationale', *Revue économique*, 36(5), 975–1000.

Raj, B. (ed.) (1990), *Advances in Econometrics and Modelling*, London: Kluwer.

Romer, P.M. (1989), 'What Determines the Rate of Growth and Technological Change?', Working Paper World Bank, Country and Economics Department, no. 279.

Soete, L. and Verspagen, B. (1992), 'Technology and Growth: the Complex Dynamics of Catching Up, Falling Behind and Taking Over', in A. Szirmai, B. van Ark and D. Pilat (eds), *Explaining Economic Growth*, Amsterdam: Elsevier.

Summers, R. and Heston, A. (1991), 'The Penn World Table (Mark 5): An Expanded Set of International Comparisons, (1950–1988)', *Quarterly Journal of Economics*, CVI, 1–41.

Verspagen, B., (1991), 'A New Empirical Approach to Catching Up or Falling Behind', *Structural Change and Economic Dynamics*, 2, 359–380.

Verspagen, B. (1992a), 'Endogenous Innovation in Neo-classical Growth Models: A Survey', *Journal of Macroeconomics*, 14(4), 631–662.

Verspagen, B. (1992b), *Uneven Growth Between Interdependent Economies: An Evolutionary View on Technology Gaps, Trade and Growth*, Maastricht: Universitaire Pers Maastricht.

Wolff, E.W. and Nadiri, I.M. (1987), 'Spillover Effects, Linkage Structure, Technical Progress, and Research and Development', C.V. Starr Center Research Report No. 87/43.

COMMENT ON VERSPAGEN

Jan Fagerberg

This paper adds to the rapidly increasing literature on convergence (or divergence) in productivity levels across countries. Following Abramovitz (1979, 1986), the central themes in this literature (and in the present paper as well) are:

1. To what extent can a trend towards convergence in GDP per capita across countries ('catching up') be shown to exist?
2. Which factors determine whether the potential for convergence, demonstrated by widely differing productivity levels across countries, is exploited or not?

The standard answer in the literature to the first of these questions is: yes, there has been some convergence, but only for 'developed countries' (sometimes identified with the current members of the OECD), and only after the Second World War. Using a statistical approach, Verspagen estimates a 'convergence parameter' for a group of 16 OECD member countries between 1903 and 1987. He finds that convergence took place between 1950 and 1980, for example, that – for this sample of countries – convergence in GDP per capita levels came to an end in the late 1970s.

The major part of the paper is devoted to the second question. Many of the early contributions in this area were of a theoretically more 'heterodox' nature, combining Schumpeterian and post-Keynesian insights (Cornwall 1976; Pavitt and Soete 1982; Fagerberg 1987). More recently, many empirical researchers in this field have applied neoclassical production functions, extended with a variable reflecting the potential for 'catch up' (and other variables as well), to cross-country samples. One central reference is Dowrick and Nguyen (1989). They applied a standard extended Cobb–Douglas production function, including capital, labour and the potential for 'catch up', to a sample of OECD countries between 1950 and 1985. Verspagen essentially adopts the same framework (without much discussion, one may add), but extends it by including R&D and patents (and in some versions technology payments and technology embodied in imports as well).

Verspagen presents two sets of tests of his extended production function model. The first is cross-sectional (23 countries between 1970–1985), the second pooled cross-sectional time series (annual data for 25 countries between 1969–1987). In the cross-sectional test (Tables 7.1 and 7.2), multicollinearity turns out to be an important problem, in particular in relation to the investment and patent variables. The results are shown to be quite sensitive to the exclusion of one or more countries. Quite different models yield almost identical explanatory power (the results for the original model – as specified by Dowrick and Nguyen – are not reported, though). Thus, even Verspagen's quite modest conclusion ('some, although, limited, support' for the variables added by him) may perhaps be questioned.

The data set for the second test combines cross-country and time-series information, and is therefore both much larger and displays more variance. This normally reduces multicollinearity, as also appears to be the case here. The investment variable now turns up as significant in all cases, but the patent variable continues to cause problems (see Table 7.4). However, pooling time-series data also introduces the familiar problems of whether parameters are constant across countries and time. This is taken into account here only to a very limited extent, by allowing parameters of 'country groupings' to vary, although there are enough degrees of freedom to test the model for each country separately (and then test these against the pooled version). As Verspagen points out, the reported results indicate that there may be important differences across countries in the way the model works. This raises many interesting questions, which are only touched upon briefly by the present paper. Some of the reported results may also be interpreted as an indication of changes in (the parameters of) the model through time: for the years 1980–85, the model predicts convergence, which was not realised (Table 7.5). In fact, the estimated model only explains a small fraction of the observed slowdown in convergence.

The paper by Verspagen represents a welcome addition to the literature in this area, both in terms of method and content. Its main finding is that for the sample of countries considered, convergence appears to have come to an end. This points clearly to the need for further research in this area. However, to explain these developments, a more refined approach, probably based on a system of equations rather than one single equation, may prove necessary.

References

Abramovitz, M. (1979), 'Rapid Growth Potential and its Realization: The Experience of Capitalist Economies in the Postwar Period', in E. Malinvaud (ed.), *Economic Growth and Resources*, London: Macmillan.

Abramovitz, M. (1986), 'Catching Up, Forging Ahead, and Falling Behind', *Journal of Economic History*, 66, 385–406.

Cornwall, J. (1976), 'Diffusion, Convergence and Kaldor's Law', *Economic Journal*, 86, 307–314.

Dowrick, S. and Nguyen, D.T. (1989), 'OECD Comparative Economic Growth 1950–85: Catch-Up and Convergence', *American Economic Review*, 79, 1010–1030.

Fagerberg, J. (1987), 'A Technology Gap Approach to Why Growth Rates Differ', *Research Policy*, 16, 87–99.

Pavitt, K. and Soete, L. (1982), 'International Differences in Economic Growth and the International Location of Innovation', in H. Giersch (ed.) (1982), *Emerging Technologies: Consequences for Economic Growth, Structural Change, and Employment*, Tübingen: J.C.B. Mohr.

8. Productivity Growth and Capital Intensity on the Sector and Industry Level: Specialisation among OECD Countries, 1970–1988

Edward N. Wolff

In a recently completed book, *Competitiveness, Convergence, and International Specialization*, David Dollar and I investigated the sources of the convergence of aggregate labour productivity observed among industrialised countries (see, for example, Maddison 1982; Abramovitz 1986; Baumol 1986; Baumol, Batey Blackman and Wolff 1989; Wolff 1991; and Barro 1991). The convergence phenomenon is usually attributed to the so-called 'advantages of backwardness', by which is meant the potential for the diffusion of technical knowledge from the leading economies to the more backward ones. The further an economy is from the technological frontier, the greater the rate of technical advance possible from such borrowing. Thus, countries further behind the leading economy in terms of labour productivity will tend to experience higher *rates* of productivity growth.

In our book, we considered two possibilities: (a) convergence of labour productivity in individual industries; and (b) specialisation of countries in industries that differ from one country to another, with modest leads in labour productivity in the country that specialises in them.[1] We first examined data for manufacturing industries and found that between the early 1960s and the early 1970s the first of these forms of development, productivity catch-up on the industry level, played the dominant role. However, after that, specialisation became the main vehicle of convergence. Indeed, after the early 1970s, convergence of labour productivity within industries slowed down considerably, and that of total factor productivity (TFP) essentially halted. There were also good reasons to believe that more rapid rates of technological advance might be associated with more rapid rates of capital formation. Our evidence supported the existence of a strong interaction effect (complementarities) between the growth in capital intensity and that of TFP.

We found remarkably similar results when we compared productivity levels of the major non-manufacturing sectors among the industrialised countries of the world. There was strong evidence of convergence in labour productivity levels for the total economy in these countries during the 1970s and early 1980s and a somewhat weaker trend at the sectoral level, but the dispersion in technology levels generally remained unchanged. Also, when looking across the ten major sectors, we found a much more varied pattern of sector leadership in the 1980s than among individual manufacturing industries, which the US still generally dominated.

We also found that variation in technology levels, capital intensity and labour productivity levels was consistently greater at the individual level than at the aggregate level. These results lend support to our hypothesis that specialisation of countries in different industries, particularly since the mid-1970s, played the critical role. The greater similarity in overall productivity levels than in those of the representative industry is attributable to the fact that countries excel in different industries, so that on average among countries aggregate productivity levels are closer than industry productivity levels. The same is true for capital intensity. We concluded that countries chose different industries for their main investment in new technology, which explains the convergence of labour productivity and TFP on the aggregate level.

In this paper, I update the results of our book using the latest (January 1992) version of the OECD International Sectoral Database (ISDB). The data run principally from 1970 to 1988. Four questions are addressed. First, has convergence continued on the aggregate level through 1988 (section 1)? Second, has country specialisation continued through the 1980s (section 2)? I also present a more formal test of the specialisation hypothesis: namely, that aggregate convergence continued after 1970 through the *uneven* development of industries in the individual OECD countries. Third, have countries invested more heavily in industries with rapidly growing TFP (section 2)? Fourth, has the interaction effect between capital investment and TFP growth continued through the 1980s (section 3)? Concluding remarks are made in section 4.

1. PATTERNS OF AGGREGATE PRODUCTIVITY GROWTH AND CAPITAL FORMATION

I will begin by presenting an overview of the aggregate performance of OECD countries from 1970 to 1990 with regard to labour productivity growth, total factor productivity and the growth in capital intensity (as defined by the capital–labour ratio). I confine the analysis to OECD countries, since I am not interested in establishing general patterns of convergence but in focusing on the role of individual sectors in this process.[2]

1.1 Labour Productivity

Table 8.1 presents results for the total economy on the basis of the January 1992 version of the OECD International Sectoral Database (ISDB). The data set covers the period from 1960 to 1989, though the period of greatest data availability is from 1970 to 1988. The data consist of GDP, already calculated in 1980 US dollar equivalents (on the basis of OECD purchasing power parity, or PPP, exchange rates), total employment (the sum of the number of employees and the number of self-employed), and gross capital stock, measured in 1980 US dollars equivalents.

I look at both catch-up, defined as the closure of the gap between follower countries and the leader in terms of productivity levels, and convergence, defined as decreasing dispersion in productivity levels among all countries in the sample. Catch-up is measured in two ways. The first index is the (unweighted) average productivity level of all countries excluding the US to that of the US (defined as 100). This measure climbed from 56 in 1970 to 75 in 1988, demonstrating substantial catch-up. The second, the ratio of the minimum productivity level to the maximum, also confirmed catch-up, as it increased from 40% to 56%. Convergence is measured by the coefficient of variation, defined as the ratio of the standard deviation to the mean, which fell from 0.26 to 0.15 over the period. This is the most direct indicator of convergence in productivity among OECD countries.[3]

The US led in terms of overall labour productivity throughout the period from 1970 to 1988. Its nearest rival in 1988 was The Netherlands, at 86% of the US level. Japan had the lowest average productivity level in 1970 but by 1988 it was ninth (out of 14), at 69% of the US level according to these data. Germany in 1988 was at 71% the US level.

The last two columns of Table 8.1 present rates of labour productivity growth over this period. A quick look at the data for the total economy suggests that those countries with lower productivity levels in 1970 (at the top of the table) experienced more rapid rates of labour productivity growth. This relation is confirmed by the correlation coefficient between the initial level of productivity and the rate of labour productivity growth (at the bottom of the table). A negative value indicates that more-backward countries grew faster. This coefficient was calculated to be −0.67 for 1970–1979 and −0.70 for 1979–1988.[4] Japan had the fastest rate of labour productivity growth in both periods and the US the lowest.

Labour productivity growth among OECD nations fell off by about

Table 8.1: Labour productivity levels relative to the US for the total economy among OECD countries, 1970–1988[a]

	Index number (US = 100)						Annual rate of lab. prod. growth (%)	
	1970	1973	1975	1979	1985	1988	1970–79	1979–88
Japan	40	46	47	55	64	69	4.18	3.37
Finland	41	44	47	52	57	63	3.34	2.93
Denmark	47	48	49	53	55	56	2.02	1.46
Norway	51	53	58	62	67	69	2.93	1.90
United Kingdom		54	53	56	60	64	1.83[b]	2.21
Sweden	52	54	55	56	58	60	1.52	1.63
France	55	59	62	69	74	78	3.30	2.13
Germany	56	58	60	67	69	71	2.91	1.45
Italy	57	60	61	69	70	74	2.79	1.61
Belgium	60	65	67	74	78	81	3.05	1.85
Australia	67	67	70	72	74	74	1.55	1.12
Netherlands	67	73	77	83	87	86	3.17	1.19
Canada	75	77	77	79	80	81	1.33	1.09
United States	100	100	100	100	100	100	0.78	0.80
Summary statistics for total economy								
Unweighted average								
(a) excluding US	56	58	60	65	69	71		
(b) including US							2.48	1.77
Coefficient of variation	0.26	0.23	0.22	0.19	0.17	0.15	0.38	0.39
Minimum/maximum	0.40	0.44	0.47	0.52	0.55	0.56		
Correlation with initial labour productivity[c]							−0.67	−0.70
Summary statistics for total industry[d]								
Unweighted average (excluding US)	54	57	59	66	71	74		
Coefficient of variation	0.26	0.23	0.22	0.18	0.15	0.14		
Minimum/maximum	0.37	0.43	0.44	0.52	0.59	0.60		

Notes
a   Source: Own computations from OECD International Sectoral Database on diskettes (1992 version). Labour productivity is defined as the ratio of GDP in 1980 US dollars to total employment (persons engaged in production). Countries are ranked by their 1970 labour productivity level (1973 for the UK).
b   UK figure for 1970–1979 based on total industry (see below).
c   Correlation coefficient between annual rate of labour productivity growth and labour productivity level at the start of each period, across all OECD countries with available data.
d   Total industry is defined as the total economy excluding producers of government services and other non-firm producers.

30% between 1970–1979 and 1979–1988. Comparisons with data from Maddison (1982) suggest that labour productivity growth peaked in the 1960–1970 period, fell in 1970–1979, and then again in the 1979–1988 period. Interestingly, the dispersion in labour productivity growth rates among countries (as measured by the coefficient of variation) showed no change between the 1970–1979 and 1979–1988 periods. This is a surprise since, according to the catch-up hypothesis, if labour productivity levels converge, so should rates of labour productivity growth, since they vary, by assumption, inversely with (initial) labour productivity levels.

Table 8.2 shows a similar set of statistics for total manufacturing. Here the results are quite different. Catch-up to the US level was considerably slower than for the total economy and confined to the 1970–1979 period, as average labour productivity in manufacturing relative to the US increased from 58 to 64%. Between 1979 and 1988, there was no further catch-up in labour productivity (and the ratio of minimum to maximum level actually declined). There was also modest convergence in manufacturing productivity levels between 1970 and 1979, as the coefficient of variation fell from 0.23 to 0.20. However, between 1979 and 1988, the coefficient of variation increased, from 0.20 to 0.23.

Results are also shown for labour productivity growth rates in manufacturing. During the 1970s, there was a clear inverse relation between initial productivity levels and productivity growth rates, with a correlation coefficient of −0.42. However, between 1979 and 1988, this relation failed to materialise. Indeed, there was *no* correlation between the two. Japan ranked first in terms of labour productivity growth in manufacturing in both 1970–1979 and 1979–1988. US labour productivity growth was slightly below average in the 1970–1979 period, but slightly above average in 1979–1988. As for the total economy, there was a significant fall-off in average labour productivity growth among OECD countries in manufacturing between the 1970s and 1980s, but, unlike the total economy, the dispersion in productivity growth rates was higher in the 1980s than the 1970s. Thus, it is clear that international performance in manufacturing was quite different than that from the total economy during the 1980s.[5]

1.2 Total Factor Productivity

I next present similar tabulations based on 'total factor productivity' or TFP. The TFP level for country h is measured using the Translog index:

$$\ln TFP^{\,h} = \ln Y^{\,h} - \bar{\alpha}\ln L^{\,h} - (1-\bar{\alpha})\ln K^{\,h} \tag{8.1}$$

where Y^h is the total output of country h, L^h is labour input, K^h is capital

Table 8.2: Labour productivity levels relative to the US for total manufacturing among OECD countries, 1970–1990[a]

	1970	1973	1975	1979	1985	1988	1970–79	1979–88	1970–79	1979–90
							Annual rate of lab. Prod. growth (%)			
		Index number (US = 100)					OECD ISDB data		BLS data[b]	
Denmark	42	41	48	48	44	39	4.25	0.90	5.39	1.16
Japan	46	49	50	62	72	78	6.00	5.66	5.95	4.01
United Kingdom	54	53	53	52	52	56	2.15	4.18	2.69	4.32
Belgium	54	56	59	70	76	78	5.47	4.35	6.87	4.87
Finland	55	51	51	56	59	65	2.81	4.89		
Italy	57	57	58	69	72	76	4.67	4.37	5.69	3.83
Sweden	58	55	58	55	54	50	2.04	2.07	3.53	2.00
Norway	59	57	59	55	52	50	1.79	2.13	3.01	2.39
Netherlands	61	63	65	74	74	71	4.67	2.76	6.26	3.01
Germany	62	59	63	67	60	55	3.58	0.91	4.47	2.10
France	64	62	65	72	65	67	4.01	2.35	4.27	3.60
Australia	68	62	67	68	63	62	2.66	2.16		
Canada	81	80	82	81	76	72	2.57	1.89	3.33	1.45
United States	100	100	100	100	100	100	2.59	3.23	2.57	3.08

Summary statistics for total manufacturing

Unweighted average

	1970	1973	1975	1979	1985	1988	1970–79	1979–88	1970–79	1979–90
(a) excluding US	58	57	60	64	63	63				
(b) including US							3.52	2.99	4.50	2.99
Coefficient of variation	0.23	0.23	0.21	0.20	0.21	0.23	0.37	0.48	0.32	0.38
Minimum/maximum	0.42	0.41	0.48	0.48	0.44	0.39				
Correlation with initial labour productivity[c]							−0.42	0.01		

Notes

a   Source: Own computations from OECD International Sectoral Database on diskettes (1992 version). Labour productivity is defined as the ratio of GDP in 1980 US dollars to total employment (persons engaged in production). Countries are ranked by their 1970 labour productivity level in manufacturing.

b   Source: Own computations from Bureau of Labor Statistics (1991), Table 1. Labour productivity is defined as output (GDP) in constant prices in each country per hour worked. No international level comparisons are available.

c   Correlation coefficient between annual rate of labour productivity growth and labour productivity level at the start of each period, across all OECD countries with available data.

input, and $\bar{\alpha}$ is the international average wage share.[6]

Total factor productivity growth is based on the Divisia measure, ρ, defined as:

$$\rho^h = \hat{Y}^h - \bar{\alpha}\hat{L}^h - (1-\bar{\alpha})\hat{K}^h \qquad (8.2)$$

where a superscript hat ($^$) indicates the rate of growth (see Gollop and Dale 1980, for a discussion of the Divisia index).[7]

The convergence in TFP levels for the total economy is even more marked than that in labour productivity levels (see Table 8.3).[8] Between 1970 and 1988, the coefficient of variation fell from 0.17 to 0.13 (com-

Table 8.3: Translog total factor productivity (TFP) levels relative to the US for the total economy and total manufacturing among OECD countries, 1970–1988[a]

| | Results for the total economy | | | | | Results for total manufacturing | | | | |
| | TFP levels[b] | | | TFP growth[c] | | TFP levels[b] | | | TFP growth[c] | |
	1970	1979	1988	1970–79	1979–88	1970	1979	1988	1970–79	1979–88
Finland	51	56	64	1.45	1.80	54	54	60	1.34	3.12
Denmark	57	61	65	1.01	1.15	49	52	44	2.22	0.11
Norway	63	68	71	1.33	0.84	57	50	42	0.00	−0.17
Sweden	63	63	66	0.43	0.98	59	52	49	0.17	1.26
United Kingdom		67	74	0.65[d]	1.38	58	53	56	0.49	2.49
Germany	70	77	78	1.36	0.57	71	73	62	1.83	0.10
France	73	82	87	1.69	1.07	69	74	65	2.22	0.57
Belgium	74	82	85	1.44	0.79	60	70	74	3.05	2.54
Netherlands	77	88	89	1.85	0.47	58	62	60	2.37	1.46
Australia	77	78	79	0.40	0.58	71	69	65	1.19	1.15
Japan	80	82	87	0.60	1.25	68	77	91[e]	2.78	3.71
Italy	84	87	88	0.71	0.52	65	68	72	2.00	2.48
Canada	85	86	83	0.52	−0.03	76	77	66[e]	1.65	0.25
United States	100	100	100	0.37	0.41	100	100	100	1.47	1.92
Summary statistics										
Unweighted average										
(a) excluding US	71	75	78			63	64	62		
(b) including US				0.98	0.84				1.63	1.50
Coefficient of variation	0.17	0.15	0.13	0.51	0.54	0.18	0.20	0.24	0.55	0.80
Minimum/maximum	0.51	0.56	0.64			0.49	0.50	0.42		
Correlation with initial TFP level				−0.96	−0.73				0.07	0.13

Notes

a Source: Own computations from OECD ISDB. TFP levels are computed according to eq. (8.1). Output is measured by GDP in 1980 US dollars, labour by total employment, and capital by gross fixed capital. Factor shares are based on the average ratio of employee compensation to GDP for the 12 countries over the 1970–1988 period. Countries are ranked by 1970 TFP level for the total economy.

b Index number, with US = 100.

c Average annual rates (in percent) based on the Tornqvist–Divisia index.

d The UK figure for 1970–1979 is based on total industry.

e 1987 is used instead of 1988.

pared to 0.15 for labour productivity). Average TFP in other countries grew from 71% of the US level to 78% (compared to 71% for labour productivity). As with labour productivity, those furthest behind had more rapid rates of growth in TFP, and the correlation coefficient between the two is −0.96 for 1970–1979 and −0.73 for 1979–1988.

The US maintained the highest level of TFP throughout the period, though Belgium, France, Italy, Japan and The Netherlands were all within

15% of the US by 1988. Japan's TFP growth was just about average (the difference with its labour productivity performance a reflection, as we shall see below, of its massive capital investment). The US had the lowest rate of TFP growth among these countries in the 1970–1979 period, and was second lowest during 1979–1988, at about half the average of all OECD countries. Average TFP growth among the countries in the sample fell off slightly between 1970–1979 and 1979–1988, though not nearly as much as labour productivity growth.

In manufacturing, the story was again different. There was rising dispersion in TFP levels, particularly between 1979 and 1988. The correlation between initial TFP level and TFP growth was slightly positive, at 0.07 in 1970–1979 and 0.13 in 1979–1988. The dispersion in TFP growth rates increased substantially between the 1970–1979 and the 1979–1988 periods. TFP growth in US manufacturing was 10% below average in the 1970s but 28% above average during the 1980s.

1.3 Capital Intensity

To complete the aggregate picture, we next present comparative results on capital–labour ratios among OECD countries in Table 8.4. According to the OECD data, the US remained the most capital-intensive country throughout the period between 1970 and 1988. However, the average capital–labour ratio among other countries increased from only 58% of the US level in 1970 to 81% in 1988. Japan is noteworthy in that its capital–labour ratio was only 20% of the US level in 1970 but reached 52% by 1988. There was general convergence in capital intensity among OECD countries, as the coefficient of variation fell from 0.29 to 0.16.

In terms of the growth in the capital–labour ratio, the results are even more telling. There was a significant inverse relation between initial capital–labour ratios and capital–labour growth, with correlation coefficients of −0.90 in the 1970–1979 period and −0.69 in the 1979–1988 period. Japan had the highest growth rate in both periods, while the US was last in 1970–1979 and second from last in 1979–1988. Average OECD growth in capital intensity also slowed down, by almost 40%, between the 1970–1979 and 1979–1988 periods. Japan also slowed down, with its rate of capital–labour growth almost falling by half between the 1970s and 1980s (from 8.5 to 4.8% points).

In manufacturing, the picture is again different. During the 1970s, there was modest convergence in capital intensity, with the coefficient of variation falling from 0.23 to 0.20, but this was followed by increasing dispersion during the 1980s. Japan had the highest capital–labour growth over the period, rising from 39% of the US level in 1970 to 69% in 1988. US capital–labour growth in manufacturing was the lowest among OECD

Table 8.4: Capital–labour ratios (K/L) *relative to the US and average annual growth rates for the total economy and manufacturing among OECD countries, 1970–1988*[a]

	Results for the total economy					Results for total manufacturing				
	K/L levels[b]			K/L growth[c]		K/L levels[b]			K/L growth[c]	
	1970	1979	1988	1970–79	1979–88	1970	1979	1988	1970–79	1979–88
Japan	20	38	52[d]	8.50	4.84[d]	39	60	69[d]	7.63	5.19[d]
Italy	40	57	66	4.93	2.59	74	103	116	6.35	4.48
France	52	67	77	3.82	2.51	83	96	106	4.25	4.22
United Kingdom	55	64	71	2.81	1.97	83	94	101	3.93	4.01
Germany	57	73	81	3.67	2.08	71	82	73	4.17	1.92
Finland	60	83	97	4.50	2.70	101	109	120	3.48	4.20
Belgium	61	78	90	3.84	2.52	78	102	114	5.72	4.30
Norway	62	80	92	3.79	2.51	107	123	152	4.23	5.45
Denmark	63	71	70	2.41	0.73	69	84	75	4.81	1.88
Sweden	65	75	80	2.59	1.56	97	113	102	4.45	1.92
Australia	71	83	86	2.73	1.28	90	97	91	3.48	2.39
Netherlands	72	87	94	3.14	1.73	117	150	150	5.46	3.08
Canada	75	81	93[d]	1.93	2.69[d]	118	113	121	2.18	3.89
United States	100	100	100	0.98	0.94	100	100	100	2.66	3.11
Summary statistics										
Unweighted average										
(a) excluding US	58	72	81			87	102	107		
(b) including US				3.55	2.19				4.49	3.57
Coefficient of variation	0.29	0.19	0.16	0.48	0.44	0.23	0.20	0.23	0.31	0.32
Minimum/maximum	0.20	0.38	0.52			0.33	0.40	0.46		
Correlation with initial TFP level				−0.90	−0.69				−0.69	0.01

Notes

a   Source: Own computations from OECD International Sectoral Database on diskettes (1992 version). Labour is measured by total employment and capital by gross fixed capital. Countries are ranked according to their capital–labour ratio for the total economy in 1970.

b   Index number, with US = 100.

c   Average annual rates (in percent).

d   1987 is used instead of 1988.

countries in the 1970–1979 period, but close to average during the 1980s. Still, the US had switched from an above-average country in terms of capital intensity in 1970 (though not the highest) to a below-average one in 1988. During the 1970s, there was a significant inverse relation between initial capital–labour ratios and their growth, with a correlation coefficient of −0.69, but during the 1980s the correlation between the two was just about zero.

From equation (8.2), the relationship between labour productivity growth, TFP growth and capital–labour growth is given by

$$\hat{\Pi}^h = \rho^h + (1 - \overline{\alpha})\hat{k}^h \tag{8.3}$$

where $\hat{\Pi}^h$ is the rate of labour productivity growth in country h and $\hat{k}^h$ is the rate of growth of country h's capital–labour ratio (K^h/L^h). From the first four tables, it is apparent that the convergence in labour productivity levels for the total economy over the 1970–1988 period has been due to convergence in both TFP levels and capital intensity. However, in manufacturing, the dispersion in labour productivity levels and capital–labour ratios remained unchanged over the 1970–1988 period, while the dispersion of TFP levels actually increased. Moreover, the substantial fall-off in labour productivity growth observed between the 1970–1979 and 1979–1988 periods for both the total economy and manufacturing was due almost entirely to the slackening pace of capital investment, while the rate of TFP growth declined only slightly between the two periods.

2. PRODUCTIVITY AND CAPITAL FORMATION ON THE INDUSTRY LEVEL

I now turn to a consideration of the behaviour of productivity movements and capital accumulation at the individual sectoral and industry level. The OECD ISDB provides data on output, employment and capital stock for ten major sectors of the economy, and nine manufacturing industries. As before, the data run mainly from 1970 to 1988. The advantage of looking at the sectoral and industry level is that it may allow us to uncover the sources of productivity movements on the aggregate level. In particular, our focus here is on whether the catch-up process on the industry level has been even over time or more jagged in appearance.

A word of caution should be given at the outset regarding country comparisons of productivity levels at the industry or sector level. These are affected by the individual industry price deflators used in each country and the corresponding intercountry exchange rates, country conventions used to measure industry output and, most importantly, by the classification scheme used in each country to aggregate the detailed sub-industry or sub-sector data to the broader industry or sector level. As a result, it is difficult to place too much confidence in precise productivity comparisons for particular industries. However, considerable experience in such comparative work suggests that the general patterns are quite reliable, particularly measures of changes over time in productivity levels.

2.1 Labour Productivity

I begin with a consideration of relative labour productivity levels between OECD countries. I have divided the non-US countries into three groupings: Japan, Germany, and 'other OECD' countries. I have singled out Japan and Germany for special treatment since they, along with the US, constitute the three major economies of the world. We begin with a consideration of the major sectors of the economy.

If we first look at the performance of Japan relative to the US, it is clear that the 71% (69/40–1) catch-up in Japanese aggregate productivity relative to the US highlighted in the first line of Table 8.5 is also manifested for most *but not all* major sectors of the economy (also see Figure 8.1). Between 1970 and 1988, Japan made spectacular gains relative to the US in mining and quarrying (73%); manufacturing (69%); trade, restaurants and hotels (104%); and finance, insurance and real estate (119%). However, Japan made only modest relative advances in agriculture (12%); utilities (electricity, gas and water, 25%); transportation and communications (6%); and actually declined in relative terms in community, social, and personal services (a loss of 5%). By 1988, Japan had surpassed the US labour productivity level in utilities; finance, insurance and real estate; and government services, but, as noted above, had achieved only 78% of the US productivity level in total manufacturing, and was still very far behind in agriculture (18% of the US level); mining and quarrying (26% of the US level); and transportation and communications (47%). Thus, it is clear that Japanese productivity advances relative to the US was quite uneven over this period.

German performance relative to the US was not as spectacular as Japan's (see also Figure 8.2). Overall, Germany's labour productivity level advanced by 28% (71/56–1) on the US level. Its largest relative gains were recorded in agriculture (85%), utilities (49%), construction (82%); and finance, insurance and real estate (61%). Relative gains were modest in other sectors and, in fact, Germany fell back in mining and quarrying (29%) and in *manufacturing* (11%). By 1988, Germany had surpassed the US only in finance, insurance and real estate; and in community, social and personal services. It was still far behind the US in the other sectors, including manufacturing (55% of the US level).[9]

With respect to other OECD countries (see Figure 8.2), the record was again mixed. Major gains were found in only mining and quarrying (a result due almost entirely to The Netherlands' very high productivity in natural gas production) and construction. Modest gains occurred in agriculture, utilities, and finance, insurance and real estate. For the other major sectors, there were only modest relative gains (for government services, a modest relative loss). With the exception of mining and quarrying, and finance, insurance and real estate, the US was still considerably ahead of the other countries in terms of average labour productivity.

We can summarise these results in two ways. The first is to compute the coefficient of variation in productivity levels for each sector across countries. These are shown in the last three columns of panel A of Table 8.5. Two patterns emerge. First, the dispersion in labour productivity levels on the aggregate level shows a substantial decline between 1970 and 1988, with the coefficient of variation dropping over 40%, from 0.26 to 0.15. However, there are substantial declines in dispersion in only six of

Table 8.5: Labour productivity levels relative to the US, by major sector and manufacturing industry among OECD countries, 1970–1988[a]

| | Productivity relative to US (Index number US = 100) | | | | | | Coefficient of variation in productivity across all OECD countries | | |
| | Japan | | Germany | | Other OECD | | | | |
	1970	1988	1970	1988	1970	1988	1970	1979	1988
A. Total economy[b]	40	69	56	71	57	71	0.26	0.19	0.15
Agriculture	16	18	22	41	41	55	0.52	0.39	0.36
Mining & quarrying[c]	10	26	14	10	32	160	1.06	1.83	1.17
Manufacturing	46	78	62	55	59	62	0.23	0.20	0.23
Utilities	86	107	44	65	52	70	0.42	0.31	0.29
Construction	43	64	41	75	46	84	0.35	0.20	0.22
Trade, restaurants[d]	34	69	55	64	62	71	0.27	0.24	0.20
Transp. & comm.[e]	45	47	50	58	49	55	0.31	0.29	0.24
Fin., insur., real est.[f]	73	159	81	131	77	100	0.28	0.21	0.29
Social, personal serv.[g]	67	63	136	161	85	87	0.49	0.45	0.29
Government services	77	101	70	72	70	68	0.25	0.25	0.26
Unweighted average:									
All industries							0.42	0.44	0.37
All industries except mining							0.35	0.28	0.28
B. All Manufacturing[h]	46	78	62	55	60	62	0.23	0.20	0.23
Basic metals	78	199	39	45	51	73	0.46	0.49	0.48
Chemicals[i]	83	170	69	59	51	66	0.35	0.42	0.43
Nonmetallic minerals[j]	56	58	58	65	60	75	0.29	0.27	0.27
Machinery & equip.[k]	33	78	60	47	58	55	0.27	0.25	0.32
Paper, print., publ.	55	95	52	61	67	77	0.24	0.21	0.23
Food, bev., tob.	56	35	68	54	62	67	0.28	0.27	0.35
Textiles	44	57	81	71	77	78	0.20	0.19	0.19
Wood & wood prod.[l]			72	54	70	77	0.26	0.18	0.23
Other industries[m]	45	46	54	41	61	62	0.64	0.53	0.71
Unweighted average:									
All industries							0.32	0.30	0.34

C. Coefficient of variation of labour productivity levels relative to the US across industries by country

	10 major sectors			9 major sectors except mining			9 manufacturing industries		
	1970	1979	1988	1970	1979	1988	1970	1979	1988
Australia	0.35	0.26	0.23	0.33	0.27	0.22			
Belgium	0.39	0.33	0.34	0.25	0.17	0.19	0.36	0.25	0.18
Canada	0.15	0.16	0.23	0.15	0.17	0.23	0.17	0.11	0.22
Denmark	0.41	0.22	1.04	0.28	0.21	0.24	0.20	0.22	0.20
Finland	0.37	0.31	0.33	0.28	0.23	0.30	0.22	0.17	0.23
France	0.39	0.31	0.35	0.27	0.21	0.24	0.22	0.15	0.28
Germany	0.59	0.47	0.54	0.52	0.41	0.44	0.19	0.14	0.17
Italy	0.63	0.57	0.49	0.63	0.57	0.49	0.23	0.15	0.19
Japan	0.49	0.43	0.53	0.40	0.39	0.48	0.28	0.49	0.61
Netherlands	0.38	1.52	0.95	0.32	0.17	0.21	0.20	0.15	0.19
Norway	0.36	0.90	1.08	0.29	0.20	0.16	0.27	0.31	0.37
Sweden	0.36	0.30	0.35	0.25	0.21	0.28	0.33	0.32	0.34
United Kingdom	0.25	0.17	0.12	0.21	0.18	0.12	0.56	0.60	0.52
Average C.V.	0.39	0.46	0.51	0.32	0.26	0.28	0.27	0.25	0.29

Notes

a Source: Own computations from the OECD International Sectoral Database on diskettes (1992 version). Labour productivity is defined as the ratio of GDP in 1980 US dollars to total employment (persons engaged in production). Computations for other OECD countries are based on the unweighted average labour productivity of countries with available data.

Exceptions:

b UK figure for 1970 is based on total industry

c Excludes Italy, all years; UK, 1988

d Only wholesale and retail trade for Japan and The Netherlands

e Excludes The Netherlands in 1970 and 1979

f Excludes The Netherlands, all years; excludes UK, 1988; for Germany, includes finance and insurance only

g Excludes The Netherlands, 1970 and 1979

h Australia is included in total manufacturing but is excluded for all individual manufacturing industries

i Excludes The Netherlands in 1970 and 1979

j Excludes The Netherlands, 1970 and 1979; excludes Norway, all years

k Excludes The Netherlands in 1970 and 1979

l Excludes Japan, The Netherlands, and UK, all years

m Excludes The Netherlands, 1970 and 1979; excludes Norway, all years.

Key:

Agriculture: agriculture, forestry and fisheries

Mining and quarrying: includes oil and natural gas extraction

Manufacturing

    Basic metals: basic metal products

    Chemicals: includes petroleum, rubber and plastic products

    Nonmetallic minerals: nonmetallic mineral products

    Machinery & equip.: machinery and equipment, including fabricated metal products, industrial and transport machinery, office and data-processing equipment, and electrical and optical equipment

    Paper, print., publ.: paper, printing and publishing

    Food, bev., tob.: food, beverage and tobacco

    Textiles: includes wearing apparel and leather industries

    Wood & wood prod.: wood and wood products, including furniture

    Other industries: other manufactured products

Utilities: electrical, gas and water

Construction

Trade, restaurants: also includes hotels

Transp. & comm.: transportation, storage and communication

Fin., insur., real est.: finance, insurance and real estate

Social, personal serv.: community, social and personal services

Government services

Figure 8.1: Japanese labour productivity relative to the US by major sector, 1970 and 1988

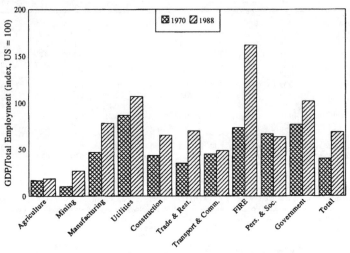

Figure 8.2: German and other OECD labour productivity relative to the US by major sector, 1970 and 1988

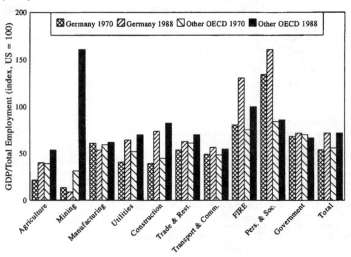

the ten sectors, and the average coefficient of variation (with or without mining) shows only a modest decline between 1970 and 1988. Second, the dispersion in productivity levels on the individual sector level, as measured by the average coefficient of variation, is substantially higher than that of the aggregate level (almost double in 1988).

The second summary approach is to compute the dispersion in sectoral productivity levels relative to the US level for each country across sectors. If sectors furthest behind the US level show the most rapid gain in productivity over time, then the dispersion in *relative* productivity levels across sectors should decline over time. Panel C of Table 8.5 shows that the coefficient of variation across all ten major sectors declines in seven out of the 13 countries between 1970 and 1988 and rises in five (and stays about the same in one). However, the average coefficient of variation increased substantially between 1970 and 1988. Since much of the variation is due to the mining sector, which in The Netherlands and Norway has extremely high labour productivity from natural gas or oil extraction, it is also useful to present the same statistics with that sector eliminated. In this case, the coefficient of variation declined in nine out of the 13 countries between 1970 and 1988, and its average value also shows a decline between 1970 and 1979 followed by a slight increase between 1979 and 1988.

Both sets of results indicate that the convergence in labour productivity observed on the aggregate level among OECD countries has been much more pronounced than at the individual sectoral level. This suggests uneven productivity developments within countries, with some sectors remaining quite backward (such as agriculture in Japan) and some modernising very quickly and even overtaking the US level (such as banking in Germany).

I next consider the individual manufacturing industries (bottom panel of Table 8.5 and Figures 8.3 and 8.4). Japan made its major gains in basic metals (157%), machinery and equipment (135%), and chemicals (106%). A substantial gain was also made in paper, printing and publishing (70%). However, relatively modest gains were recorded in nonmetallic minerals (3%), textiles (28%), and the catch-all group, other industries (2%), and in food, beverages and tobacco there was a substantial relative loss of 38 %. By 1988, Japan's labour productivity levels were far ahead of the US in basic metal products (99% greater) and chemicals (70% greater), and, indeed, in these two industries Japan had become the OECD leader in terms of productivity. However, the US led Japan in all the other industries, and, with the exception of paper, printing and publishing, Japan was still far behind the US in 1988. Indeed, according to the OECD data, in 1988 the US was still the OECD leader in food, beverages and tobacco; textiles; wood products; and machinery and equipment.

In Germany, there were no major gains. Of the nine manufacturing industries, Germany advanced relative to the US in only three and fell back in the other six. In 1988, the US was ahead of Germany in every industry. Other OECD countries made substantial gains on the US in basic metals, chemicals and nonmetallic minerals; remained at the same relative

Figure 8.3: Japanese labour productivity relative to the US by manufacturing industry, 1970 and 1988

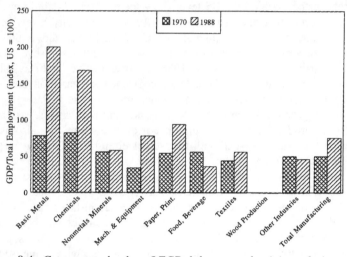

Figure 8.4: German and other OECD labour productivity relative to the US by manufacturing sector, 1970 and 1988

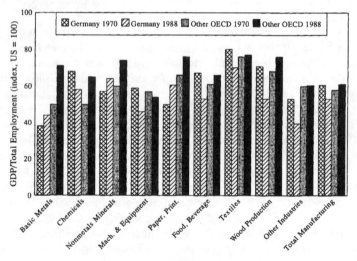

level with respect to the US in machinery and equipment, paper, printing and publishing, and food, beverages and tobacco; and actually fell further behind the US in textiles, wood, and other industries. By 1988, the US had a higher productivity level in all industries than the average of the other OECD countries. However, Finland was the OECD leader in paper, printing and publishing; and France in nonmetallic mineral products (including glass and ceramics).

The coefficient of variation of labour productivity levels across countries declined in five out of the nine manufacturing industries between 1970 and 1988 and increased in the other four. Its average value declined slightly, from 0.32 in 1970 to 0.30 in 1979, and then increased to 0.34 in 1988. The coefficient of variation of relative labour productivity levels across manufacturing industries declined in only four of the 13 countries and rose in four (remaining about the same in the others). Its average value also fell slightly between 1970 and 1979, from 0.27 to 0.25, and then increased to 0.29 in 1988. These results also give evidence of jagged productivity developments on the industry level within countries. Japan is particularly notable in both the increase of its coefficient of variation, from 0.28 in 1970 to 0.61 in 1988, and the size of the coefficient of variation in 1988. This finding, in particular, suggests intensive specialisation of Japanese manufacturing in particular industries and sub-industries.

2.2 Total Factor Productivity and Capital Intensity

Results on relative TFP levels among OECD countries by sector are, perhaps not surprisingly, similar to those for labour productivity (Table 8.6). Whereas the coefficient of variation in TFP for the total economy across countries declined from 0.17 to 0.13 between 1970 and 1980, dispersion in TFP across countries declined in only five of the ten major sectors (Panel A). The average coefficient of variation (with or without mining) shows only a modest decline between 1970 and 1988. Moreover, the average coefficient of variation is substantially higher than that of the aggregate level (more than double in 1988). The coefficient of variation in relative TFP across industries (excluding mining) by country shows a decline in nine countries (out of 13), and its average value falls modestly, from 0.33 to 0.29.

In manufacturing, the coefficient of variation in TFP levels across countries increased in eight out of the nine manufacturing industries between 1970 and 1988. The average coefficient of variation remained unchanged from 1970 to 1979, and then increased from 0.32 in 1979 to 0.36 in 1988. The coefficient of variation of relative TFP levels across manufacturing industries declined in only three countries and increased in four (remaining about the same in the other three). Its average value remained unchanged between 1970 and 1988. Japan again stands out in that its coefficient of variation increased from 0.31 in 1970 to 0.53 in 1988, suggesting intensive specialisation in Japanese manufacturing.

Results on capital–labour ratios are also shown in Table 8.6. On the aggregate level, as noted above, there was significant convergence in overall capital–labour ratios for the total economy, as the coefficient of variation fell from 0.29 in 1970 to 0.16 in 1988 (see Panel A). The same trend is reflected on the individual sectoral level, with the coefficient of variation declining in nine out of the ten major sectors, and remaining unchanged in the other. The average coefficient of variation also declined, from 0.53 to 0.45 for all ten sectors and from 0.48 to 0.40 for all except mining. Even so, its average value was considerably greater than the coefficient of variation for the total economy (over twice as great in 1988). Results are similar for the coefficient of variation of relative capital–labour ratios across sectors by country, declining in seven countries and rising in four. Its average value fell from 0.56 in 1970 to 0.52 in 1988.

In manufacturing, the coefficient of variation across countries fell in four manufacturing industries and rose in four. Its average value remained unchanged between 1970 and 1979, at 0.35, and then increased to 0.40 in

Table 8.6: TFP and capital–labour (K/L) levels relative to the US, by major sector and manufacturing industry among OECD countries, 1970–1988[a]

| | | Coefficient of variation across countries in relative | | | | | Correlation coefficient between TFP and K/L growth | |
| | | TFP levels | | | K/L levels | | | |
	1970	1979	1988	1970	1979	1988	1970–79	1979–88
A. Total economy[b]	0.17	0.15	0.13	0.29	0.19	0.16	−0.10	0.37
Agriculture	0.28	0.29	0.38	0.45	0.33	0.26	−0.65	−0.63
Mining & quarrying[c]	0.63	1.00	0.76	1.00	1.04	0.87	0.49	0.76
Manufacturing	0.19	0.20	0.23	0.23	0.20	0.23	0.58	0.41
Utilities	0.59	0.39	0.35	0.39	0.33	0.34	−0.05	−0.05
Construction	0.31	0.24	0.27	0.43	0.36	0.39	−0.54	−0.30
Trade, restaurants[d]	0.25	0.22	0.20	0.32	0.32	0.31	0.43	−0.14
Transp. & comm.[e]	0.32	0.25	0.18	0.47	0.43	0.28	−0.54	−0.78
Fin., insur., real est.[f]	0.46	0.49	0.49	0.42	0.40	0.40	−0.34	−0.20
Social, personal serv.[g]	0.51	0.46	0.39	0.74	0.69	0.63	−0.77	−0.65
Government services	0.22	0.22	0.22	0.87	0.85	0.81	0.52	0.34
Unweighted average:								
(a) All sectors	0.38	0.38	0.35	0.53	0.50	0.45	−0.08	−0.12
(b) All except mining	0.35	0.31	0.30	0.48	0.44	0.40		
B. All manufacturing[h]	0.19	0.20	0.23	0.23	0.20	0.23	0.58	0.41
Basic metals	0.42	0.48	0.45	0.31	0.26	0.28	0.45	0.50
Chemicals[i]	0.36	0.37	0.39	0.33	0.33	0.36	0.02	0.04
Nonmetallic minerals[j]	0.24	0.24	0.26	0.34	0.28	0.28	−0.23	0.36
Machinery & equip.[k]	0.23	0.25	0.33	0.29	0.21	0.21	0.40	0.43
Paper, print., publ.	0.22	0.23	0.23	0.47	0.40	0.37	0.27	0.38
Food, bev., tob.	0.30	0.30	0.34	0.26	0.22	0.25	0.22	−0.20
Textiles	0.20	0.21	0.24	0.16	0.20	0.28	−0.36	0.32
Wood & wood prod.[l]	0.26	0.24	0.30	0.29	0.26	0.35	−0.03	−0.24
Other industries[m]	0.63	0.54	0.72	0.83	1.18	1.44	−0.10	−0.03
Unweighted average:	0.32	0.32	0.36	0.35	0.35	0.40	0.07	0.17

C. Coefficient of variation of TFP levels and capital–labour ratios relative to the US across industries by country

	Total factor productivity				Capital–labour ratio			
	9 sectors[n]		9 manuf. ind.		9 sectors[n]		9 manuf. ind.	
	1970	1988	1970	1988	1970	1988	1970	1988
Australia	0.31	0.22			0.72	0.56		
Belgium	0.21	0.25	0.42	0.21	0.68	0.40	0.37	0.36
Canada	0.23	0.30	0.12	0.20	0.85	0.65	0.26	0.29
Denmark	0.39	0.41	0.17	0.17	0.32	0.63	0.32	0.36
Finland	0.17	0.12			0.45	0.41		
France	0.23	0.21	0.27	0.14	0.45	0.59	0.66	0.40
Germany	0.74	0.72	0.15	0.15	0.59	0.66	0.24	0.33
Italy	0.51	0.44	0.24	0.27	0.57	0.63	0.59	1.23
Japan	0.44	0.37	0.31	0.53	0.49	0.45	0.36	0.53
Netherlands	0.23	0.19			0.49	0.36		
Norway	0.32	0.23	0.28	0.41	0.47	0.47	0.17	0.39
Sweden	0.15	0.18	0.29	0.21	0.36	0.36	0.43	0.53
United Kingdom	0.36	0.15	0.44	0.43	0.79	0.52	0.38	0.39
Average C.V.	0.33	0.29	0.27	0.27	0.56	0.52	0.38	0.48

D. Correlation coefficient between TFP growth and capital–labour growth across industries by country

	10 major sectors		9 manuf. industries	
	1970–79	1979–88	1970–79	1979–88
Australia	−0.08	0.45		
Belgium	0.42	−0.48	−0.32	−0.55
Canada	−0.62	−0.14	−0.13	0.28
Denmark	0.05	0.94	−0.17	−0.42
Finland	−0.24	0.43		
France	−0.70	−0.79	−0.20	0.73
Germany	−0.05	−0.06	0.24	0.22
Italy	−0.66	0.08	0.39	−0.54
Japan	−0.39	−0.56	0.23	0.83
Netherlands	0.61	0.68		
Norway	0.39	−0.43	−0.48	0.28
Sweden	−0.35	0.07	−0.16	0.32
United Kingdom	−0.82	0.02	0.04	0.95
United States	0.25	−0.28	0.34	−0.04
Average correl.	−0.16	−0.01	−0.02	0.19

Notes

a Source: Own computations from OECD International Sectoral Database on diskettes (1992 version). TFP levels are computed according to eq. (8.1). Output is measured by GDP in 1980 US dollars, labour by total employment and capital by gross fixed capital. Factor shares are based on the average ratio of employee compensation to GDP by individual sector and industry for the 12 countries over the 1970–1988 period.

Exceptions:

b UK figure for 1970 is based on total industry

c Excludes Italy, all years; UK, 1988

d Excludes Australia, all years; Denmark, 1988; only wholesale and retail trade for Japan and The Netherlands

e Excludes The Netherlands in 1970 and 1979

f Excludes Italy and The Netherlands, all years; excludes UK, 1988; for Germany, includes finance and insurance only

g Excludes The Netherlands, 1970 and 1979

h Australia, Finland and The Netherlands are included in total manufacturing but are excluded for all individual manufacturing industries

i Excludes The Netherlands in 1970 and 1979

j Excludes The Netherlands, 1970 and 1979; excludes Norway, all years

k Excludes The Netherlands in 1970 and 1979

l Excludes Belgium, Italy, Japan, The Netherlands and UK, all years

m Excludes The Netherlands, 1970 and 1979; excludes Norway, all years

n Mining and quarrying sector is excluded

Key: See notes to Table 8.5.

1988. However, there is an apparent problem with the other industry category (the capital–labour ratio seems unrealistically high for Italy). If we exclude this industry, then the average coefficient of variation declined from 0.31 in 1970 to 0.27 in 1979 and then increased to 0.30 in 1988. The coefficient of variation of relative capital–labour ratios across industry by country fell in only two countries and increased in seven between 1970 and 1988. Its average increased from 0.38 to 0.48. Here, again, the 1988 value for Italy appears affected by apparent errors in the data for the other industry category. If Italy is excluded, the average coefficient of variation still climbed, though from 0.35 to 0.40.

3. RELATION BETWEEN CAPITAL–LABOUR GROWTH AND TFP GROWTH

A cursory examination of Table 8.6 suggests that there may be a connection between countries and industries that did well in terms of TFP growth and those that had superior performance in capital–labour growth. It is, of course, not surprising that there is a strong positive relation between the rate of *labour productivity growth* and capital–labour growth. This is apparent from eq. (8.3). The rate of labour productivity growth is directly related to the rate of technological progress and the rate of capital–labour growth. The latter relation is usually referred to as 'capital deepening', meaning that more capital is put into the hands of each worker, thereby increasing their output (per hour worked).

However, what is not so apparent is that there may be a positive association between the rate of *technological progress* and the rate of growth in capital intensity. In previous work (my 1991 paper), I argued that there are several ways in which capital investment and technical change may be associated. First, it is likely that substantial investment is required to adopt new inventions (the so-called 'embodiment effect' or 'vintage effect'). A second avenue is that the introduction of new capital may lead to better organisation, management and the like. A third is through learning-by-doing. A fourth is that potential technological advance may stimulate capital formation, because the opportunity to modernise equipment promises a high rate of return to investment. A fifth is through the so-called Verdoorn effect, whereby investment growth may lead to a growth in demand and thereby to the maintenance of a generally favourable economic climate for investment. These possibilities do not lead to a specific functional relation between TFP growth and the rate of capital growth but do suggest a positive correlation between the two variables (see my 1991 paper for more details).

I first computed the simple correlation coefficient between the rate of TFP growth and the rate of growth in the capital–labour ratio, for both the 1970–1979 and the 1979–1988 periods. These are shown both across country within sector or industry (Panels A and B) and across sectors or industries within country (Panel D). Here the evidence of a positive relation between TFP growth and capital–labour growth is quite mixed. For the total economy, there is a positive correlation between the two in the 1979–1988 period (correlation coefficient of 0.37) but the correlation for the 1970–1979 period is slightly negative. However, among the major sectors, most of the correlation coefficients are negative. The notable exception is the manufacturing sector, which has positive correlations in both periods (0.58 and 0.41, respectively). This suggests that countries that were investing heavily in manufacturing were also experiencing greater than average TFP growth in manufacturing. However, an examination of the individual manufacturing industries again presents a mixed picture, though, on average, the correlations are slightly positive. Correlations across industries within country also show a mixed pattern, some countries with positive coefficients and others within negative ones. Perhaps, the notable exception is Japan, with a correlation coefficient of 0.83 among manufacturing industries in the 1979–1988 period, confirming its high investment and technological progress in certain targeted industries.

A more proper channel to test this relation is through a regression framework. I used the following specification:

$$RLTFPGRT_{it}^{h} = b_0 + b_1 RLKLGRT_{i,t-1}^{h} + b_2 RELTFP_{it}^{h} + \varepsilon_t^{h} \quad (8.4)$$

where $RLTFPGRT_{it}^{h}$ is the rate of (Divisia) TFP growth in sector (or industry) i in country h at time t relative to the corresponding US rate of TFP growth; $RLKLGRT_{i,t-1}^{h}$ is the rate of capital–labour growth in sector (or industry) i in country h at time $t-1$ relative to the corresponding US growth rate; $RELTFP_{it}^{h}$ is country h's TFP relative to the US at the start of each period; and ε is a stochastic error term. Both two-year and three-year averages are used for the growth variables to reduce random noise. The regression is performed on both the sample of nine manufacturing industries and the sample of ten major sectors. We treat each industry (or sector) in each country in each period as an observation. The US is excluded from this regression equation, since the value of the dependent variable is always unity.

The key variable of interest is $RLKLGRT$, since it provides a test of the 'interaction hypothesis'. This hypothesis suggests that the rate of growth of TFP will be positively correlated with the rate of growth of the capital–labour ratio. I use the lagged value of capital–labour growth in the regression for two reasons. First, in so far as causation may run both ways, there may be a 'simultaneity bias' introduced if we use the contemporaneous value of capital–labour growth. Second, there may also be costs of adjustment associated with the introduction of new capital. The coefficient of the contemporaneous value of *RLKLGRT* may thus reflect the negative influence of adjustment costs on (contemporaneous) productivity growth.

We also include the term *RELTFP* to control for the so-called 'catch-up effect', which states that industries and countries which lagged furthest behind the US in technological sophistication had the most opportunities to imitate and purchase advanced technology and hence should exhibit the fastest rate of technology advance. Taking each industry (sector) in each country as an observation, this hypothesis implies that the rate of growth of (relative) TFP should be inversely correlated with the level of (relative) TFP at the beginning of the period.

In some specifications, country and industry dummy variables are also included to control for country-specific effects, such as the degree of trade openness, culture and government policy; and industry-specific effects, such as market structure and diffusion patterns for new technology.

The results, shown in Tables 8.7 and 8.8, generally confirm the interaction hypothesis. For the manufacturing industry sample, there is a statistically significant relation between a country's (relative) rate of TFP growth and its (relative) rate of capital–labour growth, though the significance level varies from 10% to 1%. The results are strongest for the sample that uses three-year averages for the variables. For the major sector sample, all the regression forms show a highly significant effect of increasing capital intensity on TFP growth. The magnitudes of the coefficients are also interesting. Within manufacturing, a one percentage *point* increase in the annual rate of capital–labour growth is associated with about a 0.1 percentage point (the range is 0.07 to 0.12) increase in TFP growth. Across the major sectors, a one percentage point increase in the annual rate of capital–labour growth is associated with about a 0.3 percentage point (with a range from 0.24 to 0.37) increase in TFP growth.

The results also provide confirmation of the catch-up effect, showing a highly statistically significant inverse relation between the rate of TFP convergence by industry and country and its initial TFP level, relative to the US. However, the *size* of the coefficient is much lower than for relative capital–labour growth. A one percentage point increase in initial relative TFP level is associated with only about a (negative) 0.040 percentage point change in TFP growth for the total economy and about a 0.035 percentage point change in TFP growth in manufacturing.

Table 8.7: Regression of relative TFP growth on relative TFP level and growth in relative capital intensity^a (manufacturing industry sample)

Independent variables	Dependent variable: $RLTFPGRT_{it}^h$			
	2-year average values			3-year averages
Constant	0.0037	−0.0131	−0.0509***	−0.0507***
	(1.01)	(1.43)	(4.28)	(5.99)
$RLKLGRT_{i,t-1}^h$	0.0945**	0.0742*	0.0944**	0.1151***
	(6.16)	(1.70)	(2.22)	(2.86)
$RELTFP_{it}^h$	−0.0250***	−0.0362***	−0.0422***	−0.0358***
	(2.68)	(3.53)	(3.94)	(4.14)
Country Dummies	Excluded	Included	Included	Included
Industry Dummies	Excluded	Excluded	Included	Included
R^2	0.023	0.074	0.154	0.332
$\bar{R}^2$	0.019	0.053	0.122	0.293
Std error	0.060	0.058	0.056	0.037
Sample size	550	550	550	364

Notes

a   Results are based on two-year averages for *RLKLGRT* and *RLTFPGRT* (three-year averages in the last column). The sample covers the time period from 1970 to 1988, 13 countries (excluding the US), and 9 manufacturing industries. Lags are in terms of periods (for the two-year average variables, the lag is two years). Estimated coefficients are shown next to the respective independent variable and the absolute value of the *t*-statistic is shown in parentheses. Industries and countries with missing data are excluded from the sample.

*   Significant at the 0.10 level (two-tailed test)
** Significant at the 0.05 level (two-tailed test)
*** Significant at the 0.01 level (two-tailed test)

4. CONCLUDING REMARKS

An examination of aggregate statistics, based on the coefficient of variation, shows that convergence of labour productivity, TFP and capital intensity has continued over the period from 1970 to 1988 for the total economy among OECD countries. There is also clear evidence of catch-up, indicated by both rising average productivity and capital intensity of OECD countries relative to the United States and an inverse relation (negative correlation) between initial levels and rates of growth. However, there was no or little convergence in growth *rates* of productivity, which one would expect if productivity levels converged and advantages of backwardness held sway.

On the sectoral level, the coefficient of variation of labour productivity levels, TFP levels and capital intensity was much higher, on average, than that for the overall economy. Moreover, dispersion on the sectoral level shows only a very modest decline. The same pattern is evident for the

Table 8.8: Regression of relative TFP growth on relative TFP level and growth in relative capital intensity^a (major sector sample)

Independent variables	Dependent variable: $RLTFPGRT_{it}^h$			
	2-year average values			3-year averages
Constant	-0.0068^{**}	-0.0164^{**}	-0.0083	-0.0033
	(2.77)	(2.15)	(0.88)	(0.44)
$RLKLGRT_{i,t-1}^h$	0.3479^{***}	0.3738^{***}	0.3525^{***}	0.2351^{***}
	(6.93)	(7.19)	(5.87)	(4.64)
$RELTFP_{it}^h$	-0.0369^{***}	-0.0443^{***}	-0.0464^{***}	-0.0290^{***}
	(7.08)	(7.19)	(6.59)	(5.12)
Country dummies	Excluded	Included	Included	Included
Industry dummies	Excluded	Excluded	Included	Included
R^2	0.117	0.139	0.154	0.238
$\bar{R}^2$	0.115	0.0122	0.127	0.201
Std error	0.055	0.055	0.054	0.036
Sample size	743	743	743	494

Notes

a   Results are based on two-year averages for *RLKLGRT* and *RLTFPGRT* (three-year averages in the last column). The sample covers the time period from 1970 to 1988, 13 countries (excluding the US), and 10 major sectors. Lags are in terms of periods (for the two-year average variables, the lag is two years). Estimated coefficients are shown next to the respective independent variable and the absolute value of the *t*-statistic is shown in parentheses. Industries and countries with missing data are excluded from the sample.

*   Significant at the 0.10 level (two-tailed test)
**   Significant at the 0.05 level (two-tailed test)
*** Significant at the 0.01 level (two-tailed test)

dispersion of productivity levels and capital–labour ratios relative to the United States across sectors within country. The simple correlation between TFP growth and capital–labour growth was virtually zero across sectors. However, the regression analysis, after controlling for differences in initial TFP, does show a strong positive relation between a sector's TFP growth and its rate of (lagged) capital–labour growth. Moreover, though the catch-up effect is statistically significant, about 50% of the growth of TFP from 1970 to 1988 was attributable to capital investment and only 10% to the catch-up effect, with the remainder due to other factors (results are calculated by substituting mean values of the independent variables into the regression equation results).

For total manufacturing, the convergence of productivity levels came to a halt by 1979 or so. There was a slight convergence of labour productivity levels and capital–labour ratios between 1970 and 1979, followed by a slight divergence between 1979 and 1988. On net, there was virtually no change between 1970 and 1988 in the dispersion of labour productivity levels and an actual increase in that of TFP. There is some evidence of catch-up in labour productivity levels and capital–labour ratios between 1970 and 1979 but none between 1979 and 1988. For TFP there was no catch-up in evidence either during the 1970–1979 period or the 1979–1988 period. Moreover, the coefficient of variation of growth rates of both labour productivity and TFP increased between the 1970–1979 period and the 1979–1988 period.

On the industry level, the coefficient of variation of labour productivity levels and capital–labour ratios declined slightly, on average, between 1970 and 1979 and increased somewhat between 1979 and 1988. The dispersion of TFP levels remained unchanged between 1970 and 1979 and then increased over the 1979–1988 period. The average dispersion of labour productivity, TFP and capital intensity was higher on the industry level than for total manufacturing.

As with the major sectors of the economy, there was virtually no correlation between TFP growth and capital–labour growth on the industry level. However, the regression analysis does show a strong positive relation between industry TFP growth and lagged capital–labour growth. Moreover, the catch-up effect is statistically significant in the regression analysis, though it fails to show up in the aggregate data. Additional calculations show that about 70% of the growth of TFP within manufacturing from 1970 to 1979 was attributable to capital investment and 10% to the catch-up effect and 80% to capital investment over the 1979–1988 period, with almost none of it stemming from the catch-up effect.

Perhaps the bottom line is that the simple advantages of backwardness argument as the explanation of *aggregate* convergence must be modified. The catch-up effect should show up, *if anywhere*, on the sectoral (or industry) level. This occurred very weakly among major sectors of the economy in the 1970s and 1980s and among manufacturing industries in the 1970s, but was virtually nonexistent during the 1980s within manufacturing. Instead, specialisation in particular industries in terms of investment, with its concomitant technological change, appears to be the main driving force over this period. This was particularly the case in manufacturing in the 1980s (Japan being an extreme example of this process). This has resulted in uneven or jagged productivity developments by sector and manufacturing industry within each country.

It also seems likely from other work that the advantages of backwardness effect was the primary mechanism of OECD growth from the 1950s up until the early 1970s. This might explain the high level of productivity growth among OECD countries during this period. However, as productivity levels converged, the advantages of backwardness exhausted themselves, as was particularly evident in manufacturing during the 1980s, and average productivity growth rates fell during the 1970s and again in the 1980s. Further productivity growth is now being achieved primarily through pushing out the technological frontier and, in many cases, overtaking the leader, a process that requires intense capital investment.

NOTES

1. A third possible mechanism was also considered – namely, that employment shifted over time towards industries with high productivity. We found that employment shifts played no role in the convergence of aggregate productivity.
2. See de Long (1988) and Baumol and Wolff (1988) for a discussion of the selectivity bias associated with the OECD sample.
3. Table 8.1 also shows summary statistics for total industry, defined as the total economy excluding producers of government services and other non-firm producers (such as domestic servants). The closest US concept is private GDP. Results for this series show slightly more rapid convergence and catch-up than the previous set for the total economy.
4. It should be stressed that the negative correlation coefficient does *not* by itself constitute a *test* of the convergence hypothesis but that it is indicative of such a relation. See Baumol (1986), de Long (1988), and Baumol and Wolff (1988) for further discussion.
5. The last two columns of Table 8.2 show productivity growth rates based on comparable international data from the US Bureau of Labor Statistics (1991). Results are similar to those from the OECD ISDB data.
6. I use the international factor shares in the computations throughout the paper. See Wolff (1991) for a discussion of the choice of the proper factor shares. The TFP measure is standardised by setting Y/L and Y/K to unity for the US in 1970 so that US TFP in 1970 is equal to one.
7. The Tornqvist approximation based on average period shares is employed.
8. It should be noted that differences in service life assumptions, retirement patterns, and capital prices among countries will lead to inconsistencies in (gross) capital stock estimates among countries and thus in TFP estimates.
9. The 55% figure may appear rather low, but it should be noted that productivity levels here are not adjusted for hours worked. With such an adjustment, GDP per hour worked in German manufacturing was 76% of the corresponding US level in 1988.

REFERENCES

Abramovitz, M. (1986), 'Catching Up, Forging Ahead, and Falling Behind', *Journal of Economic History*, 46, 385–406.
Barro, R.J. (1991), 'Economic Growth in a Cross Section of Countries', *Quarterly Journal of Economics*, 105, 407–443.
Baumol, W.J. (1986), 'Productivity Growth, Convergence, and Welfare: What the Long-Run Data Show', *American Economic Review*, 76, 1072–1085.
Baumol, W.J., Batey Blackman, S.A. and Wolff, E.N. (1989), *Productivity and American Leadership: The Long View*, Cambridge, MA: MIT Press.

Baumol, W.J. and Wolff, E.N. (1988), 'Productivity Growth, Convergence, and Welfare: Reply', *American Economic Review*, 78, 1155–1159.

de Long, J.B. (1988), 'Productivity Growth, Convergence, and Welfare: Comment,' *American Economic Review*, 78, 1138–1154.

de Long, J.B. and Summers, L.H. (1991), 'Equipment Investment and Economic Growth', *Quarterly Journal of Economics*, 151, 445–502.

Dollar, D. and Wolff, E.N. (1993), *Competitiveness, Convergence, and International Specialization*, Cambridge, MA: MIT Press.

Gollop, F.M. and Dale W.J. (1980), 'US Productivity Growth by Industry, 1947–73', in J.W. Kendrick and B.N. Vaccara (eds), *New Developments in Productivity Measurement and Analysis*, Chicago: University of Chicago Press.

Maddison, A. (1982), *Phases of Capitalist Development*, Oxford: Oxford University Press.

Summers, R. and Heston, A. (1988), 'A New Set of International Comparisons of Real Product and Prices: Estimates for 130 Countries, 1950–1985', *Review of Income and Wealth*, 34, 1–26.

US Department of Labor, Bureau of Labor Statistics, Office of Productivity and Technology (1991), 'Output per Hour, Hourly Compensation, and Unit Labor Costs in Manufacturing, Twelve Industrial Countries, 1950–1990 and Unit Labor Costs in Korea and Taiwan, 1970–1990', December.

Wolff, E.N. (1991), 'Capital Formation and Productivity Convergence over the Long Term', *American Economic Review*, 81, 565–579.

COMMENT ON WOLFF

Thijs ten Raa

The initiator of the productivity convergence debate, Ed Wolff, who launched his empirical results early last decade, now takes us with yet another thought-provoking result. The total factor productivity convergence of the 1970s has continued in the 1980s, but the mechanism has changed. It is no longer a technological catch-up by less-developed countries, but the result of specialisation in high-growth sectors. Professor Wolff's diagnosis of convergence is in line with the trade liberalisation that we have witnessed recently.

Professor Wolff's results are still reassuring to the United States. Total factor productivity growth in Japan has not reached American levels yet. To some extent this result may be ascribed to his methodology, however. Total factor productivity growth is measured by the residual between the output growth rate and weighted input growth rates, where the weights are the value shares of the inputs. With an appeal to the theory of international trade, these value shares are equated across countries by taking inter-national means. In this discussion, I am going to examine this methodology and its implication for the result that Japan is still lagging. I shall do so in the context of an example that is favourable to the adoption of the factor price equalisation theorem, namely a world with a common technology.

So let us consider a world economy with a CES production function,

$$F(L,K,\rho) = (\tfrac{1}{2}L^{-\rho} + \tfrac{1}{2}K^{-\rho})^{-1/\rho},$$

common to the US and Japan. Note that since the time argument does not appear on the right-hand side, technical change is absent. If factor inputs are valued by their marginal productivities, as they should be in total factor productivity growth analysis, the wage share is

$$\alpha = \tfrac{1}{2}(Y/L)^{\rho}.$$

For simplicity, let labour and capital grow exponentially in each country: $L = L_0 e^{lt}$ and $K = K_0 e^{kt}$, then the wage share reduces to

$$\alpha = \frac{e^{-\rho lt}}{e^{-\rho lt} + e^{-\rho kt}}.$$

The labour and capital growth rates may be different for the two countries. Professor Wolff pays attention to the higher growth rate of capital in Japan than in the US. The consequent abundance of capital depresses productivity. Let me stylise this fact by assuming balanced growth for the US ($k = l$), but unbalanced growth for Japan ($k > l$). Then the last expression shows that $\alpha = 1/2$ in the US, but $\alpha \to 1$ in Japan. In the latter country, capital gets so abundant that not only does its price go down, but even its value share does. (This is possible when the macroeconomic production function is CES rather than Cobb–Douglas.)

By averaging out with the US, Professor Wolff underestimates the wage share in Japan and overestimates the capital share. Since in the total factor productivity growth formula, the growth rate of capital dominates that of labour (and both are subtracted from the output growth rate), he underestimates total factor productivity growth in Japan. In other words, the high growth rate of Japanese capital may suppress total factor productivity growth, but the weight attached to it ought to be smaller than in the US and this off-setting effect is not taken into account when value shares are averaged out across countries. Japan may perform better than Professor Wolff's estimates suggest.

International trade theory may be employed to equate factor prices, but not factor shares, except possibly at the sectoral levels. One might build a case, using neoclassical paradigms, for equalisation of value shares between countries on a sector-by-sector basis. However, it is precisely the process of specialisation in sectors that may invalidate the equality of macroeconomic value shares between labour and capital across countries. It would be interesting to redo Professor Wolff's computations with the shares equalities inserted at the sectoral level, on which he builds his analysis anyway.

I am sceptical, however, as regards any use of the factor prices equalisation theorem. One of its assumptions is that at any point of time countries have access to a common technology. True, technical coefficients will differ, but only in response to scarcity conditions, not the state of technology, the book of blueprints of all conceivable techniques. In such a stylised world, any measure of total factor productivity growth that relates to technical change in Solow residual fashion ought to imply no divergence or convergence between countries, but a zero wedge. In other words, when there is access to a common technology, convergence is no issue.

In the final analysis the measurement of productivity growth and convergence is a matter of choosing factor input prices. Professor Wolff, like all leaders in the field, uses the ones based on market value shares. This may be appropriate for a pure competitive economy, but not for the real world. My preference would be to calculate the shadow prices of labour and capital through an appropriate linear program. There would be no need to assume a common technology or to equate value shares. The elasticities of substitution are endogenised by intersectoral shifts of economic activities.

The convergence field is exceptional in economics. Empirical results are ahead of methodology. It remains to be seen if my observations on the bias in Professor Wolff's work are significant. For the time being I accept his confirmation of American leadership and his diagnosis of convergence.

PART III

Microeconomic Foundations of Growth and Technology Diffusion

9. Dynamic Oligopolistic Pricing with Endogenous Change in Market Structure and Market Potential in an Epidemic Diffusion Model

Thomas Ziesemer[*]

1. INTRODUCTION

In Dosi *et al.* (1988) there is a repeated claim that economic models should be imperfectly competitive, dynamic and of the disequilibrium type. At first sight this seems to be demanding too much from one paper. However, in this paper it will be shown that adding an epidemic diffusion model to a simple static monopoly model and to duopoly models generates all three properties.

After having mainly been used as an empirical tool without explicit supply considerations, the epidemic diffusion model has begun a second career as an information technology constraint imposed on monopoly models quite common in economic theory (see Glaister 1974; Metcalfe 1981; Amable 1992; Stoneman 1983, ch. 9; and Mahajan, Muller and Bass 1990, for an introduction to the literature on 'diffusion and supply'). Glaister (1974), starting from an epidemic information diffusion assumption with an exogenous long-run equilibrium value of demand, derived a non-logistic diffusion curve skewed to higher growth rates in earlier product phases and continuous intertemporal price differentiation. Since that time the marketing literature has used it in the framework of dynamic optimisation and differential games. Metcalfe (1981) assumed an epidemic demand curve and derived a sigmoid diffusion curve using a monopoly

[*] I should like to thank Bruno Amable for correspondence, Paul Diederen, Theon van Dijk, René Kemp, Bart Verspagen and Adriaan van Zon for helpful discussions, Marc van Wegberg and Arjen van Witteloostuijn for their detailed comments on the conference version, Gene Grossman for providing me with the written version of his conference remarks and very helpful comments on the penultimate version, and Reinoud Joosten, Hans Peters and Jerry Silverberg for commenting on an earlier version of the paper. Responsibility remains entirely mine.

mark-up assumption on the supply side and the assumption that diffusion is proportional to profits. Amable (1992) extended this analysis to allow for increasing returns and competing technologies.

This literature has been developed with the intention of improving the theoretical explanation of the observed sigmoid diffusion curves. Very often these curves show a logistic or skewed diffusion pattern. Several non-epidemic approaches to explain these patterns have been tried in the literature. The introduction of learning economies is used in the models by Bass (see Mahajan, Muller and Bass 1990) and Stoneman and Ireland (1983). However, in the former the diffusion curve derived depends on the specification of an exogenously imposed shift function, which bears great similarity to the epidemic functions used in the literature mentioned above, and in the latter on a special relation between price and threshold adopter derived from the imposition of a distribution of firm size that again bears great similarity to the types of functions used in epidemic models. Soete and Turner (1984) use the assumption of N techniques in a classical growth model. At the macro level there is a classical investment function from which sectoral investment deviates positively (negatively) if the sector in question has a higher (lower) rate of profit than the average. Asymptotically, the best-practice technique approaches a 100% share of capital, K_N, in total capital, K. K_N/K follows a sigmoid diffusion curve. The way any technique α gains capital from inferior and loses capital to superior techniques bears great formal similarity with the way a product loses demand to a new product and gains from older products in the purely empirical 'law of capture' of Norton and Bass (1992). Vintages of capital with a finite horizon optimisation model to investigate intra-firm diffusion are used in Felmingham (1988). Investments made during the early periods have a correspondingly longer productive lifetime. The lower the discount rate and the higher the expected prices, the larger the investment will be. Therefore investment is first increasing, then decreasing and the vintage capital stock has a sigmoid form.

The examples given above are on the borderline between evolutionary and (neo)classical economics and the marketing hybrid of the two. A survey of the microeconomic literature can be found in Reinganum (1989). Silverberg, Dosi and Orsenigo (1988) broadly introduce the evolutionary literature and Mahajan, Muller and Bass (1990) the marketing literature. Chatterjee and Eliashberg (1990) connect the marketing literature to the microeconomic literature, thereby giving the epidemic diffusion model and the marketing literature the status of microfounded aggregates.

This paper uses Amable's version of the model (consisting of a linear estimate of a demand curve, a linear quadratic cost curve and a logistic diffusion curve) and four types of imperfectly competitive behaviour – monopolistic intertemporal profit maximisation, a dynamic Bertrand oligopoly, and a duopolistic differential game with endogenous market potential, which leads to a Stackelberg-leadership situation or a phase of pure monopoly.

Neither endogenous market potential nor endogenous change in market structure have been treated in the differential games literature using the epidemic diffusion model or similar constructs (see Mahajan, Muller and Bass 1990; Dockner and Jorgensen 1988).

The structure of the paper is as follows. In section 2 the basic elements of Amable's model are presented. Intertemporal profit maximisation results for the case of a slightly extended version of Jorgensen's (1983) pure monopoly model are derived in section 3 to facilitate the understanding of the differential game presented later. Section 4 looks at the results of an oligopolistic market structure where n firms produce homogeneous goods in an otherwise unchanged model. In section 5 it is assumed that consumers associate the product with the name of one of two firms; a differential game of profit-maximising duopolists leads to either monopoly profits for one of the firms and for the other to first positive, then zero profits and finally exit, or a Stackelberg leader–follower constellation. The Stackelberg leadership–follower constellation is analysed in section 6. In all cases variants of sigmoid diffusion curves are obtained. In section 7 the results are summarised. After introducing the models in each section I shall discuss the literature to which they are related.

2. BASIC ELEMENTS OF THE MODELS

The model consists of a linear-quadratic total cost function in output y:

$$C = c_0 y + c_1 y^2 \qquad c_0 > 0 \, , \, c_1 \gtrless 0 \qquad (9.1)$$

(where $c_1 \gtrless 0$ indicates whether unit costs are rising or falling) and a possibly correct estimate of potential market demand

$$D = a_0 - a_1 p, \quad a_0, a_1 > 0, \qquad (9.2)$$

where D is the long-run demand potential for given p. Moreover, the choice of D and y is restricted by the epidemic (information) diffusion curve:

$$\dot{y} = \beta D y (1 - y/D) = \beta y (D - y), \ \dot{y} \equiv dy/dt, \ \beta > 0. \qquad (9.3)$$

Eq. (9.3) mirrors the assumption that consumers get to know or forget the product only slowly, depending on sales already made or the number of persons who have bought the product, y, multiplied by the probability, $1 - y/D$, that they meet somebody who is part of the market potential and does not know the product. The specification used in eq. (9.3) is known as the Chow logistic (see Stoneman 1983, p. 70). Glaister used the model for the analysis of the diffusion of consumer products, and Metcalfe used it for the analysis of diffusion of production technologies. In both contributions the quantity sold and the number of adopters are identical, implying that each individual buys or hires one unit per period, an assumption also widespread in the marketing literature (see Mahajan, Muller and Bass 1990). In a later section we consider a model with two such information diffusion technologies for one firm as initiated by Amable (1992). y, D and p depend on time t.

The epidemic model considers a purely random process of diffusion of knowledge about the existence of a product or technology and the desire to buy it. The existence of two classes of individuals, one of which knows and buys the product and one that does not, is analogous to two classes of people with respect to a disease, one of which is randomly infected and the other is not. Once the product is known there is no uncertainty with respect to quality or price. The assumption of a purely random process is of course an exaggeration that emphasises the costlessness of information diffusion. In the variants that consider diffusion and supply together, labour investment of household into the search for new products, or advertisement costs of sellers are neglected (for an introduction to the epidemic diffusion models see Thirtle and Ruttan 1987, ch. 3). Efforts to analyse price policy and advertising together yield intractable differential games if goodwill dynamics are added. Therefore advertising is not considered here. Instead, the focus will be on price policy and market structure. Before one proceeds to draw managerial consequences, the above-mentioned simplifications should be taken into consideration. However, complexity sometimes requires us to treat things separately.

In Glaister (1974) β is a function of p, and D is fixed. The difference is that $\beta(p)$ allows a direct choice of the growth rate of y at each value of y, whereas in this specification the growth rate can only be indirectly influenced through the impact of the control variable p on D. In Metcalfe (1981), Batten (1987) and Amable (1992) the growth of supply depends on profits. Amable (1992) assumes that the parameters of the model are constant over time and known to the firm at each moment but not for the future. We make the same assumption in section 4, but in sections 3, 5 and 6 we add the assumption that the firm knows the constancy of parameters over time.

In the next section we shall investigate the model under the assumption of monopolistic behaviour. This is based upon Jorgensen's (1983) contribution, which serves as a reference model for the later oligopolistic models in this paper. We do not consider the microfoundation of eqs (9.2) and (9.3) (see Oren and Schwartz 1988 and Chatterjee and Eliashberg 1990 on this point) or the marketing instruments that provide the firm with estimates of them.

The logistic diffusion curve $y(t)$ derived for constant D from eq. (9.3) is an empirically well-established relation (see Rosegger 1986, ch. 9, and Coombs, Saviotti and Walsh 1987, ch. 5.6, for descriptive realism; and Mahajan, Muller and Bass 1990 and Karshenas and Stoneman 1992 for econometric estimations and tests of models) and will turn out to be the result of the monopolistic (section 3) and oligopolistic (section 4) considerations and of the change in market structure (sections 5 and 6) here. Therefore we try to contribute to the literature on diffusion and supply with special emphasis on market structure.

3. INTERTEMPORAL PROFIT MAXIMISATION WITH A SINGLE DIFFUSING TECHNOLOGY

If the monopolist producing y maximises intertemporal profits for an infinite horizon subject to eq. (9.3) because no (potential) competitor is threatening his position, the Hamiltonian for his program is

$$H = (p-c_0-c_1y)y + \lambda[\beta y(a_0-a_1p)-\beta y^2].$$

The first-order conditions for a singular solution are eqs (9.4), (9.5) and $\lim_{t \to \infty} e^{-\rho t} \lambda(t) = 0$:

$$\delta H/\delta p = y+\lambda\beta y(-a_1) = 0. \tag{9.4}$$

The economic problem here is that high prices increase temporary profits but decrease future profits by reducing the speed of diffusion. As the Hamiltonian is linear in p a singular solution is optimal for some time phase if it exists. During such a phase a singular solution requires a constant λ, following from eq. (9.4):

$$\lambda = 1/(\beta a_1).$$

The shadow price of y is the inverse of the impact of p on the growth rate of y, βa_1. The first-order condition for y is (with discount rate ρ)

$$-\delta H / \delta y = -p + c_0 + c_1 2y - \lambda [\beta (a_0 - a_1p) - 2\beta y] = \dot{\lambda} - \rho\lambda.$$

$$\tag{9.5}$$

From the solution for λ and $\dot{\lambda} = 0$ we obtain

$$-p + c_0 + c_1 2y - (\beta a_1)^{-1} [\beta(a_0 - a_1 p) - 2\beta y] = -\rho(\beta a_1)^{-1}. \quad (9.5')$$

The condition from static theory that marginal revenue should equal marginal cost is modified by two dynamic terms here, one due to diffusion and one due to discounting. Terms containing p are identical up to their sign and thus can be dropped. Then solving for y yields:

$$y^* = (-\rho/\beta - c_0 a_1 + a_0)/[2(c_1 a_1 + 1)]. \quad (9.6)$$

y^* is a constant value here. This solution differs from the solution of the static monopoly model only by the term ρ/β. The monopoly solution eq. (9.6) with diffusion is lower than the static monopoly solution because of the impatience expressed by the positive discount rate. Here is $\dot{y} = 0$ and the price is determined by $a_0 - a_1 p^* = y^*$. As a consequence in this phase the last term subtracted on the left-hand side of eq. (9.5') is negative. If ρ is close to zero, price then has to be higher than marginal cost. This is all the more the case if $\rho > 0$. For profits to be positive for all ρ we must have $a_0 - c_0 a_1 > 0$. For a static monopoly solution to exist ($\rho \to 0$) and y^* to be positive for small ρ, eq. (9.6) requires that $c_1 a_1 + 1 > 0$, which we shall assume henceforth unless noted otherwise.

However, for $y(0) < y^*$ (where $y(0)$ may be the sales to workers producing the product who are the most natural candidates to know first about the existence of the product) there must be a phase where this value is approached. This requires $\dot{y} > 0$ and therefore some $p' \leq p^*$ is sufficient to reach the singular solution. However, Jorgensen (1983) shows that for $c_1 = 0$ a most rapid approach to a singular solution reached by prices as low as possible is the optimal solution. These are introductory prices to be defined below. During such a phase y is lower than D and supply is therefore lower than estimated potential demand. In this sense there is a temporary disequilibrium due to slow diffusion. Of course, 'one can turn any disequilibrium model into an equilibrium equivalent [if an equilibrium exists] and *vice versa* by a suitable definition of the information sets and perceptions of adopting agents' (Metcalfe 1988, p. 561).

Due to the linearity of H in p a lower bound for p, p', has to be imposed at which the diffusion of knowledge takes place. Some examples of such bounds can be discussed for the purpose of illustration. If the chosen p' goes to minus infinity one obtains jumps (impulse control) in the stock variable y. As this is at variance with the idea of slow diffusion we do not consider this possibility. Free sample copies, hence $p' = 0$, are a possibility as well. However, the accompanying losses during a phase with prices lower than costs require credit that can be repaid only in the singular solution phase with positive profits, and therefore is an unnecessary complication. $p' = \max (c_0, c_0 + c_1 y^*)$ ensures non-negative profits in the introduction phase. Even $p' = p^*$ would be a candidate because y^* would be approached from any value $y(0) < y^*$.

Figure 9.1 p' is the introductory price, p* is the long-run price under dynamic optimisation

Figure 9.2 Under dynamic optimisation the logistic curve leading to D' is generated by p'. If y reaches D*, dy/dt jumps to zero

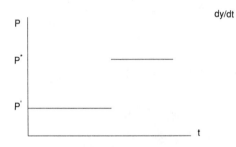
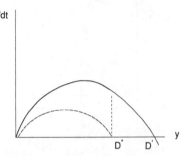

For any such value we have a diffusion process that stops increasing at y^*. For a graphical summary of the solution, see Figures 9.1 and 9.2. During the introductory phase with price p', the firm moves along the diffusion curve going through D'. Once $y^* = D^*$ is reached this curve is no longer relevant because $\dot{y}$ becomes zero as the price jumps to p^*. In spite of a jump of the price there is no corresponding jump in the quantity because the new price implies $\dot{y} = 0$. The product is no longer made better known because one prefers to have high profits now if $\rho > 0$. The equilibrium value $y^* = D^*$ belongs to a diffusion curve that has not been followed, because there was a jump from $D'(p')$ to $D^*(p^*)$. As ρ approaches zero the solution approaches that of the static Cournot monopoly. The comparison with Cournot monopoly is illustrated in Figure 9.3 for Jorgensen's case with $c_1 = 0$ and $p' = c_0$, where MR is marginal revenue, and y_m, p_m is the static monopoly solution. Starting from $y(0)$, y grows at $p' = c_0$ until y^* where p jumps to $p^* > p_m$.

Recall that Glaister (1974) regarded two prices as the more realistic case compared to the permanent intertemporal price differentiation obtained in his model. The linearity of the Hamiltonian which generates this solution with two prices is due to the insertion of a linear demand function (see Feichtinger 1982, p. 240) into the Chow logistic, which is the simplest special case of the Bass model, which in turn is the preferred one of several possible variants (see Stoneman 1983) in the marketing literature and generates a variant of discontinuous price policy in models of

Figure 9.3: Jorgenson's (1989) case: at price p' the monopolist moves to p^*,y^* *(discontinuous intertemporal price differentiation), and the static monopoly solution* $c_o = MR, p_m, y_m$

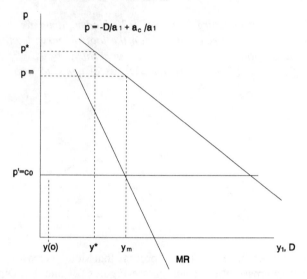

diffusion and supply. If one gives up one of these specifications the price paths will be either that

1. of Glaister (1974) (see Figure 9.4) with continuous price differentiation from low to high prices (called market penetration in the marketing literature); or
2. of Robinson and Lakhani (1975) for optimising and Metcalfe (1981) for non-optimising behaviour under supply constraints, both with continuous price differentiation from high to low prices (market skimming).

In Metcalfe's case diffusion may depend strongly on making profits, which requires high introductory prices, whereas in the Robinson and Lakhani case the fall in prices is due to falling costs and positive discount rates. The cases of continuously falling or increasing prices as well as a combination of both were contained in Spremann (1975). The specifications for the case of discontinuous price policy emphasised here will turn out below to be a starting point for tractable differential games because these are the simplest possible of all specifications used in the literature.

Figure 9.4 (a) Metcalfe's (1981) case and (b) Glaister's (1974) case of intertemporal price differentiation

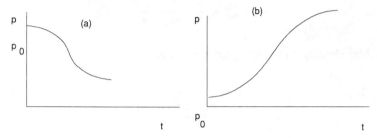

4. PRICE POLICY IN A DYNAMIC BERTRAND OLIGOPOLY

In this section we use the same model as above but assume that there are n firms introducing the new product at the same time. Patenting is excluded. Knowledge about the existence of the product again works as in eq. (9.3). However, the oligopolists now compete for the buyers, y, who know of the product:

$$y = y^1 + y^2 + ... + y^n.$$

The upper indices of the supply terms on the right-hand side of the equation are the indices of the firms. Buyers are assumed to be perfectly informed about the prices of all firms such that eq. (9.2) holds with $p = \min [p^1, p^2, ... , p^n]$. We assume that all firms have identical cost functions. As outputs y^i and prices p^i are fast variables, given the value of the slow variable y, the model is symmetric with respect to the firms and therefore they are assumed to produce the same quantities $y^i = y/n$. These assumptions are used in the following differential game:

$$\max_{p_i} \quad p_i y_i - (c_0 + c_1 y_i) y_i$$

$$\text{s.t. (9.2), (9.3) and } y_i = \frac{y}{n}, \ p_i \in \left[c_0 + c_1 y_i, \ \frac{a_1}{a_0} \right]$$

with $c_0 + c_1 y_i$ as a lower bound for p_i as in section 3. For $n = 1$ this game yields the same results as section 3. For $n > 1$ the rationing rule is $y_i = y/n$, all firms choose identical quantities and prices because they are identical in all respects. Instead of eqs (9.5') and (9.6) one gets for a singular solution:

$$p_i\left(1 - \frac{1}{n}\right) = c_0 + 2c_1\frac{y}{n} - \frac{a_0}{na_1} + \frac{\rho}{n\beta a_1} + \frac{2\beta y}{n\beta a_1}$$

which is identical to eq. (9.5') for $n = 1$, and

$$\frac{y^*}{n} = \frac{a_0 - a_1 c_0 - \dfrac{\rho}{\beta}}{n - 1 + 2(a_1 c_1 + 1)} \tag{9.7}$$

which is identical to eq. (9.6) for $n = 1$. In eq. (9.6) p dropped out because $n=1$. Therefore a solution for y was obtained which had to be approached gradually in a transition to the singular solution. For $n > 1$ p does not drop out now. Given the initial value for y/n, p is determined in the equation that is similar to eq. (9.5') and the shadow price can be determined such that a singular solution is valid from the beginning. No transition is necessary. Insertion of the price equation into the differential equation for y would allow analysis of the dynamics of y again. Under the assumption that the numerator and the denominator of the stationary solution of y are both positive one gets the same type of a curve as in Figure 9.2. In this model profits will in general be positive as in the model of section 3.

A rather similar model is that of Rao and Bass (1985), where products are also homogeneous and therefore prices have also to be identical across firms, but costs are dependent on cumulative output. The model by Eliashberg and Jeuland (1986) differs from that of Rao and Bass (1985) in that they consider differentiated products with homogeneous products as the special case of a huge impact of price differences and no learning effects in the cost functions. For that limiting case their (very complex) model is one with an exogenous market potential.

In summary, the introduction of competitors has made a continuous price policy out of what was a discontinuous price policy in the previous, monopolistic model.

5. A DUOPOLISTIC DIFFERENTIAL GAME WITH ENDOGENOUS MARKET POTENTIAL AND TRANSITION TO MONOPOLY OR STACKELBERG LEADERSHIP

In this section we investigate a differential game with two firms that differ in initial market share and have to make their own reputations. The products of the two firms considered are imperfect substitutes. The difference between the products is indicated by the name or reputation of the firms producing with identical unit cost functions

$$c = c_0 + c_1 y.$$

Consumers knowing about the product of a firm infect those consumers who do not know either of the two firms or their product. The epidemic process is then (see Amable 1992)

$$\dot{y}_i = \beta y_i (D - y_i - y_j) \quad i = 1,2 \quad j \neq i.$$

These are two diffusion processes – one for each firm's reputation or number of clients – with the same growth rates. This dynamic process imposes identical growth rates on the reputations of the two firms, which is a rather strong dynamic rigidity. However, it simplifies the analysis considerably because the difference in levels of the y_i will be determined by their initial values and the common growth rate (on the tractability of differential games with respect to the problem at hand, see Dockner and Jorgensen 1988). In the y_1–y_2-plane the duopoly then moves along a ray through the origin determined by the initial values. If a differential equation drives y_i upwards (downwards) then the firm's quantity cannot grow faster (decline slower) and by assumption it can never jump. The firm can sell less but not more than indicated by the differential equation.

Overall potential demand D is assumed to be

$$D = a_0 - a_1 p_1/2 - a_1 p_2/2.$$

This demand function can be derived as a special case of the demand functions for imperfect substitutes:

$$D_1 = e_1 - b_1 p_1 + d_1 p_2, \quad D_2 = e_2 + b_2 p_1 - 1 d_2 p_2 \quad \text{with } e_i, b_i, d_i > 0.$$

Summing left- and right-hand sides yields

$$\begin{aligned} D = D_1 + D_2 &= e_1 - b_1 p_1 + d_1 p_2 + e_1 + b_2 p_1 - d_2 p_2 \\ &= e_1 + e_2 - (b_1 - b_2) p_1 - (d_2 - d_1) p_2. \end{aligned}$$

Assuming $b_1 - b_2 = d_2 - d_1$ and defining $e_1 + e_2 \equiv a_0$ and $b_1 - b_2 = d_2 - d_1 \equiv a_1/2$, the above demand function is obtained. $a_1/2$ is positive if own-price effects are stronger then cross-price effects. For the case $p_1 = p_2$ this demand function reduces to the demand function in the monopolistic part of the paper. The assumption $b_1 - b_2 = d_2 - d_1 \equiv a_1/2$ is a strong simplification which helps to focus on differences in the initial values of market shares as the main point of interest concerning differences between firms. Which firm becomes known to the buyer is again determined solely by the epidemic random process operating on a common market potential D for both firms. Both prices have an impact on the speed of diffusion of the knowledge about the existence of the product. High prices increase current profits given a vertical short-run demand curve y_i because y_i is a slow variable, and low prices contribute to the diffusion. Therefore individual firms' intertemporal profit maximisation subject to the differential equations takes the form of a duopolistic differential game where each firm bases its own decision on expectations about the other firm's behaviour concerning price and quantity:

$$\text{Max}_{p_i, t_1} \int_0^{t_1} [p_{iy_i} - (c_0 + c_1 y_i)y_i]e^{-pt}dt, \quad i = 1,2$$

$$\text{s.t. } \dot{y}_1 = \beta y_1 (D - y_1 - y_2), \quad \dot{y}_2 = \beta y_2 (D - y_2 - y_1) \quad (9.3')$$

$$D = a_0 - a_1 p_1/2 - a_1 p_2/2$$

and

$$y_1(0) = y_{10}, \ y_2(0) = y_{20}, \ t_1 \varepsilon (0, \infty).$$

Up until now in the literature such games have only been considered for constant values of D, although endogenous D is held to be desirable (see Dockner and Jorgensen 1988). In that literature prices $p_{1,2}$ are introduced in a manner that is more reminiscent of Glaister's $\beta(p)$ function. We consider the Nash equilibrium for open-loop strategies. Whereas the marketing literature focuses on price policy and profits, we also look at diffusion and change in market structure in connection with leadership in terms of market shares.

Insertion of D into the differential equation yields the generalised Hamiltonian for firm 1:

$$H_1 = p_1 y_1 - (c_0 + c_1 y_1)y_1 + \lambda_1 \beta y_1 (a_0 - a_1 p_1/2 - a_1 p_2/2 - y_1 - y_2)$$

$$+ \mu_1 \beta y_2 (a_0 + a_1 p_1/2 - a_1 p_2/2 - y_2 - y_1).$$

The first-order conditions for a singular solution phase are the differential equations (9.3'), $\lambda_1(t_1) = \mu_1(t_1) = 0$, $H(t_1) = 0$, implying zero profits if finite t_1 exists, and

$$\delta H_1/\delta p_1 = y_1 + \lambda_1 \beta y_1 (-a_1/2) + \mu_1 \beta y_2 (-a_1/2) = 0 \qquad (9.8)$$

$$-\delta H_1/\delta y_1 = -[\, p_1 - c_0 - 2c_1 y_1 + \lambda_1 \beta (a_0 - a_1 p_1/2 - a_1 p_2/2 - y_2 - 2y_1) - \mu_1 \beta y_2 \,]$$
$$= \lambda_1 - \rho \lambda_1 \qquad (9.9)$$

(where ρ is the discount rate as in the monopolistic model) and

$$-\delta H_1/\delta y_2 = \lambda_1 \beta y_1 - \mu_1 \beta (a_0 - a_1 p_1/2 - a_1 p_2/2 - y_1) + \mu_1 \beta 2 y_2 \qquad (9.10)$$
$$= \dot{\mu}_1 - \rho \mu_1.$$

From these first-order conditions one can solve for p_1 and p_2. The results are:

$$-c_0 - (2c_1 + 4/a_1) y_1 - \rho 2/(a_1 \beta) + (2/a_1) a_0 - 4 y_2/a_1 = p_2 \qquad (9.11)$$

$$-c_0 - (2c_1 + 4/a_1) y_2 + (2/a_1) a_0 - 4 y_1/a_1 - \rho 2/(a_1 \beta) = p_1. \qquad (9.12)$$

In eqs (9.11) and (9.12) y_1 and y_2 are slow-state variables. Therefore they determine those (expected) values of prices which can be equilibrium prices of a singular solution. From the monopoly model one might have expected that there would again be a transitionary phase where imposition of values for $p_{1,2}$ would lead to such a singular solution. However, there is no reason not to be in a singular solution from the beginning because the equations for a singular solution do not yield results such as y^* in the monopoly model that must be approached slowly. The most rapid approach in this case is to begin with (correctly expected) prices as determined by eqs (9.11) and (9.12).

Insertion of D and the solutions for $p_{1,2}$ into the differential equations using $y_1 + y_2 = y$ yields after some manipulations

$$\dot{y} = \beta y \,[\, a_0 + a_1 c_0 - 2a_0 + 2\rho \,/\, \beta + y(3 + a_1 c_1) \,]. \qquad (9.13)$$

Eq. (9.13) summarises the development of the market quantity y. y_1 and y_2 differ only by their initial values and have growth rates identical to that of y. Eq. (9.13) is graphed in Figure 9.5. It has an unstable threshold value at

$$y^* = (a_0 - a_1 c_0 - 2\rho/\beta)/(3 + a_1 c_1). \qquad (9.14)$$

Again we assume that the discount rate is sufficiently low to ensure a positive solution y^* with positive numerator and denominator. As a consequence of eq. (9.14) one can draw a no-growth line $y_1 = -y_2 + y^*$ in the $y_1 - y_2$-plane (see Figures 9.6–9.8). If the game starts below that line both quantities will be decreasing, and if it starts above it both quantities will be increasing until a zero-profit line is reached. To be able to derive the zero-profit line and to understand the movement to that line we have to consider the price equations again. Price equations can be rewritten as functions of y and the initial values of y and $y_{1,2}$ in the following form:

$$p_2 = -c_0 - \rho 2/(a_1\beta) + (2/a_1)a_0 - y[(2c_1 + 4/a_1)y_{10}/y_0 + 4y_{20}/(y_0 a_1)] \qquad (9.11')$$

$$p_1 = -c_0 + (2/a_1)a_0 - \rho 2/(a_1\beta) - y[4y_{10}/(y_0 a_1) + (2c_1 + 4/a_1)y_{20}/y_0]. \qquad (9.12')$$

Prices are negatively related to the quantity y. If the initial values were below the threshold value both firms could become smaller and smaller at positive profits with no finite value of t_1 existing, because – as will be shown below – zero-profits lines will be to the right of the no-growth line. Firms would converge to atomistically small suppliers. To understand the movement to the zero-profit line it is important to recognise that in spite of the assumption that in the static demand curves a firm's own price has a stronger impact than the other firm's price, $b_1 - b_2 = d_2 - d_1 = a_1/2 > 0$, eqs (9.11) and (9.12) imply that a price is more (less) strongly affected by the other firm's quantity than by its own quantity if $c_1 \gtrless 0$:

$$|\delta p_i / \delta y_j| \gtrless |\delta p_i / \delta y_i| \quad \text{as} \quad c_1 \gtrless 0. \qquad (9.15)$$

Inserting the price equations into the zero-profit condition $p_i - c_0 - c_1 y_i = 0$ yields the zero-profit lines

$$y_i = -\frac{(1 + a_1 c_1 / 2)}{(1 + a_1 c_1 / 4)}y_j + \frac{a_0 - a_1 c_0 - \rho/\beta}{2(1 + a_1 c_1/4)}, \qquad i, j = 1,2. \ (9.16)$$

To illustrate three possible outcomes we distinguish three cases.

Case 1. For $c_1 = 0$ (see Figure 9.6) the no-growth line has intercepts

$$y^* = (a_0 - a_1 c_0 - 2\rho/\beta)/3$$

and the zero-profit lines (indicated as 11 in Figure 9.6) becomes

Figure 9.5: Dynamics of market quantity y with threshold value y. The duopoly game stops at y(t$_j$)*

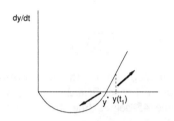

Figure 9.6: If initial value y$_1$(0) and y$_2$(0) are above the no-growth line and c$_1$=0, both firms arrive at the zero-profit line at t$_1$, the finite endogenous horizon value

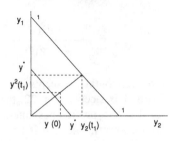

Figure 9.7: If c$_1$>0 and y$_2$>y$_1$(0) the price of firm 1 will be so low that it reaches the zero-profit line and exits or becomes a Stackelberg-follower with a zero-profit strategy

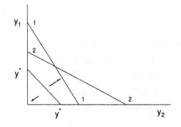

Figure 9.8: If c$_1$<0, small |c$_1$| and y$_2$>y$_1$(0) drive firm 2 towards its zero-profit line and either to exit or to a Stackelberg-follower position

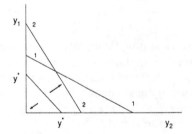

$$y_i = -y_j + (a_0 - a_1 c_0 - \rho/\beta)/2.$$

Obviously, zero-growth lines are identical for both firms in this case, have the same slope as the zero-growth line and their intercepts are larger than y*, the intercept of the no-growth line. On whichever ray the firms move to the zero-profit line, they both reach it at the same time t_1. From that point in time onwards they may have a weak preference to stay in the market, which leads to the same results as the Bertrand model of the previous section. Alternatively one or both exit.

Case 2. For $c_1 > 0$ we find that

$$y^* = (a_0 - a_1 c_0 - 2\rho/\beta)/(3 + a_1 c_1)$$

$$< y_2 \bigg|_{\substack{\pi_1 = 0 \\ y_1 = 0}} = \frac{a_0 - a_1 c_0 - \rho/\beta}{2 + a_1 c_1} < y_2 \bigg|_{\substack{\pi_2 = 0 \\ y_1 = 0}} = \frac{a_0 - a_1 c_0 - \rho/\beta}{2(1 + a_1 c_1/4)}.$$

Therefore horizontal intercepts are clearly ranked and 11, the zero-profit line of firm 1 is steeper than 22, the zero-profit line of firm 2 (see Figure 9.7). As the zero-profit lines intersect at the 45-degree line, firm 1 will reach its zero-profit line first if firm 2 has the higher initial value, and the firms therefore move along a ray that is flatter than the 45-degree line. The reason is that for $c_1 > 0$ the negative effects of one firm's quantity on the other firm's prices indicated in eq. (9.15) are stronger than the negative effects of quantities on a firm's own price. When reaching the zero-profit line firm 1 may either exit and leave a monopoly position for firm 2 or it may weakly prefer a zero-profit strategy leaving a Stackelberg-leadership position to firm 2, which we analyse below.

Case 3. For $c_1 < 0$ for small $|c_1|$ one can show that

$$y^* < y_2 \bigg|_{\substack{\pi_2 = 0 \\ y_1 = 0}} < y_2 \bigg|_{\substack{\pi_1 = 0 \\ y_1 = 0}}$$

and 11 is now flatter than 22, as shown in Figure 9.8. As a consequence, for $y_{20} > y_{10}$ firm 2 will come first to its zero-profit line because its quantity is depressing its own price more than that of firm 1. Therefore it is either optimal to exit in spite of having the larger market share or to weakly prefer a zero-profit strategy, thus leaving a Stackelberg-leader position to firm 1.

Other possible cases might exist because zero-profit lines may be below the no-growth line for $c_1 < 0$. Initial values above the zero-profit line but below the no-growth line lead to negative growth rates driving the process to the origin. There will be a phase with negative profits followed by one with positive profits. The question then is whether overall profits are positive. If a process begins above both lines it will not be started at all because profits become increasingly more negative. If the zero-profit line lies above the no-growth line an alternative to the singular solution phase might be that firms price at the corner $p_1 = e_1/d_1$, $p_2 = e_2/d_2$. Then they move back to the no-growth line with maximum speed. Arriving there they could price at the no-growth maximum profit price of the singular solution, which may yield higher discounted long-run profits. However, then the firms no longer are confronted with a diffusion problem.

6. THE STACKELBERG-LEADERSHIP PHASE

Suppose that firm 2 has gained a Stackelberg-leadership position either because $c_1 > 0$ has brought firm 1 to its zero-profit line because $y_{20} > y_{10}$ or $c_1 < 0$ has brought firm 1 to its zero-profit line because $y_{20} < y_{10}$ and it weakly prefers to stay in the market. Firm 1 may then try to produce $y_1(t_1)$, the quantity reached during the phase of the duopolistic game, provided that the differential equation does not produce negative growth rates such that consumers forget the firm. This will turn out to be no problem, because it will be shown that firm 2 goes to a higher quantity.

The problem for firm 2 from t_1 onwards then is

$$\text{Max}_{p_2} \int_{t_1}^{\infty} [p_2 \, y_2 - (c_0 + c_1 \, y_2) \, y_2] \, dt$$

$$\dot{y}_2 = \beta y_2 [a_0 - a_1 (c_0 + c_1 y_{1t_1})/2 - a_1 p_2/2 - y_2 - y_{1t_1})],$$

given t_1 and $y_{1,2}(t_1)$ from the previous phase. The current value Hamiltonian can be written as

$$H = p_2 y_2 - (c_0 + c_1 y_2) y_2$$
$$+ \lambda_2 y_2 \beta \, [a_0 - a_1 p_2 / 2 - a_1 (c_0 + c_1 y_{1t_1}) / 2 - y_{1t_1} - y_2].$$

First-order conditions for a singular solution phase are: the differential equation, $\lim_{t \to \infty} e^{-\rho t} = 0$ and

$$\delta H/\delta p_2 = y_2 + \lambda_2 \beta y_2 (-a_1/2) = 0 \tag{9.16'}$$

and

$$-\delta H/\delta y_2 = -\{p_2 - c_0 - c_1 2 y_2 + \lambda_2 \beta [a_0 - a_1 p_2/2 - a_1 (c_0 + c_1 y_{1t_1})/2 - y_{1t_1} - 2 y_2]$$
$$= \lambda_2 - \rho \lambda_2. \tag{9.17}$$

From these first-order conditions one can derive the level of the market quantity y:

$$y_2 = \frac{a_0 - a_1 c_0 - \rho/\beta}{2 \, (\, a_1 c_1 \, / \, 2 + 1)} - y_{1t_1} \, / \, 2 \tag{9.18}$$

The first term is the value of y_2 at the end of the zero-profit line of firm 1 (of the differential game phase), i.e. for $\pi_1 = 0$ and $y_1 = 0$ in the y_1–y_2-plane (see Figure 9.9). In that plane eq. (9.18) describes a straight line with slope minus 2 through

$$y_2 {\Big|}_{\substack{\pi_1=0 \\ y_1=0}}$$

Therefore it is steeper than all zero-profit lines of the differential game phase. Since y_{1t_1} is a constant and the line determined by eq. (9.18) lies to the right of the zero-profit lines of the previous phase, firm 2 moves from the zero- profit line of firm 1 parallel to the horizontal axis to the line of eq. (9.18), thus extending its market share in the Stackelberg phase because firm 1 sells less than its market reputation would allow it to, because it has changed its strategy in order to avoid running into negative profits, whereas the behaviour of firm 2 must have made both products better known during the transition to eq. (9.18), to which we turn now.

For a transition to this singular solution phase of the monopoly for the whole market one would have to define lower and upper bounds for prices of firm 2 again. Here we assume that the lower bound is the zero-profit condition. However, when the price jumps down at t_1 from its positive profit level for one of the oligopolists (firm 2 in our example) there must be a jump in $d\dot{y}/d(t_1)$. The curve of Figure 9.5 stops at $y(t_1)$. From that time onwards the curve of Figure 9.2 is valid. Its value of $d\dot{y}/dt(t_1^+)$ – where t_1^+ is the first moment of the Stackelberg phase – must be higher than the value $d\dot{y}/dt(t_1)$ of the differential game phase. There will be a jump to a different diffusion curve when p_2 is raised such that the growth stops at a value of D belonging to the monopoly price. The complete diffusion curve of the whole game is drawn in Figure 9.10. A similar curve could be derived for the case that firm 1 exits and firm 2 has a monopoly position instead of one of a Stackelberg leadership.

Whereas in Fershtman, Mahajan and Muller (1990) pioneering advantage is defined with respect to market shares of a pioneer and a competitor that turn out to be equal in the long run in their model, here market shares are constant during the differential game phase due to the dynamic rigidity. Pioneering advantage leads to exit or weak preference for staying in with zero profits of the leader if $c_1 < 0$, allowing for Stackelberg-leadership or monopoly profits in a later phase for the one who was lagging behind in terms of market share in the beginning. Only in the case of an increasing unit cost curve will the market share 'advantage' of the leader not be lost, because in the equations for prices (i.e., eqs (9.11) and (9.12) and in contrast to the properties of the demand functions D_1 and D_2) cross effects of quantities on competitors' prices are larger in that case than those on a firm's own prices. If unit cost curves are falling the quantities of a firm have a higher influence on its own price. Then higher initial quantities (pioneer advantage) lead the pioneer to his zero-profit line, Stackelberg followership or exit (optimal timing of withdrawing a product from the market). The Stackelberg leader then extends his market share. This phase is initiated by a downward jump of the price. Another example of a downward jump of the price can be found in Eliashberg and Jeuland (1986), where a monopolist decreases his price at the moment of entry of a competitor.

Figure 9.9: After firm 1 reaches the zero-profit line 11 firm 2 extends its market share in the Stackelberg phase

Figure 9.10: The differential game produces diffusion between 0 and t_2. The onset of the Stackelberg phase produces a jump at t_1, and diffusion ceases at t_2

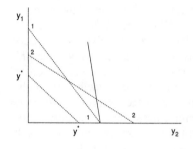

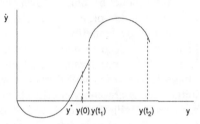

7. CONCLUSIONS

In this paper the model used by Metcalfe, Batten and Amable and in the marketing literature has been used to derive the dynamics of output and price under different behavioural assumptions than in their papers. It seems to me that the imposition of the epidemic diffusion assumption as a technological constraint on information flows is an interesting approach to dynamic imperfectly competitive disequilibrium behaviour, although I would not go as far as Batten (1987), who views this model as competing with the neoclassical growth model. The latter is a general equilibrium model whereas the Metcalfe and marketing models are partial (dis)equilibrium models. In the following we summarise the results obtained with this approach.

This paper has started from Jorgensen's (1983) version of the monopoly model. In that version there is an optimal introductory price and a jump to a long-run price that is higher than that of a static monopoly solution under a positive discount rate. This result differs from the permanent, continuous price differentiation obtained by Glaister (1974), Metcalfe

(1981) and others; disequilibrium growth is found in the introduction phase of the product but not in the phase of a singular solution.

Allowing for competition one has to make an assumption on whether or not the dynamics of the product becoming known is associated with the name of the firm. If it is not, firms compete under perfect information for the number of consumers knowing the product. Under mutually perfect information a zero-profit strategy is the only equilibrium strategy because for higher prices a competitor can always take over the whole market. As a consequence the two-prices strategy of the monopoly version of the model is replaced by a continuous price strategy. Before the diffusion process has proceeded sufficiently the firm will not be on the estimated and possibly true demand curve, and therefore the economy will be in disequilibrium.

If the product becomes known and the consumers associate the name of the firm with the product and do not know of the other firm's supply, then substitutes are imperfect. In a differential game with dynamic rigidity higher prices lead to higher instantaneous profits but slow down the diffusion. If the initial values are below a critical minimum level the quantities of both firms will decline towards zero and prices will rise. If the initial values are above a critical minimum level the quantities will grow and prices will decline. Under decreasing (increasing) cost curves the leader (follower) arrives at his zero-profit line when the other firm still makes positive profits. If it switches to a zero-profit strategy the other firm becomes Stackelberg leader, and if it exits the other firm gets a monopoly position.

In the latter case we are back in the slightly extended Jorgensen model. In short, epidemic diffusion dynamics combined with a demand and a cost function can be used in models that are imperfectly competitive, and can also be used to justify dynamic monopolistic (dis)equilibrium or Stackelberg leadership, both possibly resulting from a duopolistic differential game.

An alternative version that we shall investigate in a further paper will use individual market potentials $D_i = a_i - b_i\,p_i + b_j\,p_j$, with $b_{i,j} > 0$ and individual diffusion curves $\dot{y}_i = \beta y_i(D_i - y_i)$. In that case the dynamic rigidity will vanish and there will be competition for market potential. The main problem will presumably be the tractability of the differential game. Advertising may be added to the model by making β dependent on the expenditures for advertising. This would avoid adding additional differential equations for goodwill.

The purely empirical literature as far as it is based on the epidemic model considers the sigmoid or similar diffusion patterns which can be generated formally by the models mentioned above. In the models, however, diffusion is driven by firms' price policy, investment or output decisions. The models using price policy exhibit a great variety of possible policies. They are all based on continuous intertemporal price differentiation. To get a better impression of how all of this works it is necessary to enlarge empirical research to include the price policy and changes in market structure accompanying the diffusion process. A crucial empirical question will be how the price paths are correlated with the diffusion paths and perhaps those of other variables.

This paper has looked with somewhat neoclassical eyes at the literature connecting the epidemic diffusion model with dynamic firm behaviour and therefore ended up in marketing science, where this model is most prominent. It is clear that evolutionary economists will find this effort to be too neoclassical and will doubt the availability of the necessary information, and that neoclassical economists will shift emphasis to even better information emphasising advertising and search costs of customers. However, I share the marketing literature's view that all of these measures may improve information but will not change the character of the basic problem because advertising and search costs will increase β and will therefore increase the term in our model, but will not necessarily change results radically. However, the models might become more complicated. We hope that there are more economists outside the marketing field who like parts of all the three directions of research and are convinced that the epidemic diffusion model has something to offer to neoclassical economics and deserves the effort of extension to general equilibrium modelling which might make clear what are the exact differences between the two directions of research.

REFERENCES

Amable, B. (1992), 'Competition among Techniques in the Presence of Increasing Returns to Scale', *Journal of Evolutionary Economics*, 2, 147–158.

Batten, D. (1987), 'The Balanced Path of Economic Development: a Fable for Growth Merchants', in D. Batten, J. Casti and B. Johansson (eds), *Economic Evolution and Economic Adjustment*, Heidelberg: Springer-Verlag.

Chatterjee, R. and Eliashberg, J. (1990), 'The Innovation Diffusion Process in a Heterogeneous Population: a Micromodelling Approach', *Management Science*, 36, 1057–1079.

Coombs, R., Saviotti, P. and Walsh, V. (1987), *Economics and Technical Change*, London: Macmillan.

Dockner, E. and Jorgensen, S. (1988), 'Optimal Pricing Strategies for New Products in Dynamic Oligopolies', *Marketing Science*, 7, 315–334.

Dosi, G., Freeman, C., Nelson, R.R., Silverberg, G. and Soete, L. (eds) (1988), *Technical Change and Economic Theory*, London: Pinter.

Eliashberg, J. and Jeuland, A.P. (1986), 'The Impact of Competitive Entry in a Developing Market upon Dynamic Pricing Strategies', *Marketing Science*, 5, 20–36.

Feichtinger, G. (1982), 'Optimal Pricing in a Diffusion Model with Concave Price-Dependent Market Potential', *Operations Research Letters*, 1, 236–240.

Felmingham, B.S. (1988), 'Intra-firm Diffusion and the Wage Bargain', *Economics Letters*, 26, 89–93.

Fershtman, C., Mahajan, V. and Muller, E. (1990), 'Market Share Pioneering Advantage: a Theoretical Approach', *Management Science*, 36, 900–918.

Glaister, S. (1974), 'Advertising Policy and Returns to Scale in Markets where Information is Passed between Individuals', *Economica*, 41, 139–156.

Jorgensen, S. (1983), 'Optimal Control of a Diffusion Model of New Product Acceptance with Price-dependent Total Market Potential', *Optimal Control Applications & Methods*, 4, 269–276.

Karshenas, M. and Stoneman, P. (1992), 'A Flexible Model of Technology Diffusion Incorporating Economic Factors with an Application to the Spread of Colour Television Ownership in the UK', *Journal of Forecasting*, 11, 577–601.

Mahajan, V., Muller, E. and Bass, F.M. (1990), 'New Product Diffusion Models in Marketing: a Review and Directions for Research', *Journal of Marketing*, 54, 1–26. Reprinted in N. Nakicenovic and A. Grübler (eds), *Diffusion of Technologies and Social Behaviour*, Heidelberg: Springer-Verlag, 1991.

Metcalfe, J.S. (1981), 'Impulse and Diffusion in the Study of Technical Change', *Futures*, 13, 347–359.

Metcalfe, J.S. (1988), 'The Diffusion of Innovations: an Interpretative Survey', in G. Dosi, C. Freeman, R. Nelson, G. Silverberg and L. Soete (eds), *Technical Change and Economic Theory*, London: Pinter.

Norton, J.A. and Bass, F.M. (1992), 'Evolution of Technological Generations: The Law of Capture', *Sloan Management Review*, 66–77.

Oren, S.S. and Schwartz, R.G. (1988), 'Diffusion of New Products in Risk-sensitive Markets', *Journal of Forecasting*, 7, 273–287.

Rao, C.R. and Bass, F.M. (1985), 'Competition, Strategy, and Price Dynamics: A Theoretical and Empirical Investigation', *Journal of Marketing Research*, XXII, 283–296.

Reinganum, J.F. (1989), 'The Timing of Innovation: Research, Development, and Diffusion', in R. Schmalensee and R.D. Willig (eds), *Handbook of Industrial Organization*, I, Amsterdam: Elsevier.

Robinson, B. and Lakhani, C. (1975), 'Dynamic Price Models for New-product Planning', *Management Science*, 21, 1113–1122.

Rosegger, G. (1986), *The Economics of Production and Innovation*, London: Pergamon Press.

Silverberg, G., Dosi, G. and Orsenigo, L. (1988), 'Innovation, Diversity and Diffusion: A Self-organisation Model', *Economic Journal*, 98, 1032–1054.

Soete, L. and Turner, R. (1984), 'Technology Diffusion and the Rate of Technical Change', *Economic Journal*, 94, 612–623.

Spremann, K. (1975), 'Optimale Preispolitik bei dynamischen deterministischen Absatzmodellen', *Zeitschrift für Nationalökonomie*, 35, 63–76.

Stoneman, P. (1983), *The Economic Analysis of Technical Change*, Oxford: Oxford University Press.

Stoneman, P. and Ireland, N.J. (1983), 'The Role of Supply Factors in the Diffusion of New Process Technology', *Economic Journal*, 93, supplement, 66–78.

Thirtle, C.G. and Ruttan, V.W. (1987), *The Role of Supply and Demand in the Generation and Diffusion of Technical Change*, London: Harwood Academic Publishers.

COMMENT ON ZIESEMER

Gene Grossman

I make these remarks from the perspective of an unrepentant neoclassicist. Thomas Ziesemer asks how firms behave in a market for a new product when consumers are initially ill-informed. His model has three key assumptions: linear potential demand for the product; quadratic costs of production; and an 'epidemic diffusion' of sales. The latter means that sales grow (or shrink) at a rate proportional to the difference between 'potential sales' at the stated price and actual sales.

The author studies several different market structures. First, a single monopolistic firm chooses the time profile of prices to maximise discounted profits. It is shown that the monopolist sets the price as low as possible until potential demand reaches the desired level, and then raises the price to its steady-state or long-run level. Second, a set of n firms compete to sell a homogeneous product. Third, two firms compete to sell differentiated, but substitutable products. In this last case, the sales of each are assumed to adjust according to the difference between aggregate potential sales and the two firms' total actual sales.

I have some quibbles about details. For example, in section 4 on Bertrand oligopoly, the author assumes that a firm's share of the overall market is insensitive to the price it sets. That is, each firm sells y/n units, even if some firms charge higher prices than others. It is hard to see why this should be so. Moreover, the assumption has the effect of eliminating all competition between the firms; each firm behaves as a mini-monopolist, with an absence of strategic interaction between them. It would be more appropriate, in my view, to specify a rationing rule that divides the constrained market among the firms in relation to the (relative) prices they set.

But more fundamentally, I question the modelling strategy used here. I am concerned about the lack of explicit assumptions about the information available to consumers or the way in which they behave in the market. The assumptions about sales adjustment are essentially arbitrary and leave me with concerns about the robustness of the results.

I have no problem with an assumption that consumers learn about a product because others are using it. But why should that lead to the sales constraint in the precise form given in eq. (9.3)? Why should sales adjustment be symmetric for expansions and contractions in the size of the market? And how is it that these consumers, who one moment know nothing about the product and then learn of its existence, suddenly know (in section 4 and beyond) the prices of all the competing brands available on the market? In the case with differentiated products, what assumptions about information would be needed to generate a rate of growth of sales for a firm's product that is proportional to the difference between total potential demand *for both brands* and the total sales *of both brands*? This assumption has the rather unappealing implication that when one firm lowers its prices, the rate of growth of sales by its rival (whose price has not changed) increases.

My own approach to the same type of questions would begin with the consumer or household and would specify precisely what information they lack. Are consumers unaware of the existence of the new product or its price? Do they know the products' qualities and attributes? Second, I would specify how consumers acquire information. Do they need to watch others using the product, will they find it randomly on the shelf at the store, or do they receive messages in the form of advertisements? And do they actively search for new products or are they passive in obtaining new information? Third, I would ask what inferences consumers draw from their observations. Do they infer that low prices mean low quality, or do they realise that the introductory offer is intended to attract new customers? Once we have specified what information consumers have available and how they interpret that information, we can turn to the profit-maximising behaviour of firms. How can they best ease the constraint on sales due to imperfect information? Can they advertise their product, mail out free samples, or make low-price introductory offers?

Some of these questions have already been addressed in the industrial organisation literature on markets for new products. Several studies have looked at advertising as a means of conveying information about price or product attributes. Other studies have focused on pricing strategies that firms can use when consumers do not know much about a product. These studies also examined the inferences that consumers make when they see a low price for a product of unknown quality.

Something close to the author's epidemic diffusion could probably be given better microeconomic foundations. One could have consumers initially unaware that a new product type exists. Each consumer would have a latent demand for the good. Then consumers would meet randomly, and each would tell the other (with some probability?) about the attributes and prices of new products he had encountered. A consumer who learned about a new product would then decide how much to buy. With more than one producer we would also need to know how the consumers learn about the existence of the several brands and their differing attributes.

Why bother with this more detailed, and potentially more complicated, specification? I believe that this is the only way we can know whether specific results rest on essentially arbitrary assumptions. One thing we have learned from the burgeoning literature on markets with imperfect information is that the optimal profit-maximising behaviour of a firm depends critically on the details of the information structure and the way in which consumers acquire and interpret new information. I would feel more comfortable with conclusions about market conduct and performance if I knew that they could arise in a plausible setting in which consumers rationally pursue their own self-interest.

Paul Stoneman:
There is a long tradition in the diffusion literature of using epidemic diffusion curves to model the spread of information on the proportion of households that know of a technology. This model contains a strange learning mechanism that separates out the proportion of households that know of a technology from the amount that each household buys. Somewhere there is the assumption that households are homogeneous, though for other things you need to assume that they are heterogeneous. The diffusion or learning curve should be applied to the proportion of households that know of the technology, which will give a demand curve for each household.

Richard Nelson:
Do we need a family of models and theories of the diffusion of a new product or is a single theory adequate? Does it make sense to believe that the same set of forces that explain the diffusion of a new drug among doctors will be behind the diffusion of diesel locomotives among railroad companies? There are a lot of reasons to believe that these forces differ and the issue of whether the market is homogeneous or heterogeneous may vary a lot from case to case. Perhaps diffusion research should focus on the variables that differ from case to case.

Thomas Ziesemer:
The literature discussed by Gene Grossman makes assumptions about the use of information-gathering technologies, whereas the epidemic diffusion literature that I referred to assumes that there is almost no information on competitors. Which of these two approaches is more accurate is an empirical question that I cannot decide. I have chosen to follow the epidemic diffusion model because it fits very well, in the technology literature, to the diffusion of many products.

Gene Grossman:
I have no problem with an epidemic diffusion process, but the model could be improved by assuming that some fraction of households are aware of a product and buy a certain amount and those that don't know about it have a probability of learning about it through observing someone else using it. These probabilities could be used to build a model of how diffusion occurs through the uninformed households. I also have no problem with the assumption that households have almost no information, which is reasonable for some markets. What I would like to see though is a clear set of assumptions that are consistent with some set of micro foundations.

Reference

Tirole, J. (1988), *The Theory of Industrial Organization*, Cambridge, MA: MIT Press.

10. Games with Changing Payoffs

Reinoud Joosten, Hans Peters and Frank Thuijsman[*]

1. INTRODUCTION

A game with changing payoffs or actions is a dynamic game in which the payoffs or action sets may change from one decision moment to the next as a consequence of the actions played previously. Stochastic games, as well as differential games are, generally speaking, examples of such games. On the other hand, a repeated game is not a game with changing payoffs in this sense; although the payoffs may change over time, this is a consequence of, for instance, time discounting, and not of the actions played.

Our motivation for studying games with changing payoffs or action sets comes from the idea that by (not) performing certain actions the payoffs resulting from those actions may increase (decrease), or the set of available actions may change. Although this phenomenon may be called *learning* or *unlearning* (see Joosten *et al.* 1991), these expressions should be understood in a different way than is usual in the game-theoretic literature. By *(un)learning* we do not mean (un)learning how to play the game, nor gathering (or losing) information about the game. Rather, it should be interpreted as (un)learning how to perform a *physical* action – where *physical* can be taken in a broad sense. Let us clarify this by some examples.

In a dynamic duopoly situation a firm may choose to offer more than the Cournot–Nash equilibrium amount. The relative loss suffered may be compensated by enhancing its production technology – by the 'practical' production experience – or enlarging its market share. This is an example of a situation where (not) performing an action increases (decreases) the future payoffs resulting from that action.

An example from sports is the decathlon, where athletes may specialise in specific skills, not only depending on their own capabilities but in par-

[*] The authors thank Fernando Vega-Redondo and Thomas Ziesemer for comments and suggestions.

ticular also on the skills and specialisations of their adversaries. If a certain skill – say, high jumping – is stimulated or neglected, then future jumps will be higher or lower.

One might also think of countries competing in the world market, contemplating the adoption of new technologies. Learning-by-doing effects are to be anticipated on any adopted technology, whereas unlearning-by-not-doing effects must be anticipated on the 'traditional' activities. The experience of certain former colonies in sub-Saharan Africa (cf. Acharya 1981) may serve as an illustration in this context. Under colonialism intra-African economic ties were strongly discouraged in favour of economic ties with the coloniser. Economic structures and relationships within the colonies were transformed in the interests of the colonial power or in the interests of European settlers. African economic interests were generally disregarded, and African initiative was often heavily discouraged. For example in Kenya, Africans were prohibited from growing coffee until 1948–1949, and veterinary services for African-owned dairy cattle were withheld until 1955 (Heyer 1976). It is therefore not surprising that some of these former colonies found themselves at independence with little entrepreneurial and managerial know-how, an agricultural sector with little differentiation focused on production for the market of the coloniser, and an economy open to the coloniser, lacking important inter-industrial links and ties with neighbouring countries. The combined effects of not being able to 'learn' certain skills and processes fast enough in the post-colonial period to be competitive on the world market, and having 'unlearned' attractive alternatives which had been present in pre-colonial times, seem to have contributed to the problems which these former colonies face in industry and agriculture at present.

Such examples indicate that a variety of situations can be modelled as dynamic games with changing payoffs or changing actions. In particular, the choice a player may have between specialising on certain actions or trying to keep the spectrum of available and worthwhile actions as broad as possible, is an important feature of such games. Games like this *have* been analysed in the game-theoretic literature, mainly in the form of stochastic or differential games.

Before considering both types of games in somewhat more detail, a few words on the existing learning-by-doing models are in order. *Learning-by-doing* is the title of a pioneering paper by Arrow (1962). The existence of the possibility to learn by doing is not surprising. The novelty of learning-by-doing lies in its incorporation as a concept into economic theory. In a game-theoretic setting learning-by-doing is a different phenomenon, since learning-by-doing decisions also depend on what the other players do (see, in particular, the next section).

The purpose of this note is to present some examples of dynamic games with changing actions or payoffs. In section 2 we consider infinitely repeated matrix games where actions vanish if they have not been used for some time. Such games are a special type of stochastic game. In section 3 some differential games are analysed where each momentary action determines not only an immediate payoff but also influences a state variable which is part of the payoff function. Section 4 concludes the paper with a few remarks.

2. STOCHASTIC GAMES: VANISHING ACTIONS

A stochastic game (introduced by Shapley 1953) is characterised by a collection of states. In each state the players choose actions; these actions determine immediate payoffs as well as a probability distribution over the collection of states. The state at the next decision moment is determined on the basis of this probability distribution. The overall reward can be a discounted sum of immediate payoffs, or a limit of average payoffs; both criteria have been and are still being studied. A stochastic game clearly is an example of what we have called a dynamic game with changing actions.

Our first attempt to study (un)learning in the sense as described above, is Joosten *et al.* (1991). Two players repeatedly play a matrix game, where the entries of the matrix represent payoffs by the column player to the row player. Each player has a memory of a certain length, say r_1 and r_2 for players 1 and 2, respectively. If player 1, the row player, does not choose a certain row for r_1 consecutive times, then he loses the possibility to do so; that row is deleted from the matrix. Similarly for player 2, the column player, when he does not play a certain column for r_2 consecutive times. The payoff criterion is the limiting average payoff. Observe that this game is a stochastic game with a very special payoff/transition structure. The existence of limiting average ε-optimal strategies, for any $\varepsilon > 0$, follows from an established result in stochastic game theory (Mertens and Neyman 1981). The interesting aspect is that for some cases optimal strategies *can* be found and are relatively easy to describe. As an example, consider a 2 × 2 matrix game:

$$A = \begin{bmatrix} a & b \\ c & d \end{bmatrix}.$$

If this game has a saddlepoint, as for instance in the specification
then it is obvious that the one-shot optimal actions, namely the top row for

$$A = \begin{bmatrix} 1 & 2 \\ 0 & d \end{bmatrix},$$

player 1 and the left column for player 2, are, when repeatedly played, also optimal in the memory-restricted infinitely repeated game. In this case there is no proper 'learning-by-doing' or 'unlearning-by-not-doing'. The players concentrate on what already are their optimal strategies; by doing so, eventually they lose their suboptimal strategies, which only reinforces their incentives to play optimally – so to speak. This is similar to the one decisionmaker case, and a game-theoretic analysis sheds no further light on the situation.

The situation becomes different and more interesting if the original zero sum game does *not* have a saddlepoint, say $a \geq d > b \geq c$.

As an example, assume that both players have memory of length equal to 2. In this case, for player 1 it is optimal to start by playing each row with probability $\frac{1}{2}$. If payoff a or d is realised, then he should play his second or first row, respectively, at the next stage, and keep switching rows as long as player 2 still has both columns available; as soon as player 2 loses a column, player 1 should play the payoff maximising row. If, at the first stage, payoff c or b is realised, then player 1 should play the first row forever. Player 2 has a similar optimal strategy. The expected payoff – the value of the game – is, thus, $\frac{1}{2}(b + d)$. In this game, both players at first keep both actions alive; actually, in optimal play their first moves are chance moves, and only from the second move on do the players play deterministically.

If both players have memories of length equal to three, then the optimal strategies are somewhat more complicated but can still be described. The value of the game is equal to $v := \frac{1}{4}(a + b + c + d)$ if this number is between b and d. It is equal to b if $v < b$, and it is equal to d if $v > d$. We refer to Joosten *et al.* (1991) for more details.

For an arbitrary but finite length of memory it is not easy to calculate or describe the optimal strategies in the above games. To some extent, this is due to the discrete nature of the game; the game is played in discrete time, and actions vanish suddenly. In the next section we consider a few examples of differential games with changing payoffs. In simple cases it is possible to calculate a certain type of Nash equilibrium by optimal control methods.

3. DIFFERENTIAL GAMES: CHANGING PAYOFFS

In a differential game, the players choose actions in continuous time, thereby receiving a flow of payoffs. Such actions are called *controls*, and they are chosen subject to certain constraints, in particular with respect to a *state variable*. Such a constraint is called the *state equation* or *transition equation*. The state plays a role similar to the state in a stochastic game; in the vanishing actions games of the preceding section, states are described by keeping track, for each possible action, of the number of times that action may not be played before it is lost. Differential games are often analysed by methods provided by optimal control theory, or by dynamic programming (see for instance Starr and Ho 1969a,b).

Differential games are used to model situations like common resource extraction. Suppose two countries use a common resource over a certain period of time. At each moment, their decisions to use an amount of the resource influence their profits (in a Cournot-like fashion), as well as the remaining stock of the resource (see, for instance, McMillan 1986). An additional assumption could be that prices might increase as the amount of the resource left for the future decreases. This would imply that the pay-offs of the players change as a result of their previous actions.

3.1 An Investment Problem

In this subsection we analyse a differential game corresponding to a sty-lised economic problem of choosing between two ways to invest money. Specifically, we consider a two-player game in continuous time where at each point of time $t \in [0,\infty)$ each player has one (perfectly divisible) unit of money to invest. Each player can divide this one unit between on the one hand a project for which the payoff depends on the investments of both players, and on the other hand a project for which the payoff depends only on own investment. An investment in the first project will, moreover, result in an additional payoff stream, depending on both own investment and the investment of the opponent. This is meant to capture the idea of learning or unlearning as explained in the introduction. One may think of increasing or decreasing one's skill/technology[1] or market share. These additional payoffs constitute state variables.

Let $\alpha(t) \in [0,1]$ and $\beta(t) \in [0,1]$ denote the investment decisions at time t of players 1 and 2, respectively, in the first project. Let $g(\alpha(t), \beta(t))$ and $h(\alpha(t), \beta(t))$ denote the resulting immediate payoffs at time t for players 1 and 2, respectively. The function g can be assumed to have obvious properties, like being increasing in α and decreasing in β. Similar-ly for h. In this basic formulation, however, we do not need such assumptions. We just assume that both functions are continuously differentiable, but that assumption may also be relaxed. As functions of t, however, we require that α and β have only isolated points of discontinuity, in order to ensure the existence of the integrals below.

The immediate payoffs from investment in the second project at time t are equal to $1 - \alpha(t)$ and $1 - \beta(t)$, if $\alpha(t)$ and $\beta(t)$ are the investments in the first project, respectively. (Un)learning effects for player 1 are assumed to be captured by a state variable x depending on α as well as on β by the state equation $\dot{x}(t) = \alpha(t) - \beta(t)$ (where the dot denotes time derivative). The additional resulting payoff stream for player 1 is given by $x(t)e^{-rt}$, where r may be any real number. Here, $x(t)$ expresses the amount of 'learning' relative to the opponent, whereas e^{-rt} describes its long-run effect. Unlearning effects are stressed when r is positive; note that in that case in the long run the term $x(t)e^{-rt}$ practically vanishes, so that only short-term effects are interesting. A formulation of the problem where this is avoided, that is, where also long-term effects are interesting, is given in subsection 3.4.

Similarly, (un)learning effects for player 2 are given by a state variable y governed by the state equation $\dot{y}(t) = \beta(t) - \alpha(t)$. The corresponding additional payoff stream is given by $y(t)e^{-st}$, for some real number s. Note that $x(t) + y(t)$ is constant, so one can think of $x(t)$ as the market share of player 1 at time t. According to this interpretation, the constants x_0 and y_0 in the two maximisation problems to follow can be seen as the initial market shares, and it would be natural to choose $x_0 + y_0$ equal to 1. The case of actual learning would correspond to both initial values being set equal to 0.

We can now write down player 1's maximisation problem for any given investment plan $\beta(t)$ ($t \in [0,\infty)$) of player 2 and any discount factor ρ:

Maximise $\int_0^\infty e^{-\rho t} [g(\alpha(t),\beta(t)) + (1 - \alpha(t)) + x(t)e^{-rt}] dt$

subject to $\qquad\qquad\qquad \dot{x}(t) = \alpha(t) - \beta(t)$ (10.1)

$\qquad\qquad\qquad x(0) = x_0, \alpha(t) \in [0,1].$

Similarly, for player 2, given investments $\alpha(t)$ of player 1 at each moment $t \in [0,\infty)$:

Maximise $\int_{\sim 0}^\infty e^{-\rho t} [h(\alpha(t), \beta(t)) + (1 - \beta(t)) + y(t)e^{-st}] dt$

subject to $\qquad\qquad \dot{y}(t) = \beta(t) = \beta(t) - \alpha(t)$ (10.2)

$\qquad\qquad y(0) = y_0, \ \beta(t) \in [0,1].$

Thus, the players are assumed to maximise discounted streams of payoffs (with common discount factor ρ), given the investment plans of their opponents. The initial conditions for the state variables x and y are included to make the maximisation problems well-defined, but play no role in our analysis.

Observe that, in a seemingly more general but equivalent formulation, the terms $1 - \alpha$ and $1 - \beta$ in the objective functions could be taken into the functions g and h, respectively.

A simultaneous solution of problems (10.1) and (10.2) is a Nash equilibrium for this game. Depending on the nature of the strategies (investment plans) employed, we distinguish between open-loop strategies and closed-loop (feedback) strategies. In the latter case, strategies may depend on the state variables, and the players have the possibility to adapt their action choices while the game is being played. In the former case, a strategy depends only on time and not on the state variables. We will concentrate on open-loop strategies, which are much easier to calculate.

Solving problems (10.1) and (10.2) is a straightforward application of optimal control theory, specifically, of Pontryagin's maximum principle. The Hamiltonian corresponding to problem (10.1) is the function

$$H(\alpha, x, t, \lambda) = e^{-\rho t}[g(\alpha, \beta) + (1-\alpha) + xe^{-rt}] + \lambda[\alpha - \beta],$$

where the Lagrange multiplier (or costate variable) λ is also a function of t. Necessary conditions for a function α solving problem (10.1) are:

(a) At each t, α maximises[2] H. Thus, for an interior solution $0 < \alpha < 1$, we have $\partial H/\partial \alpha = 0$, hence

$$e^{-\rho t}[\partial g(\alpha, \beta)/\partial \alpha - 1] + \lambda = 0.$$

For a solution $\alpha = 0$ we have

$$e^{-\rho t}[\partial g(\alpha, \beta)/\partial \alpha - 1] + \lambda \leq 0,$$

and for a solution $\alpha = 1$ we have

$$e^{-\rho t}[\partial g(\alpha, \beta)/\partial \alpha - 1] + \lambda \geq 0.$$

(b) $\dot{x} = \partial H / \partial \lambda$, i.e. $\dot{x} = \alpha - \beta$.
(c) $\dot{\lambda} = -\partial H / \partial x$, i.e. $\dot{\lambda} = -e^{-(\rho+r)t}$.
(d) Transversality condition: $\lim_{t \to \infty} \lambda(t) = 0$.

Conditions (c) and (d) together imply

$$\lambda = \frac{e^{-(\rho + r)t}}{\rho + r},$$

which may be substituted in the conditions formulated in (a).

The Hamiltonian and necessary conditions for problem (10.2) look similar and therefore will not be written down explicitly.

Observe that, in general, interior solutions cannot always be expected. For an interior solution for α (and fixed β), the appropriate condition under (a) becomes

$$\frac{\partial g(\alpha,\beta)}{\partial \alpha} = 1 - \frac{e^{-rt}}{\rho + r},$$

and, assuming that the partial derivative of g with respect to α is non-negative, this condition cannot be met for low values of t if $\rho + r < 1$. In that case $\alpha = 1$ for low values of t. On the other hand, if $\rho + r \geq 1$, a necessary condition to have an interior solution α for all values of t (and β) is that $r > 0$ and the derivative $\partial g(\alpha,\beta)/\partial \alpha$ takes all values between $1 - 1/(\rho + r)$ and 1.

In the following subsections we consider a few specifications of g and h which enable us to derive exact solutions.

3.2 Bang-bang Solutions

The specification considered here allows 'bang-bang' solutions, that is solutions taking only the values 0 and 1, among the open-loop Nash equilibria. Let

$$g(\alpha,\beta) = \alpha(1 - \beta), \quad h(\alpha,\beta) = \beta(1 - \alpha).$$

The conditions in (a) – (d) of the previous section lead to

$$\alpha(t) = 0 \quad \text{if} \quad \beta(t) > \frac{e^{-rt}}{\rho + r},$$

$$\alpha(t) = 1 \quad \text{if} \quad \beta(t) < \frac{e^{-rt}}{\rho + r}$$

and analogous conditions for $\beta(t)$, depending on $\alpha(t)$. Further, α (or β) may take on arbitrary values between 0 and 1 if we have an equality sign in any of these conditions. This leads to the following description of open-loop Nash equilibria. Here, t' is the value of t for which $e^{-rt}/(\rho + r) = 1$ and t'' is the value of t for which $e^{-st}/(\rho + s) = 1$. Observe that $t' < t''$ if $r > s > 0$, provided that t' and t'' exist.

Proposition 1 With the specifications $g(\alpha,\beta) = \alpha(1 - \beta)$ and $h(\alpha,\beta) = \beta(1 - \alpha)$ and for $r > s > 0$, the open-loop Nash equilibria are combinations of strategies α and β containing only isolated discontinuities and satisfying:

(i)   For every $0 \le t < t'$: $\alpha(t) = \beta(t) = 1$.
(ii)   For $t = t'$: $\beta(t) = 1$ and $\alpha(t)$ is arbitrary.
(iii) For $t' < t < t''$: $\beta(t) = 1$, $\alpha(t) = 0$.
(iv) For $t \ge t''$: $\beta(t) = 1$ and $\alpha(t) = 0$ or $\beta(t) = 0$ and $\alpha(t) = 1$ or $\beta(t) = e^{-rt}/(\rho + r)$ and $\alpha(t) = e^{-st}/(\rho + s)$.

Thus, in this specification there are solutions taking on only the values 0 and 1. Solutions of this kind are usually called *bang-bang solutions*. Both players might start off (depending on the values of r and s relative to the common discount factor ρ) with full investment in the first (competitive) project. In the longer run, however, in equilibrium either one of the players invests fully in this project and the other one invests nothing or the investments of both players are between 0 and 1 but in the long run converge to 0. It should be noted that the solutions in Proposition 1 are formulated at each point t in time separately, so that the resulting strategies may be highly discontinuous. The first player to jump (necessarily) to zero investment is the one with the higher of the two rates r and s (as can be easily seen); at that point, it is no longer advantageous to compensate for the comparative 'unlearning' effect of investment in the first project (given that the other player still invests fully) by also investing in that project. Thus, the player with the higher of the two rates r and s is the first one 'to give up'. A plausible equilibrium would be one where after this event this player stays at a zero investment level, while his opponent stays at investment level 1.

A proof of Proposition 1 can be based on the necessary conditions stated in the previous section and will not be elaborated.

3.3 A Cobb–Douglas Case

In this subsection we assume specifications which also allow interior solutions of the players' maximisation problems, that is, open-loop Nash equilibria with investments which may be strictly between 0 and 1. To be precise, we take

$$g(\alpha,\beta) = \sqrt{\alpha(1 - \beta)}, \quad h(\alpha,\beta) = \sqrt{\beta(1 - \alpha)}.$$

The analysis of the general Cobb–Douglas case is more tedious but will not exhibit essentially different features.

The next proposition describes the open-loop Nash equilibria for the situation analogous to the one in Proposition 1. In order to make the description easier to digest, we first introduce some notation.

Assume $r \geq s > 0$ and $\rho + r \leq 1$. Then let

$$t_1 = -\frac{\ln(\rho + r)}{r} \qquad t_2 = -\frac{\ln(\rho + s)}{s}$$

$$t_3 = -\frac{\ln\frac{1}{2}(\rho + r)}{r} \qquad t_4 = -\frac{\ln\frac{1}{2}(\rho + s)}{s}.$$

It can be verified that $0 \leq t_1 \leq t_2 \leq t_4$ and that $t_1 \leq t_3 \leq t_4$.

For $t \geq 0$ define

$$v(t) = 1 - \frac{e^{-rt}}{\rho + r} \qquad w(t) = 1 - \frac{e^{-st}}{\rho + s}$$

$$\alpha^*(t) = \frac{1 - 4w^2(t)}{1 - 16v^2(t)w^2(t)} \qquad \beta^*(t) = \frac{1 - 4v^2(t)}{1 - 16v^2(t)w^2(t)}.$$

We can now state our proposition.

Proposition 2 Assume

$r \geq s > 0$ and $\rho + r \leq 1$, and $g(\alpha,\beta) = \sqrt{\alpha(1 - \beta)}$, $h(\alpha,\beta) = \sqrt{\alpha(1 - \alpha)}$.
The open-loop Nash equilibria are combinations of strategies α and β containing only isolated discontinuities and satisfying:

(i)   For $0 \leq t < t_1$: $\alpha(t) = \beta(t) = 1$.
(ii) For $t = t_1$: $\beta(t) = 1$, $\alpha(t)$ arbitrary.
(iii) For $t_1 < t < t_2$: $\beta(t) = 1$, $\alpha(t) = 0$.
(iv) For $t_2 \leq t < t_4$, there are two cases. (a) If $t_3 \leq t_2$, then $\beta(t) = 1$, $\alpha(t) = 0$. (b) If $t_2 < t_3 < t_4$, then for $t_2 \leq t \leq t_3$ there are three possibilities: $\beta(t) = 1$, $\alpha(t) = 0$, or $\beta(t) = 0$, $\alpha(t) = 1$ or $\beta(t) = \beta^*(t)$, $\alpha(t) = \alpha^*(t)$, while for $t_3 < t < t_4$: $\beta(t) = 1$, $\alpha(t) = 0$.
(v)   For $t \geq t_4$: $\beta(t) = \beta^*(t)$, $\alpha(t) = \alpha^*(t)$.

Proposition 2 describes the most general case: in all other cases with $r \geq s$, the only difference may be that the whole picture moves to the left (or, equivalently, the origin to the right). Of course, the analysis of the case $r \leq s$ is similar. The proof of Proposition 2 is again based on the conditions formulated in the previous section, and will not be given in detail.

Figure 10.1 Proposition 2

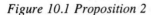

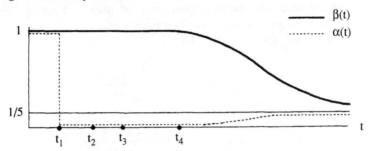

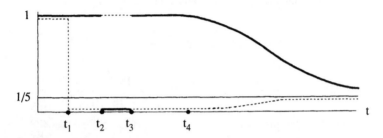

Figure 10.1 depicts some strategy combinations described by Proposition 2. Again, it should be noted that the strategies are defined for each t separately, and thus may contain any number of isolated discontinuities. In all cases, after t_4 the additional payoff effects associated with the state variables x and y decrease rapidly, causing player 1 to start investing again, while player 2 gradually decreases investments in the competitive project. In the limit, both α^* and β^* approach $1/5$.

The following proposition applies to the situation where one of the two players has a nonpositive depreciation rate of the (un)learning payoffs.

Proposition 3 Assume $g(\alpha,\beta) = \sqrt{\alpha(1-\beta)}$, $h(\alpha,\beta) = \sqrt{\beta(1-\alpha)}$, and $r \leq 0$, $s > 0$, $\rho + r \leq 1$, and $|r| < \rho$. Let, as above, $t_2 = -\ln(\rho + s)/s$. Then, for an open-loop Nash equilibrium we have:

(i) For all $t > \max\{0,t_2\}$: $\alpha(t) = 1$, $\beta(t) = 0$.
(ii) For all $0 \leq t < t_2$: $\alpha(t) = \beta(t) = 1$.

This proposition confirms the obvious intuition that the player with the nonpositive depreciation rate survives, as far as investment in the first project is concerned. If $\rho + r > 1$, then in the longer run this will still hold although, initially, the equilibrium strategies may look different (details are omitted).

3.4 An Alternative Formulation

A drawback in the formulation of the investment problem in subsection 3.1 is that the effects of the state variables x and y vanish in the long run due to the presence of the coefficients e^{-rt} and e^{-st}; there is not only relative but also absolute 'unlearning' or 'depreciation' as time goes on.[3] To avoid this, we could alternatively require

$$x(t) = \int_0^t k(t,\tau) f(\alpha(\tau), \beta(\tau)) d\tau, \tag{10.3}$$

where, as before, x is the state variable for player 1, where f describes how the state variable depends on the investment plans of both players, and where the function k reflects the depreciation or growth of the state variable. Differentiating, we obtain

$$\dot{x}(t) = \int_0^t \frac{\partial k(t,\tau)}{\partial t} f(\alpha(\tau), \beta(\tau)) d\tau + k(t,t) f(\alpha(t), \beta(t)). \tag{10.4}$$

In the special situation that $\partial k(t,\tau)/\partial t = l(t)k(t,\tau)$ for some function l depending only on t, equation (10.4) implies

$$\dot{x}(t) = x(t)l(t) + k(t,t)f(\alpha(t), \beta(t)). \tag{10.5}$$

Instead of (10.1) now consider the maximisation problem

$$\text{Maximise } \int_0^\infty e^{-\rho t} [g(\alpha(t), \beta(t)) + (1-\alpha(t)) + x(t)] dt$$

$$\text{subject to } \quad \dot{x}(t) = x(t)l(t) + k(t,t)f(\alpha(t),\beta(t)) \tag{10.6}$$

$$x(0) = x_0, \alpha(t) \in [0,1].$$

The coefficient e^{-rt} has now been removed from the objective function; instead the state equation has been replaced by (10.5). A similar formulation can be given for player 2. The corresponding Hamiltonian is now given by

$$H(\alpha, x, t, \lambda) = e^{-\rho t} [g(\alpha(t), \beta(t)) + (1-\alpha(t)) + x(t)]$$
$$+ \lambda(t)[x(t)l(t) + k(t,t)f(\alpha(t), \beta(t))],$$

with

$$\dot{\lambda} = -\frac{\partial H}{\partial x} = -e^{-\rho t} - l(t)\lambda(t)$$

as the costate equation. Again, similar expressions hold for player 2.

A simple example is obtained by assuming, in line with the preceding subsections,

$$f(\alpha(\tau), \beta(\tau)) = \alpha(\tau) - \beta(\tau),$$

and

$$k(t,\tau) = e^{r(\tau-t)}.$$

Then $l(t) = -r$ (we assume $r > 0$), and it is easily established, also using the transversality condition $\lim_{t\to\infty}\lambda(t) = 0$, that

$$\lambda(t) = \frac{e^{-\rho t}}{r + \rho}.$$

Substituting this expression for $\lambda(t)$ in the Hamiltonian and maximising at a given t and for a given strategy $\beta(t)$ of player 2 over the possible values of $\alpha(t)$, it follows easily that the maximising value of α will be independent of t. In other words (and making similar assumptions about player 2), in an open-loop Nash equilibrium the strategies of the players can be chosen constant over time, for this particular choice of the function k (and the corresponding function for player 2). For particular choices of the functions g and h (the immediate payoff functions of players 1 and 2 respectively, from investing in the first project), such an open-loop Nash equilibrium can be calculated, for instance for Cobb–Douglas payoff functions as in the preceding sections. Details are left to the reader.

4. SOME CONCLUDING REMARKS

In the foregoing, some attempts were made to study (un)learning effects in continuous-time two-person games. Here, (un)learning was to be understood in a 'physical' sense of acquiring certain skills in actions, not in the sense of (un)learning how to play the game. The main model was simple enough to enable the derivation of explicit solutions. The problem is that only slightly more sophistication in the model is bound to lead to mathematical intractibility as far as finding explicit analytical solutions is concerned.

NOTES

1. See also Cheng (1984) on this topic.
2. In what follows it is convenient to suppress t from the notation whenever this does not lead to confusion.
3. This was also pointed out to us by Fernando Vega-Redondo of Alicante University.

REFERENCES

Acharya, S.N. (1981), 'Perspectives and Problems of Development in Sub-Saharan Africa', *World Development*, 9, 109–146.
Arrow, K.J. (1962), 'The Economic Implications of Learning by Doing', *Review of Economic Studies*, 29, 155–173.
Cheng, L. (1984), 'International Competition in R&D and Technological Leadership', *Journal of International Economics*, 17, 15–40.
Heyer, J. (1976), 'Achievements, Problems and Prospects in the Agricultural Sector', in J. Heyer, J.K. Maitha and W.M. Senga (eds), *Agricultural Development in Kenya*, Oxford: Oxford University Press.
Joosten, R., Peters H. and Thuijsman F. (1991), 'Unlearning by not-doing: repeated games with vanishing actions', MERIT Research Memorandum No. 91–024, Maastricht.
McMillan, J. (1986), *Game Theory in International Economics*, Chur: Harwood Academic Publishers.
Mertens, J.F. and Neyman, A. (1981), 'Stochastic Games', *International Journal of Game Theory*, 10, 53–66.
Shapley, L.S. (1953), 'Stochastic Games', *Proceedings of the National Academy of Sciences USA*, 39, 1095–1100.
Starr, A.W. and Ho, Y.C. (1969a), 'Nonzero-sum Differential Games', *Journal of Optimization Theory and Applications*, 3, 184–206.
Starr, A.W. and Ho, Y.C. (1969b), 'Further Properties of Nonzero-sum Differential Games', *Journal of Optimization Theory and Applications*, 3, 207–219.

COMMENT ON JOOSTEN, PETERS AND THUIJSMAN

Kenneth J. Arrow and Fernando Vega-Redondo

Kenneth Arrow:

Many of the models presented at this conference are based on discrete innovations that developed as a result of stochastic processes. The telephone or the computer could be examples of this. There is also another process that was first observed by T.P. Wright 56 years ago. He noticed that the number of labour hours required to assemble an airplane frame decreased with the number of airplanes built. This observation became very well known in the aircraft industry to the extent that the government, which bought airplanes on a cost-plus basis, would use learning curves to calculate costs. Later, other researchers showed that similar phenomena could be observed in many assembly operations in manufacturing.

Presumably, a continual process of learning from repeating a task over and over again leads to better ways of performing the task. Much of the knowledge gained from this learning is tacit and difficult to codify. It is also logical to assume, as is done in this paper, that failing to perform a task will lead to unlearning.

However, I have two critical comments on this paper. The first is whether or not the zero-sum game with two players is the best way to illustrate unlearning. An alternative approach is to start from a one-person maximisation. In this case, the person is better at what he/she does and worse at what he/she does not do. The result will be similar to that of a zero-sum game with an equilibrium point, except that it is simpler to understand. The person picks the best possible option, and next time there will be an even sharper maximum than before. Hence the person will not change his or her strategy.

My other comment is on the importance of unlearning in real economic terms. I would argue that unlearning does not play a big role. For example, a realistic situation which many firms face is the need to choose between two possible strategies. One strategy leads to higher immediate payoffs, but there is a low rate of increase for future gains. The second strategy has low immediate payoffs but a high learning rate. In both cases, unlearning is not very important. The difficulty facing firms is to determine the immediate payoffs to an action and to estimate the rate of improvement through learning.

There are no doubt some examples where unlearning is important and can lead to economic regression, but in most cases a lost technique is replaced by a superior technique. We can explain the lack of importance of unlearning by turning to biology for an example where unlearning is important. The analogy is the genetic retention of many different geno-types of a species. The retention of these genotypes is of value when an environment changes back and forth from one state to another. Under these conditions, it is an advantage to have several genotypes or, for ex-ample, to be able to return to an old technology. But a cyclically variable environment is required to make retention, or unlearning, important. Under conditions of largely unidirectional change, which I would argue confronts most economic and technical change, the costs of unlearning are minor.

Fernando Vega-Redondo:
In this paper, the authors set themselves to analyse a particular case of a dynamic 'investment' game which incorporates alternative versions of (un)learning by doing. As the title of the paper indicates, the scenario considered is an example of a game with changing payoffs: future instan-taneous payoffs depend on past 'investment' actions. In this respect, it belongs to that wide of class of games which economists have been study-ing for quite some time in order to analyse issues such as industrial R&D (Reinganum 1982), joint exploitation of a common exhaustible resource (Levhari and Mirman 1980), or capital accumulation (Spence 1979).

Their main model (see section 3) involves a stylised two-player context where, at every point in time, the agents have to decide how to split a unit of resources between the following two alternative uses. On the one hand, there is an 'outside option' with a fixed marginal return; on the other, the players can resort to an 'internal option' whose instantaneous payoff also depends on the current choice of the other player. The intertemporal nature of the situation springs from two considerations. First, resources devoted to the internal option allow each player to build the stock of a certain 'asset' at a rate which depends on the partner's corresponding 'investment' decision. Second, the return of the asset is assumed to rise or decay ex-ponentially with time at a given rate.

The sketched setup represents a general theoretical context which could be particularised, or adapted, to study a number of interesting economic issues. In particular, as the authors themselves suggest, it could be used to model phenomena of learning or unlearning, conceived as increases or decreases of the current 'stock of knowledge'.

An appropriate interpretation of the rise or decay of the asset return as a process of (un)learning depends on the particular formulation adopted for the corresponding law of motion. For example, the original specification analysed in subsections 3.1 to 3.3 does not seem to fit well with this inter-pretation. In it, the stock $x(t)$ accumulated up to some time t is assumed to yield an instantaneous return of the form $x(t) \cdot e^{-rt}$, for some given $r \in \mathbb{R}$.

Thus what is assumed is that the (marginal and average) return on the asset rises or falls exponentially with time, *independently of the current stock*. This highly non-stationary specification of the returns on accumulation implies, in particular, that for $r > 0$ the intertemporal decision problem converges, in the long run, to the instantaneous problem. In the long run, therefore, current returns become pre-eminent, making irrelevant any 'investment considerations'. In the alternative case with $r < 0$, the opposite extreme situation obtains. Namely, only the accumulation decisions are relevant in the long run, all other considerations becoming progressively less significant as time advances.

An alternative specification which is more appropriate as a model of (un)learning is proposed by the authors in subsection 3.4. In it, the (marginal and average) productivity of the asset is assumed to remain constant throughout. However, it is the stock itself which is assumed to decay or rise as time proceeds, with the remaining amount at each point in time changing at a certain constant rate r (c.f. eq. (10.3) of the paper).[1] As established by eq. (10.5), if $r > 0$, this is equivalent to the usual law of motion for depreciation:

$$\dot{x}(t) = -r \cdot x(t),$$

which is postulated by the standard accumulation models. Thus, with this specification, there are strong parallels between the context analysed in this chapter and capital accumulation as studied in the literature (see again Spence 1979, or the more closely related work by Reynolds 1987). It seems likely, therefore, that any further analysis of the model would benefit significantly from exploiting these parallels.

Note

1. For simplicity, I am focusing on the case where, in the authors' notation, $k(t,\tau) = e^{r(\tau-t)}$.

References

Levhari, D. and Mirman, L. (1980), 'The Great Fish War', *Bell Journal of Economics*, 322–344.

Reinganum, J. (1982), 'A Dynamic Game of R&D: Patent Protection and Competition Behavior', *Econometrica*, 50, 671–688.

Reynolds, S. (1987), 'Capacity Investment, Preemption, and Commitment in an Infinite Horizon Model', *International Economic Review*, 28.

Spence, A.M. (1979), 'Investment Strategy and Growth in a New Market', *Bell Journal of Economics*, 10, 1–19.

11. The Method of Generalised Urn Schemes in the Analysis of Technological and Economic Dynamics

Giovanni Dosi and Yuri Kaniovski

1. INTRODUCTION

Technical change typically involves diversity amongst the agents who generate or are affected by it, various forms of learning often based on trial-and-error procedures, and mechanisms of selection which reward particular types of technologies, agents or behaviours at the expense of others.

Indeed, these appear to be general features of the competitive process driving economic dynamics. 'Competition' entails the interaction among heterogeneous firms embodying different technologies, different expectations and, quite often, displaying different behaviours. Moreover, it is often the case that technological and organisational learning is associated with various types of externalities and increasing returns.

Over the last two decades such dynamic phenomena have increasingly moved to the centre of attention within the economic discipline – especially with reference to technological change. A number of conceptual approaches and mathematical tools have been applied, often benefiting from contemporary developments in the analysis of dynamic systems in natural sciences.

In this chapter, we shall discuss some of these approaches and then focus on the basic structure and interpretation of one 'formal machinery', namely *generalised urn schemes*. In section 2, we shall outline some phenomena which are central to technological and economic dynamics and briefly review alternative formal representations. Section 3 introduces the basics of urn schemes. In the following sections we illustrate some applications to relatively simple competitive environments (section 4), and such further refinements as local feedback processes (section 5); increasing returns deriving from system compatibility (section 6) and non-

261

homogeneous environments (section 7). Finally, in the conclusion we shall point out some promising areas of application of this formal apparatus, including the economics of innovation, industrial dynamics, macro-economics and finance.

2. PROCESSES OF ECONOMIC EVOLUTION

In very general terms, the impulses driving economic change stem, first, from variations in the knowledge and physical resources upon which individual agents can draw in order to pursue their activities; second, from the process by which agents learn, adapt, invent – on the basis of whatever they perceive to be the available knowledge and resources; and third, from the interactions amongst the agents themselves. Of course, these sources of change are by no means independent. For example, learning activities obviously affect the available knowledge and the efficiency by which resources are used. Interactions may trigger learning and entail exter-nalities. And learning itself may be associated with particular forms of economic activity, such as learning-by-doing. The variety of sources and mechanisms of economic change highlighted by economic history in our view, precludes the identification of a unique or archetypical dynamic mechanism which would apply across industries, phases of development and historical contexts. Still, it might be possible (and indeed is a challen-ging area of research) to identify few relatively invariant characteristics of the processes of change and the 'formal structures' to represent them.

Some basic features of economic evolution are the following: (a) imper-fect and time-consuming microeconomic learning; (b) microheterogeneity; (c) various forms of increasing returns – especially in the accumulation of knowledge – and nonlinearities; (d) aggregate dynamics driven by both individual learning and collective selection mechanisms; (e) 'orderly' structural properties resulting from nonequilibrium fluctuations.

Let us now examine the formal representations which can account for at least some of these features of evolutionary dynamics. As a general reference, let us start from 'order-through-fluctuation' dynamics (cf. Nicolis and Prigogine 1971 and 1989; Prigogine and Stengers 1984). This is a quite broad paradigm for the interpretation of complex nonlinear processes, initially developed with reference to physical chemistry and molecular biology, but more generally emphasising the properties of self-reinforcing mechanisms and out-of-equilibrium self-organisation. Such systems turn out to be sensitive to early perturbations and display mul-tiplicity of patterns in their long-term behaviour. The cumulation of small early disturbances (or small disturbances around unstable or 'metastable' states) 'pushes' the system towards one of these patterns and thus 'selects' the structure towards which the system will eventually tend. These properties apply to a very wide class of dynamic systems, highlighting some general 'evolutionary' features extending well beyond the domain of social sciences and biology.

Other specifications of evolutionary dynamics derive from mathematical biology (see Eigen and Schuster 1979). Evolution in many of these models occurs such that some global characteristics (mean fitness for biological systems or mean 'competitiveness' in the economic analogy) 'improves' along the trajectory. In the simplest case of Fisher's selection model, 'improvements' straightforwardly imply that the mean fitness increases along the path. However, even in biology this equivalence does not hold in general (due, for example, to such phenomena as hyperselection, co-evolution, symmetry-breaking; see Allen 1988 and Silverberg 1988 for discussions directly linked to economic applications). Even more so, this *non-equivalence* between 'evolution' and 'increasing fitness', however defined, is likely to emerge whenever there is no identifiable 'fundamental law of nature' or conservation principle. Putting it another way: evolutionary dynamics – in biology as well as in economics – involves some kind of selection process grounded in the relevant distributions of agents' characteristics, on the one hand, and on some environmental criterion of 'adaptiveness', on the other. (Until recently, most economic models have avoided the issue simply by *assuming* that all the agents were perfectly 'adapted', either via some unspecified selection process that occurred just before the economist started looking at the world, or via some optimisation process that occurred in the heads of the agents themselves.) Replicator dynamics is a common formal tool to represent such selection-driven adaptation (for applications to economics, see Silverberg *et al.* 1988; and with reference to game-theoretical problems, Banerjee and Weibull 1992; Cabrales 1992; Kandori *et al.* 1990). However, even the simplest replicator processes impose quite stringent conditions on the ways selection occurs. In essence, these restrictions turn out to be negative feedbacks, that is diminishing returns, deriving from some underlying 'conservation principle'.[1] In contrast, positive feedbacks may lead to multiple limit states and generate a much richer variety of trajectories which the system may follow. For example, it is increasingly acknowledged that technological innovations are likely to involve some form of dynamic increasing returns – hence, positive feedbacks – during their development and diffusion (cf. Freeman 1982; Dosi *et al.* 1988; Anderson *et al.* 1988; David 1993; and for an interpretation of the empirical evidence, Dosi 1988). Relatedly, there is no guarantee that the particular economic outcome which happens to be historically selected from many notional alternatives will be the 'best' one, irrespective of the 'fitness' or welfare yardstick.

Concerning the mathematical tools that have been proposed within and outside economics for the analysis of the competitive process, ordinary differential equations have a paramount importance (not surprisingly, since they are also the most common language of modern science, and especially physics). They have been applied to most analyses of economic and technological dynamics (cf. Nelson and Winter 1982; Polterovich and Henkin 1988; Day 1992; the works surveyed in Boldrin 1988; and the thorough discussion in Rosser 1991; on their general applicability to economics, cf. Brock and Malliaris 1989). In particular, ordinary differential equations with trajectories on the unit simplex – that is of the replicator type – borrow, as already mentioned, an idea of selection-driven evolution from biology (cf. Silverberg *et al.* 1988).[2] On stochastic (Markov) perturbations of these equations, see Nicolis and Prigogine (1971) for general equations and Foster and Young (1990) for equations of the replicator type. However, while these continuous-time formulations work well, they involve a not-so-harmless approximation of events that are by nature discrete (the main example being a phase space which is discrete and changes by discrete increments). More intuitively, the continuous-time approximation is bound to take very literally the old saying that *natura non facet saltum.*

Moreover, from a technical point of view, the approximation involves unnecessary hypotheses of a mathematical nature (a classical example is the Lipschitz condition on the coefficients of the differential equation describing the system) and specific difficulties (such as the requirement of rigorously defining the stochastic perturbations of replicator equations). In this respect, it might be worth mentioning some recent results from evolutionary game theory showing convergence to conventional Nash-type equilibria in the continuous approximation but not in the discrete formulation (Banerjee and Weibull 1992; Dekel and Scotchmer 1991). Moreover, formal representations of selection processes in economics often rely on replicator dynamics satisfying the monotonicity condition (Friedman 1991; Samuelson and Zhang 1991; Banerjee and Weibull 1992); (loosely speaking, the monotonicity condition guarantees that, given an environment, there is no reversal in the 'forces of selection' along the trajectory). However, even in simple cases the results on limit properties obtained under replicator dynamics do not hold for more general selection processes (see, for example, Cabrales 1992). Thus one would like some machinery able to incorporate as adequately as possible such additional features as 'ugly' and badly behaved selection dynamics involving also 'jumps' and discontinuities, coevolutionary effects, and a large variety of individual processes of adaptation and innovation (without restricting assumptions about the processes driving the perturbations).

In the following, we shall assess to what extent an alternative class of models, namely *generalised urn schemes*, can fulfil these tasks. These schemes, sometimes called *nonlinear Polya processes* or *adaptive processes of growth*, generate stochastic discrete-time dynamic systems with trajectories on the set of points with rational coordinates from the unit simplex (cf. Arthur 1988; Arthur *et al.* 1983 and 1987c; Arthur and Lane 1991; Glaziev and Kaniovski 1991; Dosi *et al.* 1991; Arthur and Ruszczinski 1992). The mathematical background comes from Hill *et al.* (1980) and Arthur *et al.* (1983, 1987a and 1988). This formal apparatus enables one to handle positive and/or negative feedbacks (possibly coexisting) in the same process. In particular, these feedbacks may be of a 'local' nature in the sense that they may occur only for particular states on the trajectories (Dosi *et al.* 1991). This approach also allows the treatment of complementarities and network externalities in the adoption of competing technologies (Arthur *et al.* 1987b), whereby individual commodities – say, computers or telecomunication equipment – operate within networks requiring compatibility.[3] It must be also emphasised that although we shall focus on applications of this formalism to the economics of innovation, similar applications can easily be made in many other economic domains, such as organisational forms or strategies in business economics, cognitive models and decision rules in finance, and so on. Using the generalised urn schemes one can analyse the emergence of random market structures with more than one limit state occurring with positive probability (cf. Arthur *et al.* 1983; and Glaziev and Kaniovski 1991). Moreover, one may determine the convergence rates to the various limit states attainable with positive probability (Arthur *et al.* 1988).

We shall now analyse some of the patterns of system evolution which can be discovered by means of generalised urn schemes. In order to do so we shall use some known models of technological dynamics, and also introduce some novel modifications to highlight the complex limit structures that these models can generate.

Let us start with the simplest definition of a generalised urn scheme.

3. THE BASIC ELEMENTS OF THE THEORY OF GENERALISED URN SCHEMES

To simplify the presentation we shall restrict ourselves to the case of two competing technologies, corresponding to urn schemes with balls of two colours (Hill *et al.* 1980; Arthur *et al.* 1983). Think of an urn of infinite capacity with black and white balls. Starting with $n_w \geq 1$ white balls and

$n_b \geq 1$ black balls in the urn, a new ball is added to the urn at times $t = 1$, $2,...$. It will be white with probability $f_t(X_t)$ and black with probability $1 - f_t(X_t)$. Here $f_t(\cdot)$ is a function,[4] which maps $R(0,1)$ in $[0,1]$ ($R(0,1)$ stands for the set of rational numbers from $[0,1]$). By X_t we designate the proportion of white balls in the urn at time t. The dynamics of X_t is given by the relation

$$X_{t+1} = X_t + (t + n_w + n_b)^{-1}[\xi_t(X_t) - X_t], \quad t \geq 1, \quad X_1 = n_w(n_w + n_b)^{-1}.$$

Here $\xi_t(x)$, $t \geq 1$, are random variables independent in t, such that

$$\xi_t(x) = \begin{cases} 1 \text{ with probability } f_t(x), \\ 0 \text{ with probability } 1 - f_t(x). \end{cases}$$

Denote $\xi_t(x) - E\xi_t(x) = \xi_t(x) - f_t(x)$ by $\zeta_t(x)$. Then we have

$$X_{t+1} = X_t + (t + n_w + n_b)^{-1} \{[f_t(X_t) - X_t] + \zeta_t(X_t)\}, \quad t \geq 1, \quad X_1 = n_w(n_w+n_b)^{-1}.$$
(11.1)

Due to $E\zeta(x) = 0$, the system eq. (11.1) shifts on average at time $t \geq 1$ from a point x to the value $(t + n_w + n_b)^{-1}[f(x) - x]$. Consequently, the limit points of the sequence $\{X_t\}$ have to belong to the 'set of zeros' of the function $f_t(x) - x$ (for $x \in [0,1]$). It will really be the set of zeros if $f_t(\cdot)$ does not depend on t, i.e. $f_t(\cdot) = f(\cdot)$, $t \geq 1$, for $f(\cdot)$ a continuous function.

For the general case one needs a specific mathematical machinery to describe this 'set of zeros' (see Hill *et al.* 1980 for the case when the probabilities are discontinuous and do not depend on t, and Arthur *et al.* 1987b for the case when the probabilities are discontinuous functions and depend on t).

To summarise the properties of the above urn scheme that are important for our purposes recall the following:

1. The process X_t develops on the one-dimensional unit simplex $[0,1]$ taking (discrete) values from the set $R(0,1)$ (more precisely, at time $t+1$ it can take the values $i(t+n_w+n_b)^{-1}$, $n_w \leq i \leq n_w + t$).
2. Since in general we do not require any regularity of $f_t(\cdot)$, $t \geq 1$, the process can display a very complicated behaviours (for example, its trajectories can 'sweep off' an interval with probability 1 (see Arthur *et al.* 1987b).

3. If for a function $f(\cdot)$ one has $f_t(\cdot) = f(\cdot)+\delta_t(.)$ and $\sup_{x \varepsilon R(0,1)} |\delta_t(x)| \rightarrow$ 0 sufficiently fast as $t \rightarrow \infty$, then, for an isolated root θ of $f(x) - x$, one can have convergence of X_t to θ with positive or zero probability (we call such points *attainable* or *unattainable*) depending on whether

$$(f(x) - x)(x - \theta) \leq 0 \tag{11.2}$$

or

$$(f(x) - x)(x - \theta) \geq 0 \tag{11.3}$$

in a neighbourhood of θ (see Hill *et al.* 1980; Arthur *et al.* 1988; Dosi *et al.* 1991).

4. The convergence rate to those θ to which the process X_t converges with positive probability depends upon the smoothness of $f(\cdot)$ at θ. In particular, if the smoothness decreases from differentiability, i.e.

$$f(x) = f'(\theta)(x-\theta) + o(|x-\theta|) \text{ as } x \rightarrow \theta,$$

to the Hölder differentiability of the order $\gamma > 1/2$, i.e.

$$f(x) = f'_H(\theta)\text{sgn}(x-\theta)|x-\theta|^{\gamma} + o(|x-\theta|^{\gamma}) \text{ as } x \rightarrow \gamma,$$

the order of convergence of X_t to θ increases from $t^{-1/2}$ to $t^{-1(1+\gamma)}$ (see Kaniovski and Pflug 1992).

Now, thinking of the urn as a market and a white ball as a unit of technology A, a black ball as a unit of technology B, we can analyse the process of diffusion of A and B on the market (of infinite capacity) by means of the foregoing urn scheme. Let us first consider, however, some conceptual examples of technological dynamics in homogeneous economic environments, where competing firms, producing either one of the technologies, are operating.

4. SOME EXAMPLES OF COMPETITION UNDER GLOBAL FEEDBACKS IN A HOMOGENEOUS ECONOMIC ENVIRONMENT

We start with the simplest model which displays (global) positive feedback and, as a consequence, multiple (two in this case) patterns of limit behaviour.

Suppose that we have two competing technologies, say, A and B, and a market with imperfectly informed and risk-averse adopters.[5] The two technologies have already been introduced to the market, say $n_A \geq 1$ units of A and $n_B \geq 1$ units of B. Let us study their diffusion on the market. At time instants $t = 1, 2,...$ one new consumer adopts a unit of either technology. Since the adopters, in the example here, are imperfectly informed and risk-averse, they use some 'boundedly rational' decision rule to make their choice.[6] For example, in Arthur *et al.* (1983) and Glaziev and Kaniovski (1991), the following rule was considered:

R1 Ask an odd number $r > 1$ of the users of alternative technologies. If the majority of them use A, choose A. Otherwise choose B.

According to this rule, the technologies are symmetric. Alternatively, suppose that they are not. For example, A comes from a well-known firm with considerable 'goodwill' and B from a new and unknown one. Hence, potential users perceive a different risk in this choice and require different evidence. Assume that this corresponds to the following rule:

R2 Fix $\alpha \; \varepsilon \; [1/2,1]$. Ask $q \geq 3$ users of the technologies. If more than αq of them use A, choose A. Otherwise choose B.

Here α measures the relative uncertainty of the adopters concerning the two technologies. If $\alpha = 1/2$ and q is an odd number, then R2 converts into R1.

    Another interpretation of the choice process described by R1 and R2 is in terms of increasing returns to the technologies rather than risk-aversion of the adopters: the later adopters know that the greater the number of past adopters the bigger are the improvements which a technology has experienced (although the improvements themselves are not directly observable). Hence, in this case, sampling provides an indirect measure of unobservable technological characteristics.

    Rule R1 generates the probability to choose A as a function of its current proportion on the market, which has the following form:

$$f_t \, (x) = p_{R1}(x) + \delta_t(x). \tag{11.4}$$

Here

$$p_{R1 \, (x)} = \sum_{i=\frac{r+1}{2}}^{r} C_r^{\, i} \, x^{\, i} \, (1 - x)^{r-i},$$

$$\sup_{x \, \varepsilon \, R(0,1)} \, |\delta_t(x)| \, = O(t^{-1}),$$

and C_r^i stands for the number of combinations of i from r. The function $p_{R1}(x) - x$ has three roots 0, 1/2 and 1 on [0,1]. The root 1/2, satisfying eq. (11.3), proves to be unattainable, that is there is no feasible asymptotic market structure corresponding to it or, speaking in mathematical terms, X_t converges to this root with zero probability as $t \to \infty$ (see Glaziev and Kaniovski 1991). The roots 0 and 1, satisfying eq. (11.2), are attainable, that is X_t converges to each of them with positive probability for any ratio between $n_A \geq 1$ and $n_B \geq 1$. Moreover, the probability for A (B) to dominate in the limit (i.e. that $X_t \to 1$ ($X_t \to 0$) as $t \to \infty$) will be greater than 1/2 if the initial number of units n_A (n_B) of the technology is greater than the initial number of units of the alternative technology (for details, see Glaziev and Kaniovski 1991).

Consequently we observe here a mechanism of 'selection' which is 'history-dependent': the past shapes, in probability, the future, and this effect self-reinforces along the diffusion trajectory.

Quite similarly, rule R2 generates a function

$$f_t(x) = p_{R2}(x) + \delta_t(x),\qquad (11.5)$$

where

$$p_{R2}(x) = \sum_{i=[\alpha q]+1}^{q} C_q^i\, x^i\, (1 - x)^{q-i},$$

$$\sup_{x\,\varepsilon\,R(0,1)} |\,\delta_t(x)\,| = 0\,(t^{-1})$$

Here we denote by $[a]$ the largest integer in a. The function $p_{R2}(x) - x$ has three roots 0, θ and 1 on [0,1], where $\theta \geq 1/2$ and shifts to the right as α increases. It can be shown that, as in the previous case, this rule also generates a mechanism for establishing the dominance of one of the competing technologies (and both have a positive probability of dominating). However, in this case one cannot explicitly relate the initial frequencies of the technologies to the probabilities of dominating.

The two foregoing examples display (global) positive feedbacks. Examples of (global) negative feedbacks can be derived along similar lines.

Consider the following rules:

R3 Ask an odd number r of the users of alternative technologies. If the majority of them use A, choose B. Otherwise choose A.

R4 Fix $\alpha\,\varepsilon\,[1/2,1]$. Ask $q \geq 3$ users of the technologies. If more than αq of them use A, choose B. Otherwise choose A.

If $\alpha = 1/2$ and q is an odd number, then R4 converts into R3.

These rules may accommodate behaviours such as the search for diversity in consumption or implicitly capture the outcome of strategic behaviour on the part of the producers of the technologies aimed at the exploitation of 'market power' (cf. Dosi *et al.* 1991; Glaziev and Kaniovski 1991). We have relations here similar to eqs (11.4) and (11.5) with

$$p_{R3}(x) = \sum_{i=0}^{\frac{r-1}{2}} C_r^i \, x^i \, (1 - x)^{r-i},$$

and

$$p_{R4}(x) = \sum_{i=0}^{[\alpha q]} C_q^i \, x^i \, (1 - x)^{q-i}.$$

In both cases there is unique solution of the corresponding equations $p_{R3}(x) - x = 0$ and $p_{R4}(x) - x = 0$. For R3 it is 1/2, and for R4 the root θ is greater than 1/2 and increases with α. The negative feedback determines a limiting market structure in which both technologies are represented in the market with equal shares (R3) or they share the market in the proportion $\theta : (1 - \theta)$.

For both rules, we know the rates of convergence of X_t to the root, $\sqrt{t}(X_t - 1/2)$ for R3 or $\sqrt{t}(X_t - \theta)$ for R4 become asymptotically normal as $t \to \infty$. The means of the limit normal distributions are zero for both cases, and one can also specify the corresponding variances (see Arthur *et al.* 1983 for the case of R3). Consequently we can characterise the rate of emergence of the asymptotic market structures.[7]

More complicated $f(\cdot)$ functions appear if we introduce additional hypotheses concerning the characteristics and/or dynamics of the pool of adopters. If we assume that adopters who use some decision rule R_i are represented in the population with frequency (probability) $\alpha_i > 0$, $i = 1$, 2,..., k, ($\sum_{i=1}^{k} \alpha_i = 1$), then the function $f_t(\cdot)$, corresponding to the behaviour of the whole pool, is a randomization with weights α_i of functions $f_t^i(\cdot)$ generated by the rules R_i:

$$f_t(x) = \sum_{i=1}^{k} \alpha_i f_t^i(x), \quad x \, \varepsilon \, R(0,1), \quad t \geq 1.$$

The simplest example, with R1-adopters occurring with probability $\alpha > 0$, and R3-adopter with probability $1 - \alpha > 0$, has been considered in Dosi *et al.* (1991).

Beyond these properties of general positive and negative feedbacks, let us now consider those more complicated situations with *locally* positive and/or *locally* negative feedbacks.

5. EXAMPLES OF TECHNOLOGICAL DYNAMICS UNDER LOCAL FEEDBACKS IN HOMOGENEOUS ECONOMIC ENVIRONMENTS

Let us introduce a price dynamics for the two technologies. As in Dosi *et al.* (1991), assume that two firms (producers of A and B, respectively) use the following strategy:

up to a certain market share (usually greater than 1/2), defined by the proportion of the product of the firm among all products which have been sold until the current time, reduce the price, above that level increase it. Let us consider the simplest (linear) case of this policy which, which is depicted graphically in Figure 11.1. Here $Pr_A(x_A)$ designates the dependence of the price of technology A as a function of its proportion x_A among adopters who are using either technology. $Pr_B(x_A)$ designates the dependence of the price of the technology B as a function of x_A. (Note, that the proportions of the technologies A and B are related by: $x_A + x_B = 1$.) Define x^*_A and x^*_B as the 'critical' market shares, where producers switch from falling to rising price rules. Hence the dependence of the price of the A (B) technology on its proportion on the market $x_A(x_B)$ is given by four parameters: $Pr_A(0)$, x^*_A, $Pr_A(x^*_A)$, $Pr_A(1)(Pr_B(1)$, x^*_B, $Pr_B(1 - x^*_B)$,

Figure 11.1 Dependence of prices of A and B on the market share of A

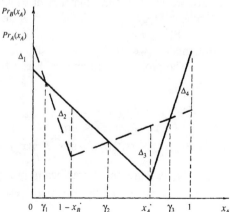

$Pr_B(0))$.[8]

This price dynamic embodies both positive and negative feedback mechanisms of diffusion. Within the domain of positive feedback the price falls with increasing market share possibly due to learning economies, dynamic increasing returns and so on, and/or, on the behavioural side, to market-penetration strategies. Then, above a certain market share, the price, driven by negative feedbacks, starts to rise, possibly due to monopolistic behaviour of the firm or to the progressive exhaustion of technological opportunities to lower production costs. Note that the model also accounts for those particular cases in which firms follow different 'non-symmetric' policies – for example, one increases the price and another lowers it, or both increase (lower) them,[9] or one increases (lowers) the price and the other follows the above general strategy. These special cases can be obtained from the general one by simply changing the relations between $Pr_A(0)$, $Pr_A(x^*_A)$, $Pr_A(1)(Pr_B(1)$, $Pr_B(1-x^*_B)$, $Pr_B(0))$.

It is natural to suppose that, in the case in which the performance of the technologies is approximately the same and potential adopters know about this, the technology which is cheaper has more chances to be sold, that is the A technology is bought if $Pr_A(x_A) - Pr_B(x_A) < 0$. However, if the prices differ only slightly, or consumers have some specific preferences (which can be characterised only statistically or on average), the adoption of the more expensive technology may happen. This case can be mathematically formalised in the following way (see also Hanson 1985). The A technology is bought if $Pr_A(x_A) - Pr_B(x_A) + \xi < 0$, where ξ is a random variable. (Consequently, the B technology is bought if $Pr_A(x_A) - Pr_B(x_A) + \xi > 0$.) To preserve the symmetry of the decision rule we should avoid the situation in which the event $Pr_B(x_A) - Pr_A(x_A) = \xi$ has nonzero probability. This is definitely not the case when the distribution of ξ possesses a density with respect to the Lebesgue measure on the set of real numbers. Consequently we shall assume that the distribution of ξ has a density in R^1. The probability $f(x_A)$ to choose the A technology, as a function of x_A, equals to $P\{\xi < Pr_B(x_A) - Pr_A(x_A)\}$. To avoid unnecessary complications in the model, we shall assume that ξ has a uniform distribution on $[-\alpha, \alpha]$. The probability to choose A as a function of x_A in this case has the form

$$f(x_A) = \begin{cases} 1 & \text{if } Pr_B(x_A) - Pr_A(x_A) \geq \alpha, \\ 0 & \text{if } Pr_B(x_A) - Pr_A(x_A) \leq -\alpha, \\ [Pr_B(x_A) - Pr_A(x_A) + \alpha]/2\alpha & \text{if } -\alpha < Pr_B(x_A) - Pr_A(x_A) < \alpha. \end{cases}$$

For $\alpha > \max_{i=1,2,3,4} \Delta_i$ this is represented graphically in Figure 11.2. Here we have three roots, θ_1, θ_2 and θ_3, of the function $f(x)-x$ on $[0,1]$. The root θ_2 satisfies eq. (11.3) and is thus unattainable, while θ_1 and θ_3, satisfy eq. (11.2) and are attainable, that is the process X_t converges to either one of them with positive probability for any initial proportions of the technologies on the market. Using results of Arthur *et al.* (1988), we find the rates of convergence to the attainable roots

$$\theta_1 = \frac{(\alpha + \Delta_1)\,(1 - x_B^*)}{2\alpha(1 - x_B^*) + \Delta_1 + \Delta_2},$$

$$\theta_3 = 1 - \frac{(\alpha + \Delta_4)\,(1 - x_A^*)}{2\alpha(1 - x_A^*) + \Delta_3 + \Delta_4}.$$

In particular,

$$\lim_{t\to\infty} P\,\{\sqrt{t}\,(X_t - \theta_i) < y,\ X_s \to \theta_i\} = P\,\{X_s \to \theta_i\}\ P\,\{N\,(0,\sigma_i^2) < y\}. \tag{11.6}$$

Also $N(0,\sigma_i^2)$ stands for a Gaussian distribution with zero mean and variance

$$\sigma_i^2 = \frac{\theta_i\,(1 - \theta_i)}{1 - 2f'\,(\theta_i)}, \tag{11.7}$$

where $f'(\cdot)$ designates the derivative of $f(\cdot)$. It can be shown that

$$f'(\theta_1) = -\frac{\Delta_1 + \Delta_2}{2\alpha\,(1 - x_B^*)} \tag{11.8}$$

and

$$f'(\theta_3) = -\frac{\Delta_3 + \Delta_4}{2\alpha\,(1 - x_A^*)} \tag{11.9}$$

One sees from eqs (11.6)–(11.9) that convergence to either θ_1 and θ_3 occurs with the rate $t^{-1/2}$, but the random fluctuations, which are determined by the variances of the corresponding limit distributions, may differ around the two roots.

In this example, the above dynamics of prices together with the described behaviour of adopters generate multiple limit patterns with slightly different rates of emergence. Under the same price dynamics and marginally

Figure 11.2   Probability of choosing A depending on its market share

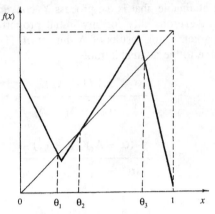

more sophisticated assumptions concerning the behaviour of adopters, one can obtain even more complicated asymptotic market structures (see Dosi *et al.* 1991). Similar considerations concerning convergence rates also apply.

6. URN SCHEMES WITH MULTIPLE ADDITIONS: A TOOL FOR ANALYSIS OF SYSTEM COMPATIBILITIES

As mentioned in section 2, quite a few modern high-technology products require compatibility. We have also hinted earlier that considering all notional combinations of new technologies as some kind of 'higher level' new technologies, although formally possible, does not look too attractive. An alternative method for handling inter-technological compatibilities has been introduced by Arthur *et al.* (1987a). For the case of two (*A* and *B*) competing technologies the argument takes the following form.

Consider Z_+^2, the set of two-dimensional vectors with non-negative integer coordinates. Introduce $\vec{\xi}_t(x)$, $t \geq 1$, $x \in R(0,1)$, independent in t, random vectors with values in Z_+^2. If $\vec{\xi}_t(x)$ takes the value $\vec{i} = (i_1, i_2)$ we can interpret this both as additions of $i_1 \geq 0$ white and of $i_2 \geq 0$ black balls to an urn of infinite capacity, or as adoptions on a market of infinite capacity of i_1 units of *A* and i_2 units of *B*.

Mathematical results similar to those presented in section 3 are obtained (see Arthur *et al.* 1987a, b and 1988). An important property of this generalisation is that $\vec{\xi}_t\,(x)$ can take the value $\vec{0} = (0,0)$ with nonzero probability. Consequently no adoption might happen at time t. Hence, taking into account that the scheme allows multiple adoptions, one sees that sequential instances of adoption do not coincide with physical time 'periods'. In other words, history may 'accelerate' by discrete jumps of variable length.

Further, let us introduce the urn model corresponding to the case when competition occurs in nonhomogeneous economic environments.

7. GENERALISED URN SCHEMES WITH NONHOMOGENEOUS ECONOMIC ENVIRONMENTS

Think of n urns of infinite capacity with black and white balls. Starting with $n_i^w \geq 1$ white balls and $n_i^b \geq 1$ black balls in the i-th urn, a ball is added to one of the urns at time instants $t = 1, 2,....$ It will be added with probability $f_i\,(\vec{X}(t))$ to the i-th urn. It will be white with probability $f_i^{\,w}\,(\vec{X}(t))$ and black with probability $f_i^{\,b}\,(\vec{X}(t))$. Here $\vec{f}\,(\cdot),\, f^{\,w}\,(\cdot),\, f^{\,b}(\cdot)$ are vector functions which map $R(\vec{0},\vec{1})$ in S_m, with $\vec{f}^{\,w}\,(\cdot) + \vec{f}^{\,b}\,(\cdot) = \vec{f}\,(\cdot)$. By $R(\vec{0},\vec{1})$ we designate the Cartesian product of m copies of $R(0,1)$ and

$$S_m = \left\{ \vec{x} \ \varepsilon \ R^{\,m}\colon x_i \geq 0, \ \sum_{i=1}^{m} x_i = 1 \right\}.$$

$\vec{X}(t)$ stands for the vector whose i-th coordinate $X_i(t)$ represents the proportion of white balls in i-th urn at time t. To introduce the dynamics of $\vec{X}(t)$11 consider $\xi^t\,(\vec{x})$, $t \geq 1, \vec{x} \ \varepsilon \ R(\vec{0},\vec{1})$, independent in t, random $m \times 2$ matrices with the elements $\xi_{i,j}^t\,(\vec{x})$, $i = 1,2,..., m, j = 1,2$, such that $P\,\{\xi_{i,1}^t(\vec{x}) = 1\} = f_i^{\,w}(\vec{x})$ and $P\,\{\xi_{i,2}^t(\vec{x}) = 1\} = f_i^{\,b}(\vec{x})$. Then the total number γ_i^t of balls in the i-th urn at time $t \geq 1$ follows the difference equation

$$\gamma_i^{t+1} = \gamma_i t + \xi_{i,t}^t\,(\vec{X}\,(t)) + \xi_{i,2}^t(\vec{X}\,(t)), \ t \geq \ 1, \ \gamma_i^1 = n_i^{\,w} + n_i^{\,b}.$$
$$(11.10)$$

Since
$$E\ [\ \xi_{i,1}^t\,(\vec{x}) + \xi_{i,2}^t\,(\vec{x})] = f_i(\vec{x}),$$
$$(11.11)$$

then, requiring that

$$\overrightarrow{f_i(x)} \geq f_i^0 > 0, \tag{11.12}$$

one has

$$f_i^0 \leq \lim_{t\to\infty} \inf \frac{\gamma_i^t}{t} \leq \lim_{t\to\infty} \sup \frac{\gamma_i^t}{t} \leq 1. \tag{11.13}$$

The number w_i^t of white balls and the number b_i^t of black balls in the urn evolve according to

$$w_i^{t+1} = w_i^t + \xi_{i,t}^t(\overrightarrow{X}(t)), \ t \geq 1, \ w_i^1 = n_i^w,$$

$$b_i^{t+1} = b_i^t + \xi_{i,2}^t(\overrightarrow{X}(t)), \ t \geq 1, \ b_i^1 = n_i^b. \tag{11.14}$$

Dividing eq. (11.14) by eq. (11.10) one has the following dynamics for the proportion of white balls in the i-th urn

$$X_i(t+1) = X_i(t) + \frac{1}{\gamma_i^t} \frac{\xi_{i,1}^t(\overrightarrow{X}(t)) - X_i(t)\,[\xi_{i,1}^t(\overrightarrow{X}(t)) + \xi_{i,2}^t(\overrightarrow{X}(t))]}{1 + (\gamma_i^t)^{-1}\,[\xi_{i,1}^t(\overrightarrow{X}(t)) + \xi_{i,2}^t(\overrightarrow{X}(t))]},$$

$$t \geq 1 \ , \ X_i(1) = \frac{n_i^w}{\gamma_i^1}. \tag{11.15}$$

Since

$$E\left\{ \frac{1}{\gamma_i^t} \left| \frac{\xi_{i,1}^t(\overrightarrow{X}(t)) - X_i(t)\,[\xi_{i,1}^t(\overrightarrow{X}(t)) + \xi_{i,2}^t(\overrightarrow{X}(t))]}{1 + (\gamma_i^t)^{-1}\,[\xi_{i,1}^t(\overrightarrow{X}(t)) + \xi_{i,2}^t(\overrightarrow{X}(t))]} \right| \overrightarrow{X}(t) = \overrightarrow{x}, \ \overrightarrow{\gamma^t} = \overrightarrow{\gamma} \right\}$$

$$= \frac{1}{\gamma_i^t} \frac{f_i^w(\overrightarrow{x}) - x f_i(\overrightarrow{x})}{1 + (\gamma_i^t)^{-1} f_i(\overrightarrow{x})},$$

relations (11.13) and (11.15) allow us to prove that $\overrightarrow{X}(t)$ converges with probability 1 as t→∞ to the set of zeros (defined properly) on $[\overrightarrow{0,1}]$ of the m-dimensional vector-function $\overrightarrow{F}(\cdot)$ whose i-th coordinate is $f_i^w(\overrightarrow{x}) - x_i f_i(\overrightarrow{x})$. Assume that both $f^{w}(\cdot)$ and $f^{b}(\cdot)$ are continuous and there is a limit X^0 for $\overrightarrow{X}(t)$. Then from equality (11.11) one can conclude that $t^{-1}\overrightarrow{\gamma}^t$ converges with probability 1 as t → ∞ and the limit $\overrightarrow{\gamma}^0$ has the form

$$\gamma_i^0 = f_i(\overrightarrow{X^0}), \quad i=1,2,...,m. \tag{11.16}$$

Using the above relations we can obtain analogous results to those of section 3 for the basic generalised urn scheme.

Figure 11.3 The price of the cheapest of the two technologies as a function of x_A

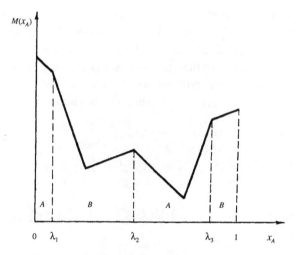

Now, suppose that we have two possible locations, 1 and 2, for the producers of two competing technologies, A and B. At each of the locations there is one firm producing A and one firm producing B. Producers use the strategy described in section 5 (with their own sets of parameters). Then for each of the locations there exists a minimum price of the technologies as a function of the current concentration of, say, A, i.e. $M(x_A) = \min (Pr_A(x_A), Pr_B(x_A))$. For the case represented by Figure 11.1, the function is graphed in Figure 11.3. Note that at points λ_i technologies reverse their order as the cheaper ones. Designate the proportion of

A for the first and the second locations by x_1 and x_2 respectively. Let λ_j^i, j = 1, 2, 3, i = 1, 2, be the points where the minimum prices switch from one technology to another. (We consider only the case in which the minimum prices for both locations have a shape similar to that presented in Figure 11.3.) Suppose that at time instants t = 1, 2,... a consumer buys a unit of either technology. He adopts the cheapest among the technologies, but, as before (section 5), because of some specific preferences or other reasons which can be taken into account statistically, he measures the difference between $M_1(x_1)$ and $M_2(x_2)$ with a random error. Here $M_i(\cdot)$ stands for the minimum price for the i-th location as a function of the market share of A at this location. A unit of a technology from the first location is bought if $M_1(x_1) - M_2(x_2) + \zeta < 0$; otherwise, that is when $M_1(x_1) - M_2(x_2) + \zeta > 0$, a unit from the second location is bought. As before, to preserve the symmetry of the decision rule we rule out the situation when that event '$M_2(x_2) - M_1(x_1) = \zeta$' has nonzero probability. Consequently we again assume that the distribution of ζ possesses a density with respect to the Lebesgue measure on the set of real numbers. The probability to choose the first location is $f_1(x_1,x_2) = P\{\zeta < M_2(x_2) - M_1(x_1)\}$. To simplify the problem let us suppose that ζ is uniformly distributed on $[-\beta, \beta]$. Then the probability to choose the first location is

$$
f_1(\overrightarrow{x}) = \begin{cases} 1 & \text{if} \quad M_2(x_2) - M_1(x_1) \geq \beta, \\ 0 & \text{if} \quad M_2(x_2) - M_1(x_1) \leq -\beta, \\ [M_2(x_2) - M_1(x_1) + \beta]/2\beta & \text{if} \quad -\beta < M_2(x_2) - M_1(x_1) < \beta. \end{cases}
$$

Suppose that $\beta > \max_{0 \leq x_i \leq 1,\ i=1,2} |M_2(x_2) - M_1(x_1)|$. Then eq. (11.11) holds with

$$
f_1^0 = \{ \min_{0 \leq x_i \leq 1,\ i=1,2} [M_2(x_2) - M_1(x_1)] + \beta \} / 2\beta
$$

and

$$
f_2^0 = 1/2 - \{ \max_{0 \leq x_i \leq 1,\ i=1,2} [M_2(x_2) - M_1(x_1)] \} / 2\beta.
$$

The simplest decision rule for choosing a specific technology when a location has been chosen is the following: a unit of $A(B)$ is adopted at the i-th location if $x_i \in I_i^A$ $x_i \in I_i^B$. Here $I_i^A = (0, \lambda_1^i)U(\lambda_2^i, \lambda_3^i)$ and $I_i^B = [\lambda_1^i,$

$\lambda_2{}^i]U[\lambda_3{}^i, 1]$. The corresponding vector-function $\vec{F}(\cdot)$ has the form

$$
\vec{F_i}(x) = \begin{cases} (1 - x_i)f_i\ (\vec{x}) \ for \ \ x_i \ \varepsilon \ I_i{}^A, \\[2ex] -x f_i(\vec{x}) \ for \ \ x_i \ \varepsilon \ I_i{}^B. \end{cases}
$$

We can show that $\vec{X}(t)$ converges (for any initial number of A and B at both locations) with probability 1 as $t \to \infty$ to a random vector $\vec{X}$. The limit takes with positive probability four values: $(\lambda_1{}^1, \lambda_1{}^2)$, $(\lambda_1{}^1, \lambda_3{}^2)$, $(\lambda_3{}^1, \lambda_1{}^2)$, $(\lambda_3{}^1, \lambda_3{}^2)$. Finally, note that one may easily refine these examples by introducing more complicated decision rules (for example, mixed strategies randomising the choice among technologies after having chosen the location, and so on).

8. CONCLUSIONS

Innovation and technology diffusion generally involve competition among different technologies, and endogenous changes in the costs and prices of technologies themselves. In the economic domain (as well as in other disciplines) the formal representation of such processes involves the dynamics of competing 'populations' (that is, technologies, firms, or even behavioural traits and 'models' of expectation formation). A growing literature in the theory of dynamical systems has begun studying the properties of the (generally nonlinear) processes in the innovation and diffusion process. Numerous models have demonstrated that multiple equilibria are a common rather than exceptional phenomena and that 'history matters', in the sense that out-of-equilibrium fluctuations may bear system-level consequences for asymptotic outcomes. Proceeding from previous results on dynamic increasing returns and the 'lock-in' of diffusion trajectories to particular technologies, we have presented a formal modelling apparatus aimed at handling the interaction between diffusion patterns, on the one hand, and endogenous preference formation and/or endogenous price formation, on the other. As examples, we presented three classes of stochastic models of market-share dynamics for a market of infinite capacity with two competing new technologies. In the first, we assumed that the adoption dynamics is essentially driven by endogenous changes in the choices of risk-averse, imperfectly informed adopters (or, in a formally equivalent analogy, by some positive or negative externality imperfectly estimated by would-be users of alternative technologies). In the second example, we considered an endogenous price dynamics of two alternative technologies driven by changes in their costs of production and/or by the intertemporal behaviours of their producers. In the third example we dealt with the same economic set-up as in the second one, but with an explicit 'spatial' representation of production.

In all of the cases, the diffusion process is allowed to embody some stochasticity, due to 'imperfect' learning from other people's choices, marginal and formally undetectable differences in users' preferences, or some inertia in adjusting between differently priced but identical-return technologies.

The formal apparatus presented here, based on the idea of the generalised urn scheme, allows quite general analytical results to be derived on the relationship between system-parameters (for example, proxies for information 'imperfection' by adopters; dynamic increasing returns and monopolistic exploitation of new technologies by their producers) and asymptotic market shares. While path-dependency applies throughout, these analytical techniques appear to be able to identify feasible limit equilibria (that is, those attainable with positive probability) and their rates of convergence.

The apparatus can also be used for numerical simulation. In this case it proves to be as general as ordinary differential equations and as easy to implement. By means of numerical simulation one can also study much more complicated and 'inductively rich' models. Still, the developed mathematical machinery serves in such numerical studies as a means of prediction and verification, revealing the general kind of behaviour one ought to expect. Yet another complementarity between the analytical exploration of these models and their numerical simulation concerns the study of their nonlimit properties, for example, the transient structures that might emerge along the trajectories and their degrees of persistence.

As the foregoing examples show, 'market imperfections' and 'informational imperfections' often tend to foster technological variety, that is, the equilibrium coexistence of different technologies and firms. Moreover, stochasticity in the choice process may well bifurcate asymptotic market-shares outcomes. Finally, corporate pricing strategies, possibly based on boundedly rational procedures and imperfect informational and systematically 'wrong' expectation-formation mechanisms, may well influence long-term outcomes.

There seem to be no *a priori* reasons to restrict this methodology to technological dynamics. In fact, with suitable modifications, it may apply as well to interdependent expectations, decisions and returns in many other economic domains. A few domains of application may well be: the evolution of strategies and organisational forms in industrial dynamics; the dynamics of location in economic geography (Arthur 1990); adaptive processes and the emergence of social norms; 'mimetic' effects and speculation on financial markets; macroeconomic coordination.[10] What we have tried to implement is a relatively general analytical apparatus able to handle some qualitative properties of dynamic stochastic processes characterised by both positive and negative feedbacks without imposing strong requirements on their smoothness. We believe that quite a few processes of economic change fall into this category, both related to technological change and also to interdependent (possibly 'disequilibrium') changes in industrial structure, and financial and product-market expectations and behaviour.

NOTES

1. In economics, profit (or utility) maximisation under a constraint of given and scarce resources clearly performs this role.
2. Of course, this does not have any implications for the sources of 'mutation' upon which environmental selection operates. For example, Silverberg *et al.* (1988) assume an exogenous drift in innovative opportunities with learning-by-using and diffusion-related externalities.
3. System compatibility implies that one ought to consider combinations amongst individual technologies. In turn, this can hardly be done by adding to the 'technological space' where choices are made from all possible combinations of technologies existing at any one time. At the very least, this procedure would lead to an enormous growth in the dimension of the phase space. For example, if N new technologies compete on the market, considering all their possible combinations would imply the 'explosion' of the dimension of the phase space up to $2^N - 1$.
4. When it does not depend on t it is called (Hill *et al.* 1980) an urn function.
5. Note that some general system properties – such as the multiplicity of limit states under positive feedbacks – are independent from the exact characterisation of microeconomic decision rules, although the latter influence both the processes and the nature of limit structures themselves.
6. A fascinating issue, which cannot be pursued here, regards the meaning of 'rationality' in environments driven by positive feedbacks and showing multiple limit states. For example, even if the agents knew the 'true' urn model, what use can they make of this cognitive representation? How could they be more than 'boundedly rational'?
7. For this particular rule one can determine an even sharper asymptotic characterisation – the law of iterated logarithm (see Arthur *et al.* 1983).
8. Note that one accounts also for the circumstances when $Pr_A(1) \leq Pr_A(x^*_A)(Pr_B(0) \leq Pr_B(1 - x^*_B))$, such as when $x^*_A = 1(x^*_B=1)$: in the case, firm $A(B)$ still reduces the price on its product as its proportion on the market increases.
9. For the case when both lower prices, see Glasiev and Kaniovski (1991) where formally the same situation is interpreted somewhat differently.
10. For some works these different domains that link at least in spirit with the approach to economic dynamics suggested here, see among others, Kirman (1991), Kuran (1991), Boyer and Orléan (1992) and Durlauf (1991).

REFERENCES

Allen, P.M. (1988), 'Evolution, Innovation and Economics', in G. Dosi, C. Freeman, R. Nelson and L. Soete (eds), *Technical Change and Economic Theory*, London: Pinter.

Anderson, P.W., Arrow, K.F. and Pines, R. (eds) (1988), *The Economy as an Evolving Complex System. SFI Studies in the Science of Complexity*, New York: Addison-Wesley.

Arthur, W.B. (1983), *On Competing Technologies and Historical Small Events: The Dynamics of Choice under Increasing Returns*, WP–83–90, Laxenburg, Austria: International Institute for Applied Systems Analysis.

Arthur, W.B. (1988), 'Self-reinforcing Mechanisms in Economics', in P.W. Anderson, K.F. Arrow and R. Pines (eds), *The Economy as an Evolving Complex System. SFI Studies in the Science of Complexity*, New York: Addison-Wesley.

Arthur, W.B. (1990), ' "Silicon Valley" Location Clusters: When do Increasing Returns Imply Monopoly?', *Mathematical Social Sciences*, 19(3), 235–251.

Arthur, W.B. and Lane, D.A. (1991), *Information Constriction and Information Contagion*, Santa Fe Institute, mimeo.

Arthur, W.B. and Ruszczinski, A. (1992), 'Strategic Pricing in Markets with Conformity Effects', *Archives of Control Sciences*, 1(37), 1–2, 7–31.

Arthur W.B., Ermoliev, Y.M. and Kaniovski, Y.M. (1983), 'The Generalised Urn Problem and Its Application', *Kibernetika*, 1, 49–56 (in Russian).

Arthur, W.B., Ermoliev, Y.M. and Kaniovski, Y.M. (1987a), 'Adaptive Process of Growth Being Modeled by Urn Schemes', *Kibernetika*, 6, 49–57 (in Russian).

Arthur, W.B., Ermoliev, Y.M. and Kaniovski, Y.M. (1987b), *Nonlinear Urn Processes: Asymptotic Behaviour and Applications*, WP–87–85, Laxenburg, Austria: International Institute for Applied Systems Analysis.

Arthur, W.B., Ermoliev, Y.M. and Kaniovski, Y.M. (1987c), 'Path Dependent Processes and the Emergence of Macro-Structure', *European Journal of Operational Research*, 30(1), 294–303.

Arthur, W.B., Ermoliev, Y.M. and Kaniovski, Y.M. (1988), *Nonlinear Adaptive Processes of Growth with General Increments: Attainable and Unattainable Components of Terminal Set*, WP–88–86, Laxenburg, Austria: International Institute for Applied Systems Analysis.

Banerjee, A. and Weibull, J.M. (1992), 'Evolution and Rationality: Some Recent Game-theoretic Results', paper presented at the *Tenth World Congress of the International Economic Association*, Moscow, August.

Boldrin, M. (1988), 'Persistent Oscillations and Chaos in Dynamic Economic Models: Notes for a Survey', in P.W. Anderson, K.F. Arrow and R. Pines (eds), *The Economy as an Evolving Complex System. SFI Studies in the Science of Complexity*, New York: Addison-Wesley.

Boyer, R. and Orléan, A. (1992), 'How Do Conventions Evolve?', *Journal of Evolutionary Economics*, 2(3), 165–177.

Brock, W.A. and Malliaris, A.G. (1989), *Differential Equations, Stability and Chaos in Dynamic Economics*, Amsterdam, North-Holland.

Cabrales, A. (1992), *Stochastic Replicator Dynamics*, Department of Economics, University of California at San Diego, mimeo.

David, P.A. (1985), 'Clio and the Economics of QWERTY', *American Economic Review, Papers and Proceedings*, 75, 332–337.

David, P.A. (1994), 'Putting the Past into the Future', *Journal of Economic Literature* (forthcoming).

Day, R. (1992), 'Irregular Growth Cycles', *American Economic Review*, 72, 406–414.

Dekel, E. and Scotchmer, S. (1991), 'On the Evolution of Optimizing Behavior', *Journal of Economic Theory*, 59, 637–666.

Dosi, G. (1988), 'Sources, Procedures and Microeconomic Effects of Innovation', *Journal of Economic Literature*, 26(3), 1120–1171.

Dosi, G., Freeman, C., Nelson, R., Silverberg, G. and Soete, L. (eds) (1988), *Technical Change and Economic Theory*, London: Pinter.

Dosi, G., Ermoliev, Y.M. and Kaniovski, Y.M. (1991), *Generalized Urn Schemes and Technological Dynamics*, WP–91–9, Laxenburg, Austria: International Institute for Applied Systems Analysis (accepted, subject to revision, by *Journal of Mathematical Economics*).

Durlauf, S.N. (1993), 'Non-ergodic Economic Growth', *Review of Economic Studies*, 60, 349-366.

Eigen, M. and Schuster, P. (1979), *The Hypercycle: A Principle of Natural Selforganisation*, Berlin: Springer Verlag.

Foster, D. and Young, H.P. (1990), 'Stochastic Evolutionary Game Dynamics', *Theoretical Population Biology*, 38, 219–232.

Freeman, C. (1982), *The Economics of Industrial Innovation*, 2nd edn, London: Pinter.

Friedman, D. (1991), 'Evolutionary Games and Economics', *Econometrica*, 59, 637–666.

Frydman, R. (1982), 'Towards an Understanding of Market Processes: Individual Expectations, Learning and Convergence to Rational Expectations Equilibrium', *American Economic Review*, 72, 652–668.

Frydman, R. and Phelps, E.S. (1983), *Individual Forecasting and Aggregate Outcomes*, Cambridge, Cambridge University Press.

Glaziev, S.Y. and Kaniovski, Y.M. (1991), 'Diffusion of Innovations Under Conditions of Uncertainty: a Stochastic Approach', in N. Nakicenovic and A. Grübler (eds), *Diffusion of Technologies and Social Behaviour*, Berlin: Springer Verlag.

Hanson, W.A. (1985), *Bandwagons and Orphans: Dynamic Pricing of Competing Systems Subject to Decreasing Costs*, PhD Dissertation, Stanford University.

Hill, B.M., Lane, D. and Sudderth, W. (1980), 'A Strong Law for Some Generalised Urn Processes', *Annals of Probability*, 8(2), 214–226.

Jordan J. (1985), 'Learning Rational Expectation: the Finite State Case', *Journal of Economic Theory*, 36, 257–276.

Kandori, M., Mailath, G.J. and Rob, R. (1990), *Learning, Mutation, and Long Run Equilibria in Games*, University of Pennsylvania, mimeo.

Kaniovski, Y. and Pflug, G. (1992), *Non-standard Limit Theorems for Stochastic Approximation and Their Applications for Urn Schemes*, WP–92–25, Laxenburg, Austria: International Institute for Applied Systems Analysis.

Kirman, A. (1991), 'Epidemics of Opinion and Speculative Bubbles in Financial Markets', in M. Taylor (ed.), *Money and Financial Markets*, London: Macmillan.

Kuran, T. (1991), 'Cognitive Limitations and Preference Evolution', *Journal of Institutional and Theoretical Economics*, 147, 241–273.

Nelson, R. and Winter, S. (1982), *An Evolutionary Theory of Economic Change*, Cambridge: Belknap Press of Harvard University Press.

Nicolis, G. and Prigogine, I. (1971), *Self-organisation in Nonequilibrium Systems: From Dissipative Structures to Order through Fluctuations*, New York: John Wiley.

Nicolis, G. and Prigogine, I. (1989), *Exploring Complexity. An Introduction*, New York: Freeman.

Polterovich, V.M. and Henkin, G.M. (1988), 'An Economic Model Interaction of Processes of Creation and Leasing of Technologies', *Ekonomika*, 24(6), 1071–1083 (in Russian).

Prigogine, I. and Stengers, I. (1984), *Order out of Chaos: Man's New Dialogue with Nature*, London: Heinemann.

Rosser, J.B. Jr (1991), *From Catastrophe to Chaos: A General Theory of Economic Discontinuities*, Boston: Kluwer.

Samuelson, L. and Zhang, J. (1991), *Evolutionary Stability in Asymmetric Games*, Tilburg University, mimeo.

Silverberg, G. (1988), 'Modelling Economic Dynamics and Technical Change: Mathematical Approaches to Self-organisation and Evolution', in G. Dosi, C. Freeman, R. Nelson, G. Silverberg and L. Soete (eds), *Technical Change and Economic Theory*, London: Pinter, 531–559.

Silverberg, G., Dosi, G. and Orsenigo, L. (1988), 'Innovation, Diversity and Diffusion: a Self-organisation Model', *Economic Journal*, 98, 1032–1054.

COMMENT ON DOSI AND KANIOVSKI

Sidney Winter

Urn schemes provide mathematical parables that show how major features of economic reality, which appear to be highly inertial, can be given scientifically compelling explanations. These mathematical techniques have been used to explain the division of markets between competing brands, technologies or network systems. Yet, these explanations are in a sense unsatisfying, for three related though distinguishable reasons.

The first reason can be illustrated by reference to historical examples, such as the QWERTY keyboard or the AC electrical distribution system in the US. The mathematics of urn schemes tells us that the historical success of particular outcomes is not inevitable. A different result could be reached if it was possible to perfectly replicate, as an experiment, the conditions which culminated in the choice of AC over DC or the QWERTY keyboard over alternatives. Repeating the experiment several times would produce a distribution of results. This means that existing reality could, for example, occur in only 10 or 20% of the experiments and lie in the tail of the distribution of outcomes. In terms of the underlying probabilistic logic of the system, some other outcome could have been more likely.

Second, whereas small interventions could have minor consequences at the present time, the mathematics suggests that the same interventions could have had major effects at key times in the past when the direction of the system had not yet been established. Thus we have the mathematical basis for the poet's remark, 'For of all sad words of tongue or pen, the saddest are these: "It might have been" '. Even as we speak, our opportunity costs for being in one place versus another include foregone small interventions in ongoing situations which, taken at the right time, could strongly shape the futures of our personal lives, our countries, the planet, or intelligent life in the universe.

Third, determinism could be recovered, perhaps, by searching for the underlying causes of the stochastic events, but it would be an unsatisfying type of determinism. The outcome of a coin toss could be determined in advance if the proper data was obtained about the physical conditions of the toss and of other influencing factors. In the same sense, given the proper data, one could find the deterministic explanations for the individual random choices represented in this stochastic model, but presumably these explanations would not be 'good' reasons in the sense that they would make the specific outcome comprehensible in human terms. Diverse examples such as VCR standards, automobile accidents, or the outbreak of the First World War are similar in this respect. These are situations in which the outcome may be deterministic, but it is the result of an entirely different category of deterministic events than those one was trying to understand.

As a corollary of each of these different reasons why mathematical explanations are unsatisfying, we can note that they all share the tendency to weaken the presumption of optimality that attaches to observed events. These types of mathematical models create serious reasons for doubting the Panglossian interpretation that existing conditions that are hard to change must be about right. Instead, just because something exists and is hard to change does not mean that it is about right, or even that it was a highly probable outcome of the system that generated it.

From an *ex ante* point of view, the lesson to be learned from these models is that we should evaluate conditions when there is a small number of balls in the urn and try to scrape up a few extra balls of the colour that one prefers and throw them in, since that could influence the outcome.

Though I've called these explanations unsatisfying, perhaps a more accurate description is that they are *not reassuring*. They indicate that the world is not the best of all possible worlds and is perhaps not working out as it should. Instead, an important explanation for the observed outcomes is nonlinearities and stochastic factors. These explanations should be quite satisfying, however, to economic historians, as they point to the need for an accurate account of specific events, which in turn elevates the value of history in the economics profession.

The significant contribution of the paper to economics lies in its application of the mathematical apparatus to some interesting and specific economic questions. Several examples are given below.

The paper raises the idea that diffusion processes can be guided by information, which itself is determined by random sampling of the results of previous adoptions. In addition, random variation is raised as one explanation of differences in preferences or in choice between two technologies with different prices, but the paper more closely examines the pricing behaviour for competing technologies as an important source of the nonlinear patterns that are crucial to the particular attractors.

The example of pricing behaviour in the model is a very plausible account of how competing firms which produce the same good decide to market their goods. It basically says that it is good to price low up to some point in order to deliberately encourage the diffusion of the innovation and then to raise the price once monopoly conditions develop. This is probably a reasonable account of a combination of increasing returns in production and a deliberate strategy of 'penetration pricing'.

Other kinds of applications for the model are briefly referred to in the paper but are not spelled out. One interesting line for further exploration is as follows. The concept of increasing returns can explain why the advantages of a technology can grow with the fraction of adopters, but there is the problem of accounting for diminishing returns outside of monopoly conditions. Given learning effects or increasing returns, an alternative explanation is needed for the diminishing appeal of a technology. One possibility is to reject the assumption of a homogeneous pool of adopters and to examine what would happen if there are differences in adopters, so that some will tend to favour one technology over another. In this case, a technology would diffuse quickly among those who are naturally disposed to adopt it, and then run into difficulty as it encounters the limit of this group and tries to diffuse into another population.

As a final comment, I should like to note that it would be very interesting to have good simulations for this approach to show the rates at which the patterns in the model develop. This would help our understanding of the subject matter.

Richard Nelson:
The topic that we should discuss here is not only this specific urn scheme, but the whole class of models that extend beyond this, including models that involve dynamic increasing returns and other alternative formulations.

Robert Ayres:
From my particular perspective the news brought by this type of model is the best possible news for the following reasons. If you are concerned about the direction of economic development from an environmental perspective, and if you believe that everything with a lot of inertia is the best of all possible worlds, then you have little choice but to believe economic models that conclude that it is going to be very costly to change. On the other hand, if you believe, as I do, that the economic system is not very close to equilibrium in the sense that we have made all the best technological choices, then there may be a number of opportunities to save on pollution and energy while simultaneously saving on money.

Sidney Winter:
Some of us prefer to model stochastic processes in discrete time, not because we think that it is more realistic, as Yuri appears to believe, but because it is easier from a technical point of view. But it is possible to rescale the time axis and hence the rate at which real time flows. By this means, the rates at which proportions change can remain constant, or

change in some other specified way, while still producing the same asymptotic results.

Gerald Silverberg:

I would just like to return to Robert Ayres's question on the inevitability of lock-in and the costs of switching between various asymptotic states. One limitation of applying the Polya urn scheme to reality is that it is necessary to assume an infinite population. This makes lock-in inevitable and prevents escape from an asymptotic regime. But of course, as you mentioned in the beginning of your talk, much of technological dynamics is related to replicator schemes which are traditionally applied to constant populations. In this case, even if you have multiple attracting states, there is always a finite probability of escaping from one of those states in a stochastic model. If you wait long enough, escape is certain. So an interesting question that has not been asked frequently enough in this context is: when are Polya urns applicable to an economic or real world problem and when are replicator dynamics of another kind applicable? This would certainly change our pessimism or optimism about our policy options in a highly nonlinear world.

Yuri Kaniovski:

The model is definitely only applicable to technologies that are produced in large quantities, where it is possible to imagine the existence of asymptotes. The model is not applicable to nuclear reactors, for example. As for replicator equations, I mentioned this analogy because both trace the proportions relative to quantities. This contrasts with branching processes, where only trivial results are possible where the concentration is either one or zero, depending on the eigenvalue. But in pure replicator dynamics, the same effect basically occurs because you assume continuity of the phase space. The discrete increments are hidden in a continuous time formulation. The proximity of two states cannot be determined because of the continuity of the phase space. For each time t, there is a discrete and finite number of possible states. There is a Markov process but it is finite but non-stationary.

Gerald Silverberg:

You can have a Markov process in which a ball must be removed for every ball that is added.

Yuri Kaniovski:

This can be done up to a certain extent, but I must avoid the case where it is possible to get a negative number of balls. This can be done for some special cases, but not in general. In this case I would introduce a mechanism for births and deaths, which would be more interesting. To stress again, the cycles that you mentioned are somehow hidden in the continuous time formulation because of the continuity of phase space.

Richard Nelson:

There are other types of urn schemes that are not addressed in this paper but which lead to similar kinds of phenomena, though they can point in different directions. In this spirit, let me propose that if economists had based their views on how industries and technologies developed on these kinds of models, then some of our industrial and other economic policies, based on the assumption that it is almost always best to let the market decide, would be very different. Instead, we would believe that the market decides in a very random – and in the long run – a socially pernicious way. In this case it might be irresponsible not to make some public decisions about the future direction of an industry or a technology. However, the discussion would not be on whether or not one could pick winners, but if one could effectively make winners.

12. What has been the Matter with Neoclassical Growth Theory?

Richard R. Nelson[*]

1. INTRODUCTION

After a hiatus of many years, formal growth theory now is back in fashion. The authors of the recent theoretical papers almost certainly were moved by a variety of motives. It is clear, however, that a number of the authors recognised that there was something the matter with the earlier generation of neoclassical growth models. They wanted to call attention to these analytic problems and to try to fix them.

Virtually all of the earlier generation of growth models had placed technological advance at the centre of the stage as the key factor behind rising labour productivity and income levels. However, most of the earlier formal growth models were mute, or incoherent, regarding the sources of technical advance. A central objective of many of the new essays in growth theory is to make technological advance endogenous, the result of investments by firms in R&D and, perhaps, other activities (see, for example, Aghion and Howitt 1992; Grossman and Helpman 1991; Romer 1990).

There are two different aspects of the modelling that make technological advance endogenous. First, in these models R&D investments are profitable for firms because they are able to make proprietary at least a portion of the value of the increased productivity or better product performance won through R&D. Second, to square with the recognition that technology is in some degree proprietary, and also that support of R&D is feasible only if price exceeds production cost by some margin, markets are assumed to be imperfectly, not perfectly, competitive. (For a good statement see Romer 1991.)

The endogenising of technical advance in these models in this way has

[*] A number of people have commented helpfully on earlier drafts of this essay. In view of the controversial nature of much of the argument, as one would expect some of my respondents were more in accord with my line than were others, but all commented constructively. I particularly want to thank the following, without implicating them in any way: Moses Abramovitz, John Kendrick, Zvi Griliches, Robert Solow, Paul Romer, Franco Malerba and Theo van de Klundert.

been complemented by the building in or the deduction of other phenomena. Thus some of the models treat technical advance as a process of 'creative destruction' in which a new technology obsoletes older ones (see Aghion and Howitt 1992). In many of the models there are 'externalities' from investments in R&D or in other activities, for example, education (see Lucas 1988). Up-front R&D investments, and in some models, spillovers, generate economies of scale. And in many of these models the rate of investment in new plant and equipment affects the steady-state growth rate, whereas in the older generation of neoclassical growth models the steady-state growth rate was independent of the investment rate.

The new models provide a number of angles for analysing how and why growth rates may vary over time. They also contain a number of components relevant for analysing cross-country differences in levels of productivity as well as growth rates. In particular, they signal that differential access to proprietary technology, economies of scale, and durable influences of the investment rate on growth rates, can lead to large and stubborn international differences in productivity and living standards.

The characterisation above does not do justice to the elegance of some of the new growth models, nor does it lay out the variety. (For more extended and systematic reviews see Romer 1991; Verspagen 1992.) However, it suffices to bring out two points. First, these models are different from most of the earlier ones, and in ways that make them more 'realistic' in the sense of capturing, at least in stylised form, features of growth that most economists studying the topic empirically have known to be important. Clearly one of the things that has been the matter with most of the older neoclassical growth theory is that it did not come to grips with the fact that technical advance is largely endogenous, or with a variety of ramifications of that fact.

However, second, this brief review also suffices to highlight that the phenomena incorporated in the new models, and neglected in many of the old ones, scarcely represent novel new insights or ideas. The basic notions that 'technical change is largely endogenous', 'technology is to at least some extent proprietary, and market structures supporting technical advance are not perfectly competitive', 'new technology often obsoletes old technology', 'growth fueled by technical advance involves externalities and economies of scale', and 'the investment rate may matter in the long run', scarcely smack of novelty. All have been part of the body of understanding of those studying economic growth for a long time. Indeed, as I shall show in the next section, Abramovitz put forth most of these propositions in his review article on the economics of growth, written over forty years ago, in 1952.

This last observation suggests that the question of 'What has been the matter with neoclassical growth theory?' might be posed in a different way from that of the authors of the new essays. While it certainly is useful to identify and fix particular limitations of the older formal models, one can ask a broader question: 'Why such a lag in incorporation of understandings long held by scholars of economic growth into formal growth theory?'. One also can ask 'What, if anything, is gained when understandings that are widely held are incorporated in formal theories?'. And one also can ask 'Where do these new models still seem to get things somewhat wrong in the light of what currently is known, and what understandings presently held by scholars of economic growth are missed in them?'.

These are the questions this essay is about. But before getting into them, I need to lay out the view of theory in economics that lies behind both the way I pose the questions, and the manner of my answers.

Some of the authors of the recent theoretical papers have put forth the argument that the theory they are presenting is 'new', but I noted that the basic ideas that have been incorporated into these models have been around for a long time. What the recent papers have done is to formalise them in particular ways. The authors of these papers might respond that, while the ideas had been around among empirical researchers, they were not incorporated in 'growth theory'. I would reply by acknowledging that the incorporation of these ideas in *formal* models may be new, but arguing that empirical scholars of economic growth long have had a theory of that process that contained those ideas in a central way, although not in a formalised manner. To associate economic theory in general with formal economic theory is too narrow a view.

Sidney Winter and I have argued (1982) that, perhaps because the subject matter and the operative mechanisms of economics are so complex, theorising in economics tends to proceed on at least two levels of formality, not one. We have called these levels appreciative theory and formal theory.

Appreciative theorising tends to be close to empirical work and provides both guidance and interpretation. Mostly it is expressed verbally and is the analyst's articulation of what he or she thinks really is going on. Appreciative theory is very much an abstract body of reasoning. Certain variables and relationships are treated as important, and others are ignored. There generally is explicit causal argument. However, appreciative theorising tends to stay relatively close to the empirical substance.

In contrast, formal theorising almost always proceeds at some intellectual distance from what is known empirically, and where it does appeal to data for support, the appeal generally is to 'stylised facts', or reasonably good 'statistical fits'. If the hallmark of appreciative theory is storytelling that is close to the empirical nitty-gritty, the hallmark of formal theorising is an abstract structure set up to enable one to explore, find and check logical connections. Appreciative theorising is rich, but often will contain logical gaps and sometimes inconsistencies. Good formal theorising usually will contain fewer strictly logical gaps and will be mostly consistent. Also, the logical inferences will tend to reach further than those of appreciative theorising. But formal theory generally will be significantly more distant from the empirical nitty gritty.

Winter and I have argued that when the intellectual enterprise in economics is going well, empirical research, appreciative theorising, and formal theorising work together or rather, empirical work and appreciative theorising work together, and appreciative and formal theorising work together. Empirical findings or facts seldom influence formal theorising directly. Rather, in the first instance they influence appreciative theorising. In turn, appreciative theorising provides challenges to formal theory to encompass its understandings in stylised form. The attempt to do so may identify gaps or inconsistencies in the verbal stories, and suggest new mechanisms and connections to explore. In turn the empirical and appreciative theoretical research enterprise may be reoriented.

According to the above view, formal theory can lead, taking appreciative theorising and empirical work into new arenas or in new directions. On the other hand, formal theory can follow appreciative theory, correcting, and fine tuning it. I am proposing that, to a considerable extent, the 'new' neoclassical growth theory has been picking up ideas from the broad body of appreciative theories and formalising these in particular ways. Some of the authors of the new formal models are reasonably generous about acknowledging this; others less so.

Which brings me back to my three questions. First, why the lag? At least one proponent of the new growth theory (see Romer 1991) has suggested that a principal reason is that the analytic tools needed to model non-competitive general equilibrium were not available until recently. I would propose that a more important reason is that most of the economists doing formal modelling were paying only sporadic attention to appreciative theorising about growth, and thus it took a long time before they took aboard the key understandings and began to reflect on how some of them might be formalised. What is the gain of formalisation? I doubt that the new formal growth theory will change very much the basic understandings about economic growth of those who have been studying it closely, since they already mostly know what the models teach, although it may sharpen some of the ideas and call attention to new angles. However, the new formal modelling may play a powerful positive role in spreading those basic understandings to the economics community more broadly, and in making them theoretically respectable, thus making research in this field more attractive to young scholars. That would be a big plus.

What important aspects of appreciative theory about economic growth shared by scholars in the field have the new formal models got somewhat wrong or simply missed? A number of different things, and discussion of these will form the analytic heart of this essay.

I shall develop my case as follows. First, in section 2, I present an analytic history of 'theorising about growth' from the early 1950s to the early l990s, focusing in particular on the pattern of interaction (or lack of it) between appreciative and formal theorising. Towards the end of this section, I shall highlight the set of puzzles about economic growth that currently is worrying the research enterprise, and what I consider to be the more interesting appreciative theoretic approaches to these puzzles. In section 3, I explore these approaches in more detail. In particular, I elaborate some of the new understandings about the nature of technology and technical advance, about how to think about the capabilities of business firms, and about economic institutions more broadly. I propose that there are the makings here of a powerful theory of economic growth that is concerned with the variables behind those focused on in neoclassical growth theory, new as well as old. Finally, a reprise.

2. POSTWAR THEORISING ABOUT ECONOMIC GROWTH: CAUSES FOR SATISFACTION AND CONCERN

In this section I will develop three themes. First, in the period since the Second World War our understanding of growth has increased greatly. However, by and large the empirical research and associated appreciative theorising has proceeded on its own with only limited contributions from formal growth theory. Second, since the 1970s important limitations of our understanding of economic growth have become increasingly evident. Economists have yet to achieve a persuasive and satisfying explanation for why growth in the advanced industrial nations and, in particular, in the United States has been so much slower in the 1970s and 1980s than in the 1950s and 1960s, for the overtaking by Japan of the many European economies and, perhaps, the United States, or for the uneven growth performance among nations more generally. Third, in struggling with these questions, economists (and other scholars interested in economic growth) increasingly are looking behind the variables that were the principal focus in earlier research. I shall develop the argument that the 'new growth theory' is incorporating a portion of what was learned prior to the 1980s, but is not in touch with recent directions of appreciative theorising.

2.1 The Postwar Resurgence of the Research on Economic Growth

Economic growth of course was a central interest of Adam Smith, and many of the Classical economists of the nineteenth century. However, during the first half of the twentieth century the topic dropped out of vogue, as microeconomic analysis increasingly came under the sway of partial and general equilibrium theory, and, with the Great Depression, macroeconomic analysis became obsessed with unemployment. After the Second World War a number of economists again became interested in economic growth. The new surge of research on economic growth was not kindled by any arresting new theory in economics. On the other hand, a principal motivation for new research was the availability of new economic statistics, particularly the national income and product statistics, which Simon Kuznets pioneered and which for the first time enabled economists to measure growth at a national level.

In 1952 *A Survey of Contemporary Economics* was published, which attempted to assess the state of the discipline then. It contained an article on the economics of growth by Moses Abramovitz, and for my purposes there are two important features of that article. First, Abramovitz begins with a statement about the absence of any coherent modern growth theory: 'Unlike most of the topics treated in the *Survey*, the problem with economic growth lacks any organised and genuinely known body of doctrine whose recent development might furnish the subject of this essay'. The reader will of course note that Abramovitz was writing a few years before the publication of the Solow (1956) and Swan (1956) pieces which are reputed to have established modern growth theory, and be tempted to take his statement as an indication that those articles filled an intellectual vacuum.

But the other noteworthy aspect of Abramovitz's essay is the up-to-date character, by contemporary standards, of the issues and relationships that he discusses. It is as if most of what neoclassical growth theory later taught already was known. Thus there is a clear statement of the logic behind modern growth accounting. Abramovitz notes that economists long have professed a theory that the level of output is determined by the quantity of inputs (land, labour and capital) and factors that affect their productivity (the state of the arts, industrial and financial organisation, the legal system, and so on). Therefore, at one level at least, economic growth can be understood as a function of changes in or improvements in these 'immediate determinants of output'. Abramovitz also proposes that analysis of growth simply at this level is not completely satisfactory, and that a satisfactory theory of growth must come to grips with the forces behind changes in the immediate determinants.

His essay goes on to analyse the forces affecting the expansion of the traditional factors of production: land, labour, capital. He has a separate section on capital formation as a cause of economic growth, and on the factors that influence the rate of capital formation. Among other features of his discussion, Abramovitz refers to the view common in economics that the marginal productivity of capital will be high or low depending on the ratio of capital to other factors, and will diminish as capital grows relative to them – clearly this characteristic of the 'old' neoclassical growth theory did not come as news. But he then goes on to argue that increases in economic efficiency as the scale of output grows may offset diminishing returns – a feature built into some of the 'new' neoclassical growth theory.

Abramovitz states that, in his view at least, 'technical improvement' must account for 'a very large share, if not the bulk, of the increase in output'. Thus while the empirical evidence that persuaded others of the economics community on this was not yet in, Abramovitz could not have been surprised by it. Abramovitz clearly sees technical advance as 'endogenous', resulting largely from investments aimed to create and exploit it, and anticipates the concept of 'knowledge capital' as follows: 'And insofar as new applied knowledge results from the deliberate direction of revenues to its discovery and use, the stock of knowledge is increased by a process identical with that which produces increases in the stock of material equipment'. Referring to Schumpeter he observes, 'with the development of industrial research departments of corporations ... almost all engineering work is undertaken only in conjunction with the deliberate entrepreneurial decision'. Some of the proponents of the new growth theory have argued that, until recently, analysts of growth were hung up on a growth theory that assumed perfect competition, but Abramovitz clearly did not have that hang up. Abramovitz also recognised that the investments that yield new proprietary technology also generate externalities, at least with time, 'as experience is gained and knowledge of the new art becomes widespread'.

Abramovitz highlights the interdependence of technical progress and the expansion of other factors as sources of growth. Thus he observes that changes in the effective supply of land often may be attributed 'to invention and increase of knowledge generally', which makes it possible to employ previously unusable land. Regarding technical progress and capital formation, 'the two factors are indeed closely related'. Vintage models would not have come as news to Abramovitz. 'The actual exploitation of new knowledge virtually always involves some gross investment (in material equipment)'.

Abramovitz goes on to imbed his analyses of expansion of the traditional inputs to production, and of technical advance as the major factor augmenting their productivity, in a discussion of 'enterprise' and 'institutions'. He already had focused on modern corporations as key actors in technical progress, and in investing in material equipment. He then observes that 'the role of enterprise has been slighted by traditional theory because of the theory's generally static character which leads easily to assumptions about perfect knowledge, and rational calculation of profit'. He goes on to suggest that, if one finds Schumpeter's analysis persuasive, one is compelled to recognise that 'the marginal productivity of capital depends on enterprise to such a degree' that to neglect it is to miss the whole point of capitalist economic development. Here Abramovitz is, in the view I will espouse, far ahead of developments in even the 'new' neoclassical growth theory, at least as that work has developed to date.

He also is far out in front in his discussion of the broader cultural and institutional factors surrounding and supporting enterprise. Here he expresses the judgement that the broader context is key, and also his concerns that 'The general conclusion suggested by this survey of the factors controlling the vigor of enterprise is that a vast deal of emphasis must be placed on forces that, in the ordinary conception of the bounds of economics, would have to be classed as political, psychological, or sociological'. Abramovitz thus flags the challenge for economists, and stresses that, to unravel the mysteries of economic growth, economists have got to get into these issues. Mostly of course we have not. The focus of almost all research on economic growth since Abramovitz wrote has been on his 'immediate' determinants.

I have dwelt at some length on Abramovitz's essay, pointing to its modern tone as well as to its richness. Abramovitz clearly is, and was, a remarkable scholar. But in his 1952 essay he does not present his theorising about growth as particularly original. Indeed he writes as if he were recounting notions long held in economics, and held at the time he was writing by other scholars getting into the study of economic growth, for example, Simon Kuznets.

At the time Abramovitz wrote, a number of economists were hard at work doing empirical research on growth using the new National Income and Product accounts, and other new data. By the mid-1950s the results of that research, probing the immediate determinants of growth, began to come in. Papers by Schmookler (1952), Schultz (1953), Fabricant (1954), Kendrick (1956) and Abramovitz himself (1956), all reported that the growth of output experienced in the United States had been significantly greater than reasonably could be attributed to input growth.

In these papers the contribution of total input growth was estimated by weighing the different inputs by their prices, a practice apparently considered so reasonable and obvious that few of the authors even bothered to rationalise it explicitly. (While not recognised by many at the time, an earlier paper by Tinbergen, 1942, had anticipated much of the methodology.) The excess of output growth over input growth was attributed to a variety of factors. Technological advance, increasing returns to scale, investments in human capital, the allocation of resources from lower to higher productivity activities, all were recognised as parts of the story, but these authors clearly put heavy stress on the former. It is important to recognise that this finding, and a reasonable methodology for estimating 'growth of total factor productivity', were public before Solow's 1957 empirical piece reporting that 'technical advance' accounted for the lion's share of the growth of output per worker that the US had experienced.

Edward Denison's research and writings based on growth accounting, which began to get published in the early 1960s, enormously increased our understanding of economic growth, at least at the level that Abramovitz had referred to as the 'immediate determinants'. Regarding growth in the United States, Denison's (1962) conclusions basically were consistent with those published earlier by the scholars cited above, and his contribution mainly involved an ingenious and painstaking attempt to break down the sources of total factor productivity growth into the various components mentioned above. Other economists followed along the same track, developing other kinds of disaggregation and exploring different measures of factor marginal productivity (see, for example, Jorgenson and Griliches 1967). Later in the 1960s Denison (1967) extended his framework to examination of growth in the European economies, with findings that were quite similar to what had been found about the US (see also Domar 1963).

However, this study also probed at the reasons why European worker productivity was significantly lower than American (in the early 1960s roughly half). The key finding here was as remarkable as the earlier finding that growth of total factor productivity accounted for the bulk of productivity growth. It was that differences in inputs per worker could account for only a small share of the differences between American and European productivity levels, and that apparently European nations were operating at significantly lower levels of 'total factor productivity' than the Americans.

Denison's work came after the publication of Solow's theoretical and empirical essays on growth. However, there is little evidence that these articles influenced him much. Denison footnotes only the Solow empirical article, and the substance of the footnotes is about differences in statistical details.

While most of the new work on economic growth was focused at the macro or economy-wide level, some was oriented to the sectoral or industry level. Thus during the early 1960s economists came to learn that the significant inter-industry differences in rates of labour productivity growth, of which they long had been aware, largely were associated with differences in rates of growth of total factor productivity, again interpreted as largely reflecting differences in rates of technical advance. The new availability of industry-level R&D data permitted Terleckyj (1960) to explore the connections. His work showed a reasonably strong relationship (by the standards of economists) between industry total factor productivity growth and industry R&D intensity. Kendrick (1973), Kendrick and Grossman (1980), Edwin Mansfield (1968), and Dale Jorgenson *et al.* (1980) also did important work exploring cross-industry differences in growth and the factors behind the differences.

Other parts of the research enterprise focused on various other sources of growth. Two are important to mention here.

Stimulated by the work of Theodore Schultz (1961) and, later, Gary Becker (1962), a sizable cluster of research grew up concerned with 'human capital'. That work analysed investments in human capital through both formal education and work experience. Portions of this research clearly recognised externalities, in some cases of a 'network' variety (as it has come to be called), in some cases because workers may leave the firms that trained them carrying those skills (which deters firms from investing in much training), and in some cases because the work some of them do – for example R&D – generates externalities.

Another sizable cluster of research grew up around the topic of technical change. That work proceeded with a number of different styles, from econometric (Griliches 1957, 1960; Mansfield 1968; and Mansfield *et al.* 1971, 1977), to historical (Rosenberg 1976; Freeman 1982). Jacob Schmookler (1966) did pioneering work using patents as a measure of inventive input. The research by scholars working in this field covered a range of topics from those stimulated by Schumpeter (do industries where the firms are large and have considerable market power experience more rapid technical advance than more fragmented industries?), to more general factors that are associated with inter-industry differences in technical advance, to the connections between science and technology, to the difference between private and social returns to R&D.

These kinds of analyses certainly alerted many economists to the fact that private returns to education or to R&D might not measure well the contribution of expansions in these 'stocks' to economic output. Some economists also argued that investment in new plant and equipment contributed more to growth than the private rate of return indicated, because new capital embodied new technology and enabled experience to accumulate and further advance, or because such investment often was associated with the shift of labour from lower- to higher-value activities, and so on.

My discussion above of the Renaissance and blooming of research on economic growth during the 1950s and 1960s hardly mentions developments in formal growth theory. As I noted, the enterprise was well on its way before the publication of Solow's and Swan's theoretical essays. And most of the basic theoretical ideas that guided its development already were there.

By that I certainly do not mean that the early works of Abramovitz and Kendrick or Denison proceeded independently of economic theory, or even neoclassical theory. But the production function idea had been around for a long time, as had the idea that the change in output could be explained in terms of changes in the inputs of the production function and changes in productivity. Abramovitz treats these ideas as essentially 'old hat' in his 1952 essay. The notion that, in growth accounting, the output increase stemming from an increase in an input might be approximated by the price of that input was a simple application of neoclassical factor remuneration theory. The idea that the difference between output growth and the factor price weighted growth of input measures growth of 'total factor productivity' did not depend on formal neoclassical growth theory.

And most of the appreciative theory that developed in connection with the new clusters of work on human capital and on technical change was developed endogenously to these research enterprises. Thus, the notion that it might be useful to distinguish between firm-specific and general skills was developed quite naturally in research concerned with incentives for firms, and individuals, to pay for different types of training. The idea that one could *measure* a stock of 'human capital' flowed from that work. The research on technical advance developed a collection of theoretical concepts specific to it. These included the notion of an R&D capital stock, and models of diffusion and of learning processes. A number of economists concerned with technical change came to see it as an evolutionary process, and tried to model it, and growth fuelled by technical change, as such.

The interesting question is what formal neoclassical growth theory contributed to the overall research endeavour during this period. Perhaps a prior question is 'What did the authors of the key early theoretical pieces think they were contributing?'.

Regarding Solow's 1956 article, the record is clear both because that essay clearly sets out what it is about, and because Solow returned to reflect on that work in his 1987 Nobel lecture. The model was put forth not so much as an 'explanation' of growth, but as a criticism of, an alternative to, the models of Harrod and Domar which had argued that it was very unlikely that economic growth was compatible with sustained full employment of both labour and capital. The Harrod–Domar models assume that input coefficients are technologically determined, and not flexible and potentially responsive to changes in factor–price ratios. Solow pointed out that if, in contrast, one assumed that the capital–labour ratio that firms would employ was sensitive (enough) to factor prices, then the Harrod–Domar problem disappeared. Whatever the savings rate, and whatever the rate of growth of the labour force, if the capital–labour ratio firms employed was sufficiently responsive to the factor–price ratio, growth with full employment of both labour and capital was achievable. The point, and orientation, of Swan's 1956 piece is virtually identical.

Thus Solow's article (and Swan's too) basically was aimed to rid thinking about long-run economic growth of the heavy Keynesian concerns about unemployment and inflation that the Harrod and Domar models were focused upon, and to bring 'neoclassical' thinking, which increasingly was dominating microeconomic theory, to bear on analysis of growth. However, as the earlier discussion indicates, while the Harrod–Domar concerns may have been influential in the theoretical discourse by economists about growth, they had little influence on empirically oriented scholars. Abramovitz mentions the Harrod and Domar articles only in a footnote towards the end of his essay.

Actually a good case can be made that purging growth theory of the Harrod–Domar concerns may not have been a good thing, in that it led to a relatively sharp separation of analysis of unemployment and inflation (main- line macroeconomics) from analysis of long-run economic growth. Angus Maddison (1967) well may have been quite right when he argued that an important reason for the rapid growth experienced during the 1950s and 1960s was that governments had learned to keep demand growing rapidly, but not so rapidly as to generate strong inflationary pressures. It may be no happenstance that the slowdown in growth rates since the early 1970s has been associated with higher rates of unemployment than marked the l960s and also surges of inflation and stop-and-start macroeconomic policies (see Nelson 1981, Boltho 1982, and van de Klundert and Schalk l978, for such a diagnosis).

In any case, it is fair to say that neither Solow nor Swan considered their original articles as basically about the sources of long-run growth of labour productivity. Indeed, except for one small subsection, Solow's article basically describes a context within which, in equilibrium, labour, capital and output all grow at the same rate and labour productivity is constant. In that subsection Solow introduces neutral technical advance to the picture, but he does not highlight technical advance as a source of growth. Solow's association with that proposition is in his 1957 empirical paper, not his 1956 theoretical one.

Both Solow and Swan derive the result that, within models of the sort they used, the rate of equilibrium growth of output is determined by the rate of growth of labour input and the rate of technical advance (if that is admitted), and is independent of the savings rate. Indeed if one believes that one of the main contributions of formal theorising is generating 'theorems' that are not obvious in prevailing appreciative theory, then the insensitivity of the dynamic equilibrium growth rate to the savings rate might be regarded as an important contribution of formal neoclassical growth theory to the thinking on growth. However, that theorem seems to have had very little impact on empirical research, perhaps because economists never have taken seriously that we are on a dynamic equilibrium growth path, perhaps because of the empirical work that seemed to show that growth rates and savings (investment) rates are correlated.

If the very earliest formal neoclassical growth models were more concerned with taking on Harrod–Domar than with developing a theory of the sources of long-run growth, subsequent models surely were aimed at the latter objective. What did they add?

One of Solow's early follow-on efforts (1959) was concerned with treating technical advance as requiring embodiment in new physical capital. Salter (1966) developed a similar model. While the basic idea was not new – recall Abramovitz's discussion of it – a case can be made that working through the formal logic did enable economists to see that increases or decreases in the investment could have much greater effects on the growth rate – in the short and medium run – than the simple growth-accounting models would lead one to believe. Putty-clay models, (see, for example, Solow *et al.* 1966) while devilishly difficult to implement econometrically, further sharpened this understanding or belief.

During the 1960s formal growth models were developed which treated elasticities of substitution as variables, and enabled economists to think more clearly about the effects of 'diminishing returns' setting in strongly or weakly as one factor grew relative to another. Some of these models also admitted non-neutral technical advance. Application of duality theory using a model that treated both elasticities of substitution and biases of technical advance as variables to be estimated (see, for example, Jorgenson 1986) certainly is an example of an analytic development that could not have occurred without the presence of formal neoclassical growth theory, and it opened up the possibility for a much richer analysis of the relationships between changes in input coefficents and changes in relative factor prices. One can question whether the way it was employed did permit the simultaneous estimation of elasticities of substitution and bias of technical advance that the users of the technique said it did. But the conclusions of such studies, for example that in many industries technical advance was both energy and capital using, certainly were interesting ones.

These theoretical insights are not trivial, but neither did they change the basic course of thinking about growth. I can give other examples of the contributions of formal neoclassical growth theory to the general enterprise of research on economic growth as it was practiced during the 1960s and 1970s. However, they would not change the picture I am drawing, which is that formal theory added wrinkles rather than contributing important new ideas. That is, formal neoclassical theory acted largely as handmaiden, not leader, of an empirical research enterprise whose basic theoretical orientation already had been set by the early 1950s.

It is useful to reflect on why formal growth theory contributed relatively little. I already have signalled my conjecture on this. It is that 'old' neoclassical growth theory did little more than to translate into a specific growth context bodies of formal theory that had been around for some time, or to formalise in relatively straightforward form appreciative ideas (like human capital). But appreciative theorising already had taken aboard these ideas, and for the most part was staying reasonably close to well-established formal theory, and was unlikely to be subject to serious logical blunders. The 'old' formal neoclassical growth theory seldom ventured to explore the more complex ideas that analysts of growth were developing in verbal form, and which departed from the safe haven of traditional well-known theory. Here the contribution of formal theorising could have been more substantial.

I would propose that the major contribution the old neoclassical growth theory did make to research on growth was to make that field much more legitimate than it had been, even sexy, and thus to attract many more young economists to its pursuit than would have come, absent the development of formal neoclassical growth theory. One of the tones of Abramovitz's 1952 review piece is that of isolation from the contemporary mainstream of economics. Reading it, it is difficult to imagine the surge of young economists coming into the field in the late 1950s and 1960s. It is quite possible that, absent Solow's 1957 article which expressly grounded the empirical calculations in formal neoclassical growth theory, the empirical work of Kendrick and Denison, which involved vastly more digging and calculating, would have received much less attention.

I think there were important limitations on the appreciative theory used to guide and interpret research on economic growth during the 1950s and 1960s. Formal growth theory shared those limitations. A central one was that growth theory was basically about what Abramovitz called the immediate determinants of growth. Exploration of the factors behind these immediate determinants was not well oriented by any theory, appreciative or formal. General neoclassic theory, and this is what broadly guided appreciative growth theory as well as formal growth theory, is basically about inputs, outputs, prices, equilibrium configurations and associated phenomena. It is not well oriented towards considering things like technologies, firms as productive organisations, or institutions. But I am getting ahead of my story.

In any case, studies of growth conducted in the 1950s, 1960s and early 1970s enormously increased our understanding of economic growth. Most of their findings have not been overturned by subsequent studies. The other side of this coin is that subsequent studies following the same line have added little that is new. By the early 1970s there is clear evidence that research of the sort I have described above was experiencing sharply diminishing returns.

2.2 The Sea-change of the 1970s

This fact was obscured by the sea-change in economic growth that occurred during the late 1960s and early 1970s. By the middle of the 1970s, the key question facing analysts of economic growth was not how to explain the relatively rapid growth that had been experienced by most countries, particularly in the early postwar period, but rather 'Why has growth slowed down so significantly?'.

It was natural that the early studies of the productivity growth slowdown used the same methodology that had been employed in the earlier studies of growth, and focused on much the same variables (see, for example, Denison 1974, Griliches 1980).

Denison's style of analysis showed that, given neoclassical assumptions, while some of the slowdown could be attributed to a fall-off in the rate of physical investment, the principal culprit was a collapse in the rate of growth of total factor productivity. A number of ingenious explanations were put forth as to why higher energy prices, which were contemporaneous, should have both deterred physical investment (energy and physical capital were complements) and reduced the economic value of technical advance that followed along old lines (technical advance was energy using). (For a discussion see Jorgenson 1986.) However, somehow the explanations were never completely convincing. And as relative energy prices declined while slow growth continued, the attempts to explain why growth had slowed so much from the heyday of the 1960s shifted to other factors.

One body of research and theorising that gradually emerged was oriented to the slowdown of growth in Europe and Japan as these nations approached US productivity and income levels. Economists were not alone in observing that, at the end of the Second World War, Europe and Japan were far behind the United States technologically, and in many cases in the organisation and management of modern business enterprises. Thus there were major opportunities for these nations to increase their labour and total factor productivity by adopting American practice, and the physical investments needed to do this were highly profitable. According to this theory, the very rapid growth after the Second World War in Europe and Japan can be explained largely as this catching up or 'convergence' process (see, for example, Baumol 1986). The other side of this coin is that, as these nations caught up with the United States, opportunities for further rapid growth through emulation diminished. This is why slower growth in Europe and Japan, which set in during the late 1960s, was inevitable.

This theory is one level 'deeper' than growth accounting. It purports to provide an explanation for some of the observed changes in the immediate sources of growth over the postwar era. The explanation basically is that when one country has a significant lead over another in technology or organisation – factors that show up in a total factor productivity difference – there are opportunities for rapid relatively inexpensive growth in the lagging country.

Yet it is apparent that this 'explanation' only pushes the questions back a stage, and in a way that raises major puzzles for someone who has simple neoclassical theory, or more specifically the first generation of neoclassical growth models, in his head. In its standard form, that theory presumes that 'technology' is a public good. It is interesting that the early Denison findings (which were replicated in many subsequent studies) showing large differences in total factor productivity among nations did not either spur the theorists to consider factors other than technology that might lie behind total factor productivity, or to expressly abandon the assumption that technology is a public good in any simple sense of that term. One of the virtues of the 'new growth theory' is that it does recognise proprietary aspects of technology.

Of course, the reason why Denison's findings did not cause a theoretical stir among those working in the field is that most of them already held an appreciative theory that recognised private aspects of technology as well as public. That theory also harboured other variables that influenced total factor productivity, in particular firm organisation and management.

However, even if one has in mind a theory that recognises these things, the empirical phenomena of convergence still raises major puzzles. One is this. The American lead in total factor productivity over Europe and Japan was not a temporary aberration of the Second World War and its aftermath, but dates back many years; it certainly was there before the First World War. Yet there is no evidence of significant convergence during the inter-war period. What then was different about the postwar period that it did erode? One explanation put forth by Gavin Wright and myself (1992), and foreshadowed by Abramovitz in the 1986 article, is that the post-Second World War environment of relatively open trade in manufactured goods and natural resources, and free international flow of both financial and physical capital, made the postwar era far more conducive to convergence among nations with the requisite skills and institutions than the interwar period. While some may find this argument persuasive, it is apparent that it is a complex one about the role of national and international institutions in the growth process.

Another puzzle is this. While Europe and Japan did rapidly adopt US technology and organisation after 1955 or so, and countries like Korea and Taiwan experienced rapid growth through similar mechanisms, why has growth in India, or Peru, or Nigeria, been so slow? In terms of the immediate or proximate sources of growth, growth of both total factor productivity and physical capital has been far faster in the rapidly developing countries than in the slowly growing ones, but this only pushes the puzzle back a stage. What is it about the firms or the system of institutions more generally in the former but not the latter that enables rapid adoption of world-class practice?

Empirical research on convergence has begun to identify some of the factors, or at least the correlates (see, for example, Barro 1991; DeLong and Summers 1991; Mankiw, Romer and Weil 1992). Relatively high levels of education seems a necessary if not a sufficient condition for a poor country to catch up rapidly, a conclusion that most economists would not find completely surprising, but one that implies a more complex relationship between education and command of technology and organisation than economists really have thought through. Also, the answer only pushes the question back a stage.

Why can some countries support effective mass education and others not? We are back again to Abramovitz's questions about culture and institutions.

The fraction of GNP going to investment in new machinery and equipment also matters. However, estimates of the sensitivity of the rate of catchup to physical investment suggest strongly that the principal gain from high investment is rapid modernisation. The fact that nations have differed significantly in their investment rates may well be signalling that the key factor behind the scenes is Abramovitz's (1986) absorptive capacity, of which educational attainments most likely is one important component. In the post-Second World War era, Western Europe was marked by both high and rising educational attainments and high investment rates.

If convergence theory begins to provide a satisfying answer to the question of why growth slowed in Europe and Japan, it does not help with the question of 'Why has growth in the US been so slow?'. Throughout the postwar period, or at least up to very recently, the US has been the leading nation technologically, not a follower. Hence the fact that other nations were catching up with the United States and increasingly were forced to develop new technology themselves if they were to continue rapid growth should not have been a factor slowing US growth but, if anything, a positive boost enabling the US to begin drawing on technologies developed initially by others.

One body of writing has taken the fall-off in total factor productivity growth in the US as an indication that frontier technical advance has slowed down. Reminiscent of Schumpeter's theory of long waves, some economists argued that the rapid economic growth in the United States after the Second World War was fuelled by the explosive development of a number of new technologies in electronics, materials, aviation, and various fields of chemistry, and that the slowdown in total factor productivity growth after 1970 is evidence that by that time further development of these technologies was running into diminishing returns. Economists such as Scherer (1983) and Griliches (1980) searched for evidence that the rate of return on R&D had fallen. The evidence was mixed. In any case, this argument, if one reflects on it, is a theory about the nature of technical change: that it proceeds through the opening up of new broad fields, that these are progressively moved out, and that the overall rate of technical progress in effect depends on the balance between the rate of working down old trajectories and the rate of establishment of new ones. This obviously is a much more detailed view than that contained in even today's formal growth models.

A number of economists found the argument that 'technical change has slowed down' not really persuasive, in view of the explosion of computer technology, biotech, fibre optics and other fields. Rather, the slow growth problem was seen to reside in the failure of American firms and other institutions to develop and exploit the new technologies effectively (see, for example, Freeman and Perez 1988).

During the 1980s research on continuing slow growth in the United States began to take on another look as other countries, especially Japan, began to surpass the United States in various fields where for decades American industry had reigned supreme. Arguments began to be put forth that what was happening in the United States was similar to what had happened in Great Britain around the turn of the century (see, for example, Lazonick 1990). Institutional structures that have been effective in one era, and when they were young, had become ineffective as the nature of technologies and world competition had changed, and as those institutions had grown older and more rigid.

Several different groups of scholars, coming from very different intellectual starting points, have argued that there are several features of the Japanese institutional structure that give it major advantages over the American. (For an eclectic survey see Dertouzos *et al.* 1989.) One cluster is associated with firms. Here long-term commitments of workers and firms to each other and broadly defined job categories, which together are conducive to significant firm investments in continuing worker training, low hierarchies and relatively easy communication across functional units like R&D and production, which enable faster and easier introduction of new products and facilitate continuing improvement of products and processes, and willingness of management to make investments that pay off only some distance down the road, are factors cited by many writers. The researchers investigating the production of complex multi-component products like automobiles also tend to mention 'just in time' delivery of inputs and close relationships with suppliers – what they often call Toyotism – and contrast this with Fordism or old-style American mass production (see, for example, Womack *et al.* 1990; Aoki 1990).

In turn it is recognised that several aspects of the broader Japanese institutional environment complement or support these kinds of behaviour and structure of Japanese firms: labour markets in which there is little mobility of personnel from firm to firm; capital markets that provide patient money. Some but not all writers place emphasis on close and cooperative working relationships between the Japanese government and Japanese industry and, under governmental auspices, cooperative precompetitive R&D arrangements between firms that otherwise compete. The writers who stress these later factors tend to be oriented towards understanding the factors behind Japanese strength in electronics, rather than in automobiles.

I do not refer to these bodies of newly developing appreciative growth theory because I necessarily agree with all the particular details they espouse. Rather, I simply want to point out that for the reasons I referred to above – diminishing returns to continuing research on the immediate or proximate sources of growth, the puzzling phenomena of slower growth in the 1970s and 1980s than earlier, slow growth in the country at the frontier as well as among the followers, and indications that the US just might be being overtaken by another national economy – the emphasis in much recent work has been on factors that lie behind the variables in growth accounting, which had been the central focus of research on growth during the earlier periods. These include prominently the processes of technical advance and what is required to master technology, the nature of firms, and of institutions more broadly. This is a very different agenda from that which marked the 1950s and 1960s.

2.3 The New Neoclassical Growth Theories in Perspective

It is somewhat puzzling why formal growth theory dropped out of fashion in the 1970s and early 1980s. It certainly was not because of lack of interesting and important empirical and policy puzzles. The most likely cause was that formal growth theorising along the same old lines had run into sharply diminishing returns, just as had empirical research along the old lines, and formal theorists knew it. Possibly also there is something to Paul Romer's suggestion (1991) mentioned earlier that theorists understood that technical change needed to be made endogenous in growth models, and that that required explicit treatment of imperfect competition, and that, until certain developments in industrial organisational theory in the late 1970s (in particular Dixit and Stiglitz 1977) and early 1980s, it was not clear how to encompass imperfect competition within a general equilibrium model.

In any case, the new neoclassical growth models surely represent an important advance over the early generation of formal growth models. They have taken on board a number of features of appreciative theory that were lacking in the old models. There is no question that the rash of new growth theory is making research on economic growth fashionable again, and attracting into the field many bright new minds. This certainly is a major contribution.

The new formal growth theoretic work has brought formal theory significantly closer to appreciative theorising, or at least that part of appreciative theorising that is concerned with what Abramovitz called the 'immediate' determinants of economic growth. However, I suggested above that an important portion of research concerned with economic growth recently has been directed towards topics and variables with which neoclassical theory does not deal, or deals with in a superficial fashion. One way of thinking about this research is to see it as probing at factors behind the immediate sources. While there is no logical reason why economic theory does not address these topics, as Abramovitz stated in his 1952 essay, standard economic theory then did not really treat topics like the nature of technology, what determines the capabilities of firms, or the role of institutions more broadly. Nor does much of more recent theory address them effectively.

3. THE NEW FOCUS ON TECHNOLOGY, FIRMS AND ECONOMIC GROWTH

I already have tipped my hand regarding the areas of research on economic growth that I think most promising and important. We need to improve our understanding of the nature of technology and of technical advance as a process. We must find a way of seeing into the capabilities of the firms and other organisations that employ the technologies and the material inputs that are the immediate determinants of growth, as well as play a major role in their creation. And we must better comprehend the economic institutions that mould, support, and constrain firms and other organisations in their own actions and interactions with each other. This may sound like a collection of interesting cats and dogs as contrasted with a comprehensive and integrated strategy for getting behind the immediate sources of growth, but I want to propose that it has a chance of becoming the latter.

In the first place, while in the standard treatments technical advance is viewed as one among a number of sources of economic growth, albeit perhaps quantitatively the most important single one, a strong case can be made for singling out technical advance as the leading force behind growth, with other factors in supporting roles. The case involves a number of connected arguments.

One of these was noted earlier. The inclination of economists to 'divide up' the credit for growth, as we do in growth accounting, represses some very strong complementarities. From the time of Solow's 1957 piece, and even before, economists have been wont to ask how much of growth of output per worker hour, say the doubling between 1909 and 1949 which was Solow's focus, could be attributed to the growth of capital per work hour (which also roughly doubled), how much to the increases in educational attainments of the work-force that were achieved over this period (which also were impressive), and, after accounting for these, how much should be attributed to technical advance. It turned out that, under Solow's calculations, only a small fraction could be attributed to greater capital intensity, and since he did not include rising educational attainments or other factors in his calculation, better than four-fifths was attributed to technical advance. Denison, who looked at a slightly different time interval, but whose major difference with Solow was that he did include education and several other variables, was able to assign more of the credit to these factors, and hence attributed less to technical advance.

But if one reflects on it, this attempt to 'divide up the credit' makes little sense. In 1929 no one had any well worked through idea as to how productively to double capital per worker. To do so required that a series of new machine designs be conceived, drawn up, tested, debugged and improved. That is, the increases in capital intensity that clearly added to worker productivity would have been largely worthless without the development of new technology. It also is highly likely that a large share of the increase in average educational attainments achieved over the period, and particularly the sharply rising fraction of the work-force with post-secondary training, had value largely in activities contributing to technical advance, and in working in areas where technology was new and often changing.

The central proposition above, that expansion of the capital–labour ratio to levels beyond actual experience, or (to give another example) the increases in the energy intensity of production that occurred over the period in question, required new technology, calls for rethinking about how one 'draws' production functions. The argument is that, to the extent production functions are constrained by known technology, they do not permit productive increase in an input that takes factor ratios beyond what has been experienced in the past, but that new technology must be developed to enable this. Atkinson and Stiglitz (1969) in fact proposed something like this some time ago. So did Paul David (1975). This proposition is built deeply into Nelson and Winter's (1982) evolutionary growth theory. In the formulations of Kaldor (1957) and Scott (1989), investment and the development of new technology are presumed to go together.

Under this characterisation, for countries at the technological frontier it is necessary to see prevailing technology as a binding constraint not only on total factor productivity, but also on the ability of the economy to employ productively the increases in the factors of production that are increasing most rapidly, or which are easiest to increase. One might note that, if one adopts this point of view, the proposal by Solow and Swan – that an economy can maintain full employment of both labour and capital even if the latter is growing significantly faster than the former if wage rates rise relative to the cost of capital – can be seen as insufficient. In addition, new technology must be developed to enable the progressive increases in capital intensity.

When inputs to a process are strongly complementary it often is difficult to assign any one of them a lead role. However, a case can be made that the advance of technology plays the lead role in the drama of economic growth, with the conventional factors in the production function playing supporting roles. The argument is that, when technical advance is occurring or the opportunities are clearly beckoning, there are strong inducements to make the complementary investments in physical and human capital. On the other hand, simply investing in physical and human capital will not necessarily induce the advances in technology that will make them productive.

I note that Kaldor and Scott appear to put the asymmetry the other way. Both presume the key driving force is investment and that, given investment, the new technology will come. In countries significantly behind the technological frontier, investing in human and physical capital very well may be the key to being able to adapt more productive technology. For countries at the technological frontier, however, I would argue the case for the kind of asymmetry I purpose, rather than that implicitly proposed by Kaldor and Scott.

In any case, if one accepts the argument about strong complementarities, gone is the clean distinction between 'moving along a production function' (in a capital using direction) and a 'shift' in the production function, that has been the hallmark of neoclassical growth theorising since the mid-1950s. Growth of total factor productivity, to employ that now old concept, remains an interesting statistic, but under this view it is no longer interpretable as a measure of the economic impact of technical advance.

The comfortable notion that one could measure the economic impact of technical advance through what was happening to total factor productivity undoubtedly has been a central reason why most economists never have bothered to probe deeply into the question 'What is technology anyhow?'. There are of course a few simple metaphors about that. The notion that prevailing technology is like 'a set of extant blueprints' is quite common, and does provide a rationale for the theoretical proposition that prevailing technology defines the bounds on the production set. The notion that technology is 'knowledge' also has been around for some time, and, to the extent that knowing is a matter of degree, suggests a less sharp boundary between the technologically feasible and the infeasible.

Scholars of technical advance have for some time recognised the inadequacy of the 'blueprint' metaphor, which suggests not only a sharp-edged production set, but also that anyone with access to the relevant documentation could operate a technology. While there is, indeed, a lot about modern technologies that is described in blueprints, texts, pictures and equations, for most technologies access to these documents provides only a start on what it takes to make a technology work. A lot of the 'knowledge', to employ the second metaphor, apparently is not written down. Further, it is increasingly apparent that for many technologies much of the 'knowledge' is 'know how', that is in the fingers rather than in the head. (For good discussions see Pavitt 1987; Dosi 1988.) As a result, command over a technology involves a considerable amount of learning by doing and using. Of course, it is not one or the other, and any model that makes it such misses important elements. For most technologies there is elaborate documentation, and command requires access. For many, the documentation can only be understood by people with professional training whose general analytic knowledge enables the specifics of a particular technology to be grasped. But almost always command of a technology requires hands-on experience. And, to anticipate a point I shall develop shortly, that experience almost always is organisational.

These elements of appreciative theory carry over to developing understanding of how technical advance comes about. Scholars of technical advance long have known the importance of investments in R&D, generally involving the employment of professionals trained in the relevant underlying engineering and scientific disciplines, and also that investments in R&D often flowed into investments in new equipment and work-force training to get the new technology into practice. They now are coming to recognise that in many fields, the ability to do R&D effectively requires not only professional training, but also experience in doing R&D in that field. The learning that occurs through operation of a technology, and the learning to do effective R&D, often interact strongly, with the former feeding back to influence R&D teams who have learned to work with their colleagues in production and marketing. When this occurs technological advance can become a cumulative learning process in which particular products and processes get improved over time through the interaction of learning through experience and in R&D.

The mechanisms sketched above may be supplemented by others, for example the development of complementary products and services and investments in specialised skills, and lead to the lock-in of particular broad technologies and lock-out of substitutes. Brian Arthur (1988, 1989), and Paul David (1985, 1992), among others, have analysed this phenomenon. Earlier Sidney Winter and I had identified it, and argued that a consequence is that at any time technologies tend to evolve along particular trajectories in a strongly path-dependent manner. This narrowness of technological development occurs at an economy-wide level, but is particularly strong at the level of the firm.

This brings me to the second broad topic I have listed at the top of the agenda for research on growth. We need to develop a much better theory of organisational, specifically firm, capabilities than economists now have.

While study of technical advance now has a relatively longstanding tradition in economics, study of firms only recently has come to be considered a serious and interesting topic by most economists. There are a number of reasons for this. An important one is that, unlike scholars of business management and strategy, the interest of economists is mostly in variables at a level of aggregation well above that of individual firms, often macroeconomic, and even our 'microeconomics' is about industry-level variables rather than firm-level ones. But perhaps a more basic reason is that we economists tend to work with theories that suggest that, at the levels of aggregation we are interested in, what firms do can be presumed to be determined by constraints, opportunities and incentives provided by the environment they are in.

This is exactly the case with 'the theory of the firm' in standard microeconomics, which is the same 'theory of the firm' built into neoclassical growth theory both old and new. In that theory the constraint on firm total factor productivity is the state of technology, assumed to be a public good in the old neoclassical growth theory, but containing a proprietary element in the new, associated with firm-specific investments. Given public technology, and opportunities to invest in proprietary technologies, firms choose what to do so as to maximise profits, given prevailing market conditions. Thus, there is no call to look carefully at firms, *per se*. They are simply puppets dancing to the tune played by the market.

However, under the appreciative theory sketched above, mastery of a technology is more like a skill that needs to be learned whose control requires practice than most neoclassical theorising is wont to admit, and the entity that learns and practices is the firm. Mastery of technique is organisational rather than individual in several respects. The practice of complex technologies inherently involves organisation and management. The way a firm organises to implement a common broad technology can make an enormous difference. This is a key finding of most of the recent work comparing US and Japanese auto production. Further, the competence resides in the organisation and not simply in the set of individuals who happen to be in that organisation at any time in that, usually, individuals can be replaced with little noticeable effect on firm performance.

Studies of American and Japanese firms of the sort mentioned earlier have been perhaps the most important stimulus to new thinking about firms. Another major stimulus has been Chandler's pioneering historical work on the rise of the modern corporation (1962, 1977, 1990). Particularly Chandler's work has led to the development of a small body of writings that see key firm capabilities as dynamic, rather than static, involving the ability to learn, adapt to changes in the environment, and innovate, and not simply to perform well given prevailing practice and conditions (see Dosi *et al.* 1992). This new body of writings on firms is, of course, quite conformable with the new theorising about cumulative technical advance sketched above.

Study of individual firms operating over time clearly shows strong path dependencies, and in most cases a considerable amount of continuity, as predicted by that theory. A firm's strategy, to use Chandler's term, represents a long-term bet about how to navigate. Different firms make different bets. While a strategy generally does not uniquely determine what a firm will do in particular cases, which can be sensitive to contingencies, it certainly guides these actions along certain lines. The way a firm is organised – its structure to use Chandler's term again – partly reflects decisions made to implement a broad strategy. But once a structure is in place it itself certainly moulds and constrains the choices a firm can regard as possible. From this point of view, the basic behaviour of firms, like the path of a battleship, does not turn easily. The troubles US automobile firms are having in changing their ways certainly supports this view.

There are signs lately that economists are paying more attention to firms, but a scrutiny of the new literature indicates strongly that the hang-ups caused by adherence to neoclassical theory are very strong. Few contemporary economists seem able to see firms as the key actors in economic growth in the sense that Schumpeter did, or more recently Chandler. Recall Abramovitz's citation of Schumpeter's argument that the productivity of capital, or R&D for that matter, is largely a function of enterprise. A good theory of technical advance requires a larger set of actors than firms, but firms need to be central active players in that theory, and not simply puppets. In most modern economies the lion's share of R&D expenditure is made by business firms. Similarly, a good theory of what determines investment in new plant and equipment, and what explains intercountry differences, would seem to require a much more sophisticated treatment of firms and firm differences than we presently have. In most modern economies a large share of business investment is covered by business savings, which usually exceed household savings. Similarly, business investments in training often account for a large share of the total.

It is natural that 'firms' play the central role in the theory of production, because they are the organisations that carry out production. Of course, it must be recognised that firms in the sense above may in some sectors include governmental organisations or not-for-profit ones, like hospitals in the provision of medical care, and schools. This could take me into a discussion of the fact that in doing growth theory economists usually have manufacturing in mind, despite the fact that manufacturing accounts for only a quarter or so of employment in most high-income countries today. However, I will not go in that direction but, rather, will proceed as if all firms were like manufacturing firms, and all technology was like manufacturing technology.

What firms do, and the technologies they employ and develop, are of course influenced to a considerable extent by the environment they are in, which brings me to the third topic in my agenda. Economists are inclined to define the environment in terms of markets. In turn behind markets are demanders of products and suppliers of inputs (who may be individuals or organisations like other firms) and their preferences and the constraints they face. Of course most economists also understand that public policies are important, but for the most part these are treated as acting through markets or directly through influencing individual incentives and constraints.

However, in recent years at least some economists have become cognisant of aspects of the environment not really considered in the simple treatment. There are entities out there like universities that may do research that feeds into technical advance in industry, and whose teaching programmes affect the supply of scientists and engineers, government agencies financing certain kinds of R&D, and others setting standards, banks and banking systems, and a variety of organisations and laws which affect labour supply, and demand. Patent, regulatory and liability laws are part of the environment. And so also are a variety of widely shared beliefs and values and customs that affect common expectations about what should be done, and what will be done, in a particular context.

This is an extraordinarily complex bag of things, and it may be foolhardy to give a name to the collection. But many scholars have called them all 'institutions'.

One can question what is common about them. Some economists and other scholars have employed the language of game theory and attempted to define institutions as 'the rules of the game', with the connotation that all that participate in a particular activity play that particular game, and that the rules define what they and others can do, and what they and others will be motivated to do under the rules (see, for example, North 1990). This seems to fit laws, and customs, and law-like government policies.

It does not directly seem to fit the 'organisations' in the environment, like universities and banking systems. However, some analysts see these as players in the game, who have plays special to them and their activities, and who therefore in a way define part of the 'rules of the game' for the other players. The case for calling these entities institutions can be made another way. While, according to the definition above, particular organisations would not be considered as institutions, generally accepted forms of governance and structure of kinds of organisations might be. Thus to the extent that Harvard or the University of California at Berkeley are taken as models of what research universities should be, and other kindred universities model themselves after them, one can speak of research universities as institutions. In this same sense one also can see corporate forms widely prevalent in an economy as institutions, to the extent that there is as it were a belief that these forms are right and appropriate. This clearly is the intended meaning of scholars who have argued that American firms are stuck in their old common ways and beliefs.

Of course institutions are not constant. They do change, if perhaps slowly. Chandler, among others, has argued that to a considerable extent a nation's economic institutions are shaped by its firms, through their individual actions, and through their collective political activities. In his monumental study of the rise of the modern corporation in the United States, Great Britain and Germany, Chandler (1990) describes the broad institutional differences among the three countries, and recognises, even highlights, that these are a part of the reason why firms in the three different countries came to differ in significant respects. But he argues that the institutional structures themselves were to a considerable extent moulded by the activities of firms.

Chandler's argument that institutions are what they are in large part because of the demands and actions of parties who have an interest in them is a special version of a general theory of institutions, and institutional change, that began to be espoused by some economists over a decade ago and which came to be called 'the new institutional economics'. (Many years earlier Marx put forth a similar theory, but with different undertones.) Much of the recent writing has focused on the structure of law, and in particular property rights, where writers such as Demsetz (1967) proposed that the law was sufficiently responsive to changes in economic conditions that it could be regarded at any time as 'optimal', at least to a first approximation.

The body of writing which posits the responsiveness of institutions is somewhat at odds with an older body of analysis of economic institutions, which stresses that they tend to be stable, and slow to change. From this point of view international differences in institutions stem from and reinforce what may be quite deep differences in values, expectations, culture and politics. A variant of this point of view is that prevailing institutions, while possibly originally brought into place for reasons that had to do with enhancing economic efficiency, soon acquire strong vested interests. Therefore they may be difficult to change even after changed circumstances have made them counterproductive. Thus Veblen (1915) argued that Britain lost her place at the economic forefront to Germany in large part because the institutions brought in place to support her early lead became obsolete but difficult to change.

In his 1952 article Abramovitz flagged broad national institutions, supporting or constraining industry, as at once something economists need to understand if they are to understand growth, and a topic whose exploration will require economists to step over the traditional boundaries of our discipline. In my view getting a good intellectual grip on institutions is going to be harder than getting a better model of technological change, or firm capabilities, and their dynamics, simply because 'institutions' are so diffuse. But as Abramovitz said forty years ago, if we are to understand growth we will have to somehow understand institutions.

Those who know me and my work may be surprised that in the discussion above I have not been pushing evolutionary theory, at least not explicitly. But of course I have been implicitly. More and more students of technical advance have been arguing that that process must be regarded as evolutionary, in the sense that it proceeds through the generation and trial of new alternatives competing with each other and with prevailing practice, with winners and losers determined in actual contest. Students of how the modern corporation came into being also often use evolutionary language, to connote the trial and error nature of that process.

It would seem apparent that technologies and business firms should be understood as coevolving. In some of the models Sidney Winter and I have developed there is a coevolutionary process involving technologies and firms, with the technologies possessed by firms influencing their profitability and hence their investment and growth, but also with particular firms being the generators of particular new technologies. The discussion above, building on Chandler's analysis, of course paints a much more complex and subtle picture of the connections between technologies and firms and their coevolution.

Students of institutional change also have been wont to use evolutionary language. And clearly institutions affect technical advance – many modern technologies depend on universities and professional societies for important activities that lead to their advancement, and some might not have been developed at all in the absence of the evolution of the modern research university. The intertwining of firms and labour and capital markets was an important theme that was developed above. Thus institutions are an essential, and perhaps slowest moving, part of the coevolutionary process of economic growth.

Can formal theorising help us to understand these processes better? Yes, it certainly can. But as yet the new growth theories have not got into this task.

4. A REPRISE

Understanding economic growth better surely should be of very top priority for economic research during the 1990s. There is so much that we do not understand. The slowdown in growth in the United States after the 1960s remains a puzzle. Economists still have no clue regarding whether that slow growth reflects a general falling off of technological progress which will affect productivity growth in all countries as they approach American levels, or whether a good share of the cause is specific to the United States which will soon be surpassed by other economies. We have a somewhat better understanding of why growth rates in Europe and Japan slowed after the late 1960s. However, our understanding of why Japan moved from the bottom of the pack of advanced industrial nations in the early 1960s to close to the top of the pack by 1990 is not very strong. Nor is it understood very well why Great Britain has continued her relative decline.

Limitations on space have prevented me from more than simply mentioning the extremely uneven performance among nations that were very poor as of 1960. Some, like Korea and Taiwan, have grown rapidly and seem to be becoming sophisticated industrial powers. The less-developed nations which have not had that successful experience naturally look to Korea and Taiwan, but it is not very clear exactly what went on in those economies that others can readily imitate.

The surge of writings that is coming to be called 'the new growth theory' partly reflects this growing awareness among economists that economic growth remains very imperfectly understood. The presence of this new theoretical literature, and the empirical work it is beginning to spawn, surely will pull a larger fraction of the coming generation of economists into the study of economic growth, and this is a big plus. Some of the things contained within the new growth theories also are helpful since they bring formal theorising closer to the understanding of those who have been doing research in this field. This certainly will mean that new economists will be better informed. And it also increases the chance that analytic work actually will shed some light in places where appreciative theorising currently is weak or confused.

However, if my discussion in the preceding section is at all on the mark, a good portion of the recent appreciative theorising about economic growth is exploring the factors behind the immediate sources of growth, which are the focus of the new growth models as well as the older ones. I propose that technical change, firm capabilities, and national institutions ought to be high on the agenda for formal growth theorising.

While the new formal neoclassical growth theories do treat technological change in a richer and more sophisticated way than did earlier neoclassical theory, there still is a large gap between the formal treatment in these recent papers and what economists studying technology and technical change know. The appreciative theory that has been developed over the years is quite complex, and not all that easy to model. That could be regarded as a stimulating intellectual challenge. To meet it those who are engaged in formal modelling need to pay closer attention to the work of economists who have been studying technical advance.

I have argued that understanding the capabilities of firms better probably is a prerequisite for significant improvement in our understanding of economic growth. The new growth models contain the same stylised, stripped down, inadequate view of firms that was in the old growth theory. There is enough empirical work and appreciative theorising about firms, now, not only to point to the inadequacies of contemporary standard treatments, but also to indicate some interesting paths that formal modelling might pursue.

The same kind of criticism applies to economic institutions. These are repressed in both the new neoclassical growth theory and the old. Yet virtually all scholars who have looked in any detail at the processes of economic growth, and at the factors that seem to lie behind the different growth performances of different countries, have fastened on 'institutions' as centrally important variables. As indicated in the earlier discussion, there are major analytic problems here. Economists who are talking about institutions presently do not even have a satisfactory theoretical way of describing them. There would seem to be very high returns from careful, informed, formal theorising here.

The 'new' neoclassical growth models continue to treat economic growth as a smooth process involving continuing equilibrium, in the sense that that term is used in neoclassical theory more broadly. Those models do not attempt to build in the trial and error, learning by doing, evolutionary process that almost all detailed empirical work reveals, although some new models treat some aspects of that. The coevolution of technology, firms and institutions would seem a fascinating and potentially fruitful arena for formal modelling. There is a special challenge here because formal evolutionary modelling involves the throwing away of the equilibrium notions that have so long served as the intellectual unifier of economic theorising.

I want to conclude by returning to an opening theme. The economic research enterprise works well when appreciative and formal theorising about a subject are interacting effectively. One of the reasons, I believe, why progress in understanding the major puzzles about growth proceeded so slowly during the 1970s and 1980s is that formal theorising failed to stay up with appreciative theorising and hence lent it little help. The indications are that at least some of this new generation of formal growth theorists are paying attention to empirical work and appreciative theorising linked to that work. This promises better for the 1990s.

REFERENCES

Abramovitz, M. (1952), 'Economics in Growth', in B. Haley (ed.), *A Survey of Contemporary Economies, Vol. II*, Homewood: Published for the American Economic Association by Richard D. Irwin, Inc., 132–178.

Abramovitz, M. (1956), 'Resource and Output Trends in the United States Since 1870', *American Economic Review*, 46, 5–23.

Abramovitz, M. (1986), 'Catching Up, Forging Ahead, and Falling Behind', *Journal of Economic History*, 46, 385–406.

Aghion, P. and Howitt, P. (1992), 'Model of Growth Through Creative Destruction', *Econometrica*, 60, 323–351.

Aoki, M. (1990), 'Towards an Economic Model of the Japanese Firm', *Journal of Economic Literature*, 28, 1–27.

Arthur, B. (1988), 'Competing Technologies: An Overview', in G. Dosi, C. Freeman, R. Nelson, G. Silverberg and L. Soete (eds), *Technical Change and Economic Theory*, London: Pinter Publishers.

Arthur, B. (1989), 'Competing Technologies, Increasing Returns, and Lock-in by Historically Small Events', *The Economic Journal*, 99, 106–113.

Atkinson, A. and Stiglitz, J. (1969), 'A New View of Technical Change', *Economic Journal*, 79, 573–578.

Barro, R. (1991), 'Economic Growth in a Cross Section of Countries', *Quarterly Journal of Economics*, 106, 407–444.

Baumol, W. (1986), 'Productivity Growth, Convergence, and Welfare: What the Long Run Data Show', *American Economic Review*, 76, 1072–1085.

Becker, G. (1962), 'Investment in Human Capital: A Theoretical Analyses', *Journal of Political Economy*, 70, 9–44.

Boltho, A. (1982), *The European Economy Growth and Crisis*, Oxford: Oxford University Press.

Chandler, A. (1962), *Strategy and Structure: Chapters in the History of the Industrial Enterprise*, Cambridge: MIT Press.

Chandler, A. (1977), *The Visible Hand: The Managerial Revolution in American Business*, Cambridge Mass.: Belknap Press.

Chandler, A. (1990), *Scale and Scope: The Dynamics of Industrial Capitalism*, Cambridge: Harvard University Press.

David, P. (1975), *Technical Choice, Innovation, and Economic Growth*, Cambridge: Cambridge University Press.

David, P. (1985), 'Clio and the Economics of QWERTY', *American Economic Review Papers and Proceedings*, 75, 332–337.

David, P. (1992), 'Heroes, Herds and Hysteresis in Technological History', *Industrial and Corporate Change*, 1, 129–179.

Davis, L. and North, D. (1971), *Institutional Change and American Economic Growth*, London: Cambridge University Press.

DeLong, J. and Summers, L. (1991), 'Equipment Investment and Economic Growth', *Quarterly Journal of Economics*, 106, 445–502.

Demsetz, H. (1967), 'Towards a Theory of Property Rights', *American Economic Review Papers and Proceedings*, 57, 347–359.

Denison, E. (1962), *The Sources of Economic Growth in the United States and the Alternatives Before Us*, New York: Committee for Economic Development.

Denison, E. (1967), *Why Growth Rates Differ: Postwar Experience in the Nine Western Countries*, Washington DC: Brookings Institution.

Denison, E. (1974), *Accounting for United States Economic Growth, 1929–1969*, Washington DC: Brookings Institution.

Dertouzos, M., Lester, R. and Solow, R. (1989), *Made in America*, Cambridge: MIT Press.

Dixit, A. and Stiglitz, J. (1977), 'Monopolistic Competition and Optimum Product Diversity', *American Economic Review*, 76, 297–308.

Domar, E. (1963), 'On Total Factor Productivity and All That', *Journal of Political Economy*, 71, 586–588.

Dosi, G. (1982), 'Technological Paradigms and Technological Trajectories: A Suggested Interpretation of the Determinants and Directions of Technical Change', *Research Policy*, 11, 147–162.

Dosi, G. (1988), 'Sources, Procedures, and Microeconomic Effects of Innovation', *Journal of Economic Literature*, 26, 126–171.

Dosi, G., Freeman, C., Nelson, R., Silverberg, G. and Soete, L. (eds) (1988), *Technical Change and Economic Theory*, London: Pinter Publishers.

Dosi, G., Teece, D., Winter, S. (1992), 'Towards a Theory of Corporate Coherence' in Dosi, G., Giannetti, R., and Toninelli, A., *Technology and Enterprise in Historical Perspective*, Oxford: Oxford University Press.

Ethier, W. (1992), 'National and International Return to Scale in the Modern Theory of International Trade', *American Economic Review*, 72, 389–405.

Fabricant, S. (1954), *Economic Progress and Economic Change*, New York: NBER, 34th Annual Report of the NBER.

Freeman, C. (1982), *The Economics of Industrial Innovation*, London: Penguin.

Freeman, C. and Perez, C. (1988), 'Structural Crisis of Adjustment: Business Cycles and Investment Behaviour', in Dosi *et al.*, *Technical Change and Economic Theory*.

Gollop, F. and Jorgenson, D. (1980), 'U.S. Productivity Growth by Industry, in New Developments in Productivity Measurement and Analysis', in J.W. Kendrick and B.N.

Vacara (eds), *Studies in Income and Wealth*, 44, Chicago: University of Chicago Press.

Griliches, Z. (1957), 'Hybrid Corn: An Exploration in the Economics of Technological Change', *Econometrica*, 25, 501–522.

Griliches, Z. (1973), 'Research Expenditures and Growth Accounting' in B. Williams (ed.), *Science and Technology in Economic Growth*, New York: Wiley.

Griliches, Z. (1980), 'R & D and the Productivity Slowdown', *American Economics Review*, 70, 343–348.

Grossman, G. and Helpman, E. (1990), 'Comparative Advantage and Long Run Growth', *American Economic Review*, 89, 796–815.

Grossman, G. and Helpman, E. (1991), 'Quality Ladders in the Theory of Growth', *Review of Economic Studies*, 58, 86–91.

Hodgson, G. (1988), *Economics and Institutions*, Cambridge: Policy Press.

Jorgenson, D. (1986), 'The Great Transition: Energy and Economic Change', *Energy Journal*, 7, 1–13.

Jorgenson, D. and Griliches, Z. (1967), 'The Explanation of Productivity Growth', *Review of Economic Studies*, 34, 249–283.

Jorgenson, D., Griliches, Z. and Fraumeni, B. (1980), *Substitution and Technical Change in Production*, Cambridge, Mass.: Harvard Inst. Econ. Research Discussion Paper No. 752.

Kaldor, N. (1957), 'A Model of Economic Growth', *Economic Journal*, 67, 591–624.

Kendrick, J. (1956), 'Productivity Trends: Capital and Labour', Review of Economics and Statistics, 38, 248–257.

Kendrick, J. (1961), *Productivity Trends in the United States*, New York: NBER; Princeton: Princeton University Press.

Kendrick, J. (1973), *Postwar Productivity Trends in the United States, 1948–1969*, New York: NBER/Columbia University Press.

Kendrick, J. and Grossman, E. (1980), *Productivity in the United States: Trends and Cycles*, Baltimore: Johns Hopkins Press.

Klundert, T. van de and van Schalk, A. (1978), 'Demand and Supply as Factors Determining Economic Growth', *The Economist*, 126, 370–389.

Kuznets, S. (1946), 'National Income, A Summary of Findings', *National Bureau of Economic Research*, New York.

Kuznets, S. (1966), *Modern Economic Growth: Rate, Structure and Spread*, New Haven, Conn.: Yale University Press.

Langlois, R. (1986), *Economies as a Process: Essays in the New Institutional Economics*, New York: Cambridge University Press.

Lazonick, W. (1990), *Competitive Advantage on the Shop Floor*, Cambridge: Harvard University Press.

Lucas, R. (1988), 'On the Mechanisms of Economic Development', *Journal of Monetary Economics*, 22, 3–42.

Maddison, A. (1967), *Economic Growth in the West: Comparative Experience in Europe and North America*, New York: W.W. Norton.

Mankiw, N., Romer, D. and Weil, D. (1992), 'A Contribution to the Empirics of Economic Growth', *Quarterly Journal of Economics*, 107, 407–437.

Mansfield, E. (1968), *Industrial Research and Technological Innovation. An Econometric Analysis*, New York: W.W. Norton.

Mansfield, E., Rapoport, J. and Romeo, A. (1977), *The Production and Application of New Industrial Technology*, New York: W.W. Norton.

Mansfield, E., Rapoport, J. and Schnee, J. (1971), *Research and Development in the Modern Corporation*, New York: W.W. Norton.

Mansfield, E., Schwartz, M., Samuel and Wagner S., (1980), 'Imitation Costs and Patents: An Empirical Analysis', mimeographed.

Metcalfe, S. and Gibbons, M. (1989), 'Technology, Variety, and Organization', *Research on Technological Innovations, Management and Policy*, 4, JAI Press, 153–193.

Nelson, R. (1981), 'Research on Productivity Growth and Differences', *Journal of Economic Literature*, 19, 1029–1064.

Nelson, R. and Winter, S. (1982), *An Evolutionary Theory of Economic Change*, Cambridge, Mass.: Harvard University Press.

Nelson, R. and Wright, G. (1992), 'The Rise and Fall of American Technology Leadership: The Postwar Era in Historical Perspective', *Journal of Economic Literature*, 30, 1931–1964.

North, D. (1990), *Institutions, Institutional Change and Economic Performance*, Cambridge: Cambridge University Press.

Pavitt, K. (1987), *On the Nature of Technology*, Lecture given at the University of Sussex.

Romer, P. (1986), 'Increasing Returns and Long Run Growth', *Journal of Political Economy*, 94, 1002–1037.

Romer, P. (1987), 'Growth Based on Increasing Returns due to Specialisation', *American Economic Review*, 77, 56–62.

Romer, P. (1990), 'Endogenous Technological Change', *Journal of Political Economy*, 98, 71–102.

Romer P. (1991), 'Increasing Returns and New Developments in the Theory of Growth', in W. Barnett, B. Cornet, J. d'Aspermont and A. Mas-Colell (eds), *Equilibrium Theory and Applications*, Cambridge: Cambridge University Press.

Romer, P. (1992), 'Idea Gaps and Object Gaps in Economics Development', Paper prepared for the World Bank Conference: How Do National Policies Affect Long Run Growth?.

Rosenberg, N. (1969), 'The Direction of Technological Change: Inducement Mechanisms and Focusing Devices', *Economic Development and Cultural Change*, 19, 1–24.

Rosenberg, N. (1976), *Perspectives on Technology*, Cambridge: Cambridge University Press.

Rosenberg, N. (1982), *Inside the Black Box: Technology and Economics*, Cambridge: Cambridge University Press.

Salter, W. (1966), *Productivity and Technical Change*, 2nd edn, Cambridge: Cambridge University Press.

Scherer, F. (1983), 'R & D Declining Productivity Growth', *American Economic Review*, 73, 215–218.

Schmookler, J. (1952), 'The Changing Efficiency of the American Economy', *Review of Economical Statistics*, 34, 214–231.

Schmookler, J. (1966), *Invention and Economic Growth*, Cambridge, Mass.: Harvard University Press.

Schotter, A. (1981), *The Economic Theory of Social Institutions*, Cambridge: Cambridge University Press.

Schultz, T. (1953), *The Economic Organization of Agriculture*, N.Y., McGraw Hill.

Schultz, T. (1961), 'Investment in Human Capital', *American Economic Review*, 51, 1–17.

Schumpeter, J. (1950), *Capitalism, Socialism, and Democracy*, 3rd edn, New York:

Harper & Row.

Scott, M. (1989), *A New View of Economic Growth*, Oxford: Oxford University Press.

Shell, K. (1967), 'A Model of Inventive Activity and Capital Accumulation', in Karl Shell (ed.), *Essays in the Theory of Optimal Economic Growth*, Cambridge, Mass.: MIT Press.

Silverberg, G., Dosi, G. and Orsenigo, L. (1988), 'Innovation, Diversity, and Diffusion: A Self-Organisation Model', *Economic Journal*, 98, 1032–1054.

Soete, L. and Turner, R. (1984), 'Technological Diffusion and the Rate of Technical Change', *The Economic Journal*, 94, 612–623.

Solow, R. (1956), 'A Contribution to the Theory of Economic Growth', *Quarterly Journal of Economics*, 70, 65–94.

Solow, R. (1957), 'Technical Change and the Aggregate Production Function', *Review of Economics and Statistics*, 39, 214–31.

Solow, R. (1959), 'Investment and Technical Change' in K.J. Arrow, S. Karlin and P. Suppes (eds), *Mathematical Methods in the Social Sciences*, Stanford: Stanford University Press.

Solow, R. (1970), *Growth Theory: An Exposition*, Oxford: Clarendon Press.

Solow, R., Tobin, J. and von Weizsäcker, C. (1966), 'Neoclassical Growth with Fixed Factor Propositions', *Review of Economic Studies*, 33, 79–115.

Sugden, R. (1989), 'Spontaneous Order', *Journal of Economic Perspectives*, 3, 85–97.

Swan, T. (1956), 'Economic Growth and Capital Accumulation', *Economic Record*, 32, 334–361.

Terleckyj, N. (1960), 'Sources of Productivity Advance: A Pilot Study of Manufacturing Industries, 1899–1953', PhD. Dissertation, Columbia University.

Tinbergen, J. (1942), 'Zur Theorie der langfristigen Wirtschaftsentwicklung', *Weltwirtschaftliches Archiv*, 55, 511–549. English translation: 'On the Theory of Trend Movements', in L.H. Klassen, L.M. Koyck and H.J. Witteveen (eds), *J. Tinbergen, Selected Essays*, Amsterdam: North-Holland, 1959.

Veblen, T. (1915), *Imperial Germany and the Industrial Revolution*, New York: Macmillan.

Verspagen, B. (1992), 'Endogenous Innovation in Neo-classical Growth Models: A Survey' *Journal of Macroeconomics*, 14, 631–662.

Williamson, O. (1985), *The Economic Institutions of Capitalism*, New York: Free Press.

Winter, S. (1991), 'On Coase, Competence, and the Corporation' in E. Williamson and S. Winter (eds), *The Nature of the Firm: Origins, Evolution and Development*, New York: Oxford University Press.

Womack, J., Jones, D. and Roos, D. (1990), *The Machine that Changed the World*, New York: Macmillan.

Author Index

Acharya 245, 257
Aghion 21, 33, 42, 75, 106, 125,
    143, 290, 291, 320
Allen 75, 106, 108, 263, 282
Allyn 11
Amable 2-4, 20, 21, 26, 38, 42,
    74, 127, 143, 217-220, 227,
    235, 237
Ammerman 14, 15, 18
Anant 75, 108, 146
Anderson 263, 282
Aoki 143, 308, 320
Arrow 3, 4, 9, 19, 20, 28, 29,
    42, 111, 113, 127, 152, 245,
    257, 258, 282, 324
Arthur 265-268, 270, 273, 274,
    280, 282, 313, 320
Atkinson 311, 320
Ayres 107, 287, 288
Azariadis 39, 40, 42, 125, 143
Bairoch 121-123, 143
Bak 95, 106
Baker 100, 101, 103, 104
Banerjee 263, 264, 282
Barro 22, 38, 42, 158, 179, 185,
    210, 306, 320
Basawa 103, 106
Bass 217-221, 223, 226, 238
Batey Blackman 155, 180, 185,
    210
Batten 220, 235, 237
Baumol 38, 42, 46, 92, 106,
    145, 155, 156, 158, 162, 179,

    180, 185, 187, 210, 211, 304,
    320
Becker 40, 42, 299, 320
Bellman 56
Benhabib 92, 106, 126, 128,
    129, 143
Bernard 39, 42, 149, 153
Bernstein 158, 180
Bertrand 218, 225, 231, 240
Boldrin 264, 282
Boltho 301, 320
Boserup 48, 62, 66, 69
Boyer 143, 281, 282
Brezis 126, 143
Brock 92, 106, 264, 282
Cabrales 263, 264, 282
Cavalli-Sforza 14, 15, 18
Chandler 314, 316, 317, 321
Chatterjee 218, 221, 237
Chen 95, 106
Cheng 75, 106, 125, 126, 143,
    248, 257
Chiaromonte 128, 129, 143
Chow 220, 223
Clark 76, 98, 100, 101, 103, 107
Cohen 159, 180
Conlisk 128, 143
Coombs 221, 237
Cornwall 155, 180, 182, 183
Cournot 223, 244, 248
Cox 100, 103, 107
Cunningham 64
Dale 190, 211, 299

325

Davis 321
Day 3, 45-47, 53, 57, 60, 62,
    64-66, 68, 69, 71, 72, 110,
    114, 264, 283
De Long 38, 42, 121, 143, 187,
    211
Dechert 92, 106
Dekel 264, 283
Demsetz 316, 321
Denison 1, 119, 143, 298, 300,
    303-305, 310, 321
Dertouzos 307, 321
Diederen 4, 217
Dinopoulos 75, 106, 108, 125,
    126, 143, 146
Dixit 309, 321
Dockner 219, 227, 228, 237
Dollar 185, 187, 211
Domar 298, 300-302, 321
Dosi 1-4, 12, 14, 41, 42, 75,
    119, 124, 128, 129, 131, 133,
    136, 143-145, 146, 147, 150,
    153, 154, 165, 180, 217, 218,
    237, 238, 261, 263, 265, 267,
    270, 271, 274, 282-285, 312,
    314, 320, 321, 324
Dowrick 156, 160-162, 180,
    182, 183
Drazen 39, 40, 42, 125, 143
Durlauf 29, 39, 42, 68, 121,
    127, 128, 144, 149, 153, 281,
    283
Easterly 121, 123, 144
Egidi 131, 144
Eigen 263, 283
Eliashberg 218, 221, 226, 235,
    237, 238
Elliott 74
Englmann 112, 113, 115
Ermoliev 282, 283
Ethier 31, 42, 321
Fabiani 2, 3, 14, 119, 129, 136,
    144, 147

Fabricant 297, 321
Fagerberg 38, 42, 144, 154, 155,
    158, 159, 180, 182, 184
Feichtinger 223, 238
Felmingham 218, 238
Fershtman 234, 238
Fisher 77, 107, 263
Foster 264, 280, 283
Freeman 1, 41, 42, 76, 98, 103,
    107, 136, 143-145, 180, 237,
    238, 263, 282, 283, 284, 299,
    307, 320, 321
Friedman 264, 283
Frischtak 77, 108
Frydman 283
Gavin 305
Georgescu-Roegen 63
Gerschenkron 155, 180
Gibbons 323
Gille 41, 42
Glaister 217, 220, 223-225, 228,
    235, 238
Glaziev 265, 268-270, 283
Gollop 190, 211, 321
Goodwin 77, 84, 87, 107, 108
Graddy 126, 145
Grassberger 92, 107
Griliches 2, 158, 161, 180, 290,
    298, 299, 304, 307, 322
Grossman 21, 22, 30, 42, 75,
    107, 125, 126, 144, 217, 240,
    242, 243, 290, 299, 322
Guellec 20, 21, 26, 42
Haavelmo 40, 42
Hahn 23, 42
Hall 154, 158, 180
Hanson 272, 283
Harrod 10, 40, 300-302
Haustein 98, 99, 101, 100, 101,
    103, 107
Heiner 131, 144
Helliwell 158, 175, 180
Helpman 4, 21, 22, 30, 42, 75,

107, 125, 126, 144, 290, 322
Henkin 75, 107, 264, 284
Herodotus 49
Heston 2, 37, 43, 177, 181, 211
Heyer 245, 257
Hildenbrand 69, 106
Hill 108, 265-267, 283, 323
Hirschman 127
Ho 248, 257
Hodgson 322
Hofbauer 81, 107
Hölder 267
Howitt 21, 33, 42, 75, 106, 125, 143, 290, 291, 320
Hulten 180
Innij 132
Ireland 162, 169, 171, 218, 239
Isabelle 94, 107
Isiodon 126, 143
Iwai 75, 107, 128, 144
Jeuland 226, 235, 238
Johnson 39, 42, 68, 121, 128, 144
Jones 324
Joosten 4, 217, 244, 246, 247, 257, 258
Jordan 283
Jorgensen 219, 220, 222, 223, 227, 228, 235-238
Jorgenson 224, 298, 299, 302, 304, 321, 322
Jovanovic 126, 128, 129, 143, 144
Justman 126, 144
Kalahari 71
Kaldor 20, 28, 42, 145, 183, 311, 322
Kandori 263, 283
Kaniovski 4, 75, 261, 265, 267-270, 272, 282, 283, 285, 288
Karshenas 221, 238
Kendrick 1, 180, 211, 290, 297,

299, 300, 303, 321, 322
Kennedy 11, 18
Kennel 94, 107
Kim 47, 62
King 40, 43, 137, 138, 144, 145
Kirman 281, 283
Kleinknecht 76, 98, 100, 103, 107, 108
Klepper 126, 145
Klundert 4, 20, 44, 290, 301, 322
Kondratieff 76, 85, 87, 104, 107-110
Krugman 126, 143
Kuran 281, 283
Kutta 81
Kuznets 76, 77, 107, 295, 297, 322
Lach 126, 144
Laffargue 20, 43
Lagrange 250
Lakhani 224, 238
Landes 119, 145
Lane 265, 282, 283
Langlois 322
Lazonick 307, 322
Lehnert 3, 11, 14, 15, 74, 93, 108-110, 115, 127, 136
Lester 321
Levhari 259, 260
Levine 38, 43, 144, 158, 162, 181
Levinthal 159, 180
Lewis 100, 103, 107, 135, 145
Lichtenberg 155, 158, 159, 161, 181
Lipschitz 264
Lorenz 92, 107
Lucas 22, 31, 35, 43, 120, 145, 291, 322
Lundvall 145
Maddison 2, 35, 43, 119, 122,

124, 145, 157, 181, 185, 189,
    211, 301, 322
Mahajan 217-221, 234, 238
Mailath 283
Mairesse 158, 180
Malliaris 92, 106, 264, 282
Malthus 46, 47, 66
Mankiw 38-40, 43, 155, 158,
    181, 306, 322
Mansfield 75, 107, 299, 322,
    323
March 131
Marchetti 108
Marglin 15, 18
Markov 264, 288
Marshall 28, 64
Martin 18, 20, 22, 42, 43, 158,
    179, 180
Marx 69, 154, 316
Matsuyama 40, 43
McMillan 248, 257
Mensch 76, 98, 99, 108
Mertens 246, 257
Metcalfe 128, 145, 217, 220,
    222, 224, 225, 224, 235, 238,
    323
Metz 77, 108
Mirman 259, 260
Mohnen 154, 158, 161, 165, 181
Montroll 74, 108
Mosekilde 76, 108
Muller 217-221, 234, 238
Murphy 29, 40, 42, 43, 127, 145
Nadiri 158, 180, 181
Nakicenovic 77, 83, 108, 238,
    283
Nelson 1-4, 54, 63, 72, 75, 108,
    109, 113, 120, 126, 128, 129,
    131, 143, 144, 145, 151, 153,
    154, 159, 180, 181, 237, 238,
    242, 264, 282-284, 287, 289,
    290, 301, 311, 320, 321, 323
Neuwirth 98, 99, 101, 100, 103,

107
Neyman 246, 257
Nguyen 156, 160-162, 180, 182,
    183
Nicolis 262, 264, 283, 284
North 19, 41-43, 106, 282, 316,
    321-324
Norton 218, 238, 322, 323
Oren 221, 238
Orléan 281, 282
Orsenigo 128, 133, 146, 218,
    238, 284, 324
Palm 147, 150
Pasinetti 145
Patel 155, 158, 159, 178, 181
Pavitt 144, 145, 154, 180, 182,
    184, 312, 323
Perez 41, 42, 144, 145, 307, 321
Peters 4, 217, 244, 257, 258
Pflug 267, 283
Phelps 126, 145, 283
Plosser 137, 138, 145
Polterovich 75, 107, 264, 284
Poullier 119, 143
Prigogine 262, 264, 283, 284
Pry 77, 107
Raj 180, 181
Rao 103, 106, 226, 238
Rapoport 322, 323
Rebelo 25, 30, 43, 137, 138,
    144, 145
Reinganum 218, 238, 259, 260
Renelt 38, 43, 158, 162, 181
Reynolds 260
Rob 126, 144, 283
Robinson 224, 238
Robson 40, 43
Romer 12, 18, 21, 28-32, 38-40,
    43, 109, 113-115, 125, 126,
    145, 151, 155, 158, 159, 181,
    290, 291, 293, 306, 308, 322,
    323
Rosegger 221, 238

Rosenberg 29, 43, 77, 108, 119,
    146, 299, 323
Rosser 264, 284
Runge 81
Ruszczinski 265, 282
Ruttan 220, 239
Sahal 98, 108
Sala-i-Martin 20, 22, 42, 43,
    158, 179
Salter 302, 323
Samuelson 264, 284
Saviotti 221, 237
Schalk 301, 322
Scherer 307, 323
Schmookler 297, 299, 323
Schotman 149, 153
Schotter 323
Schultz 297, 299, 323
Schumpeter 1, 13, 74, 76, 104,
    107, 108, 148, 296, 297, 299,
    307, 314, 323
Schuster 263, 283
Schwartz 221, 238, 323
Scotchmer 264, 283
Scott 66, 146, 311, 324
Segerstrom 75, 108, 125, 146
Shapley 246, 257
Shell 11, 12, 19, 62, 324
Sheshinski 28, 43
Shleifer 29, 40, 43, 127, 145
Sigmund 81, 107
Silverberg 1, 3, 11, 14, 15, 74,
    75, 77, 78, 87, 93, 108-110,
    113, 115, 127, 128, 133, 136,
    143-146, 180, 217, 218, 237,
    238, 263, 264, 283, 284, 288,
    320, 321, 324
Smith 1, 10, 19, 40, 46, 154,
    295
Soete 1, 75, 76, 82, 87, 93, 98,
    103, 107, 108, 110, 121, 143-
    146, 154, 155, 158, 159, 178,

180-182, 184, 218, 237, 238,
    282-284, 320, 321, 324
Solomou 98, 108
Solow 1, 2, 10-12, 19, 20, 23,
    26, 29, 38-40, 43, 52, 63, 66,
    69, 120, 125, 126, 128, 138,
    146, 158, 159, 213, 290, 295,
    298, 300-303, 310, 311, 321,
    324
Spence 259, 260
Spiegel 126, 143
Spremann 224, 238
Starr 181, 248, 257
Stengers 262, 284
Sterman 76, 108
Stiglitz 112, 127, 146, 309, 311,
    320, 321
Stoneman 217, 218, 220, 221,
    223, 238, 239, 242
Sugden 324
Summers 2, 37, 38, 42, 43, 143,
    177, 181, 211, 306, 321
Swan 295, 300, 301, 311, 324
Takayasu 95, 108
Tang 95, 106
Teece 321
Terleckyj 299, 324
Teubal 126, 144
Thirtle 220, 239
Thuijsman 4, 244, 257, 258
Tinbergen 10, 11, 19, 297, 324
Tirole 243
Turner 75, 77, 82, 87, 93, 108,
    110, 218, 238, 324
Uzawa 40, 44
Vaccara 180, 211
Van de Klundert 4, 20, 44, 290,
    301
van Dijk 149, 153, 217
van Duijn 98, 101, 103, 108
Veblen 317, 324
Vega-Redondo 244, 255, 258,

259
Verspagen 3, 20, 44, 121, 124,
    126, 146, 154, 156, 159, 165,
    170, 181, 182, 183, 217, 291,
    324
von Hippel 75, 108
von Weizsäcker 11, 19, 324
Walsh 221, 237
Walter 45, 46, 60, 62
Weibull 263, 264, 282
Weil 38-40, 43, 44, 155, 158,
    181, 306, 322
Wiesenfeld 95, 106
Williamson 324
Winter 2, 75, 108, 120, 128,
    129, 131, 145, 154, 159, 181,
    264, 283, 285, 287, 292, 293,
    311, 313, 317, 321, 323, 324
Wolf 92, 108
Wolff 3, 145, 155, 158, 180,
    181, 185, 187, 190, 210-214
Wolfson 150, 151
Womack 308, 324
Wright 258, 305, 323
Young 11, 19, 28, 44, 126, 146,
    264, 283, 293, 303, 307
Zamagni 143, 146
Zervos 38, 43
Zhang 264, 284
Ziesemer 4, 217, 240, 242, 244
Zou 45, 53, 60, 62, 63

Subject Index

accounting 1, 2, 35, 76, 97, 143,
    287, 295, 298, 300, 302, 305,
    308, 310, 321, 322
acquisition of knowledge 13, 14
adaptation 263, 264
adaptive processes 265, 281, 282
adjustment costs 133, 147, 206
adopters 220, 268, 270-273, 279,
    280, 287
adoption 212, 245, 265, 272,
    275, 279, 306
advanced industrial nations 294,
    318
advertising 220, 236-238, 241
aerospace 178
Africa 123, 124, 245, 257
agriculture 14, 15, 46, 71, 195,
    196, 195, 199, 202, 245, 323
allocation 15, 23, 31, 32, 34, 45,
    120, 128, 141, 298
allocation, optimal 31, 120, 128,
    141
American firms 307, 316
appreciative theory 109, 292-
    294, 300, 301, 303, 305, 309,
    312, 313, 319
archaeologists 46, 49
Argentina 124
Asia 14, 123, 124
Australia 157, 162, 169, 188,
    190, 191, 193, 196, 203
Austria 108, 157, 162, 169, 171,
    282, 283

available knowledge 28, 262
backwardness 140, 180, 185,
    207, 209
balanced growth 52-54, 213
Baltic sea 68
bandwagon dynamics 76
bargaining equation 112, 113
behavioural rules 56, 57, 131
Belgium 157, 162, 169, 171,
    188, 190, 191, 193, 196, 203
Bertrand model 231
Bertrand oligopoly 218, 225,
    240
big bang 109
biology 258, 262-264, 283
Britain 115, 122, 124, 125, 307,
    316-318
business cycles 42, 74, 106-108,
    111, 143, 145, 321
California 45, 63, 282, 316
Canada 157, 162, 165, 169, 171,
    181, 188, 190, 191, 193, 196,
    203
capital accumulation 19, 20, 23,
    24, 36, 37, 45, 46, 53, 54, 60,
    61, 65, 66, 110, 119, 126,
    141, 158, 194, 259, 260, 324
capital expansion 14-16
capital formation 12, 75, 185,
    186, 194, 204, 211, 296
capital intensity 185, 186, 192-
    194, 201, 204, 206, 207, 209,
    310, 311

capital/labour ratio 52, 53
capital markets 14, 308, 318
capital mobility 37
capital/output ratio 80
capital per worker 23, 310
capital stock 52, 53, 60, 66, 77-
    79, 81-83, 96, 160, 161, 187,
    190, 194, 218, 300
capital/worker ratio 23, 78
capitalist 43, 57, 76, 108, 145,
    179, 181, 183, 211, 297
capitalist countries 57
capitalist economy 76
cash flow 132
catching up 2, 24 119, 121, 123,
    124, 126, 127, 129, 131, 145,
    146, 149, 179, 181, 182, 183,
    210, 304, 306, 320
CES production function 212
changing payoffs 244, 245, 247,
    248, 259
chaos 62, 92-95, 105-108, 114,
    282, 284
China 17, 123, 124
classical economists 45, 47, 65,
    154, 295
classical growth 46, 181, 218,
    324
classical investment function
    218
clustering 76, 77, 98, 100, 101,
    103-105
coevolutionary effects 264
coevolutionary process 317, 318
communication networks 22
comparative advantages 140
competence 314, 324
competition 2-4, 20, 21, 25, 26,
    28, 29, 68, 74, 75, 104, 108,
    126, 140, 144, 146, 236-238,
    240, 257, 260, 261, 267, 275,
    279, 296, 307, 309, 321

competition, imperfect 3, 21, 74,
    126, 309
competition, international 140,
    257
competition, perfect 20, 21, 25,
    26, 28, 29, 296
competition, technological 4, 75,
    144
competitiveness 119, 132, 133,
    140, 143, 146, 185, 211, 263
competitors 14, 226, 234, 242
complementarities 28, 121, 127,
    185, 265, 310, 311
complexity 18, 45, 47, 62, 64,
    71, 114, 220, 282, 284
computer models 111
computer science 151
computer theorists 111
consumption 21, 23, 25, 26, 36,
    107, 270
consumption good 21
convergence 1-3, 20, 37, 39, 40,
    42, 55, 66, 68, 70, 92, 119,
    121, 138, 140, 143-146, 149-
    151, 153-158, 171, 176, 175,
    177, 179, 180, 182, 183, 185-
    187, 189, 190, 192, 194, 199,
    202, 206-214, 264, 265, 267,
    270, 273, 274, 280, 283, 304-
    306, 320
correlation dimension 93, 92, 93,
    92, 114
cost of information 12
costs of production 240, 280
costs of unlearning 259
Cournot, monopoly 223
Cournot-Nash equilibrium 244
creative destruction 1, 33, 42,
    74-76, 104, 106, 108, 143,
    148, 291, 320
decision rule 268, 270, 272, 278
decreasing returns 1, 28, 29, 65,
    148

demand curve 217, 218, 228, 236, 242
demand curve, epidemic 217
demand function 133, 223, 227
demand, intersectoral 127
demand, potential 222, 227, 240, 241
demoeconomic function 47, 52
demoeconomic growth 46
demographic transition zone 66
Denmark 157, 162, 169, 171, 188, 190, 191, 193, 196, 203
depreciation 39, 160, 161, 254, 255, 260
determinants of growth 297, 303, 309
developed countries 38, 124, 135, 147, 156, 170, 182, 212
developed European countries 169, 177
developing countries 123, 124, 135, 147, 156, 306
development blocks 50, 54
development patterns 51, 119, 121, 125, 141
development process 121
development, stages of 46, 50, 56
differential game 219, 225, 226, 228, 234-236, 248
diffusion 1, 4, 9, 14-17, 22, 49, 73-77, 82, 83, 87, 90, 104, 107, 108, 110, 112, 115, 120, 126, 133, 135, 138, 140, 144-146, 152, 159, 183, 185, 206, 215, 217-224, 227, 228, 233-243, 263, 264, 267-269, 272, 279, 280, 283, 284, 286, 300, 324
diffusion of innovation 135, 145
diffusion of knowledge 14, 73, 126, 144, 159, 220, 222

diffusion of production 220
disaggregation 298
diseconomies 46-51, 55, 59, 62
disembodied knowledge spill-overs 159-161, 164, 170, 175, 177
disequilibrium 1, 108, 128, 217, 222, 235, 236, 281
disequilibrium behaviour 235
divergence 3, 20, 37, 39, 66, 68, 119, 121, 129, 138, 140, 141, 146, 149, 150, 151, 154-157, 171, 182, 208, 213
divergent growth 148
division of labour 10, 28, 30, 31, 40
duopolistic differential game 219, 226, 228, 236
duopoly 217, 227, 231, 244
dynamic equilibrium growth 302
dynamic firm behaviour 237
dynamic game 4, 244, 246, 260
dynamic increasing returns 30, 263, 272, 279, 280, 287
dynamic model 77, 104
dynamic programming 248
dynamical systems 68, 91, 106, 107, 279
economic activity 46, 51, 97, 104, 105, 179, 262
economic agents 21, 147
economic change 74, 108, 145, 181, 262, 281, 283, 321-323
economic development 42, 43, 49, 62, 68, 71, 76, 107, 119, 141, 143, 145, 237, 287, 297, 321-323
economic dynamics 146, 181, 261, 281, 284
economic efficiency 55, 296, 317

economic environments 267,
    271, 275
economic growth 19, 28, 42-45,
    55-57, 62, 63, 74, 75, 107,
    108, 143, 144, 145, 146, 177,
    179-181, 183, 184, 210, 211,
    283, 291-304, 307, 309, 310,
    311, 314, 318-324
economic history 64, 65, 71,
    179, 183, 210, 262, 320
economic institutions 294, 309,
    316, 317, 319, 324
economic theory 1, 4, 42, 65,
    110, 143-145, 180, 217, 237,
    238, 245, 282, 283, 284, 292,
    300, 309, 320, 321, 323
economics of innovation 1, 126,
    136, 262, 265
economies of scale 21, 28, 291
education 21, 38, 45, 119, 126,
    136, 158, 161, 291, 299, 306,
    310
educational attainments 306, 310
efficiency 24, 51-56, 133, 262,
    296, 317, 323
elasticity of production 25, 30
elasticity of substitution 25
embodied knowledge spillovers
    159, 165, 169
employment 77-79, 82, 112,
    113, 133-135, 145, 184, 185,
    188, 187, 190, 191, 193, 194,
    196, 203, 300, 301, 311, 312,
    315
employment rate 112, 113
employment share 78, 79, 82
endogenous growth 2, 20-28, 30,
    33, 35-37, 39-43, 75, 104
endogenous market potential
    219, 226
endogenous preference formation
    279
energy 48, 83, 107, 108, 287,

302, 304, 310, 322
engineering 72, 75, 159, 178,
    296, 312
England 18
enterprise 1, 143, 146, 161, 293,
    294, 296, 297, 299, 302, 303,
    314, 320, 321
entrants 134, 148
epidemic diffusion 217-220,
    235-237, 240-243
equilibrium growth 20, 23, 38,
    301, 302
equilibrium model 127, 235, 309
equilibrium path 32, 39
equilibrium strategy 236
equilibrium theory 295, 323
equilibrium value 217, 223
Europe 14, 15, 18, 124, 304-
    306, 318, 322
European 15, 169, 170, 177,
    180, 245, 282, 294, 298, 320
European countries 169, 170,
    177
evolution 42, 45, 46, 54-57, 64,
    71, 74, 76, 107, 145, 237,
    238, 262-265, 280, 282-284,
    318, 324
evolutionary economics 112,
    144, 148, 237, 282
evolutionary game 264, 283
evolutionary growth theory 311
evolutionary model 74, 107,
    138, 144, 146
evolutionary theory 14, 108,
    145, 150, 181, 283, 317, 323
exchange rates 132, 135, 136,
    148, 187, 194
exogenous growth 12, 29
expectations 41, 77, 112, 127,
    131, 136, 228, 261, 280, 281,
    283, 315, 317
experience 1, 17, 51, 179, 183,
    185, 194, 244, 245, 296, 299,

310, 312, 313, 318, 321, 322
exponential growth 45
exports 134, 140
external diseconomies 47, 50,
    51, 59, 62
external effects 37, 40, 41
externalities 12, 21, 28, 33, 35,
    38, 42, 52, 56, 66, 125, 127,
    131, 136, 140, 143, 154, 261,
    262, 264, 265, 291, 296, 299
feedback 11, 41, 80, 97, 115,
    136, 147, 150, 153, 250, 261,
    267, 270, 272
fertility 42, 66, 71
final good 22, 26, 27, 30, 31,
    33, 34, 36
finance 18, 42, 127, 143, 146,
    196, 195, 196, 203, 262, 265
financial markets 281, 283
Finland 157, 162, 169, 171, 188,
    190, 191, 193, 196, 200, 203
fixed capital 154, 159, 161, 177,
    191, 193, 203
fixed investment 136, 165
Fordism 308
forecast 17, 24, 114
forging ahead 119, 124, 129,
    179, 183, 210, 320
formal theory 292, 293, 302,
    303, 309
France 122, 157, 162, 169-171,
    178, 188, 190, 191, 193, 196,
    201, 203
free trade 126
game 4, 49, 219, 225, 226, 228,
    230, 231, 233-236, 244-248,
    250, 256, 257, 258-260, 263,
    264, 282, 283, 316
game theory 246, 257, 264, 316
gap 42, 54, 121, 122, 130, 140,
    184, 187, 319
GDP 22, 34, 37-40, 123, 124,

156, 157, 165, 178, 182, 188,
    187, 190, 191, 196, 195, 203
general equilibrium 1, 2, 125,
    128, 141, 235, 237, 293, 295,
    309
Germany 122, 124, 157, 162,
    169-171, 178, 181, 188, 187,
    190, 191, 193, 195, 196, 195,
    199, 203, 316, 317, 324
global convergence 39, 40, 42,
    144
GNP 86, 122, 123, 149, 153,
    306
goodwill 13, 220, 236, 268
government 42, 161, 162, 188,
    187, 195, 196, 195, 202, 206,
    258, 308, 315, 316
government services 188, 187,
    195, 196, 195, 202
Great Britain 115, 122, 307,
    316, 318
Great Depression 295
Greece 162, 169
growth accounting 1, 2, 35, 143,
    295, 298, 300, 305, 308, 310,
    322
growth analysis 15, 212
growth models 20-22, 27, 28,
    30, 35, 37, 39-42, 44, 75, 76,
    120, 141, 148, 150, 154, 158,
    159, 181, 290, 291, 302, 305,
    307-309, 319, 324
growth of output 21, 155, 163,
    164, 297, 298, 301, 310
growth of technology 32
growth path 37, 38, 52, 54, 127,
    159, 162, 302
growth patterns 121, 125, 148,
    149, 158, 177
growth performance 119, 294
growth process 2, 3, 9, 23, 49,
    50, 98, 158, 306

growth rate differentials 22, 146
growth regimes 39, 40, 143
growth theory 1, 9, 20, 22, 37,
  40, 44-46, 48, 52, 56, 120,
  127, 140, 141, 155, 158, 290-
  297, 299-303, 305, 308, 309,
  311, 313, 315, 318, 319, 324
growth trajectories 54, 127
Hamiltonian 221, 223, 228, 233,
  250, 251, 255, 256
heterogeneous agents 120, 128,
  138
heterogeneous firms 135, 261
heterogeneous learning 129
human capital 2, 22, 25, 26, 31-
  33, 35-40, 42, 50-52, 126,
  143, 155, 158, 159, 298-300,
  303, 311, 320, 323
human capital accumulation 37
Iceland 162, 164, 169, 171
imitation 3, 14-16, 74-76, 107,
  112, 120, 126, 128-132, 135,
  140, 144, 148, 150, 151, 153,
  158, 159, 175, 177, 323
imperfect information 133, 241,
  242
imports 134, 140, 165, 177, 178,
  182
increasing returns 1, 3, 10, 11,
  18, 19, 21, 22, 25-28, 30-32,
  35, 43, 44, 125, 126-128, 141,
  145, 165, 218, 237, 261-263,
  268, 272, 279, 280, 282, 286,
  287, 298, 320, 323
India 122, 306
industrial economics 21, 136
industrial nations 294, 318
industrial research 296, 322
industrial revolution 121, 143,
  324
industrialized countries 181
industry 3, 108, 185, 186, 188,
  187, 191, 194-196, 200, 199,

201-203, 204-207, 206, 209,
  211, 245, 258, 289, 298, 299,
  307, 308, 313, 315, 317, 321
inflation 76, 301
information 10-15, 18, 22, 36,
  46, 133, 148, 175, 183, 217,
  219, 220, 222, 235-238, 240-
  244, 280, 282, 286
information diffusion 217, 220
information economies 46
information technology 217
infrastructural capital 60, 66
infrastructure 3, 22, 45, 46, 48,
  49, 52, 53, 57-62, 66
innovation 1, 2, 11, 18, 21, 22,
  30, 31, 33-35, 41, 42, 44, 74-
  77, 79-82, 85, 88, 89, 88-90,
  89, 90, 93, 92, 95-101, 103,
  104, 107-109, 110, 114, 115,
  120, 125, 126, 128-130, 132,
  135, 136, 140, 141, 143, 144-
  146, 148, 153, 154, 159, 164,
  165, 175, 177, 180, 181, 184,
  237, 238, 262, 264, 265, 279,
  282-284, 286, 321, 322, 324
innovation rate 35, 90, 93, 97,
  100, 103, 110
innovation time series 98, 99,
  101, 104, 114
innovator 35, 159
institutional change 43, 71, 119,
  120, 316, 318, 321, 323
institutional economics 316, 322
institutional factors 41, 297
intermediate good 21, 30-33, 75,
  159, 165, 177
internal diseconomies 48-51
international economics 22, 257
international specialization 143,
  185, 211
intertemporal externality 27, 35
invention 18, 106, 126, 296, 323
investment rate 38, 291

Ireland 162, 169, 171, 218, 239
Japan 122, 124, 125, 153, 157,
  162, 169-171, 177, 178, 188,
  187, 190, 189, 191-193, 192,
  195, 196, 195, 199, 201, 203,
  205, 209, 212, 213, 294, 304-
  307, 318
Japanese manufacturing 201
Kenya 245, 257
Keynesian 135, 146, 153, 182,
  301
knowledge accumulation 27, 28,
  35, 155, 158, 177, 262
knowledge creation 11, 12, 17,
  33, 165
knowledge spillovers 155, 159-
  161, 164, 165, 169, 170, 175,
  177
knowledge stock 12, 32, 159,
  160, 178, 259, 296
Korea 156, 162, 164, 169-171,
  211, 306, 318
labour force 26, 35, 78, 79, 148,
  301
labour productivity 54, 68, 77,
  80, 82, 112, 121, 129, 134,
  135, 160-162, 169, 170, 174-
  176, 185-188, 187, 189, 190,
  189-196, 195, 196, 199, 200,
  201, 204, 207-209, 290, 298,
  301
labour productivity growth 135,
  186, 188, 187, 189, 190, 189,
  192-194, 204, 298
labour productivity level 188,
  190, 195
laggard 125, 126, 131
laggard countries 125, 126
leader 187, 199, 200, 210, 219,
  232, 234-236, 303
leadership 127, 143, 180, 186,
  210, 214, 219, 226, 228, 232-

234, 236, 257, 323
learning by doing 1, 16, 17, 28,
  42, 43, 51, 146, 257, 259,
  312, 319
learning curve 112, 242
learning economies 218, 272
learning effects 20, 226, 249,
  256, 287
learning mechanism 242
learning process 72, 75, 115,
  313
learning rate 258
lifecycles 83
local convergence 39, 40, 121
logistic 4, 83, 98, 108, 217, 218,
  220, 221, 223
long waves 76, 77, 85, 104, 107,
  108, 110, 144, 307
macro dynamics 88
macroeconomic growth theory
  45
macroeconomics 1, 43, 44, 115,
  181, 262, 301, 324
Malthusian 49, 54, 65, 66
manufacturing 108, 180, 185,
  186, 189-196, 199-203, 205-
  209, 211, 258, 315, 324
marginal productivity 15, 21,
  23-25, 47, 296-298
market equilibrium 2, 26, 30, 35
market penetration 224
market potential 217, 219, 220,
  226, 228, 236, 238
market power 148, 270, 299
market share 83, 133, 148, 226,
  232, 234, 235, 238, 244, 248,
  249, 271, 272, 274, 278
market skimming 224
market structure 1, 145, 206,
  217, 219-221, 228, 237, 269,
  270

marketing literature 217, 218, 220, 223, 224, 228, 235, 237
Markov process 288
Marshallian externalities 21
mass production 308
Methodenstreit 65
methodology 98, 212, 214, 280, 298, 304
microheterogeneity 262
migration 15
mining and quarrying 196, 195, 196, 203
mixed strategy 65
mobility 37, 45, 308
modern growth theory 295
monopolist 31, 221, 224, 235, 240
monopolistic behaviour 220, 272
monopoly 13, 22, 31, 33, 34, 217, 219, 222-224, 226, 229, 232, 234-236, 282, 286, 287
monopoly profits 13, 33, 34, 219, 234
multiple equilibria 39, 40, 279
multiplier 24, 76, 250
Nash equilibrium 228, 244, 247, 250, 254, 256
national accounts 134
negative feedback 135, 263, 265, 269, 271, 272, 281
neoclassical growth 20-23, 29, 37, 38, 44, 52, 235, 290-297, 300, 302, 303, 305, 308, 309, 311, 313, 319, 324
neoclassical theory 38, 154, 300, 303, 305, 309, 314, 319
Netherlands 1, 152, 157, 162, 169, 171, 188, 187, 190, 191, 193, 196, 195, 199, 203
new growth theory 22, 37, 40, 120, 155, 293, 294, 296, 305, 309, 318
Nigeria 306

nonconvexities 18
nonequilibrium 262, 283
nonlinear 3, 17, 76, 90-92, 94, 95, 94, 96, 101, 105, 107, 108, 111, 112, 114, 115, 126, 129, 135, 262, 265, 279, 282, 286, 288
nonlinearity 62, 93
nonstationary 131, 150
Norway 157, 162, 169, 171, 188, 190, 191, 193, 196, 199, 203
OECD 2, 3, 38, 121, 122, 149, 155, 156, 165, 178, 180, 182, 183, 185, 186, 187, 188, 187, 190, 189, 191-193, 192, 194-196, 195, 196, 199, 200, 199-203, 207, 209
old growth theory 319
oligopolistic market structure 219
oligopoly 219, 225, 240
optimal control theory 248, 250
optimal growth 33, 43, 55
optimal innovation rate 35
organisation 16, 45, 46, 49, 56, 97, 140, 204, 238, 241, 262, 283, 284, 295, 304-306, 314, 324
output growth 52, 112, 158, 212, 213, 298, 300
patent stock 161, 175
patent system 32
patent variable 170, 171, 183
patents 32, 38, 107, 158, 162, 164, 170, 176, 175, 177, 178, 180, 182, 299, 323
patterns of growth 55, 119-121, 124
payoffs 244-250, 254, 258, 259
per capita income 23, 24, 37, 54, 66, 110, 119, 124, 149, 150, 155, 156, 177

perfect foresight 2, 127
perfect information 236
Peru 306
Phillips curve 77, 115
physical capital 25, 26, 31, 35-37, 39, 148, 302, 304-306, 311
physical investment 26, 304, 306
pioneer 234, 235
ploughback investment 83
Poisson 11, 34, 75, 80, 87, 88, 93, 96-101, 100, 101, 103-105, 108, 110, 130, 137, 138, 151
Poisson distribution 101, 103, 130, 137, 138
Poisson parameter 80, 96-98, 100
Poisson process 34, 75, 80, 87, 88, 99, 100, 104, 105, 151
policy 12, 14, 22, 23, 33, 40, 42, 43, 143, 144, 184, 206, 220, 223-225, 226, 228, 236-238, 271, 288, 308, 321-323
pollution 287
Pontryagin's maximum principle 250
population growth 28, 46, 47, 52, 54, 65, 66, 72, 110
population level 51, 53, 55, 65, 66
Portugal 162, 169, 171
positive externality 22, 29, 32, 35, 36
positive feedback 115, 267, 272
postwar growth 156, 177, 179
preference function 58
price, consumer 135
price differentiation 217, 224, 223-225, 235, 237
price differentiation, intertemporal 217, 224, 223, 225, 237

price dynamics 238, 271, 273, 280
price equalisation theorem 212
price, optimal introductory 235
price policy 220, 223-226, 228, 236, 237
price policy, discontinuous 223, 224, 226
prices, introductory 222, 224
pricing strategies 237, 238, 241, 280
process innovations 100
product innovations 100
product, intermediate 33, 34
product, joint 17, 74
product variety 30, 35
production function 2, 10, 14, 15, 19-21, 23-26, 28-33, 36, 43, 47, 48, 51, 52-54, 58, 60, 61, 75, 120, 125, 126, 128, 146, 154, 160, 164, 171, 182, 212, 213, 300, 311, 324
production function, aggregate 14, 15, 19, 43, 146, 324
production function, classical 52
production function, homogeneous 52, 60
production function, macroeconomic 213
production function, neoclassical 10
production of knowledge 11, 12
production set 312
production technology 46, 48, 244
productivity, aggregate 86, 89, 185, 186, 195
productivity, average labour 189, 196
productivity convergence 211, 212
productivity growth 38, 42, 74,

84-86, 88, 89, 88, 89, 88, 90,
  89, 92, 95, 96, 97, 112, 113,
  115, 135, 143, 158, 179-181,
  185, 186, 188, 187, 189, 190,
  189, 190, 192-194, 204, 206,
  209-213, 298, 299, 304, 306,
  307, 318, 320-323
productivity levels 152, 182,
  185, 186, 188, 187, 189, 190,
  189, 190, 194, 195, 196, 195,
  196, 198, 199, 201, 207-209,
  298
productivity levels, sectoral 199
productivity of capital 24, 25,
  296, 297, 314
productivity paradox 88, 115
productivity slowdown 1, 43,
  110, 112, 180, 322
products, consumer 220
products, differentiated 133, 226,
  241
profit maximisation 218, 219,
  221, 228
profit maximisers 147
profit rate 78, 84, 97
profit, rate of 76, 77, 110, 112,
  218
profit strategy 231, 232, 236
profitability 75, 77, 82, 85, 97,
  112, 317
property rights 45, 316, 321
proprietary technology 291, 296
public good 13, 26, 35, 130,
  305, 313
public policy 40
purchasing power parity 2, 187
R&D, business 162, 164, 170,
  175, 176, 175, 178
R&D capital stock 300
R&D data 178, 299
R&D expenditure 38, 112, 314
R&D funds 162
R&D, imported 165, 178

R&D, industrial 259
R&D intensities 165, 178
R&D investment 97, 154, 181
R&D, precompetitive 308
R&D, sectoral 165
R&D spillovers 154, 155, 158,
  165
R&D stock 161-164, 176
rational agents 120, 127
rational representative agent 128
rationality 2, 127, 131, 141, 268,
  282
rationality, bounded 131
rationing rule 225, 240
real estate 196, 195, 196
real wage 65, 66, 79
recession 170
redistribution mechanism 15
regime switching 51, 52, 57
relative labour productivity 160,
  170, 195, 201
Renaissance 68, 299
reorganisation 49, 51, 54
repeated game 244, 247
replication 49-51
replicator dynamics 81, 133,
  263, 264, 282, 288
residual 2, 120, 212, 213
resource allocation 45, 120
resources, available 65
return, rate of 13, 204, 299, 307
returns, diminishing 1, 2, 47, 48,
  110, 263, 287, 296, 302, 304,
  307, 308
returns to scale 11, 21, 25, 26,
  28-30, 35, 42, 148, 165, 237,
  238, 298
revolution 18, 121, 143, 321,
  324
risk 25, 32, 238, 268, 279
rival 32, 111, 150, 187, 241
runs test 99
Russia 69, 122

savings 23-25, 29, 39, 46, 52, 53, 61, 69, 300-302, 315
Scandinavia 124
scarcity 47, 110, 113, 213
Schumpeterian competition 104, 108
Schumpeterian dynamics 75, 76, 107, 144
Schumpeterian economic growth 75
science 12, 72, 151, 154, 159, 178, 237, 238, 264, 282, 299, 322
scientists 46, 315
selection mechanisms 120, 262
selection process 51, 263
shadow price 221, 226
simplex 264-266
simulation 65, 68, 135-139, 147, 149, 150, 280
skills 10, 36, 148, 244, 245, 256, 299, 300, 305, 313
social infrastructure 46, 48, 52, 60, 62
social production 58
socioeconomic 46, 50, 55, 57
South Korea 156, 162, 164, 169-171
specialisation 1, 3, 74, 140, 185, 186, 201, 209, 212, 213, 323
spectral density 85-87, 89, 90, 95
spectral pattern 87, 88, 105
spectral power 85, 98
speed of diffusion 221, 228
spillover, learning 28
spillovers 1, 2, 32, 154, 155, 158-161, 164, 165, 169, 170, 176, 175, 177, 291
stable attractor 66, 68, 69
stable equilibria 39
Stackelberg 219, 226, 231-236

standard of living 48, 51, 53, 54
static monopoly 217, 222-224, 235
stationary 34, 45, 47, 52, 65, 82, 85, 98, 100, 133, 136, 138, 147, 149, 150, 226, 260, 288
stationary equilibrium 34, 136
stationary state 45, 47, 52, 65, 138
steady state 3, 47, 52, 54, 75, 78, 104
stochastic game 246, 248
stochastic macroeconomic modelling 98
stochastic model 147, 285, 288
stochastic process 80, 92, 94, 104, 105, 128-130, 149
strategy 65, 120, 129, 136, 231, 232, 234, 236, 238, 240, 247, 250, 254, 256, 258, 260, 271, 272, 277, 286, 309, 313, 314, 321
structural change 54, 60, 145, 146, 181, 184
substitutes, imperfect 226, 227
substitution 25, 53, 54, 62, 77, 107, 108, 214, 302, 322
Sweden 122, 157, 162, 169, 171, 188, 190, 191, 193, 196, 203
Switzerland 157, 162, 169, 171
tacit knowledge 9, 16, 17
Taiwan 211, 306, 318
technical change 1, 2, 10, 20, 21, 24, 39-44, 69, 72, 74, 75, 107, 108, 120, 128, 136, 143-146, 180, 204, 212, 213, 237-239, 259, 261, 282, 283, 284, 291, 299, 300, 307, 308, 319-324
technical knowledge 185
technical progress 10, 19, 20, 23, 24, 26, 28-30, 33, 38, 41,

74, 108, 126, 138, 180, 181, 296, 297, 307
technical progress, exogenous 24, 29, 138
technological change 33, 38, 41, 43, 46, 49, 50, 62, 107, 120, 144, 145, 154, 155, 158, 159, 175, 180, 181, 209, 261, 281, 317, 319, 322, 323
technological characteristics 268
technological expectations 112, 127
technological externalities 28, 125
technological frontier 177, 185, 210, 311
technological gap 130
technological imitation 158, 177
technological knowledge 130, 155
technological lags 126
technological opportunities 128, 130, 138, 272
technological progress 10, 18, 20, 107, 144, 204, 205, 318
technological regimes 51, 108
technological shocks 129, 135
technologies, competing 218, 265, 267, 269, 274, 277, 282, 286, 320
technologies, complex 314
technologies, distribution of 82
technologies, new 56, 72, 79, 82, 83, 158, 159, 245, 265, 274, 279, 280, 307, 317
technology, coevolution of 320
technology indicators 155, 158, 159, 177
technology, production of 32
technology transfer 2, 165
theory of growth 19, 295, 322, 323
total factor productivity (TFP)
185, 191
trade 11, 12, 22, 40, 42, 68, 75, 119, 122, 126, 134, 140, 144, 146, 180, 181, 195, 196, 195, 202, 203, 206, 212, 213, 305, 321
trade, international 22, 42, 75, 144, 146, 180, 212, 213, 321
trade liberalisation 212
trade openness 206
trade theory 213
traditional neoclassical growth 20-22, 29
transition 54-57, 66, 71, 72, 151, 226, 234, 246, 248, 322
transversality 250, 256
trend 3, 19, 20, 23, 24, 29, 34, 99-101, 103-105, 110, 137, 138, 147, 149, 156, 157, 171, 175, 177, 182, 186, 202, 324
underinvestment 13
unemployment 42, 82, 84, 85, 107, 295, 301
UNESCO 178
uneven growth 181, 294
unit cost 227, 234
United Kingdom 157, 162, 169-171, 178, 188, 190, 191, 193, 196, 203
unlearning 4, 244, 245, 247-249, 252, 255, 257-259
urban 49, 68
urn 4, 261, 265-268, 274-277, 280, 282, 283, 285-289
USA 108, 122, 124, 138, 157, 161, 170, 176-178, 257
USSR 124
utility 21, 25-27, 29, 30, 32, 36, 263
utility function 25, 27, 30, 32, 36
vintage 82, 204, 218, 296
wage 34, 65, 66, 79, 112, 113,

132, 135, 190, 212, 213, 238, 311
wage bargaining equation 112
wage rate 79, 112, 113
wage share 65, 190, 212, 213
weak preference 231, 234
white noise 88, 90, 91, 95, 134
world economy 2, 125, 136, 147, 181, 212
world growth rate 122
world market 135, 245
World War II 110
Yugoslavia 162, 169